27ʰ.9.06

RACE CODE WAR

By Khari Enaharo

African American Images
Chicago, Illinois

Front cover illustration by Angelo Williams

Copyright © 2003 by Khari Enaharo

All rights reserved.

First Edition, First Printing

Printed in the United States of America

ISBN: 0-913543-84-5

WHY THIS BOOK?

This book is designed to increase awareness of Black and White people as to the role of communication in the continuing practice of racism and racial alienation. It is also designed to expose the use of racially loaded and color-coded language.

The social changes that came about as a result of the civil rights movement forced hardcore racist language, symbols and images to go underground. Hardcore racist language and symbols, words such as nigger, blackey, shine, and the Confederate flag were so much an integral part of apartheid in North America that they had to be altered or go completely out of general usage. The forced language and symbolic changes were a part of the sweeping deconstruction of Western-style White apartheid. While the practice of apartheid was dismantled, White supremacy domination did not go out of business.

Those people who believe in and practice White supremacy domination evolved a new type of linguistic communication to transmit messages about Black people, using coded language. This happened for three basic reasons. First, the communication system is so deeply entrenched in derogatory color and racial bias that the transmission of racially based messages was relatively easy.

Second, the color and racial bias that is embedded deep within the language has never been sufficiently identified, challenged or rooted out. The third reason is that racists have not demonstrated a desire or shown the will to stop the practice of racism and, as a result, have discovered new ways to communicate in order to continue.

For these reasons it was possible for a coded language to evolve as a spin-off from hardcore racial communication. Some people might refer to this new code language format as political correctness. However, the words, symbols and images are much more than politically correct language; they are used to label, brand, demean and degrade Black people as criminals, rapists, whores, and many other belittling stereotypes.

Far too frequently Black and White people regurgitate this as if the words, images and symbols were correct. This perception has a tremendous impact on the development and implementation of social policy. In addition the spiritual, psychological, economic and political damage that it has done to Black people is simply too great to measure.

But it has had its greatest impact on the will and the ability of Black people to sustain unity and to develop systems of self-reliance. Many Black and White people may not be cognizant of how language is used as a form of racialized communication to foster a derogatory perception of targeted racial populations. However, it is incumbent on all people to become sensitized to this practice and stop the use of racial communication if we are to make this nation and world a healthy place in which to live.

It is the intent of this work to show how words, symbols, colors and images are used to nurture and sustain the practice of modern racism. Some of these racial codes are exposed, explained and examined in this book. My objective is to show how words, symbols, colors and images are used in a systematic manner to hide racism. This racialized form of communication is part of a long-running history that has had the affect of an undeclared racial war on the development of Black people here and abroad.

This work does not seek to demonize any racial population. I do not believe nor could I prove that all White people are White supremacists or practice racial domination. However, it appears that those who do believe and practice White supremacy/racial domination are extremely powerful and very effective.

I seek to expose racist and color-based discrimination practices that are detrimental to humanistic growth and development of all people. Those individuals or groups that wish to eliminate and correct racial injustice must support efforts to dismantle language/communications that foster racism and White supremacy.

Any form of communication that helps to maintain ideologies, practices, philosophies and functional systems of racial supremacy must be discarded. The ultimate goal of this effort is to help establish a world based on justice for all people, free of any form of racial supremacy, racial code words, symbols, images and color-coded language.

RACE CODE WAR

IN THE BEGINNING WAS THE WORD

INTRODUCTION

THE DEBT I OWE

There is a debt that I owe. Every human being owes a debt to those who have gone before to make a way or to clear a path. I owe the greatest debt to my parents Isabelle Dawson MCcrimmon-Braden, Walter MCcrimmon Sr. and my sister Devoylia MCcrimmon.

More than any book, job or classroom settings, they shaped my life.

They exhibited the highest examples of dignity, charity, love, morality, spirituality, intellectualism and service to humanity. They were the living manifestation of each of these virtues. I owe a great debt to my living siblings Arletta (Akira) MCcrimmon, Charles MCcrimmon (thanks for your special gift of support and belief in me) Walter MCcrimmon Jr, Arvetta (Jahara) MCcrimmon, Martha MCcrimmon and to my Aunt Vivian Stevens, Penny and Roy Gaffney, Edward "Pop" Braden and Uncle William Dawson.

To my nephews and nieces Charles Dwight, Kenneth Jameil (God grant his safe return), Curtis, Khari-Ben, Akena, Akeba, Yvette, Alexis, Walter (Fat-Fat) III, Abdullah, Nkenge, Ronald, Arif, Amirah, Quinton, Yolanda, John, Iyanna, Tylisha, Kabeera and Kadijah. To my cousins Brenda, Keith, Pinky, Michael, Langston, Arlethia, Maggie, Edith, Tudy, Vernon, Myron, Bobby, Barbara, Bruce, Beverly and their spouses and children.

Also I want to give special recognition to the following individuals for their inspiration, encouragement and support. Joyce Mitchell, Alberta Richardson, S. Yolanda Robinson, Gerlinde Higginbotham, Allen Huff (*Mr. Style Over Substance*), John Hardiman, Todd Hadden, Fran Frazier, Ako Kambon, Shirley Bridges, Carolyn Sims-Modena, Carol Nowell, Cynthia Bland-Jones, Donna Yvonne Dillard-Webb, Dr. Norma Mullins, Charles Richardson, Billy (The Big Guy) Joe Smith, and Dr. Gregory Thomas. Special thank you to Dr. Jawanza Kunjufu for his incredible expertise, patience and commitment to Black people and to this project. Finally, the greatest debt that I owe is to the great *God* of the universe. Without this awesome power I could do or be nothing. *This is the debt I owe.*

WHO I AM

My journey in life began in Dayton, Ohio, under the all seeing- eye and powerfully intelligent mind of my loving parents. Their greatest words of advice were to use my mind and skills to address the racial and social conditions of Black people here and abroad. That thinking always guided my academic, professional management and social development. My background includes more than thirty years of community involvement, management experience and public relations/ communications work.

I received a Bachelor's degree from Wilberforce University in Wilberforce, Ohio, and a Master's degree from Antioch University in Yellow Springs, Ohio. My community involvement is extensive. I served as the developer and organizer of three Columbus Black Political Conventions. The programs that emerged from the Conventions led to the development of 50 community action initiatives and the establishment of 25 organizations. I was also appointed the City of Columbus Director of Human Services from 1983-1987.

Since 1991, I have hosted a weekly radio talk show that was originally titled "Express Yourself." In 1996 it was changed to "Straight Talk Live on WCKX 107.5." I hosted my own cable television show for14 years and was a guest newspaper columnist and magazine writer.

I have read the works, attended the lectures and had the privilege of engaging in many private conversations with giant thinkers such as Mr. Neely Fuller, whom I believe is one of the most comprehensive thinkers on issues of race, racism and White supremacy. Mr. Fuller has been responsible for the advancement of the study of White supremacy domination.

I have also read the works and listened to the lectures of outstanding scholars and great thinkers such as Dr. Welsing, Dr. John Henrik Clarke, Dr. Chancellor Williams, Dr. Yosef ben-Jochannan, Dr. Earl Ofari Hutchinson, J.A. Rogers, Marcus Garvey, Malcolm X and many others. I have increased my understanding of these works by carefully studying communication interaction. This provided an opportunity to assess the power of words, symbols and images and color in modern racial relations. All of my conclusions, interpretations and opinions are based on both historical and present-day communication between Black people and White people.

STICKS and STONES

"Sticks and stones may break my bones but words can never hurt me"
This old saying has been used for many years as a social shield against the horrors of racism. Black parents had the first part of the equation correct. They knew that Black children would have to fight off a powerful onslaught of name calling from White supremacists and from other Black people trained to think and act in a self-destructive manner. These cute little sayings were used to strengthen the minds and the will power of Black people. During the pre-civil rights era, White supremacists called Black people derogatory names such as niggers, coons, heathens and savages.

Distorted racial images were used on products such as soap, watermelons, liquor, shoe polish, baking powder, soup cans, pancake boxes and rice. Black parents taught their children not to pay attention to name calling and derogatory images. Black children were told to focus their energies on actions and deeds. They were told not to allow words to impact their lives. They were told words could not hurt. That is the reason why Black people have not paid attention to words and symbols. While this approach helps to lessen the impact of certain social debasements in the early years, it does not fully prepare Black people to deal with modern racism.

Words can hurt and kill.
Words and images impact the quality of human life.
The Jewish people understand the power of words. In 1933 they thought the propaganda machine of Dr. Josef Goebbels in Nazi Germany was a joke. Many of them mistakenly believed that his words and images would have no lasting impact on the thinking of the German people. They thought this little, twisted man would go away and people would not believe such radical rubbish. They were *dead* wrong. They did not have a full understanding of the power of words and images to frame social thought.

The Nazi word machine fully understood the power of words and images. They knew that words, images and messages repeated and unchallenged are believed by most of the people most of the time. That is one of the reasons why Jews established the Anti-Defamation League and react with intensive passion to every word and statement that contains racially destructive references and passages. They know the power of language. Black people have not fully understood this lesson. Black people often use words to look cute and to impress White people. Black people must develop a mature understanding of how to use words.

CHAPTER ONE
HIDDEN in PLAIN SIGHT

UNTANGLING the WEB

To some it might seem that the author of this book has a color hang up or a racial phobia. It may be that such hang-ups and phobias are needed, in a constructive sense, to untangle the deep web of White supremacy indoctrination. The indoctrination is so deep and sophisticated that Black males and White males exposed to the same information can receive completely different sets of racial images, words and symbols. The Black male will come away with derogatory words, images and symbols in his mind. He will never fully understand why he feels inferior, oppressed, depressed and self- destructive.

The Black man will come to believe in his own inferiority, degradation and slave status. He will act against himself and against his people with self- and race-destructive behaviors. He will never know what triggers this destructive behavior. He will not understand the nature of this oppression until the images, words, colors, symbols and messages that are deeply embedded in his psyche are decoded and unscrambled to reveal their hidden derogatory racial and color meaning.

On the other side, the White male, hearing and seeing the same derogatory words, images and symbols, will perceive the Black male on that basis. The words, symbols and images that he has of himself will be completely different. The White man is imaged as a god on earth. There are thousands of pictures depicting Jesus and God in his image. Some of the greatest symbols of supernatural male power, such as Superman and Mighty Thor with his big hammer, are in his image. The White man is told and reminded in millions of subliminal and overt ways that he and his people are smarter and that they are born to rule. The White male will never understand the nature of White supremacy/domination and how it impacts the Black male and shapes his own thinking and beliefs until the hidden racial messages, images, words and symbols are decoded.

To reverse this condition and recapture their own minds, Black people must fight through the deep level of racial and color

1

indoctrination. They must decode the racial environment and untangle the deep web of White supremacy/domination. They must use and develop independent thinking tools to understand how racially based communication tools are used to maintain the existing racial order of things.

RACIAL COMMUNICATIONS

Communications between Unequal People Can Never Be Equal

What is the role of language and communications in maintaining the racial order of things? Language interaction between Black and White people within the framework of the existing racial order is inherently unequal. White people interact with Black people from a functionally superior position. Black people respond to White people from an inferior social position. Even in the year 2003 White people still tell Black people what to do in nearly every facet of life. This reality is true and is a fact of life despite the denials of many Black and White people. Black people literally depend on White people for survival and have not shown a collective belief that they can do it for themselves.

The belief in self-development has been stamped out and destroyed by White supremacy/domination. It was destroyed during slavery, reinforced during post-slavery, reintroduced during the era of Jim Crow segregation and discrimination and postulated through purposeful social neglect into the new millennium. If this social reality did not exist, Black people would own and control wealth and resources at the 15 percent level or an equal percentage based on their population. They would own and control all of the productive capacities necessary to meet the needs of all black people here and abroad. They would independently own, support and control fifteen percent of the hospitals, financial institutions, major manufacturing corporations, universities and so forth.

This kind of ownership and control takes place when people have a core belief in their own worthiness and strength as human beings. Such people share the same traditions and have confidence in their capacity to develop and solve problems by depending on each other and working together. They see themselves as the rulers of their own destiny, as people who share an unbreakable relationship and have enough trust in each other to work together in the spirit of a shared vision.

Communications are at the very heart of it all. When the language ingredients needed to build a new mindset and humanity are taken away, collective confidence is destroyed. The belief in unity is destroyed and self-development can never happen. This is the social outcome of a communication system that by its very nature perpetuates racial and color bias. This type of language interaction is called racial communications. It is the written, oral, physical and visual language interaction between White and Black people under the system of White supremacy/domination. Racial communication is the language of White superiority and Black inferiority. It is the interaction between a population in charge and a population that follows orders.

White people still control the economic, cultural, political, educational, media / entertainment, labor, religious, health and medicine, technological and governmental systems. This condition in itself does not make it racist. *It is racist if this level of power and domination was achieved using racism, racial domination and discrimination.* If racial discrimination, racial domination or racism was used to achieve this level of power, then control is based on race. In interactions between White and Black people, the racial and color factor is still-despite millions of denials-the most important ingredient in terms of who is superior and who is inferior. Under the existing system, the color White is superior and powerful and the color Black is inferior and powerless. The communication interaction between Blacks and Whites is a direct reflection of the superior and inferior power relationship. Race-based communication systems support and sustain the existence of White superiority and control versus black dependency and inferiority. *White people interact with Black people from a command and control position.* Racial communication defines Black people as the problem, as menaces to society and genetically inferior people who must be trained, retrained, contained, managed or eventually discarded. The state of White and Black race relations can be summed up this way: *White people are in charge and still on the top and black people are dependent and still on the bottom.* This kind of domineering and controlling relationship is seen consistently in the majority of situations where White people and Black people interact in the year 2003. This racial arrangement still exists regardless of temporary political agreements or minor economic concessions. Whether in South Africa, Washington, D.C., or Detroit, areas where Black people are supposed to be in charge, Black people are still dependent on the expertise, money, technology and thinking of White people.

Racially coded systems of language and communication are used in the modern era to maintain domination. The racial codification and colorization of words, images and symbols is one of the most effective and still largely undetected methods of transmitting derogatory racial messages. Racially coded communications, i.e., *racial code words, racial images, racial symbols, hidden racial messages, word bombs and racial colorizations and racial rituals,* are the workable tools that promote White supremacy.

What is White supremacy? It is the practice of white racial domination of Black and nonwhite people. The chief tools are fear, violence, dependency and deception. The concept and practice are based on the classification of people according to race or genetic similarities and the assignment of superiority and inferiority based on those racial classifications. The idea and practice of White supremacy have been passed down through generations in the same way as a royal birthright, property inheritance or cultural heritage.

The status quo is now portrayed by White supremacists as the normal state of existence, a sort of manifest destiny and the divine right to rule. This domination has remained intact despite a myriad of revolutions, civil wars, geopolitical conflicts and world wars. It is still the most powerful and the most enduring political, economic and social force on the planet. Its sovereignty has never been dethroned.

White supremacy/domination has been devastating to the history, culture, economics and political development of Black people. It has disabled Black people, destroyed Black unity and Black culture. The greatest evidence of this is that after more than 400 years of social interaction, Black people still remain economically, politically and socially dependent for their survival. Despite all of the public appearances, Black people have never been allowed to really be in charge or control.

The basic creed of a racist is that Black people must be fooled, managed and kept at a controllable level. This is part of an historical allegiance and racist tradition that those individuals, groups and populations that believe in racism promise to protect, defend and uphold

4

it. The common thread of this racist agenda is that *no matter what the issue, program or geographical location, White people must dominate, be in control or in charge.*

Over the course of time, White supremacy/domination has undergone major revisions. Neely Fuller in his 1984 groundbreaking book, *The United Independent Compensatory Code / System / Concept,* indicated that White supremacy has gone through four stages: establish, expand, maintain, and refine. In 2003 it has advanced to a superfine stage where language and communication tools are used as the chief weapons to *hide racism in plain sight.* Racism has not been eliminated. It is like a very resistant virus in that it has *mutated* its form.

RACISM HIDDEN IN PLAIN SIGHT

Black people must begin to understand how to decode racism in the superfine stage. The first and most basic understanding is that modern racism is hidden in plain sight and is nothing short of a continuous campaign that has the effect of racial warfare implemented in broad daylight for all to see. How is racism hidden in plain sight? What is meant by the term "in plain sight"? It means that racism is in full view, and everyone sees it and some even acknowledge it, but very few know or understand what to do about it or how to decode it when they see it.

Many have been mentally conditioned to look the other way or to incorrectly interpret what they see as something other than racism. Their mindset has been trained not to see the reality that is placed in full view. This is an old magician's trick. Words, symbols, images and colors have effectively retrained the mind so that reality has been interpreted to be something it isn't and never has been. In the 21st century what is obvious to a blind man is not so obvious to a brainwashed individual.

The following are examples of how racism is hidden in plain sight.

Selling the Suburban Lifestyle

Suburban communities exist because White people ran away from Black people. This is a simple and undiluted fact. It was the implementation of a race-based activity in plain sight. The creation of the suburbs was primarily a racial decision that led to a pattern of racial migration.

It was clear that these communities were being constructed primarily for White populations escaping Black populations even though there were no public proclamations that uttered those words. Some Black people caught onto to it initially when they labeled this behavior pattern as *"White flight."*

This observation never really quite stuck because the propaganda machine was so effective at rebutting the charges of racism. Coded images and language phrases were used to conceal this racial reality. White racial migration from the central city to the outlying suburbs was billed as modern living, beautiful suburbia and the affluent lifestyle, middleclass America, upscale housing communities, trendy neighborhoods and the good life. It was sold as a migration pattern stimulated by the desire for better economic and social lifestyles. Racially based migratory patterns were effectively defended, totally deflected and powerfully imaged in such a way that it appeared to be something other than what it was then or today. Public relations rationales such as green fields are easier to develop than the rust belt and toxic brownfields were developed to bend the truth to obscene proportions.

Imaging the Caribbean Islands

The second example is evident in how well-known tourist locations like San Juan, Puerto Rico, and the Caribbean islands are publicly imaged. The people living in these locations are programmed to use soft language and placid images to falsify a racist and deadly past. The official tourist guides and media material give the impression that the islands were civilized by heroic and honorable people.

There are huge statues on the islands of Nassau, Bahamas, and in locations such as San Juan, Puerto Rico, that honor White men as the great liberators and builders of civilization. In reality many of these men were great murderers and racist plunderers. The tourists are taken to see the forts and houses that were really used as military headquarters to conquer, destroy and enslave the original habitants. Stone structures are imaged as wonderfully exciting and historical tourist sites. Superbly colored brochures emphasize sexy, romantic and historical images. Racial conquering and genocide is sold to the public with coded words such as *progress* and *expansion of Western civilization*. Tourists are rarely told the real truth about the racist reasons and purposes for such things as the forts and houses. This kind of historical interpretation is rarely allowed. It is usually censored or deleted.

What is told is that the conquerors were liberators who made great contributions to mankind by civilizing the people and making the island inhabitable. While it is true that Western technology benefited material development, it is also true that these colonizers have the blood of thousands, maybe millions, of peaceful and innocent people on their hands. This whitewashed, racist-free portrayal completely removes or greatly minimizes the gory and barbaric past. This ugly distortion of history makes racism appear as human evolution and social progress. It is subtly portrayed as the White man's manifest destiny to dominate nonwhite people. The new imaging is done to continue to reel in billions of mostly White and Asian tourist dollars. The Black and Brown locals are trained to give scripted language accounts and glossy images of the history of the island to hide the horrible legacy of racism and social degradation.

This kind of false presentation is perpetuated in the silhouettes of the large public symbols of racial imperialism such as the forts, prisons, slave chains, memorial statues and ships. These open racist symbols are the clear public remnants of imperialism, racism, slavery and colonialism. However, the racist history is shielded and hidden because of the effective use of coded racial images and language.

Racial propaganda is done under the banner of public relations, marketing and promotion. The objective is to plant false images and histories that lure White people to the islands. Their egos must be fed and many must feel comfortable in the knowledge that domination is still in effect. Black politicians convince the local population to go along with this because the White and Asian tourist trade brings badly needed jobs and income. They are reminded that revealing the truth about the racist past in the media, brochures, in the museums and on statues would drive White and Asian people with big money away. Many people would not come to the island if the unfiltered racial history were constantly presented in all media outlets and formats. The inhabitants of the island would be labeled as a hostile and rebellious population.

RACE CODE WAR

Economic investment would cease, and a push for the military overthrow of the government would commence. White domination is protected and hidden behind a veneer of Black control. The most powerful forces on the islands are the financial, manufacturing and tourist industries that are still White dominated and controlled. In order for Black people to participate in the economic system, they must pretend that this control does not exist. They must go along with the fabrication and hide racism in plain sight to get the crumbs reserved for Black and other nonwhite people.

Commercial Financial Institutions

The next example is of a senior vice president for commercial lending that believes in and practices covert White supremacy. According to the official job description, his/her role is to loan money to help the economic and physical development of a neighborhood or existing commercial area. The senior vice president will laugh and smile all day long with his Black co-workers. He will treat Black members of the management team with the utmost courtesy. He will give wonderful Christmas gifts at the company party. However, he will continue to make racially based lending decisions and will use the most elaborate charts and financial analyses to justify the denial or approval of loan applications. He will also use public relations and economic code language to justify racially based lending policies. Terms like *project feasibility, cash flow analysis, creditworthiness, debt-to- income ratio, market studies* and a host of other coded phrases hide his racist lending practices. The vice president is adept at arguing about why the bank cannot make a $500,000 loan to a small Black business. At the same time, he will find creative ways to fund $15,000,000 for a development activity that benefits areas in the predominantly White communities.

The inner city exists because the areas where Black people live in large numbers have been economically discarded. The bank vice president knowingly recommends and implements fiscal actions that keep Black communities in an underdeveloped state. He purposely denies requests for loans that could redevelop or stimulate their commercial viability. This same financial institution will brag about its branch operations in the Black community. In reality it is an operation that siphons off dollars in the community. These financial institutions

8

do not reinvest at the same level they take money out of the area. They will not even make loans that improve the commercial standing of the community in which the branch operations are located. Black people deposit billions of dollars in these banks, yet they get back only a small portion of what they have deposited in the form of development loans to improve their communities. This is racism in plain sight that has the effect of racial warfare against the growth and development of Black people. Why? Racist actions such as these keep Black people and their living environments stunted, dependent and moving backward.

The Urban Downtown

The urban downtown is one of the most blatant examples of racism in plain sight. The large buildings towering over the central city landscape are clear evidence of the hoarding of money, capital and material resources based on race. These structures were built because White banks hoarded money and White businessmen were given preference over Black businessmen. Black entrepreneurs were denied capital and adequate financing to maintain, expand and improve the quality of life in the Black neighborhoods. Black people have deposited billions of dollars into White-controlled financial institutions and to this day have received back only a pittance of what has been deposited.

A quick comparison between Black and White communities makes it very clear as to what has been and what is still going on. Money taken out of Black neighborhoods has historically been used to build up White communities. The individuals that run these institutions have historically and to the present day made financial decisions based on race. Based on the lack of interest in the redevelopment of the Black community, it appears that the large developers are making their economic investment decisions based on race. No mathematical model or scientific reasoning can explain this disparity other than racism.

It is no accident of history that nearly every major development is in or near White-dominated areas and communities. As a matter of record, whenever Black people move into an area in large numbers, White businesses move out in large numbers, leaving behind an abandoned community.

This is an act of purposeful disinvestments in the area, and the record is in plain view for all to see. It is a clear pattern of racist investments, disinvestments and loans. Only one reason can account for this kind of economic disparity and that is massive discrimination based on race. There is no logical or statistical reason. Racism in plain sight is covered up by a barrage of words designed to tell a lie that is believable.

The 2000 Republican National Convention
The final example is the 2000 Republican National Convention. The dominant racial code word was the term *inclusion* and it served as the new password. It went like this: "Let's make these people believe that things have changed. Let's put them on stage as dancers and singers. Let's give them the impression that we want to include them in what we do." Convention leaders wanted their group to understand that they were behind in using the latest techniques of racial management. They were behind other political parties and needed more training in code words, images, symbols and colors.

Other political parties had developed advanced techniques on code wording, with terms like *diversity* and *equal opportunity,* and had become experts at cooling out, redirecting aspirations and controlling Black rage. The leaders of the Party understood and knew how to bridge the deficit. Racially coded phrases such as *leave no children behind* were employed to set the stage.

The language on both sides was so coded that during the first presidential debate, the Democratic candidate, Al Gore, openly accused the Republican candidate, George Bush, of *talking in code*. Both candidates used heavily coded phrases and slogans. Does the slogan *leave no child behind, when decoded, mean leave "those" children behind?* Does the Gore slogan *I will fight for working class families*, when decoded, mean *I will fight for the White families left out of the economic good time?* According to political pundits, it was the White suburban household voter that had to be convinced that Gore was worthy to be the commander-in-chief.

The codified communications included the following symbols and words:

Tools	Symbols	Decoded Meaning
Spiritualism	Black church choir	we are one in the Lord
Music	Black entertainment	we share a common culture
Preaching	Black entertainment	we believe in the Word together
Politics	Black people giving major speeches	we accept Black leadership

Hidden in Plain Sight

The message is that we are all Americans. Mr. Bush said "I'm a uniter not a divider " to sell the American image of unity and color blindness. This example of deception and confusion illustrates how racism can be hidden in plain sight despite all of the anti-discrimination laws on the books. It is hidden through the use of deceptive speech, thought, behavior and actions. Black people do not understand how it works in the modern social context and therefore have not updated their struggle methodologies.

Black people are still employing the same strategies used to fight racial apartheid and racial segregation. Racism is no longer out in the open as it was in the sixties. The modern form of racism is hidden in such things as racially coded speeches to justify why inner city ghettos still have not been eliminated. It is hidden in the racial and color symbolism of big-budget motion pictures like "Godzilla," "Artificial Intelligence (A.I.)" and "Planet of The Apes." It is hidden in the development of policies and practices that devalue and depreciate the people, land and resources in Black communities.

Racism is hidden in the politics that keep Black schools inferior. Racism has gone into deep cover behind a wall of *black faces, anti-discrimination laws, diversity, equal opportunity, inclusion and other coded words and phrases.* Even the use of the words racism and White supremacy/domination have become taboo and quietly removed from the discussion. Racism is officially protected in glib talk. Racial propaganda is so effective that many have been convinced that race and racism no longer exist and that it is not a valid excuse for the deplorable conditions that still exist in many Black communities and nations. The argument goes like this: "You (Black people) are responsible for the condition of your community."

The reality is that Black people are not responsible for the existence of these social conditions. They do not own any major financial institutions or any Fortune 500 corporations. Black people do not own major capital and stock investment houses to bring massive dollars into their communities. Black people have no self-reliant organization capable of uniting and solving their collective problems. If Black people are going to develop, they must understand how to deal with modern racism hidden in plain sight.

RACISM in PLAIN SIGHT CHART

The following chart shows how racism in plain sight has the effect of a program of racial warfare against the development of Black people. For example, the continued existence of inferior and poor quality schools from generation to generation results in a constantly under-educated population. When a community is flooded with drugs and guns, it creates a massive destabilization that destroys the social and cultural fabric of a people or community. *This is racism in plain sight and it has the affect of racial warfare against the development of Black people here and abroad.* The charts below provide additional evidence and illustrations of how racism in plain sight has the effect of a program of racial warfare.

Evidence of Racism in Plain Sight	Social Impact
Economics - Constant denial of bank loans in Black neighborhoods	Accelerates deterioration of the Black community
Education - Poor quality schools and miseducation	Generations of uneducated / unskilled people
Politics - No real representation or control of political finances	Maintenance of political powerlessness
Health - Poor health care, AIDS, no hospital ownership	Genocide, lower life expectancy, disease
Media - Lack of ownership, proliferation of racist images	Racial profiling, stereotyping as criminals
Housing - Maintenance of substandard housing / homelessness	Creation of ghetto and inner city blight
Law - Injustice in the courts and by the police	Record rate of incarceration of Black males
Labor - Chronic high unemployment rate	Climate of hopelessness, lack of capital for economic development
Sex - Interracial sex, homosexuality, bisexuality, pornography	Poor male / female relations, low marital rates
Food - Poor quality, high sugar and lack of store ownership	Poor health, lack of physical development
Clothing - Socially degrading apparel / lack of store ownership	Stereotyping and labeling as gang bangers / Thugs
Technology - Maintenance of low-grade technology	Digital divide, backward state of development

Hidden in Plain Sight

Historical Evidence of Racism in Plain Sight As Racial Warfare
The Chattel Slave Trade
Colonialism on the African Continent
Imperialism Against the African People
Racial Apartheid
Institutional Racism
Racial Segregation
Economic Rape of Mother Africa
Perpetuation of Poverty and Economic Depravity
Enfranchisement of Corrupt Politicians
Massive Extermination Programs Here and Abroad
The Welfare Dependency State
Policy of Ghettoization/Inner Cities
Importation and Experimentation of Diseases in Africa and the Caribbean
Maintaining Inferior Schools
Substandard Housing and Slums
High Unemployment and Underemployment
Financial Neglect of Black Communities Here and Abroad
Burdening of Massive Debts Against Black People Here and Abroad
Construction of Illegal Governments
Destruction of a Black Economy
Assassination of Independent Black Leadership
Brutal Overthrow of Independent Black Governments
Mass Starvation of Millions of Black People
Breakdown of the Social Infrastructure System
Continuation of Wars and Destabilization Campaigns in Africa/ North/South
    America
Theft of Black History
Destruction of Black Civilization
Elimination of Black Languages in North America
Elimination of Black Culture from North American Black People
Massive Incarceration of Black People
Importation and Introduction of Illegal Drugs into Black Communities
Massive Rape of Black Women
Destruction of the Black Family
Divisions Among Black People Based on Skin Color and other factors
Black Inferiorization Process
White Superiorization Process
Elimination of Original Black Religions
Derogatory Stereotyping of Black People
Black on Black Religious, Tribal, Community and Gang Warfare

RACE CODE WAR

Lynching, Murders and Castration of Black People
Use of Brutal Occupation Forces in Black Communities Here and Abroad
Sexual Imaging, Glorification and Exploitation of Black Women As Prostitutes
Sexual Imaging, Glorification and Exploitation of Black Men As Stud Animals
Wholesale Theft of Land Owned, Operated or Controlled by Black People
Introduction of a White Religious God
Continued Political Disenfranchisement
Criminalization of the Black Male
Mammy Imaging of Black Females
Dark Skin, Nappy Hair, Thick Lips and Broad Noses as Ugly and Undesirable
Permanent Black Underclass
Racial Imaging As Clowns, Buffoons and Child-like Beings
Imaging of Black Males As Savages, Animals and The Dark Menace
Low Rate of Black Homeownership
The Digital Divide
Gang banging and Drive-by Shootings
Proliferation, Glorification and Exploitation of Gangsta Rap
Proliferation of Illegal Weapons in the Black Community
Racial Profiling
Police Brutality

CHAPTER TWO
SPEAKING IN CODE

CODE TALKING

In the modern social order the development of codification is used for many purposes. Codes come in many covert formats, including secret slogans, military operations, political speeches and numbers. There are money codes, clothing/design codes, music codes, color codes, advertising slogan codes, movie title codes, card game codes and many hidden codes in children's fairy tales. Codes are plentiful in such things as riddles and crossword puzzles, cattle brands, quilts and flags. Organized crime leaders use codes to carry out their illegal operations. Major League baseball managers, NFL football and NBA basketball coaches use code language to fool the opponent. All of these operations-and many more-transmit coded messages beneath the human radar screen.

Codes are also used in more public ways to establish standards and regulate public and private conduct, comportment and social interaction. The standardized codes of conduct or rules of the game have become the bible for what is acceptable or legal and what is unacceptable or illegal. Standards of conduct and norms of social interaction are written in a coded format. When new legislation is passed that amends, reinterprets or abolishes an existing standard of behavior it is a revision, or a revised code.

Law schools train attorneys to understand the standards and codes. They are taught to understand how to decipher the meaning and intent of a law. Legal language is not classified as a secret form of communication. However, it is a codified way of thinking, writing, speaking and behavior. According to *Webster's New Collegiate Dictionary*, the definition of a code and some of its applications are as follows:

Code
A system of signals for communication. A system of symbols as letters, numbers or words used to represent assigned and often secret meanings.

Code Book
A book containing an alphabetical list of words or expressions with their code group equivalents for use in secret communications.

Code Word
A code name or code group.

Code Name
A word made to serve as a code designation.

Codify
To reduce to a code, classify and systematize.

EXAMPLES OF PUBLIC CODES
Legislative Codes
Codes of Conduct
Financial Codes
Business Codes
Sale Codes
Tax Codes

EXAMPLES OF SECURITY CODES
Bank Account Codes
House Alarm Codes
Fire Alarm Codes
Business Security Codes
Security codes are used to protect items, services, information and resources. The codes are often numerical or a combination of letters and numbers. This type of code is used for a specific instrument, function or purpose.

EXAMPLE OF SECRET CODES
Military Codes

EXAMPLES OF CLOAK-AND-DAGGER CODES
Intelligence Codes
Spy Operations

Speaking in Code

COVERT CODES

Covert codes are crafted forms of linguistic communication used in secret, concealed or deceptive activities. They are part of a deceptive language pattern used most often in intelligence, economic or military espionage operations. Code language is indispensable and is very important to the success or failure of a mission. A code word has a purposely disguised intention that is recognized by the people trained to decode its meaning. Coded language is protected and shielded because it uses common words that are part of everyday conversation. Some covert codes are wrapped in language familiar in certain industries, professions or activities. Strange words are minimized so that no unintended signals or special alert are given to the opposition.

BREAKING the CODE: MANY LOOK; FEW WILL SEE

To comprehend how to break a code it is vital to have some awareness of the ways that are used to obscure messages. Words, sentences, paragraphs or essays and forms of visual communications may contain letters, numbers or slogans that infer different meanings. In the code world a single letter or number could represent many things. A designated number can mean a safe house at a drop-off location or it could stand for a boat that might be used as part of a getaway scheme.

The uses of code in language are endless. Sentences and paragraphs or slogans often contain multiple words, spellings of words and word associations that are close enough for the intended party to understand the real meaning. Letters, words, near spellings and other spellings are intentionally placed within the body of other sentences, paragraphs or slogans to conceal intended messages. Not all of the reading material has a coded purpose or contains a hidden message. In a highly organized social structure it cannot be taken for granted that coded messages are not there. Political, commercial and racial messages are frequently coded. Many are sent using an *anagrammed* format to hide or to jumble a phrase.

The subconscious mind reads the sentences, phrases and letters and picks-up on the meaning of the intended message. On the surface it may not make a lot of sense; however, the deeper subconscious mind gets the meaning and then moves the body to the beat of the message. The goal is to find the anagrams that are the racial triggers used to relay race messages. According to *Webster's New Collegiate Dictionary,* the word anagrams means *"to rearrange letters of a text in order to discover the hidden meaning."*

There are slogans and speeches wherein the race themes cannot be detected using only the anagram method. There are other methods including word associations, trigger words in statements, racial images, racial symbols, race code words, sexual codes words, religious code words, economic code words, political code words, symbol decodification, color codes, racial embeds, near spellings, other spellings, number associations, sound-alike and read-alike phrases, letter tracking/placement and so forth.

In a racially coded environment, it is very important to understand that most messages are not just funny jingles made up to amuse people. These are powerfully effective forms of communication that are developed by experts in the areas of propaganda, public manipulation and subliminal communications.

The goal of the decodification process is to find out what other spellings, near-spellings (words spelled close to the spelling of other words so that meaning is very clear), word associations or sound-alike or read-alike words are embodied in an original word or sentence. When a slogan has a number of discovered hidden spellings or words related to the same or a closely related subject, it is clear that there is an intended message.

To give the benefit of the doubt, it is possible that the hidden spellings and words may have been an accident or an unintended outcome. However, the developers of slogans know or should know what other spellings/words are hidden within their work. When a significant number of hidden racial stereotypical or trigger words are discovered in a slogan or speech, it raises the question as to whether it is an accident or purposeful.

Among the easiest ways to hide a message are with the use of reshuffled letters, one- or two-word discoveries, alternative, sound- or read-alike words, near spellings and word associations that are woven within the body of the slogan. The reshuffled letters may start with the first letter in each word of a slogan or title of a presentation. If these letters are arranged in a certain fashion, they could spell out a word or give a signal for an action. The one-or two-word spellings that are discovered in the slogan or speech often trigger mechanisms to create within an individual a certain mental or emotional response.

The discovery of one word does not necessarily imply that there is a hidden message unless it is found to be a coded reference to activate something. The technique of alternative words requires that a word be purposely placed so that it most likely has a double or triple meaning. The near-spellings or spellings that are close enough to the spelling of another word are also ways to conceal information and intent. Such spellings are close enough to other words to mentally and perceptually activate the other supposedly unintended declaration. Word association enables the mind to relate words to other spellings and images that carry different messages.

Sound-alike and read-alike words and spellings are used to alert, correlate and draw mental attention to another or opposite point of view. The following are examples of slogans that contain other words, spellings and near spellings hidden within the body of the phrases. These spellings, near spellings or word associations are actual wordings found within each speech or slogan. There are also other words, spellings or near spellings within each of the slogans that are not presented here. The following are short examples of racial, war, religious, sexual and political anagrams and the word association process.

Racial Anagram in the Following Spelling
Neighbor
N e i g h b o r = the underlined letters form the anagram
The hidden word is Negro

Social Anagrams in the Following Spelling
Good
What are the other words in this spelling?
Go
God
Do
Dog

Word Associations in the Spelling of "Good"
Good = honorable, esteemed, bad, ugly, pretty
Dog = chase after, chase away, guard, cat, obedience, friendship,
Do = sex, work, play and perform
Go = active, travel, proceed and depart

Letter Tracking and Number Anagrams
The first letters of words in a slogan can often reveal if the slogan is a racial, religious, economic or political message. Track the first letters of each word within a slogan to see if they reveal a pattern. Review the second letters in each word of the slogan, and so on if necessary, to determine if there is a hidden message.

Track the first or second letters of the title of a speech or the name of a book or movie, high points in the speech or catch phrases in the movie. Reshuffle the order and find out how many words/spellings originated from this process. In more detailed codes the letters are often jumbled from word to word. One code might use the sixth letter of the third word and another might use the eighth letter of the fifth word.

The result of this scenario could be the code, and it could trigger a designed action. These examples are generally part of highly complex codes that require extensive training to decipher. Most of the coded words for public consumption are far less intricate and easier to discern:

Corporate, Allegiance, Responsibility and Efficiency = Care or Race = Race/Care

Renew The Spirit And Manifest The Energy = RTSAMTE = Matters. *Message is Race Matters*

Never Offend a Good Earning Resident = NOGER = Negro.

Well-known statements, jingles, slogans or catchphrases offer further demonstrations of ways to decode words, hidden messages and alternative meanings. By no means are the methods used here the only ways to develop or use decodification mechanisms. This approach is only a start. The first example is taken from a speech on the "War Against Terrorism" given by President George W. Bush to Congress following the events of September 11, 2001.

President Bush used the slogan "Axis of Evil" to label Iran, Iraq and North Korea as evil predators. The use of the word Axis triggers the term Axis Powers as in World War II. The Axis Powers were against the Allies (America, Russia and England). This political and military confederation consisted mainly of Germany, Japan and Italy. The anagram method is used to deduce other spellings or near spellings that are contained in the examples below. Revealed are the *actual spellings or close spellings* that are found in the body of the slogan, word or statement.

	Decodification of Hidden Spellings/Words
Phrase	**Selected Decoded Words, Spellings**
Axis of Evil =	Ax - To chop down or suddenly remove
	Axis = Nazi Germany or Axis Powers or Hitler-like situation
	Evil = Devil, blackness or darkest day
	Eve = Garden of Eden or Babylon or Persia/Iraq
	Vile = Foul, obscene, detestable, sickening
	Sex = Male gender
	Lives/Live = The shedding of blood or lives lost
	Foil = To stop or thwart the menace
	Oil = oil fields in Iraq and Caspian Sea area
	Seal = Approval
	Sale = The sale of oil
	Sail = Sea
	Fiels or Fields = oil fields
	Oval = Oval room

The next message to be decoded is *the only thing we have to fear is fear itself.* This was part of a very powerful message delivered by the President of the United States, Franklin Delano Roosevelt in 1933 during his inaugural address and at the depth of the Great Depression. This statement is loaded with deep war, geographical and political meanings. In the coded spelling of the United States the V with a horizontal extension serves as the letter U, and the B turned around is the letter D. Listed below are words and spellings that are derived from this statement.

RACE CODE WAR

Phrase /Slogan   **Selected decoded words and spellings and near spellings**

The only thing we have to fear is fear itself

Roosevelt = Roosevelt
Stalin = Soviet Leader
Togo = Tojo
Harbor = Pearl Harbor
Earl Habor = Pearl Harbor
Englan = England
Hitler = Nazi Germany dictator
Aolf = Adolf Hitler
Rising Svn = Rising Sun/Japan
Bear = Soviet Union
Vniteb States = United States
Nvssolini = Mussolini
Rea r = Battle strategy
Oil = Planes
Tub = Sea vessel
Allies = Russia, England and U.S.
Rvssia = Ally
Italy = Italy = Axis
Soviet = Soviet
Union = Soviet Union
Ear = Spying/shig = ships/Pearl Harbor
Air Fore = Air Force

Slogan   **Decoded words and spellings and near spellings**

Like a good neighbor State Farm is there

Negro
Nigger
Master
Dog
God
Segregation
Integration
Sothern = southern
Northerm = northern
Shoot
Rob
Steal
Trash
Reloate = Relocate
Great fear
Lesser breed = Lesser breeds
Genes
Rasist = Racist

Speaking in Code

Slogan	Selected decoded words and spellings and near spellings

Maxwell House is good to the last drop

God
Deuil = Devil
Dead
Past
Death
Worship
Esus = Jesus
Ghost = Holy Ghost
Hell
Satam = Satan
Sex = sin
Life
Praise
Pit Hell = Pit of Hell
Health
Eterity = eternity
Darth = Dark

Decoded words and spellings and near spellings

Fly the friendly skies of United

deth = death
die / dies
The end of life
Life/shit
risk/risky
flies/fly/sky
fry/fries
he/she
lies/lie
need insure = need insurance
neer = near ded = near dead
insure = insurance
ensure
deed
destrution = destruction

RACE CODE WAR

Slogan   **Decoded words and spellings and near spellings**

Finger lickin' good

Niger = Nigger
Nigger
Negro
Dick
Lick
God
Dr. King
Dog
Dong
Ding
King
Kong
Koon

This slogan was developed in 1964 under the brand name of Kentucky Fried Chicken, or KFC.

Slogan   **Decoded words and spellings and near spellings**

Let your fingers do the walking

Niggers
Dr. King
Rights = civil rights
Washington
Negroes
Whites
Walking/walk = civil rights marches
Talking = speeches
Kenned - President Kennedy
Sit-In – sit-ins
Klu
Klan
King
Kong
Dong
Ding

24

Speaking in Code

This came out in 1964 under the brand name of Yellow Pages. The commercial was broadcast during the height of the Civil Rights Movement.

Slogan	Decoded words and spellings and near spellings
Make it a Blockbuster night	Black
	Osama Bin Lebem = Osama Bin Laden
	Negroes
	Gun
	Christ
	Christian
	Mose = Moses / Reb Sea = Red Sea
	Black Garter /nilon = nylon
	Black Stocking
	Girble = girdle
	Robber
	G-String
	Cunt
	Bitch
	Lick
	Masturbation
	Urine
	Shit
	Suck
	Meat
	Hitler
	Sabbam Husien = Saddam Hussien
	Clitoris
	Belt
	Stock
	Girls
	Islam
	Arab
	Oral
	Men
	Kock = cock
	Chasite = chastity belt
	Muslin = Muslim
	China
	A. Sharon
	Israel
	Geore Bush = George Bush
	Al Gore
	B. Clintom = Bill Clinton
	Carter = Jimmy Carter
	Reagan = Ronald Reagan
	Religion = Christianity and Islam

RACE CODE WAR

The number of spellings, near spellings and word associations is amazing. From a total of five words, connotations cover many racial, sexual, religious, political and military subjects. This message was aired during the NFL Super Bowl in 2002, the Super Bowl after the tragic incidents of September 11, 2001.

Slogan	Decoded words and spellings and near
The ultimate driving machine	Negr = Negro
	Mate
	Male = black male
	He - man
	Niger
	Blach = black
	Vietnam
	China
	India/Indian
	Iran
	German
	A. Hitler
	Churhil = Churchill
	Urine
	Time
	Mine
	Mad
	Avis = Axis

Word Associations

Word associations are words that can have hidden spellings or a spelling close to another word, or it can sound or read like another word or phrase in order to make a subtle or overt reference to people, things, places and events. The following examples reveal other messages by using anagrams and the word association method.

Speaking in Code

A Diamond Is Forever
Man
Dar or dark
Ever = Eternal
Die = Immortality
Dead = Millions die in Afria or Africa
Afria = South Africa
Mines = Millions die for diamonds in the mines of South Africa

Put a tiger in your tank
Niger = nigger and nation in Africa
Tiger = jungle and Africa
Tank = gun power
King Tut = Egyptian Pharaoh
Egypt = rig = oil rig

We brings good things to life
God = ultimate power
Lord = Jesus
White = White people
Dog = man's best friend
Ring = angelic halo
Wings = angels

You're in good hands with Allstate
God = ultimate power
Lord = Jesus
Dad = provider and first to die
Dog = man's best friend
Hands = control
All = everything
State = earthly power
You = the only person in the world
Land = subsistence
Own = business or residence
Die and will = death planning
Estate = money transfer
Niger = niggers

Word Associations

Cigarette brands	Decoded message
Doral = Lord, Rod, Oral, Al, Do, Lora, Or = Lora do oral to Al and Rod	
Pall Mall = Pal, Pell, All, Lap, Pale, Male = pale male or White male	
Lucky Strike = Lick, Suck, Luck, Lucy, Juicy, Key, Kiler or Killer = kill her	

CHAPTER THREE

RACE CODE WORDS

Racially identifiable language is used to distinguish or classify an individual or a population based on race or color. Terms such as African American identify a racial population. Racial code language is comprised of non-racially identifiable words that are used as substitute or surrogate verbal and written communication that is used to deceive, glorify, demonize, degrade or stereotype racial populations and their living environments.

Racial code words are non-racially identifiable words, terms, phrases, and sentences or slogans that are as used as surrogate language to identify, marginalize, mislead, glorify, demonize, degrade, smear, label and stereotype racial populations and their living environments. A non-racially identifiable word is a word that on the surface has no specific racial group identity or individual designation. A racially identifiable term is African American, Black American or Chinese. It is clear as to what is meant by the use of these words.

An example of a non-racially identifiable word or term is "inner city." At first glance, the words inner and city say nothing about race or issues related to it. These words define a geographical location. However, this term has been defined and imaged in a derogatory manner, and it is linked almost exclusively to Black people and their living environments. Therefore, the term is racial and it has derogatory racial implications and racist meanings. It is used in a clandestine, disguised or concealed manner to convey racist messages about target racial populations and their living environments.

The racial code wording process produces perceptions that are generally misleading, racist and demeaning. What determines if a word or term is a racial code word? The basic criterion is that if the word is used repeatedly in context with or to identify certain racial populations and /or their living environments it is a racial code word.

One example of race code wording is found in the way the print media handles stories about drug busts that occur in neighborhoods largely populated by Black people. If the words used to describe the incident consistently implicate all of the people and the whole neighborhood in a derogatory manner, they are code words or phrases that are being used to hide the underlying racist perception of the community.

Words such as black and nigger are often prohibited from use in the media, so non-racially identifiable words with derogatory meanings are used as substitute language to say or to imply the same thing. For example, the phrase *drugs infested* is frequently used when describing drug raids in certain Black neighborhoods. This is an ugly phrase that has a sweeping identification tag that implicates all of the residents. All Black people are not drug dealers. All Black communities are not drug infested, and besides, there is no set standard as to what constitutes an infested community. If this word is to be used, it must have some criterion to determine when infestation has occurred. The use of this word has no purpose other than as a racial code word. The language must be correct and tell the whole truth at all times.

The word infestation is a broad term that smears everything and everybody. It says that everyone in the community uses, sells or buys illegal drugs.

Words and images are integral parts of the perceptual experience. Therefore, instead of identifying the community as black or nigger and run the risk of being called racist, a code word with the same racial meaning is just as effective. Images, symbols and colors that are consistently attached to repetitive verbal descriptions establish mental impressions.

A racial code word may not contain any direct racial references on the surface. However, connecting the words to specific images, symbols and colors create a potent message. Racial and color bias have been deeply embedded within the basic core of our language. In the dictionary and thesaurus you will find numerous derogatory associations between black and dark and an equal number of positive associations between white and light or bright. A *white* knight is a good knight. A *black* knight is a *bad* knight. *Angel* food cake is heavenly, and dark cake is *devils'* food. Associations are part of the racial conditioning process. The values of good, bad, inferior and superior are also attached to colors. Code words are developed, interpreted and decoded by individuals or groups with the same mindset, values and understanding. It is easy to communicate when the audience speaks the same language.

The modern racist speaks in code about most things that are racial. It is amazing how innocent-sounding words that seem to have no apparent racial meaning or identity can, over a period of time, become racially derogatory references. In proper circles crude and unrefined racial language is banned and will not be openly tolerated. Why risk calling a Black male or female a socially unacceptable name or direct racial word such as *nigger* when they can be called racial code words using socially acceptable language with terms such as *lowering the property value* or social *disinvestments.* An effective racist can now kill two birds with one stone and not be detected. They are even bold enough to use racial codes to enlist the support of unsuspecting Black people.

Far too many Black people repeat a word without understanding what is being said. This gives the racist a way out. They can claim that Black people use these words to describe their own kind so how could they be racist? A code word is also a protective device because it can be used to deflect charges of racism.

Code words make life that much better for a smart racist. He/she can talk about and control Black people without them raising hell or knowing what to do about it. ***Code talkers can use coded language to call a Black man a nigger to his face and get him to laugh about it and accept it.*** In the White supremacist culture, code language is difficult to distinguish.

Many of the common words that are used to describe Black people are also used to describe other populations. This can be tricky and off- setting. For example, Irish radicals were also labeled as drug dealers. White hippies in the 1960s were labeled acid heads.

However, the difference in both of these examples is that the entire race, its history and culture were not trashed, labeled, stereotyped and degraded. White people that degrade other White people usually are engaged in a temporary struggle, power grab or social correction. This does not mean that they do not hate each other or will not kill each other during the struggle. However, in crises or during wartime, they do not trash their race or each other on the basis of color.

The continued use of racial code language is borne out in the findings of a recent study published in the November 2002 edition of the Demography Journal in a study by Maria Krysan, a University of Illinois at Chicago Sociologist, who examined the responses of 1600 randomly selected White residents in three cities.

Whites Who Say They'd Flee: Who Are They, and Why Would They Leave? Abstract: Questions have been raised about whether white flight—one factor contributing to U.S. residential segregation—is driven by racial, race-associated, or neutral ethnocentric concerns. When asked why they might leave, Whites focused on the negative features of integrated neighborhoods.

This study revealed that many White people interviewed in Detroit, Boston and Atlanta said they would move if their neighborhoods reached varying levels of racial integration. Some of the reasons given included a healthy sprinkling of language such as declining property values, graffiti, crime and drug use. In decoded words it means that they believe that with more racial integration it is the same as the expansion of the inner city.

NAME DISCRIMINATION

The racial code wording process also includes the codifying and labeling of the names of members of targeted racial groups/ populations. According to Marianne Anthe of BET.COM Black people are quietly being racially discriminated against based on their names. Anthe reveals that the results of an employment hiring study conducted between mid 2001 –mid 2002 by Marianna Bertrand of the University of Chicago and Sendhil Mullainathan of MIT, indicate that White-named applicants were selected 50% more often than Black-named applicants with the same qualifications. The study found that there was clear evidence of discrimination against Black names such as Aisha, Keisha, Tamika, Kenya, Latonya and Ebony. This is another way in which the racial coding is used to practice modern racism beneath the radar screen. Black people are racially coded by name, zip code and other means in order to weed them out of the process for employment, housing, loans, educational grants and other life giving resources.

RACE CODE WORDS for BLACK PEOPLE

Following are a small sampling of frequently used racial code words. *This is by no means a complete listing of all racial code words.* The list is only a small beginning, a starting point to begin to understand how common words that on the surface have no direct racial identity or definition are used as coded language to foster racist thought, practices and images. These words and terms must be exposed and challenged, discontinued or clearly redefined. Most if not all of these words have become part of a language that conducts racial warfare against Black people. The list is always changing, with new words being added that must be decoded.

State's Rights

This is an old Southern word that was used in racial management conversations between groups of White supremacists. The Southerner said to the Northerner, *"Look, we want to handle our Negroes, without you riding our backs or looking over our shoulder. You are in violation of our agreement! There is no set standard for handling these people. You have a New York method and I have a Mississippi method. It all amounts to the same thing so why are we fighting over whose method is the best."* The state's rights argument was that each locale could handle its own race situation best.

The latest version of the racial management philosophical struggle was manifested in December 2002 over Mississippi Senator Trent Lott's comments at an event celebrating the 100th birthday of former racial segregationist, South Carolina Senator Strom Thurmond. The short battle that followed was an excellent example of the code talk between the north and the south. Trent Lott breached the code by speaking in a harder core racial language. Lott was probably so giddy about the recent political power gains achieved in the November 2002 elections that he let his language game slip below the racial radar screen.

Lott said the following: "I want to say this about my friend. When Strom Thurmond ran for president, we voted for him. We're proud of it. And if the rest of the country had followed our lead, we wouldn't have had all of these problems over these years, either."

His words are a classic mixture of code and hardcore language. The phrases, *we voted, these problems, our lead* and *rest of the country* are harder edged code wordings because of the context in which they were used. His comments were used in the glorification of racial segregation.

His use of code words like these problems is the same as saying those people or them niggers. The wording of these problems activated the old states rights issue. If you would let us handle these people our way we would not have had all of this racial mess in the nation. We're proud of it means White people that believe in the old model of white supremacy/racial domination.

The rest of the country when decoded means that if the rest of the White people would have listened to us we wouldn't be in this situation. His cover was blown and was trapped because he stepped outside of the code and recklessly used harder-edged language when the racial antennas were very high or at least were on special alert. For this major blunder Lott had to be removed from his position as the Senate Majority Leader.

Mud Slinging/Dirty

At first glance this would not be perceived as a racial code word. Wet dirt is mud, a substance no one wants on clothes. On the surface throwing mud could be an act of fun or an act of anger and hostility. Generally speaking, however, throwing mud is considered a hostile act. Dirt and mud are interesting words. Dirt is usually light to dark brown; when it is wet, it is very dark or black. Mud has been the subject of many racial jokes. On the positive side, all life comes from dirt. The earth is land or dirt, sea and air. Everything that is life giving and live saving comes from the dirt. Our final resting place is under the dirt. Dirt is really a good thing. Without it, life as we know it would not exist. The wettest dirt, or mud, helps crops to grow, and the darker the dirt, the richer the soil.

In the present social order mud and dirt are considered bad things. In a racial social order words like dirt and mud have far more than just ecological, mineral, biological or chemical meaning. In the racial context "dirt" means an evil deed against another person.

To get dirt on someone means to get or use harmful information to destroy an individual or group. Why use the word dirt to express an act of evil? Why not just call it harmful information?

Why is there a perceptual association between a dark-colored substance and an evil deed?

When dark colors are associated with evil, it is logical to conclude that dirt is a bad thing. Dirt does have its unimpressive side. It has the power to smear a material or alter the look of a substance. The removal of dirt helps to maintain a healthy living environment because it prevents the spread of disease. However, dirt like any other earthly substance, must be used within a positive context.

If the goal is to get clothes free of unwanted substances, the use of the word dirt is correct. However, in a racially codified social environment, the word dirt is associated with other racially derogatory meanings. Mudslinging is the act of throwing liquid blackness. This is another of the many ways of casting aspersions at black people. This kind of thinking is inherent in the psychological make-up of a racist mind. The blackening of one's name and reputation is the same as slinging mud. The affiliation of dark and black to evil, inferiority and badness is conjured up again. The act of slinging mud is the act of trying to blacken, nigrify, darken and downgrade. It is the color of mud that creates the reaction. If mud were white, the use of the term would be very different.

This same linkage occurs with dark-colored raisins, blackbirds and roaches. These and other images were used in countless television and radio commercials. The racist mind will always associate color with the worth of a racial population. A racist will use these kinds of artificially manufactured affiliations to convey racial messages. To be hit with a mud stain is to be hit with a stain of blackness. In White supremacist folklore the blackest stain is the worst and most frightening. White, brown, blue, red, purple or yellow are tolerable, but no stain is more feared than the black stain. In a racist context to be hit with the black stain means to be mentally, spiritually and physically overwhelmed by darkness and blackness. Black and dark colors have inescapable negative associations, just as light and white have unavoidable positive connectedness. A racist mindset will seek to relate the value of a color with the value of a group of people. Seemingly harmless statements when placed under the sharp eye of the racial microscope have extremely detrimental social reverberations. This selected list is an example of terms using the word "dirty" to express racial meaning.

DIRTY WORDS	**RACIAL MEANING**
Down and dirty	Dark and ugly
Dirty dog	Low down
Dirty old man	Dark side old man
Dirty old woman	Dark side old woman
Sex is dirty	Sex is smut (blackness)
You have dirty mind	You have a smut filled mind
Dirty bitch	Dark female
You like to play dirty	You like to play on the dark side

Walk on the Wild Side
This means to go across the tracks to the Black community or seek to have sex with a Black man or Black woman. Walk on the wild side is the same as saying walk on the savage side of life.
Go see what life is like in the jungle. Go see the primitive and backward Black people, a wild and untamed people. These undomesticated areas of town are full of wild sex, drugs, guns, murder, loud music and vibrant colors.

Troublemaker
This term means black male. Black men are considered criminals. Whether they hang around on corners or come down the street. It is the same as a criminal walking down the street or trouble walking through the door. Troublemaker is a tag of criminality. Even professional Black men have to endure these kinds of verbal assaults. It is not unusual for these men to hear statements like "stay out of trouble this weekend, Ronnie," which on the surface sound harmless. However, the subtle reference to the word trouble is indeed very troubling for Black males who are thought of as criminals and associated with crime in the street, high crime and the crime rate.

Race Code Words

The word trouble is part of a quiet yet powerful assumption that Black males are more likely to get into trouble because they are prone to violent behavior and illegal and immoral acts. The whole concept of driving, flying, walking and shopping while Black is based on the racist imaging of Black people and the Black male in particular as troublemakers.

You Rule

This is a new term designed to make Whites feel that they are still in charge and on top. In this statement the word "you" means a White individual. The word "rule" means in charge. Put together, the tag means White people are in charge and in control. This is designed to calm the mounting fears about the growing number of nonwhites invading the White terrain. This fear is based on data that suggests the White population especially in the United States, will shrink drastically over the next 30 years. It is estimated that the White population in America will no longer amount to a strong majority. Latinos, Asians and others will swamp the countryside and populate old and new cities. The coming decline of the White population was forecast in the 1972 movie "Executive Action" that starred Burt Lancaster and Robert Ryan. The movie dealt with the "conspiracy" surrounding the assassination of President John Kennedy in Dallas, Texas. One of the revealing and important statements in the film occurred between Lancaster and Ryan.

During a walk outside of the mansion where the conspirators planned the assassination, Ryan told Lancaster, that his group feared Kennedy would stop the Vietnam War. They did not want the war in Indochina stopped because the "things we learn here can be used to eliminate our excess population such as blacks..." These words were very chilling, instructive and prophetic. This motion picture did not have great circulation, but it sent a clear message to those who needed to know about racial warfare and population reduction. These kind, soft, race-based strategies have been used to maintain control and dominance. In the past it was a safe bet that a war or an intelligence operation would be launched to depopulate various populations. The rise of nonwhite populations is a threat to the command and control of White supremacists. Statements like you rule are designed as statements of reassurance.

RACE CODE WAR

Men in Black

Men dressed in black suits, dark sunglasses and black hats, all of the classic elements of the dark menace, are either from another planet or are protecting Earth from an alien invasion. It depends which version one wants to follow. According to most UFO literature, men in black are evil, strange and menacing.

The motion picture of the same name with actors Will Smith and Tommy Lee Jones is a different version. They portrayed the MIB (Men in Black) as defenders against the dark alien evil. However, these "men" go around threatening regular American citizens if they try to reveal what they know about the existence of the alien presence on earth. The MIB are the ever-present dark menace that each White family has been taught to fear and mistrust. These men dressed in black are coming to invade White communities and destroy the White genetic seed. This thinking is used in Ufology lore to send racial messages. It uses alien abductions as a cover for racist thinking. The Men in Black story is similar to the theme of the Prince of Darkness or the Princess of Darkness. It is another warning sign to White populations of the dark menace. When the message is decoded, it means that the men in black are Black males who are the real-life dark menace. These are the increasing numbers of Black and other dark skin males who date and have sex with White females. If this continues, there is the possibility of destroying the concept of a White race. White supremacists use these mediums as message boards to alert White people of the coming dangers of too much interaction with Black and other **dark, n**onwhite people.

Cloning

This is a new code word that must be studied very carefully. It was introduced as a non-racial word, and it is very similar to the Nazi practice of eugenics or creation of the master race. What is the purpose of cloning? Is it to make up for the declining population of White people in countries such as America, Britain and France? Who will be cloned and for what purpose?

Does this also mean that larger numbers of Black people will become **the victims** of genocide?

Race Code Words

Master Plan

This expression relates to such words as dominate, superior, control, command, overlord, godhead, god almighty, super and supreme. Only the master can develop a master plan.

A comprehensive plan can be created and developed by many groups. However, a master plan can only be conceived by the master. In White thought, the word "master" means White supremacist. Therefore, only those persons classified as White supremacists can develop a master plan. In decoded language the master plan is a plan for the establishment, maintenance and expansion of White supremacy, domination and control of the known universe. Whenever the term master plan is used, it furthers the subliminal mental association between subservience and White domination. To do master planning means in effect to keep the master in power and in charge. There are very few if any so-called Black master plans. And those plans never call for the dismantling and elimination of White supremacy. There are no Black masters so there can be no Black master plan. This term master plan must be discarded immediately.

The phrase must be discarded or redefined because each time it is used it triggers and reinforces the idea that master means White male and White God because Jesus is White and is called Lord and Master. Many Christian hymns are written using the word master. The word master was used to define White men during the chattel slavery period. The White man was called master. The use of the word master immediately triggers a mental association between God, White man and slave master. Under White supremacy, all three terms, God, White man and slave master, have the same meaning. This includes the effective majority of words and phrases that have the word master.

For example, the Masters Golf Tournament, until two black men, Tiger Woods and V. J. Singh, won, was considered the supreme White male event. Other examples include such terms as: mastery, master stroke, a masterpiece, masterful, a mastermind, master's degree, master race, master sergeant, master of ceremonies, master bedroom, master chef, masterful, master key and so forth. This word has so many very powerful racial and color meanings that it is effectively dissociated from its abstract meaning.

All words beginning or ending with the word master must be understood before using them in a sentence or statement. The best strategy is to discard the use of the word until it is redefined within the context of liberation language. This word has no place in the dialogue of thought that strives to eliminate all race and color language except in the honest descriptions of people, things and locations. Replacement terms could include the following: effective, competent, knowledgeable, understanding, capable, efficient, accomplished, adept, proficient and professional. These are acceptable and reasonable replacements.

Mob

This word used to be associated with the Mafia. However, in later years it also came to mean a gathering of Black people. When Whites encounter groups of Black people at various social events or outdoor festivals, they have a tendency to leave early or leave before the show or event is over. The deeper into the night, the more Whites will feel uncomfortable about the presence of large numbers of Black or dark people. Many Whites seem to feel or show a sense of being overwhelmed, intimidated and frightened.

They will pack up the children and the husband/wife will rush along in order to leave. While in the car, they will say, "My God, I'm glad we got out of there before all of them cut loose. I don't mind being around some, but too many of them makes me very nervous and uncomfortable." It is an old saying that Black folks come late and White folks leave early. The two groups are like ships passing in the sea. While this does not apply to all Whites and Blacks, it does apply to the effective majority of White/Black interactions here and abroad. The level of racial tolerance is still very low despite the claims of social reformers. The word mob was used by a newspaper reporter to describe a large gathering of predominantly Black people at a music festival in Columbus, Ohio.

The article, written by Curtis *Schieber, appeare*d in the Columbus Dispatch on Tuesday, July 25, 2000. It was about the Jazz & Rib Festival, an outdoor food and music festival held annually in Columbus, Ohio. He seemed very "concerned" by the huge crowd that came to see White jazz saxophonist Kenny G. He called the huge and largely African American crowd a "mob scene."

What was the basis for this statement? Why was the word mob used? This word is normally associated with huge displays of anti-social behavior. The crowd was estimated at 300,000 people. Yet there were no major reports of unruly behavior, fist- fights, guns being drawn, riots or any other disorderly conduct. The huge crowd seemed to have a good time. Everyone was friendly and very accommodating. There was nothing in this summer assemblage that even resembled a mob scene. So why was the largely Black crowd labeled a mob scene?

It is interesting that when large numbers of White people assemble for major events such as auto races they are never labeled as mobs or mob scenes. The use of the phrase mob scene is an expression of fear, intimidation and a feeling of being overwhelmed. This seems to be an unspoken mental and emotional dynamic that occurs when many White people are exposed to large numbers of Black people.

The perception is based on racial images and symbols that create fear in the minds of White people. The equation is simple. Black is evil, and therefore Black people are evil and criminal-minded. If they gather in large numbers, there will be problems. Therefore, large gatherings of Black people automatically mean trouble and must be monitored. This is probably the reason why the effective majority of Whites still go to White clubs, bars and restaurants and Blacks still go to Black bars and restaurants. When terms like mob or mob scene are used to describe large, peaceful gatherings of Black people, they validate the White supremacists' derogatory depictions of Black people.

Defeat the Dark Side

This is part of a collection of subtle race-based messages designed to establish and reinforce the belief that Black people are the dark enemies of White mankind. What is a dark force? Is it a nonhuman force? Is it robots, mutants or what? What color is the alien or nonhuman force? If it is a human or humanoid force, what color is it? The only known intelligent forces in the universe are human. There are no known mechanical armies that are engaged in battle against human forces (that is, so far as it is known). Therefore, defeat the dark side must be alluding to some human force that is dark or nonwhite. This human force has been defined as the dark force. If it is dark and human it is classified as nonwhite. The objective is to keep the public thinking that dark and Black people are the evil, vicious enemy forces who will one day overtake and overthrow White domination. This kind of racial propaganda keeps the policies of racial warfare alive and well, fighting against Africa and Black communities here and abroad.

White supremacists use many slogans to express fears about the dark menace. These sayings include popular slogans like "defeat the dark side." These and other sayings are used to rev up the fears of White people about the dark menace. This slogan means to defeat dark and Black people. It perpetuates the thought, triggered in the minds of millions of whites, that Black people are the enemies and must be watched and carefully managed. White people are conditioned to believe that Black people are the number-one threat to their system. The White supremacist will use the least obvious method of communication to send a race-based coded message. Who would ever look for hidden racial messages in adventure-filled stories that are as American as apple pie, yet this is one of the first places to look when decoding race-based information.

Black Plague in the Dark Ages
This term has been linked to the AIDS situation on the continent of Africa. When the 13th annual AIDS conference convened in Durban, South Africa, the headlines screamed that the AIDS virus would wipe out an entire generation of African people. The White-oriented media quickly pronounced doom in Africa by saying that the AIDS situation was similar to the black plague in the dark ages. This was a double race code word hit. The terms black and dark combined to produce a double whammy effect. This language immediately triggers a link to Africa without ever publicly saying that Black people are a threat to national security because they are the largest *ca*rriers of the AIDS virus.

Race Code Words

This word association was carried in every major White newspaper and in some large Black weeklies; it connected AIDS, black plague, Dark Ages and Black people. The White supremacist clearly understood the message; however, with most black people it flew right over their heads. This is a classic illustration of racial code wording linking derogatory words with derogatory situations and repeatedly associating them with certain groups and individuals.

The real message is that Black people both here and abroad are threats to the national security of the United States of America. When the U.S. government issued an intelligence finding through an Executive Order that said the AIDS virus was a threat to the national security, it also said that Africa and Black communities around the world-because of high rates of AIDS-were national security threats. This meant that Black people abroad might be barred from coming into this country and possibly those living in the U.S. could be subjected to mandatory AIDS testing. Those individuals who refuse could be locked up and/or internalized for long period*s of time. N*obody wants a black *plague or* a return to the Dark Ages because of *diseases assoc*iated with Dark Continent. This action is designed to further create a climate that would justify the recolonization of Black people in Africa and **other parts of the w**orld.

The Dark Continent

This is a racial reference to Black people that when it is decoded implies savage, backward and primitive. It has nothing to do with the lack of sunshine on the Continent. Africa has more days of sunshine than any other geographical location. The phrase "dark continent" in decoded language means "backward ass niggers." There is no counter-term such as the light, bright or white Continent. The word dark has a clear racial and color meaning that is associated with evil, blackness, dark or Black people.

AIDS-Ravaged Nation or Community

This term is used to define Black nations and Black communities. The word ravaged sounds very similar to the word savaged. When this word is connected to the Continent, it reads much like a substitute term for the word savage that subtly implies brutality, wild people, murderers, cannibals and rapists. It is no accident that this word was linked with Africa.

There are other words that could be used to communicate the truth much more effectively.

For example, one could say that African communities have been purposefully victimized by germ warfare diseases that were more than likely developed in non-Black-owned and controlled laboratories.

Sub-Saharan Nations

This term has been designed to talk openly about Black people and Black nations in a highly derogatory context. Derogatory racial language such as nigger country or nigger nation can be coded by using the term Sub-Saharan. The word sub means below, less than or to take away from. The term means that the Black nation-states are inferior to other half-white Arab nation-states. It tells the world not to confuse this part of Africa with the half/white or White part of Africa. It leads one to believe that Black people have had very little to do with the positive modern developments occurring on the Continent. Sub-Saharan says that the Black people in Africa had nothing to due with the development and existence of the ancient empires of Algeria, Morocco, Tunisia, Egypt and Libya because they lived below the North African region. The implication is that Black people have lived in the same regions and area for thousands of years and did not live up or down the Nile River Valley and did not help to develop any of these regions.

Sub-Saharan is also designed to remove from the minds of modern day audiences the links between the ancient and modern Black world. The thousands of years of Black dynasties of mighty Egypt are attributed to the brown skinned and White Arabs and White people from Europe. There are millions of historical facts that document Black people as the supreme architects of the ancient Egyptian dynasties. The term Sub-Saharan is also used to separate the powerful developments and innovations of Black people from progressive modern-day developments on the Continent, that is to say, Blacks have had nothing to do with the development of Saudi Arabia and other developed areas on the Continent.

Race Code Words

The term Sub-Saharan really means land of the savages. It means that King Kong is chasing a White blonde woman named Faye Ray around the Continent. It means Rwanda, Burundi, Sierra Leone, Botswana, Zimbabwe, South Africa (under so-called Black rule), Angola, Senegal, Uganda, Swaziland, Lesotho, Namibia, Malawi, Kenya, Ethiopia, Eritrea, Somalia, Cameroon, Ghana, Ivory Coast, Gabon, Congo, Nigeria, Niger, Mozambique, Zambia, Tanzania, Sudan, Chad, Liberia, Gambia, Guinea Bissau, Togo, Benin, Mali and Madagascar.

All of these areas in the White supremacist mindset are nigger countries. They will be kept on the bottom of the totem pole just as Black people are kept on the bottom all over the planet. These are Black-ruled nations with no hope for the future. These nations are the poorest and most devastated nations in the world according to the *United Nations Human Development Report 2000*. The term Sub-Saharan is also another derogatory label that categorizes Black people as inferior and hopeless. This term is similar to the creation of the phrase Middle East, which is a term used to separate this area from the African Continent. The word Sub-Saharan has been used to hide the White supremacist's race war against Black people. The White supremacist can blame the Black people and say that these people can never be civilized and develop on their own merit. They must be managed with kid gloves and then we can only hope for the best because they are so backward and unintelligent. Their potential is limited because of their genetic inferiority. They will only develop to a limited degree no matter how many resources are pumped into their communities or areas. This is why it is better that they are eliminated or the population is significantly reduced.

If this would have happened in the Balkans or in Eastern Europe or in Mexico, with White people, the reaction would have been different.

The White supremacists are well aware of the damage this deadly virus is having on the African Continent. The intentional neglect toward Black people regarding the prevention of the spread of the deadly AIDS virus was purposeful. Purposeful neglect and indifference are part of whole or limited extermination. The AIDS epidemic is estimated to take out entire generations of Black people in Africa, India, Indonesia, Fiji Islands, the Caribbean, Canada, Australia, South America, the United States and other areas where Black people reside in significant numbers.

On April 06, 2001 former Congresswoman Cynthia McKinney (D) GA sponsored a forum on the plunder and rape of Africa.

In her opening comments she said the following:

> *Their investigations into the activities of Western governments and Western businessmen in postcolonial Africa provide clear evidence of the West's long-standing propensity for cruelty, avarice, and treachery. The misconduct of Western nations in Africa is not due to momentary lapses, individual defects, or errors of common human frailty. Instead, they form part of a long-term malignant policy designed to access and plunder Africa's wealth at the expense of Africa's people. In short, the accounts you are about to hear provide an indictment of Western activities in Africa.*

The goal is to wipe out indigenous power on the Continent, thus controlling the riches of Africa. This also keeps the most effective Black people, those living in the United States, from becoming aroused and looking toward the African Continent for help, dual citizenship and mutual economic development. In the new millennium the most powerful and effective Black people on the planet are almost totally disconnected from Black people in Africa. This is quite a contrast to the hopes of Black people in the sixties and seventies when Black people from Africa and America were reuniting and developing international bridge-building activities. Black people were even developing dual citizenship relationships with African nations.

The talk at that time was a great coming forth of the mighty African nations. Africa was viewed as the hope and future of the Black world, with its diamonds, oil and other plentiful natural resources. However, talk of building relationships did not go unnoticed by White supremacists. They paid close attention to the growing Black awareness and pressures on white-ruled South Africa, Rhodesia and other parts of the Continent.

They were keenly aware of the activism of Black people here in the U.S. and Canada who staged such huge activities as African

Race Code Words

Liberation Day. They heard the call for a united Black world and began to put a grand strategy in place to destroy the hopes and dreams of Black people here and abroad. The White supremacist went to work to dislodge and destroy these budding Black unity relationships. They supported efforts to destroy Black nations by supplying millions of rounds of ammunition and military hardware to ferment civil war and massive killings.

They helped to stagnate and downgrade the African economies thus creating extreme poverty, extreme starvation, extreme homelessness and the control of African economic imports and exports. They permitted such things as AIDS and the Ebola virus, the assassination of Black leaders, the fermenting of family and tribal disputes, the dearth of foreign aid and development funds, the overburdening of nations with insurmountable debt, the corruption of political leaders who were given bank accounts in foreign nations where most of them either died or were imprisoned before they could ever use the money.

The West financed the weapons for internal destruction and the flow of drugs to addict millions. The lack of a modern economic infrastructure, the destruction of school systems and the exportation of the most talented and educated to White countries contributed to the massive decline of African nations. Every imaginable human ill on the African Continent can be traced to the workings of the collective White supremacy. The goal was to destroy Africa as a base for Black people from all over the world. Such a base would allow the Black world to develop and control massive resources for development. This would mean trade programs, joint academic institutions, cultural sharing and development, one-world Black ideology, independent Black world media, collective economic development programs, a rewriting of Black history, the development of technology, and the establishment of a protectorate system for the sanctity of Black life all over the planet. This would create the same kind of development as Jews accomplished in the state of Israel, The Irish in Ireland, Italians in Italy and Germans in Germany. The other goal was to keep Black people in a hopeless and degraded position in the new century.

Africa, wholly developed by Black people, would become one of the strongest areas of the world. The field of athletics teaches us a lot about the ability of Black people to effectively dominate on an equal playing stage. The White supremacist is aware that if Africa develops and is controlled by Black people, Black people all over the world will move forward to take their rightful place on the world stage. That means that black people in Indonesia, Fiji Islands, China, India and so forth will be called to reunite with their black brethren. The destruction of Africa, on the other hand means that Black people in America will be less likely to connect with African causes in the future. Blacks in America will see themselves more as American citizens and less as members of a united Black people worldwide. They also will not see the connection between their plight in America and the Black plight in Africa. Thus, the incredible carnage in Rwanda, the Congo and other locations went without shouts above a whisper, especially among Black people. Millions of Black people disappear and yet no major effort has been made to find out why? This would not have happened to White people without a major international outcry.

No appreciable sound was heard from voices in the Black communities in America, in India, on the Fiji Islands, in Indonesia or in South America. This has been part of a five-hundred-year campaign to disconnect Black people all over the world. It is the goal of the White supremacist to destroy the base and bonding of Black people in order to reduce their numbers here and abroad.

Abortion
This word is cloaked in walls and walls of deceptive language. Black people must not be deceived by the synthetic arguments about when life begins. This is a misleading diversion for the sake of public drama. The abortion debate is calculated racial propaganda designed to deflect and confuse black populations.

The real issue is not over when the life of the fetus begins but which racial management philosophy will be used to control the development of black people. When the issue of abortion is decoded, it is no more than an argument among White supremacists over how to manage and control the development of blacks and other nonwhites.

Unfortunately, Black people have not successfully decoded this argument. They have not flushed out the hidden or even subtle meanings in the tightly cloaked argument. White supremacists have effectively masked this public spat as a disagreement over the right to choose vs. the right to life. Both these positions are very clever disguises and have worked effectively.

Race Code Words

The two-sided argument is based on the old Soviet Union vs. America / Communism vs. Capitalism script. One side poses as a left-wing liberal and the other as a right-wing conservative. These are two sides of the same coin pretending to be radically different. It is a virtuoso con game because both groups have the same goal of White supremacy domination. The game works this way.

The liberal side pretends to have a greater tolerance for things like interracial relationships, Black economic development and social intermingling. They even design a litany of government-funded programs to create the illusion of meaningful change. In reality White supremacists are haunted by the possibility of Black racial unity and unlimited economic development.

They see this as a serious threat to the continued existence of White supremacy. That is why when all the dust has cleared and the shouting is over, and in spite of all the special government-funded programs, the power relationship between Blacks and Whites has not change to any appreciable degree. Remember, when dealing with a White supremacist, the real issue is always power, based on racial domination. The objective is to control through deception.

In the area of sex and family relations, they use the language of abortion to debate the issue of the management of nonwhite birth control. One side uses their liberal credentials to push the concept that women have the right to choose an a*bortion. Their slogan is pro choice or t*he woman's right to choose.

Racists use these kinds of trigger words to appeal mainly to nonwhite females. The hidden message t*o the nonwhite female is: He (black male) won't be around to help raise the baby. We have seen that reality and therefore you will have to carry **the** burden all by yourself!* Their goal is to reduce and/or contain the birth rate of nonwhite people through abortion and other methods of birth control. Their concern is that if the birth rate is not controlled, there will be too many nonwhites on the planet. They will spill out of their ghettos and reservations and genetically annihilate and numerically overwhelm White people. Abortion helps to reduce the number of Black and nonwhites.

Therefore, birth control is a useful tool for the perpetuation of White supremacy. Under the liberal model, abortion is marketed toward the nonwhite female. Other groups are called conservatives, and their role is to oppose abortion. Conservatives want to conserve or keep White supremacy domination just as it is currently being implemented. They do not want to restrict the number of nonwhites. They want to use them as economic, political and social slaves. They need more nonwhite babies to starve, miseducate, incarcerate, infect with various diseases, keep addicted to drugs and brainwash. It keeps the White economy working. The White Government superstructure has benefited greatly from Black people involved in the multi-billion-dollar prison/ industrial complex. And, predictably, this is the province of the law-and-order White conservatives.

The right-wing conservative argues for the elimination of abortion. They use a *disguised argument* called the right to life to skillfully hide the real meaning. The right to life con game is also marketed to the Black and nonwhite female. This side uses a very strong emot*ional and moral argument. They equate abortion with murder in language that suggests t*hat abortion is homicide. It is tinged with a sense of religious cultism. This is the same group that supports monetary cuts to social programs that are designed to help nonwhites enjoy the right to life. In other words, while they holler for the right to life, they support efforts that destroy and reduce the quality of life for newborn Black children. This is a direct and purposeful contradiction that confuses many Black people. When this is decoded, it turns out to be a racial argument among White supremacists about how to manage the development or underdevelopment of nonwhite people-especially Black populations.

Affirmative Action
The concept of affirmative action began as a corrective approach to racism in education, employment and other areas. In the early days of affirmative action it was used as a process to achieve limited compensatory relief. The objective was to produce justice for victims of injustice. However, in recent years this term h*as become a code word for giving somethi*ng for nothing to Blacks. Therefore, affirmative action is viewed as a sort of Black welfare handout program. It has become a trigger word to signal that Blacks are getting something they have not worked for or honestly earned. It has been used to rally White interests against Black people. In reality the greatest beneficiaries of affirmative action programs have been White **female**s.

50

Race Code Words

At Risk
This is a term associated with the social condition and problems of Black people. It conveys the more-than-subtle message that the survivability rate of Black people is in question. The concept of at risk also suggests that Black people are a dangerous and self-destructive population without social or political direction, a mindless group of childlike beings bent on destruction and mayhem. They are dangerous to be around and a threat to the existence of other people. When this term is used, it is a clear indication of a population or community's survival being threatened.

Birth Control
The term birth control decoded means to control the birth rate of Black people. The term birth control was first publicized as a new vehicle to unleash greater sexuality. The fear of unwanted pregnancies was removed from the act of sexual intercourse with the introduction of the birth control pill. It was sold as the great sexual liberator. *The propaganda read, You can now have as much sex as you want* without getting pregnant. This was used to disguise the real purpose of reducing the Black and nonwhite birth rate. The White supremacist implemented containment programs all over the world by linking trade, investment, military arms, material aid and financial support to rates of birth control. The Continent of Africa, South America, India, China, Indonesia and other nonwhite populations were inundated with tons of birth control pills, literature and birth control training programs. Foreign monetary policies were tied to birth control activity. Birth control is part of the White supremacist's nonwhite population containment operation. Other containment activities include starvation, illiteracy, war, drugs, disease and genocide.

Inclusion
This is another code word used largely in political and legal circles. It means allowing a few Blacks to participate with White people. This word is a racial illusionist term used to pacify Black people. It is also becoming a marginal word to create conflict among nonwhites. The term inclusion fosters competition between Asians, Latinos and Black people. This is done with the purpose of minimizing nonwhite participation while pretending to embrace it. Inclusion is a dynamic

action word designed to create and foster the notion of effective participation. It is, however, an illusionary word that frustrates nonwhites and pits them against each other for the leftover crumbs. The term inclusion also implies a subservien*t relationship that means I'll take care of you Black people so do*n't worry about a thing. This code word has nurtured the rise of the so-called Black nerd, a racial creation of White supremacy and part of a process that selects and recruits some of the most talented Black minds.

They are exposed to the best White-controlled institutions and placed in good positions so that their minds may be used in the interest of White supremacy. They are totally alienated from Black people and totally in love with White people. They even hate their Black skins and humble Black beginnings. They see no relation between themselves and Black people on the Continent. They do not wish to be called or classified as Black. This is nothing new, but at this critical juncture in history it could have major consequences that set the progress of Black people back many years. Inclusion is a code word for a brain drain that is designed to steal some of the best Black minds. It is a slickly designed **divide-and-conquer** strategy.

Undesirables

This word has a larger meaning; when decoded it means Black people. The White supremacists project Black people as undesirables because in the White worldview Black people are unacceptable. They are considered the lowest of the low, the last on the totem pole. Blacks are still invisible except for a few select Black personages leaving the impression that much in this society has changed.

However, the facts simply do not support this assumption. According to the June, 2000, *Human Rights Watch Report*, which included data on the rate of male incarceration, Black males are imprisoned for drug offenses in some American states at 57 times the rate of White males, even though White males use, sell and distribute drugs, including *crack cocaine, at nearly five times the rate of African American males.* This is also true for Black females who are imprisoned for drug offenses nearly eight times as often as White women for the same offense.

Race Code Words

Using words like undesirables helps set the tone for the justification of such incredible injustice. This term is also frequently used to paint an especially derogatory image of Black males. One example of this was the media's racial imaging of Black males during the Puerto Rican Festival in Central Park, New York, on June 19, 20, and 21, 2000. The NBC news reporters kept playing the same video shots over and over again of Black men throwing water and groping light-skinned and White females. This was to portray Black males as rapist, lusting after White females.

However, in the new era Black males have been given a green light to openly touch White and near-white females. This kind of Black-White sexual interaction has been sanctioned, and Black men have been given license to dance and engage in lewd sexual behaviors in the open with White women. Interracial touching and hot sexual interaction has also been allowed at other large outdoor events such as Mardi Gras in New Orleans and the Florida Spring Break. White males have engaged in these "rites of passage" events for many years, and they have not been called undesirables or animals.

White males have gone to Florida to engage in open wild, lewd and immoral sexual behavior for years, and the media have proclaimed this activity as simply the boys need to work off some steam and have a little fun in the sun. At these events White males regularly gorge themselves on wet tee-shirt contests and groping White females. The media sees White females, without any prodding or coercion, fully expose their bodies and have sex in public. This sexual activity regularly happens at the Mardi Gras, the Florida Fantasy Festival and Havasu River, which is south of the Mexican border, and the Colorado River. However, cries of undesirables, vicious savages and vicious rapists are not heard.

Such cries are only heard when Black males very foolishly try to duplicate the worst behavior of White people by engaging in the same kind of immoral and mindless behavior. Black males began in the1980s attending some of these mostly White events. They learned that the old rules had been relaxed a little because the White supremacist strategy no longer called for the same kind of physical reaction to Black hands touching the "sacred" body parts of White females.

In the 1940s, 1950s, 1960s and 1970s Black men did not openly touch White females, especially on or near private parts. In the late

1980s Black males got the new message and started showing up in greater numbers at these sexually driven events. They were allowed to watch and in some cases touch White women's body parts. The new game plan was designed to efface the "caveman" image of the racist, beating up Black males for just touching or looking at White females.

The racists wanted to erase the impression that just one look at a White female meant certain pain and death for Black men. The old model of racism was out the door. The new model was the name of the game. During the Puerto Rican Festival, White, light-skinned and some Black females accused a number of Black males of groping them and tearing away their clothes. The Black males were called beasts, animals and a host of other derogatory epitaphs.

This same kind (or even worse) behavior takes place at such predominantly White events as the Mardi Gras festival in New Orleans and Fantasy Festival in Florida. These events feature in full public view thousands of sexual acts such as breast flashing, oral sex, cross dressing, posing and walking around totally nude, masturbating, sexual intercourse and other voyeuristic behavior. These lewd behaviors are rarely mentioned in a derogatory way in the media, and the events are glorified and sold as sexual fun and frolic by responsible adults.

If any of this sexually lewd and irresponsible behavior is wrong, then all of it should be classified as unacceptable. To do less is to perpetuate a racial image that shows Black men to be animals and undesirable, creatures that should be banned and locked up because they are a menace to society. Undesirable is a powerful word. It means that Black males are not wanted because they are less than human and uncivilized. They are undesirable in terms of moving into White communities, professions and business relationships.

Smut

This word is used to identify pornographic material and sexually explicit acts. Smut is darkened ash from old furnaces. It is very black in color. Therefore, the use of the term implies that sex is dirty and black or nasty. That it is trashy and low life. When pornography became a huge business in the late 1960s there were very few Black people doing filmed sex acts. It should have been called "snow" because of the large number of White people in pornography films and videos. It would have been more correct. The labeling and equating of explicit sex with blackness is a pure act of racism. It implies that all sexual activity is dark and black. The word smut has begun to make a comeback in the year 2002 in the new language of the porn industry.

Divide (Digital or Racial)

This is a new code word. It has been applied with the word racial to form terms such as racial divide and digital divide (which also means racial divide). The word divide clearly is a reference to the division between Black and White people. The inference is that Blacks are the reason for the so-called divide. Black people are so hung-up on race that they hate Whites and want to be segregated. They are also responsible for not wanting to integrate into the mainstream of society. They are the reason Whites do not want to live around them and be involved in what they do.

Guess Who's Coming to Dinner

This is a code word for Black people moving into a neighborhood, entering a new work area, a Black and White romantic relationship or some related racial activity. This word was used in the movies and comic stints during the early '60s to late '70s. It also meant that Back males were coming after White women.

Teeming Slum

The word slum is a code word to describe an area of town that is overcrowded with Black and other dark-skinned nonwhite people. The word slum has become synonymous with the concept of being Black. A slum area is an inferior, backward and disease-filled area. It is an area where modern-day savages reside.

The Underclass

This code word is designed to define poor Black people. The term underclass assumes that Black people constitute an economic class. Blacks do not control the development of production or the distribution of resources, and they do not constitute a class. A class is based on how the material gains from the production of goods and services are divided.

If a group of people own nothing and produce nothing, they have nothing to divide. They cannot be classified as anything other than a non-class group and a social commodity to be bought and sold by the different classes of people. They are merely a surplus population. The notion of class when applied to Black people is clearly a misnomer. Black people are really the dependent wards of White people.

The word underclass is used all over the globe to define Black youth and Black poor who live in the so-called inner city. The word "under" means to be on the lower level, on the bottom.

This term gained great prominence during the 1980s as a means to define in a derogatory manner the condition of Black people. The use of the word by Black scholars is very troubling. It connotes the idea of being below, low level, subservient and slave-like. It is the same as labeling Black people as a slave population.

The Old, Central or Close-in Suburbs

The term old suburb is a new and developing code word that means that White people have or are abandoning a domain and Black people are moving in. Black people are buying homes in communities and Whites are moving out of certain suburban communities. The suburb has historically been a code word for White. However, given the changing nature of words in racially charged environments, the word had to be changed to reflect the dynamics of the changing social order. Therefore, a new word is emerging to signal that White people are again migrating away from Black people. That word, according to the Wednesday, September 29, 2000, edition of *USA Today* is *far-flung or new suburb*. The new strategy for moving away from Black people is the far-flung suburb.

According to the 2000 census data and 2002 desegregation reports from Harvard University and other academic institutions, a new pattern of racial segregation is emerging. The White middle-class has rejected the notion of racial integration and continues to move far away from Black people. This is the basis for the term far-flung suburbs. The old notion of suburban and urban is dead. The new identification will be based on what kind of suburb? The far-flung suburb is clearly a White-dominated community. If it is an old suburb, it contains new Black populations and what is left of aging or very poor White people.

Race Code Words

Civil Rights

When this code term is used, it usually is in reference to Black people. This term was attached to Black people in the early 1940s when they began to push for an end to White apartheid rule in America. The civil rights struggle has become an historical relic. It does not have the same meaning since the rules of the race game have significantly changed. However, it is still used to racially assign and paint the struggle of Black people.

Trash Talking

This slogan along with such phrases as trash minutes gained prominence with the increased presence or domination of Black athletes in certain sports. It has gained its greatest reputation in the NBA and the NFL. It is a term used primarily against Black athletes to defame the mental manipulation process used by them in competitive sports. When this reference is used, it means that the participants are engaging in garbage and dirt talking. It is a form of talk that exhibits low character and a conversation level that has zero content. When White athletes talked loudly and extensively, especially during professional baseball games, it was called "chatter."

It was praised as a psychological tool to disrupt the concentration and thinking ability of the opponent. When Black males engaged in "chatter" and took it to a higher and more intense level, it was reclassified as trash talk with zero content, functioning at the garbage level. The correlation between trash and Black people is indeed a very interesting and revealing affiliation. Until very recently, the majority of the nation's trash containers were dark or black in color. It is still true that the vast majority of trash containers in the backyard and office are still dark or black. Many of these containers are shaped like dark or black penises. What is the association between the Black reproductive organ and trash? The relationship is that the product that emanates from the Black reproductive organ is trash, garbage and therefore no-good. That means Black people are born as garbage and are throwaway surplus.

The color and shape of the trash receptacle is a clear signal of how much the social order values the life of a newborn Black or dark child. The only way this can be corrected is for the Black child to denounce his/her blackness or to try and "whiten up" the color of the newborn child with interracial or lighter-skin relationships. The dark black individual is at the lowest scale. He or she is considered closer to animal life, devils and junk. They are tolerated as sideshow freaks in the same manner as exotic animals are prized.

Even the great Michael Jordan with his "perfect black" is considered as much a sexual creature and big black animal with his tongue hanging out as he is a great athlete. Today, Shaquille O'Neal is the big, black lovable gorilla with the big, black penis that jams the brown ball into the white nets with force and power. Shaq is often portrayed as a big kid, meaning that he is physically developed but not mentally prepared. In a slew of recent television and Internet commercials he was linked to hamburgers. The linking of a very large, very dark-skinned male with the word ham is interesting. The use of the word ham, other than as a description of meat, is from the Holy Bible. In the Bible, Ham was a Black male. Could there be any association between Ham in the Bible and the use of Big Black Shaq?

Impoverish

This word has been used for many years to define locations that are home to large Black populations. It is designed to undercut the value of Black people and their living environments. The homes and communities lose property value. They simply say that it is a low-income area in a state of poverty and bad times. The impoverishment exists because of economic plunder, racial discrimination and racist hoarding. Black people were and still are denied access to the resources needed to build their communities. However, many of the Black people with some resources or access have decided to flee from Black people and move to where White people reside. They have become supporters of Black impoverishment.

Minorities (Minority)

This code word is designed to make Whites appear more dominant than nonwhites.

This is done to make Black people feel inferior to Whites and to give the appearance that Whites represent the majority of the world's population. The reality is that Whites are less than 20 percent of the world's population. The term minority also means that Blacks are less in number and are inferior.

Nightmare

This word has very little to do with night or nighttime. It is another reference to the correlation between darkness, blackness and evil. A nightmare is not a daydream or even a dream. Both of these words have reference to constructive or positive activities. A daydream is usually associated with romance, money or some affirmative event. Notice that the word includes "day" which means light or bright and in White supremacy thinking it is closely associated with whiteness and White race. The term "night" is connected with evil, blackness and Black people.

Reverse Discrimination

This term more than any other has been used to justify the White supremacist's attempt to avoid efforts to rectify the wrongs of slavery, Jim Crow segregation, discrimination, apartheid and racism. The celebrated case of Alan Bakke was used to set-up the case for the bogus reverse discrimination claim and rhetoric. It is virtually impossible for Black people to discriminate against White people in any meaningful way. White people control and dominate all of the life-giving and life-saving institutions.

Black people do not have the power or the position to discriminate against White people. If discrimination did occur, it would be because powerful White people used Black people as bait to anger ordinary Whites to radically oppose affirmative action. White people control the social order and therefore if any level of discrimination took place it would be a result of their actions. Affirmative action was a compensatory program designed to combat the impact of racism, especially in the areas of employment, business and education.

High-risk population

This is a newer code for Black and other nonwhite populations. The term high risk means that Black people are dangerous. They are prone to engage in unsavory and violent activities. Therefore, they must be watched and controlled. Black people are classified as a threat to the maintenance of order. The term high risk means that they are a menace and threatening by virtue of their sheer existence. They must be treated as an alien force to be pacified or to be conquered and destroyed. They must be viewed as a detriment to the growth and development of society. This expression of racism is common among many racists.

Racists will constantly refer to how bad, awful or uncivilized Black people are. This is especially notable when numbers of Black people move into or live in predominantly White communities. The constant complaint is how bad the community is and how it has gone downhill since the Black population came on the scene. The language reduces Black people and especially Black children to the level of little savages without manners and without hope. What are Black people at high risk of? Are they at high risk of the implementation of an intricate program of social, cultural and physical genocide?

Cannibal

This is an old code word for Black men in the jungle. When this word is used, it is always a subtle or overt reference to an uncivilized Black population. There are many sources of this word association from Tarzan the Ape Man books and movies to songs like "In the jungle," which symbolize conquering the savages of Africa and civilizing them enough to function as semi-human beings. During the 1930s when White supremacists were more brazen in their racist portrayals of Black people, it was common to find pictures of Black people with bones coming out of their noses ready to eat the poor White settlers stewing in a boiling hot pot. This old notion of cannibalism is still in the minds of millions of Whites and, for that matter, millions of Blacks. The word cannibal is a direct reference to the word dark. During one nightly newscast, a famous CBS news anchor introduced a story about Africa, using the term *deepest Africa*. This phrase is close enough to evoke the association of racist terms like *darkest Africa or the Dark Continent*.

Jungle

This is a code word for wild Black males. The jungle is a place for savages and the uncivilized.
This reference is similar to the concept of the cannibal. After all, isn't this where all of the cannibals are located: in the jungle? According to

Race Code Words

Webster's New Collegiate Dictionary the word jungle means "an impenetrable thicket or masses of vegetation." This is far from the racial meaning ascribed to the term jungle. When one thinks of jungle, one immediately harkens back to the old Tarzan movies that featured the wild Black men and crazy Black women.

The Downtrodden
This is a code word for Black and poor people. Particular interest should be given to the word "down" because of its long-term association with Black people. The language is designed to portray Black people as beneath Whites in all areas of life. Thousands of word combinations that use the down word in social description contexts are generally making reference to the color black or a Black and nonwhite population. The word trodden means to tread. The use of this word is also quite interesting. The term implies that Black people are low-life beings who tread on the goddess of the society or, better put, White society.

Credit Worthy or Credibility
This is a racial code word that is used in an economic context to keep Black people in a materially deficient state. The concept of credit worthiness has more to do with the level of trust and belief in the viability of the individual than it does with such things as economic payback schedules. The idea of being credit worthy is synonymous with the idea of being a worthy, virtuous red-blooded American. Under White supremacy, no Black individual is worthy. Only a White man or White woman can be sanctioned as worthy.

Transvestite
This word has become associated with Black males, particularly in the last few years. When this term was originally used, it was associated widely with the behavior and lifestyle of White homosexuals. However, in the last few years, this word has come to mean Black men dressing up as females and imitating White females. They are trying to resemble White women. They do not dress like Black women in other parts of the world. They do not dress in Black wrap or other culturally based black garments. They dress like Greta Garbo, Marilyn Monroe and so forth. The White supremacist desires to put Black men in dresses to

reduce their manhood so that they become less of a threat. This is part of the reason for the explosion of Black males in drag. Black men that dress as females have been allowed to star in television shows, appear in movies and become big-time celebrities.

Vouchers
This is a code term for inner city youth going to White or whiter school systems with portable vouchers. According to *Webster's New Collegiate Dictionary*, a voucher is "a documentary record of a business transaction." The vouchers are new signals that suggest the Blacks are coming. Instead of providing an effective education in predominantly Black schools, another phony race-assistance program is implemented. It implies that all Black schools are grossly inferior and uncivilized. This is a part of what racism does as it plays on the legitimate desires of Black people to set up programs to help their children succeed.

Crack Baby
This term is applied to Black children who are born victims of the chemical conspiracy. This term condemns little Black children to a life of abuse. It also justifies the actions of some to push the concept of sterilization of Black and nonwhite people.

Ethnic
The term ethnic is another old word in new bottles that define race in different contexts. This word has gathered steam on the supermarket shelves. It started being used to identify hair care products and other related items. It defines an area in the store that sells products for Black people, usually clothing or hair care items. This is very interesting because most hair care products are geared toward the development of a better White look. The "ethnic" word is a code for *if you want to look Black or if you are Black, you should buy this product.*
It is another way of saying Black without dealing with the baggage of racism that is attached to it. In the world of pornography, for example, the word ethnic does not sell. They openly use the term Black or African American as part of their marketing approach. The word ethnic is a soft racial marketing code word to make Black products more acceptable and tolerable to White consumers. Dr. Frances Cress Welsing, writes

that many White people really do not like their skin color and will risk their health to get darker pigmentation.

The purchase of Black products allows the illusion of color identification. The purchase of African or Black label products gives too much exposure for some White people to off-handed remarks that they are trying to be Black. This is what happened to many White people who wore hip hop clothes, baggy pants, hair braids, bought black rap music and affected other Black identification items. They were accused of wanting to be Black. This is of course an old accusation. Many White people have desired deeper or black color for centuries. Although seeking more skin pigmentation, they are not willing to give up the benefits of Whiteness in modern society. From the ancient Greeks and Romans to the Europeans of the Dark Ages, the worship of Blackness was institutionalized.

Only in the last 350 years have Whites in a highly organized and deceptive manner attempted to conceal this great desire to be and look Black. According to the research of Dr. Welsing and others, this great desire for dark skin or to look Black comes out in many ways: sun tanning, large eyes and bigger lips, hair braiding, body movement and dance, body look, body building with deep color tans, padded and bigger buttocks, black or dark stockings, wearing darker clothes, black cars (when decoded, Black penis symbols), Black talk, Black art, Black architecture, Black science and Black music. It is very interesting to watch White shoppers at various music stores go to the rhythm and blues section to purchase so-called Black music.

Whites assume an interesting look, as if saying, "I am not a racist. I just want to satisfy this great hunger I have for cultural diversity. I'm not ready to admit that it means anything other than liking different music from time to time." Music has the power to impact and alter the mind. When listening to music, the listener can identify with or take a peek inside the history and culture of the people that originated the song.

White people that quietly listen to Black music are secretly being seduced and influenced by the words, sound and rhythm. Overt White supremacist groups like the White Citizens Council opposed the Elvis Presley imitation of Black music. They believed it could lead to the disintegration of the "White social order." The code word "ethnic" exposes a real desire to be Black or darker. The hidden desires are cloaked with these kinds of words that help to conceal the strong desire for color.

White Collar Criminal

This is the code phrase generally reserved for White male criminal activity. A white-collar crime means a sophisticated criminal act that requires great thinking, organizational skills and mental concentration. The white collar and the white shirt are color-coded symbols of White superiority and power. The white-collar crime is considered the stuff of glamour criminals and the theme of glossing movies. The white-collar criminal is praised and glorified. In decoded color and racial language, the white collar represents the White mindset, the White way of doing things and White people.

In the existing racial/color climate when the words white or black are used in any context they must be closely examined to determine their real or hidden meaning. A white-collar crime is vastly different from a street crime, which decoded means a crime committed by a Black male. The white-collar crime is the diamond heist, insurance fraud, stock swindle or insider trading scam. The term white collar came into high use during the late fifties and early sixties with the growth and expansion of the white middleclass, which was considered a superior, educated workforce. The white shirt was used to signal the superiority of the large White workforce.

The majority of the so-called white-collar workers were White, quiet, dedicated and intelligent. Today the image has been slightly altered. One or two light-skinned Black people, Hispanics or others flash in the video/photo. This is used as a cover against charges of racism and noninclusion. However, the term white collar has fallen on hard times in recent years because of the coloration of the new work force. When a Black individual wears a white collar or white shirt, he or she is submitting to the will and thinking that developed the concept of the white collar/ white shirt. In short, wearing a white shirt that covers the heart region of the body is part of the emotional attachment to the Whitening process.

The white shirt gives a Black male a feeling of being restricted, controlled and contained within a false social identity. When the Black male puts on a white shirt, he is in full uniform and ready to play the game according to the White male's rules. This is a daily mental manipulation that has very little to do with physically wearing a shirt. With the growth of a new workforce of varying colors, the white shirt look had to change.

They have now moved away from the white shirt look so prevalent once in major White-dominated corporations such as the IBM Company. The new look is confusing and misdirecting. The clothing pattern does not seem to have a sense of organization or purpose. Is this an attempt to misdirect the nonwhite masses? Is this an effort to make them believe that the atmosphere is more tolerant of their existence and more open to their growth and development? It this a way to accommodate and manipulate the colored workforce by creating a greater variation of color in the workplace.

The so-called *business causal looks* have more to do with the invasion of the colored workforce than a productivity motivation scheme. Is this an adjustment to a more color-based social environment? Does it seek to manage color? It is a way to accommodate the colored psyche without losing control and staying in charge. The key color to the business causal look is khaki, which is primarily a brown color.

The *dress down look* is either darker in color, as in jeans, sweatshirts and/or looser-fitting clothes similar in style but not in color to traditional African or nonwhite clothing. Notice the evolution of the term dress at a time when more color is worn in the workplace. The so called "trendy" or "designer" look, which is a code word for White people, shows the direct influence of colored people on the psyche of White people. And it is also an attempt to hide the influence of Black people in the workplace.

The message of White supremacy is taking a different course and concentration at least temporarily. There is an attempt to make nonwhites believe that the workplace is now an equal-opportunity environment with freedom and justice for all. This is another racial illusion. The real goal is to maintain control without the rigid, inflexible color codes of the past. It is part of the whole dynamic of reworking the racial system by using racial codes to slip the message underneath without the victim suspecting anything.

RACE CODE WAR

The White supremacist knows that "hardcore cold whiteness" will not work in a new environment mixed heavily with people of various colors. This is why so much is hidden in code. In the old days of the white collar, the White worker was the highest paid employee. He or she wore a white shirt as a symbol of higher ranking. The white-collar wearer had higher social and economic status. The wearing of a dark suit with the white shirt is a very interesting racial and color dichotomy. This seemed to show a desire to have a physically black or dark body to cover the whiteness. However, the wearing of the white shirt meant that on the inside, from the head down to the waist, white and dominant.

Diversity

This is the code word that replaces the use of coded terms like racial/ color integration and equal opportunity. It simply means that Black people are now needed to sit deeper in the window in order to give the "illusion of inclusion." This entails the visible level of nonwhite involvement in the project, company or development scheme to make nonwhites believe that they enjoy active participation.

Them / Those People

This code term classifies Black people as some sort of aliens unlike human beings. These, them, those and the classic you people phrase are derogatory references to people of color. These terms get a hostile reaction from Black people every time they are used. They imply that Blacks are less than White people or are foreigners with a disease or a plague. The terms say that Black people are not like other civilized folks. We don't want to have to associate with them any more than necessary. It is clearly a nasty term designed to strike at the self-esteem of a group of people. It is a code with a hard edge, and it really can sting when used in a social confrontation context. When Black public housing residents across the nation sought to move out of the central city into suburban areas, they were met with this type of racially resistant language. The statements ranged from, "We don't want those people," and "these children have special needs" (as if all children don't have special needs) to "crime is coming into the area."

Race Code Words

Loss and/or Decline in Property Value

Code terms used to indicate the devaluation of property and living environments based on race or color. The property argument is a ruse for hiding the real reason why the value of the land or capital is decreased when Black people move into or live in an area. It says that if Black people move into an area, the property values will automatically or eventually depreciate. It doesn't matter if the income of the Black people in the neighborhood is the same or higher than the Whites and the houses are kept up. In a race-based social order, Black does not have the value of White. A Black individual may purchase a house in a rich White community or subdivision. The value of the property stays high so long as the community remains White. If it changes to all Black, the value of property in all likelihood will depreciate or not increase in value at the same rate. The occupant is Black and therefore it changes the value because in general Blacks are less valuable than Whites. Value is based on race and color. A White neighborhood will have or retain more of its value than an all Black neighborhood.

The value of White life and material possessions is higher than for Black. It is not the land or even its use but who is on the land that accounts for the difference. The notion that Black is inferior and therefore of lesser or no value is reflected most blatantly and historically in the real estate industry. How often do White Realtors maneuver White people away from investing and living in Black areas or communities close to Black people with just the hint that "they" (code word for Black) are moving into the neighborhood? When White people leave in great numbers, the area declines in value. When they move to a new area, that location, the land, houses and community, appreciates in value. The word "value" means White.

The level of nonwhite value is based on its degree of physical proximity to the color white. The so-called Asian population has higher value not just because it is the best trained but primarily because it is closest to whiteness in skin color. Asians also comprise the largest number on a percentage basis of nonwhites moving into suburban areas. The color yellow is the next level down from white, and in some quarters Asians still are considered little slant-eyed bastards. Despite these drawbacks, they are still preferred over Black people.

White supremacists do business with Blacks and Asians and interact because it is in their best interests. The Japanese had begun to resist White demands for greater access to their economy. They extolled the virtues of being Japanese and had even started to brag again about being racially and economically superior. The Japanese consistently resisted the demand for greater market penetration of Western goods and services. The White economic hammer began to come down. Talk of curbing imports, increasing tariffs and even subtle hints of military action reduced resistance.

The Japanese even though very stubborn had no choice but to open up their markets to greater White penetration. The once stable Japanese market began to falter along with the rest of oriental Asia and brown Asia. As their economies reemerge, the dialogue about racial superiority that was once so prevalent is totally absent. In the final summation, it does not matter how many cars Yellow people produce. If they do not have the White seal of approval, nothing can be produced or sold in any White nation. If they were to proceed without White approval, they would be portrayed once again as the Yellow Peril. This same justification was used very effectively in the 1940s when military force was employed to destroy their economic capacity. Under the system of global domination, White supremacists determine what is valuable and what is not valuable. The true meaning of power is the ability to set standards and rules that the rest of the world must follow.

Crossover

This is a soft racial code word for Black or other nonwhites gaining acceptance in the White economic market. This word is usually used in conjunction with the entertainment industry. Historically, the music, motion picture and fashion industries were segregated. At one time soul singer James Brown's music was limited to Black audiences. Motown was one of the first Black dominated organizations to reach beyond the Black music market into some sections of the White music marketplace. James Brown's music was labeled race music. Today it is called funk or rhythm and blues, which are soft racial codes for saying that it is "nigger music." The word crossover gained greater utilization with the emergence of labels like Motown. The crossover word was a code to White people that Black people wanted to be economically and socially integrated and that their music posed no social threat.

The term crossover means to come over to the other side. Black people wanted to come to where White people were. They wanted to work, sleep and live next to White people. They wanted to show that they could clean up their language, appearance and mannerisms in order to be accepted. It was a signal that they wanted social acceptance and to be viewed without regard for race. The crossover word is part of the package of communication that came from a generation of integration-based language.

The crossover tag eased the restrictions on Black and White social interactions. It also allowed White people to feel even more superior because Black people were once again begging for entry into their world. They wanted to blend in and, if possible, become invisible. One of the biggest examples in the early stages of crossover was the big splash about the relationship between the White actress Racquel Welch and the legendary Black NFL professional football player Jim Brown. In the 1967 motion picture "Long Rifles" even the title of the movie was a racial and sexual code term for the power of the long Black penis. It also connoted that black men had larger sexual organs. A rifle is long, the color is usually black or dark and it shoots explosive sperm, or firepower. The film played heavily on the social taboo of Black men fornicating with beautiful White females on the big screen. Jim Brown played the hero who got the White woman even though she died in the end.

To placate the White audiences she had to be killed. Big black Jim Brown could be allowed to walk away with the woman classified as the most beautiful "female in the world." It was an instant replay of the King Kong syndrome all over again. During this era, Racquel Welch was the number-one White sex siren and a top female box office attraction. The casting of big Black Brown with Welch played on the widely held belief that Black males wanted and, if allowed, would get White females. This was one of the first big screen depictions of Black males and White females being involved sexually. Before this movie, Black men interacted with White females much like actor Sidney Poitier did in the motion picture "Lilies of the Field." He acted like a eunuch with no interest in women. The White female had no contact and displayed no sexual interest in the black male. The interracial match up between Jim Brown and Raquel Welch set off a storm of controversy in 1967.

This did not repeat itself to any great degree until the coming of the new Black male leads in the early to mid-1990s. Even in the year 2003, except in a very few instances, Black men do not relate to White females in major motion pictures as on-screen lovers with romantic interests. There are notable exceptions such as Laurence Fishbourne in the movie "Othello" and Wesley Snipes in Spike Lee's "Jungle Fever," which did well in terms of critical appeal. However, neither picture was a great commercial success. As a general rule, these crossover romantic movies have not done well at the box office or even in video sales.

The exception to the rule was part two of "Mission Impossible," which featured a White male, actor Tom Cruise, cast with a very light skinned and caucasoid-appearing Black female. (This movie also had an interesting mountain-top scene at the beginning that depicted Cruise as the crucified Christ figure.) The word crossover automatically gives a coded warning that the motion picture is about racial relations.

The crossover word has also been used recently to describe Hispanic pop music artists, trying to appeal to the White music market. The crossover artists are still considered secondary performers. This is why White pop star Brittany Spears will always be bigger than Janet Jackson. It doesn't matter that Brittany is no more than an imitation of Jackson; her Whiteness assures top billing. Poor Janet went through extreme efforts to make herself more appealing to White audiences. She started posing as and looking like a White sex symbol and wound up with a smaller nose, lips and lighter color to Whiten-up her physical appearance.

The crossover artist is a cultural adaptation who tries to gain the attention of White people for a small moment in time. This desire of people of color will be used by White supremacists as a cover to pretend that they will tolerate Blacks and other nonwhites. They will

70

quickly say that they collect Black, Hispanic or Asian music or see nonwhite movies. This little maneuver is effective in opening up mental and emotional doors for social, political, economic and racial manipulation. This says to the nonwhite victim, "Hey, this guy or gal is not a racist, they enjoy Black culture and appreciate other contributions of Black people."

Remember the thought-provoking words of the ultimate crossover superstar Michael Jackson in July, 2002, when he boldly proclaimed that the music business is racist and treats Black artists differently from white artists. These words came from a man who has gone to great lengths to appeal to White audiences. Michael openly acknowledged what many crossover stars have pretended did not exist: racism and color domination. And this dynamic admission came after years of sacrifice and some say self-mutilation in order to be accepted by White people or to become White. What he discovered was that in spite of his efforts to please and join in, he is hated and rejected more now than ever before.

In November, 2002, the White-dominated Fox News had big fun with Jackson's latest round of irresponsible behavior in Germany when a news videotape clip showed the star holding his baby son over a fourth-floor railing at a German hotel. The incident took place in Berlin, Germany. Jackson, even in his state of mind, understood the cost of trying to be liked by people other than his kith and kin. To crossover means to shed any resemblance of real Blackness and become as White as possible.

A White supremacist will listen to Black music, watch Black people play sports and even root hard for them to win. Yet he will go right out and implement policies and programs that impact adversely on the growth and development of Black people. The term crossover acts in the same way. It provides many racists with cover and allows them to hide their true selves, enjoy the fruits of color and still implement deeds that keep Blacks and other nonwhites in positions of inferiority and confusion. The lists below include examples of terms used to define racially identified and racially targeted music.

RACE CODE WAR

SOFT RACIAL CODE WORDS   DECODED MEANING

Rock and Roll Music	White people copying Black music
Crossover Music	Black music seeking acceptance by White people
Rhythm and Blues Music	Black music
Country Music	Rural or Appalachian White people
Classical Music	Maximum income White people
Jazz Music	Searching Black people
Soul Music	Mainstream Black people
Popular/Pop Music	Mainstream White people
Blues Music	Southern or Southern-based Black people
Bluegrass Music	Deep rural White people
World Music	Nonwhite and non-American music
Rap Music	Tough Black youth
Folk Music	Artistic and pacifist White people
Funk Music	Deep-beat Black music/ jungle music
Teen Bop Music	Mainstream White youth
Reggae Music	Blacks in the Caribbean/ Black drug music
Hard Rock/ Acid Music	Hardcore White youth
Rock Music	Disenchanted White youth
Opera Music	Rich White people
Show Music	Affluent White families
New Age Music	Mystical White people
Alternative Music	Folk-based White people

RACE- AND COLOR-IDENTIFIED WORDS

Spanish Music
The British Sound
African Music
Latin Music
Hispanic Music
Oriental Music
Native American Music
Indian Music
Italian Music
Irish Music
Welsh Music
Russian Music
Polynesian Sound
Middle Eastern Music
Scottish Music
Jewish Music
French Music

Race Code Words

Caribbean Music
German Music
Arab Music
Greek Music

Inner City

This term was designed by White sociologists and literally regurgitated by Black academicians in the late sixties as an alternative term to the word ghetto. The term inner city has been visually associated with broken down homes, rodents and crime. It has the image of drug busts, featuring gold-toothed baggy pants gang-bang Negro males lying on the ground under heavily armed White police control. In the 1970s the inner city term gained wide acceptance and surpassed the horrible images associated with the word ghetto. It conjures up images of wild, half-crazed drug-dealing and crime-oriented Black youth. The term has very little to do with geographical location. If it were simply a matter of geography, there would be equal references to the outer city, upper city or lower city. It is clear that an inner city has a wholly different meaning. The meaning is racial.

The term inner city appeared to be less threatening. In the early seventies inner city became an acceptable term as used by Marvin Gaye in his super classic "What's Goin' On" album. Inner city was an expression of oppression, and it was a call to rally against tyrannical forces. In the late1980s the inner city label became a euphemism for Black thugs, hoods and criminals. It blamed Blacks for their social problems and shifted the focus away from White supremacy.

The inner city term is now taking on a new context, as some White people (mostly White homosexuals and middle-aged Whites with money) desire to relocate back into these communities. They are tired of driving ten to eighty miles a day. Some racists fear that Black people will begin to control water and sewage systems, street lighting and so forth. They do not want central power in the hands of Black people. The code for taking back the city is wrapped up in the language of revitalization. These areas are attractive again. They are now coded by phrases like the *neglected and under-served market.* The rhetoric is quietly changing. As more White people resettle into the so-called inner city, it will become known as the central city, the new urbanism or some other fancy-sounding code term to indicate that the new pioneer has arrived, resettled the area and run the savages out.

Wherever Black people relocate, the area will be redefined with inner city language to besmirch and denigrate. As Black people expand into the old suburban areas, the question of declining and impoverished suburbs has begun to appear in the social lexicon. A classic example of this was the political battle against something called *tax incentive financing,* or *TIF* that took place in Columbus, Ohio, in the summer and fall of 1999. The battle was between the owner of the Northland Mall and the owner of a new mall area called the Polaris. The issue was whether the Columbus City Council should have granted the new Polaris development a tax-incentive financing package. The TIF allows for normal tax payments that go to the city to be used to make targeted infrastructure improvements for things such as lights, streets and sewage disposal.

The owner claimed that if the TIF were allowed to stand, the old Northland Mall would have to close because it would not be able to complete with the new Polaris development in the far- flung suburbs. The old Northland Mall did close in October, 2002. The Northland Mall was located in the old suburbs, which were now inhabited by large numbers of Black people. The owner of the Northland Mall asked the local citizens through a petition drive to rescind the City Council-approved TIF. He promised that if the TIF were defeated, he would invest 70 million dollars in the renovation of Northland Mall.

The petition drive netted 14,000 signatures, which were enough to put it on the ballot to repeal the Polaris TIF. The move to repeal the Columbus City Council action was defeated on the November ballot. This battle was portrayed in the Columbus media as a battle between titans, with control of the local retail industry at stake. While this was playing out, two other less publicized media events had occurred regarding the Northland Mall and its owner. A pager business had sued Northland for terminating their lease.

They accused the Northland Mall management group of racism. They accused them of revoking the lease because the pager business was bringing in too many young Blacks that were hanging around the store. The pager company felt that the Northland management had viewed their business as a menace to the operation of the mall. This suit was eventually settled out of court with neither side taking blame.

Race Code Words

The second incident occurred when owner Dick Jacobs allegedly put on a Klu Klux Klan hood as a practical joke in front of a former president of the Cleveland Chapter of the NAACP and a former City Council president, George Forbes. All of this drama provided a backdrop for the real issue. The Northland was an enclosed shopping mall constructed 35 years before in what was then a pricey White Columbus suburban area. This area had drastically changed over the years. As higher income White homeowners moved further out, Black people moved into the area.

At the same time as this great racial migration, the shopping areas, including the Northland Mall, began to decay. The businesses began to relocate or go out of business. This deterioration happened as more of Northland's shoppers and residents became Black. Less than five miles down the road, a brand new super-sized modern shopping-business complex called Easton had sprung up. Both the Polaris and Easton were shopping centers heavily geared toward the White shopper with higher income. The shopping malls became racial codes and symbols for White shoppers. Northland, with all of its problems and social issues, became a code for Black shoppers. The Black shoppers were labeled riff-raff and troublemakers.

The real reason for the decay was that Black folks moved in and White folks moved out. This pattern is nationwide. It is hidden in race code words that scare away investors and White homeowners. In the process of leaving they depreciate the value of the land and disinvest in the infrastructure. The reverse happens when Whites move back into an area. The price of the housing stock goes up.

The term inner city is a race term, and it follows Black people no matter where they go. The new sayings are the *inner city is expanding, urban sprawl* or now *urban scrawl.* Decoded it means that the niggers are coming to the suburbs and bringing decay. It is part of the new urban woefulnes' language. The whole sprawl issue is wrapped around the question of color. For years White people have run from Black people. They move quickly if the area appears to attract large numbers of Black people. Code words such as lowering *academic standards and lowering property values* are used to justify relocation.

This is not about physical development. Expansion has been occurring for years, with White people moving and building new communities. This is about who is coming to the suburbs, or *guess who's coming to dinner* or *there goes the neighborhood* or *not in my backyard (NIMBY)*. The newest migration pattern features public housing residents, tax-credits housing and other poor Black people leaving the inner city for the promised land of the suburbs. This has created a hell on wheels for Whites because they thought they had moved out of the reach of Black people. The following are selected examples of racial code words for the movement of Black people into previously White communities.

RACIAL CODE SAYINGS FOR BLACK EXPANSION
Guess Who's Coming to Dinner
There Goes the Neighborhood
Lower Property Values
Inner City Is Expanding
Inner City Is Spreading
Urban Sprawl
Crime is Spreading
Increased Crime in the Neighborhood
Not in My Backyard
You Can't Get Away from Them
Them people
Those people
Lowering of Academic Standards
For Sale
Far-Flung Suburbs

Quotas
The term quota is code for giving Blacks special treatment. This word has become the lightening rod in the White conservative attack against affirmative action. The word quota when decoded means a nigger getting something for free at the expense of White people. This word, along with the concept of affirmative action, stirred up the notion that every White deal had to include a Black individual of business. This would have destroyed the tight network of White supremacy, the so-called good old boys' network. This word was attacked furiously in the courts, media and political circles.

Race Code Words

The system of quotas has always been used in the White world to keep Blacks and other nonwhites at bay. And as long as this was the practice, the word quota never evoked any particular reverence and did not create any controversies. It only became an active word when it had a racial connotation attached to it. To a White supremacist, this word says that the old boy or old girl network would be broken up and/or confused if this were to happen, and White domination would suffer a severe blow.

Preferences
This is code for Blacks receiving favored treatment over White people. The term preference means that Black people get special treatment. This has been used to image Black people as targets for social agitation.

Race Card
This term is new to the lexicon of racism. It is one of the terms designed by the White conservative movement and came of age during the infamous murder trial of O.J. Simpson in 1995. It is used to belittle or poke fun at the serious charge of racism. It is an excellent propaganda tool designed to deflect and downplay the devastating impact of racism in real life social interaction. If a charge of racism is made, it gets poked fun at by saying, "Oh there you go again, playing the race card." This is an effective shielding mechanism for hiding the hand that threw the racial rock. Race card dialogue dilutes serious attempts at racial reformation and conciliation. It essentially says that race is not an issue or a problem and is only being used because the accuser has no other grounds to gain sympathy and support.

The race card statement says that racism does not exist or does not exist at the level the accuser indicates and that it is a lame excuse and only exists in the mind of the victim. It has now become a convenient excuse for blaming someone else for personal problems and social shortcomings. The race card argument further adds validity to the notion that Black people really are lazy and dysfunctional and want others to take care of them. It also has the effect of dismissing hundreds of years of racist history as nothing but profane ranting from a do-nothing group of people. The race card term is a very dangerous statement' and it must not be trivialized because it is a brilliant and powerful two-word statement that obliterates the impact of racism.

Athletic Ability

This is code for a Black athlete and is used chiefly by White television sports broadcasters. It is a term that is applied 90% of the time when talking about a Black athlete. This code is designed to portray Black men as horses or studs with strong bodies and weak brains. Most high-performance sports require the use of the body *and* the mind.

Time to take out the trash

■ **After 10 days of jabbering, Michael Johnson and Maurice Greene meet in a spicy 200-meter showdown.**

By Todd Jones
Dispatch Sports Reporter

SACRAMENTO, Calif. — The beating of war drums began 10 days ago and the sound has thumped relentlessly ever since.

Today, the noise stops. A starter's pistol will be raised, an expected sellout crowd of more than 23,000 in Hornet Stadium will fall silent and a national TV audience will sit riveted by the sight of two men side by side in the starting blocks of the 200 meters.

Yes, finally, in the final event of the U.S. Olympic Track and Field Trials, it's time for Michael Johnson vs. Maurice Greene. And like good ice cream, one scoop isn't enough. Fans probably will get to see them race head-to-head twice because they're in the same 200 semifinal heat, in lanes 4 and 5. The top four in each of the two heats advance to the final at 8:48 p.m. (EDT).

The two rivals, who have lobbed trash-talk mortars at each other throughout the trials, crossed paths yesterday before Greene won the third preliminary heat (in 20.29 seconds) and Johnson won the fourth (19.89) to advance to the semifinals at 7 tonight.

"It kind of reminded me of a heavyweight title fight," said Brian Lewis, who won the fifth preliminary heat in 20.56. "There was a lot of me-mugging. That's part of the game. They were staring at each other face to face. They were laughing. No words."

After winning their heats, there were few words. Greene, who had the fourth-best time of 34 prelimi-

U.S. Olympic Track and Field Trials
7, tonight
TV: NBC (Ch. 4)

nary participants, refused to talk to reporters, which happens about once every solar eclipse. Johnson, after snapping off the day's best time, did an interview with NBC and a brief one with USA Track and Field officials in which he ignored the topic of running against Greene.

"I'm not going to talk about that. It's silly," he said.

Inger Miller previously had stoked the fire in her own 200-meter showdown against Marion Jones, set for a semifinal heat tonight at 7:40 and an 8:36 final. But Miller, the reigning 200 world champion, also refused to speak with reporters after winning her heat in 23.13. She did speak to a USATF official.

"I don't care how anybody else ran, just myself," said Miller, who ran so easily she said she watched herself on the stadium's huge replay screen during the race.

Jones won her heat with the best time (22.62) of the 26 women in five heats. Miller's time was fourth best, which is why they'll be lined up together in lanes 4 and 5 during a semifinal. The first- and fourth-best times in the preliminaries gain spots in the same semifinal heat; the second- and third-best preliminary times advance to the other heat.

Jones distanced herself from the previous week's trash talk by Miller, taking a more subtle approach.

"None of you have ever heard me say bad things about anybody," Jones said. "I'm tired of all this trash talking. If you're going to talk, put up. If you're going to talk, come out to the track ready to run. That's all I'm asking."

The women's 200 final follows finals in the women's pole vault, women's 100-meter hurdles, men's high jump, men's triple jump, men's discus, men's and women's 800 meters and men's 110-meter hurdles. Those events, however, might as well be held on Venus.

All everyone is talking about is

Associated Press
Michael Johnson, left, ran his 200-meter heat in 19.89 seconds. Maurice Greene, right, won his heat in 20.29.

Johnson (world record-holder in the 200 and 400) vs. Greene (reigning world champion in the 200 and 100, in which he holds the world record). Never mind that the third-place finisher also receives a spot on the U.S. Olympic team. Johnson-Greene is so hot it's drawing comments from other athletes, too.

"They have a tendency to make excuses when they lose," Lewis said. "If I win, they'll be making more excuses."

Johnson has been bothered by a sore Achilles' tendon. John Capel, running next to him yesterday, noticed something about Johnson during the race.

"About 50 meters he started hobbling a little bit," Capel said.

Still, Johnson's 19.89 was the second-fastest time run in the world this year (behind his own 19.71) and the 13th fastest ever. Greene, who

watched the performance on a TV next to the track, did a rooster strut out of the stadium as soon as the race ended.

"(My Achilles') went away on the straights," Johnson said. "Hopefully, it will be OK. I felt it through the curve and then it went away. I'm not sure what to say now. I felt it cramp a little in the curve. I was able to finish the race. I hope the schedule (today) won't be a problem, but I don't know right now."

Johnson immediately wrapped his right foot after his race and also had a wrap just above his right knee. Perhaps he was just trying to think about. Maybe he really injured. Not much was said about it, for a change.

"After (today), they'll shut up," Lewis said.

The caption Time to take out the trash placed above the heads of two black males is very disturbing. This header and photo arrangement imply that black males garbage and trash are somehow intertwined. Is this a racial message? Think about it!

Race Code Words

Even in boxing the mind operates at a highly efficient level. The mind is required to think fast and react even faster. Mind and body must operate in a cohesive manner. Boxers have to think fast and far ahead, as in a chess game. They must be able to anticipate an opponent's body and hand moves 30 jabs and punches into the future. Boxing demands great energy efficiency, high mental concentration and physical precision. A good boxer must understand the physics of movement and angles, and he/she must know the finer points of the human anatomy just as well as a medical doctor. The boxer must understand how to apply pressure against the opponent with the precision of an engineer.

Boxers must know how to use psychology to manage pain and also to intimidate the opponent. This element of the sport is rarely discussed. It is because Black pugilists have excelled at this game. Black men like Mike Tyson or Sonny Liston were labeled as having animal or savage instincts. They are never given credit for knowledge of movement, speed, power and angles, anatomy, psychology, biology and pain management. When White announcers call prize fights, they describe Black fighters as a *stable of fighters* or as *stable mates.*

This is code for the breeding of high-performance animals. These are nothing but animalistic terms used by White sports and talk show announcers without being corrected or challenged. These words perpetuate the belief that Black athletes are big, dumb, physical and sexual creatures. "All these dumb nigger jocks want to do is have sex and play sports."

The promotional lead-up to the June, 2002, world heavyweight championship fight between Lennox Lewis and Mike Tyson in Memphis, Tennessee, was one the most glaring examples of Black men being cast as animals. The White media's interpretation of the events during the pre-fight promotion was a real throwback to old days of overt racism. This event got out of control. Tyson and Lewis were not supposed to actually punch each other. However, everything went haywire and a scuffle involving several Black males broke out. It was as if the White media were able to satisfy a great hunger for openly castigating Black males as savages and animals. All of the Black men in the scuffle were called wild, crazy and "ghetto." Mike Tyson's comments and behavior were highly undignified and totally unacceptable.

However, his behavior was used as a cover to subtly label another Black man as a cannibal. Racist jokes about Tyson's stupid and senseless ear-biting incident in a boxing match against former heavyweight champion Evander Holyfield ran the gamut of bad taste. The real tragedy was that far too many Black sportscasters joined in the fun. They must have forgotten that just a few years earlier all Black men were portrayed as cannibals. When they joined in the process of poking fun, many did not realize that the racists were also laughing at them while using Mike Tyson as a poster boy for the demonization of Black males.

Black men and now Black women have been bred to box and play basketball and football. Only recently with the emergence of Tiger Woods, has there been a small groundswell for golf. When Black people become stronger in the golf game, the language will reflect an emphasis on physical ability rather than thinking skill, that is, if a racist has anything to do with the play-by-play announcement. This is already happening, with greater emphasis on Tiger's ability to hit the ball hard and long. This is a physical attribute. The term athletic ability is usually not applied to White athletes. They are called blue-collar or hard-working athletes. They are not born with animalistic talents. They are more hard working or cerebral. There is much greater emphasis on thinking, figuring things out, coordination and organization. Even in the sports leagues that are Black dominated, if there is a White superstar, the racially phrased commentaries and distinctions are noticeably different to the discerning mind.

The classic example is the description back in the 1980s of National Basketball Association star Larry Bird that he was so great and smart that he had "radar in the back of his head so that he could see the basketball." As great as Michael Jordan was, little emphasis was ever, at least publicly, given to the power of his intellect. It was always his competitive nature, strong desire to win, amazing hang time, spectacular dunks and body moves.

We rarely heard mention of Jordan's incredible ability to think and intellectualize the complexities of life and the game. Basketball is a game of quick and accurate thinking at a high level of speed and intense interaction. However, when listening to or watching the games, the term most frequently used is that he or she has great athletic ability. It is similar to the statements of a White sportscaster who once said that

Race Code Words

Blacks were bred to become good athletes. This contrasts sharply with the usual sack of words used to describe White athletes, with their *cerebral approach to the game.* In effect, the White athlete is a thinker, a human being and an athletic performer. He is a whole individual.

The Black athlete is a superior animal bred for high performance on the field. Off the field he is a criminal, intellectually deficient and mentally inferior. This is close to the thinking of the White slave masters in the old South. Black men and women were bred to have babies and do the manual labor but not to develop superior intellects.

This is reflected even in the number of managerial and ownership positions in professional sports. During the bidding for the purchase of the Cleveland Browns there was an example of how athletic ability and not the ability to think carries over after football playing days. Football great Jim Brown played his whole career for the Cleveland Browns. In his bid to purchase the new franchise, he was rebuffed with some of the worst White radio talk-show commentary ever aired, which bordered on racist slander.

Brown and the other Black bidders were dismissed early because their bids were not serious and they did have the capacity to run a complex organization. The franchise went to a group with no visible Blacks in ownership roles despite the fact that more than 60 % of the NFL football players are Black athletes. The term athletic ability discards the idea of brainpower because it says that Blacks are naturally born athletes. This casts doubt on their intellectual ability.

This Guy's a Stud

This code is the same as the phrase athletic ability. The stud word is a throwback to the chattel slavery system when Black men and women were bred as cattle. This was a standard practice during chattel slavery. Black men were used to impregnate Black females to produce more slaves to raise cotton and take care of the master. The best- conditioned slaves brought the highest prices at the slave auction. The breeding process idea and philosophy have continued in competitive athletics. The White brain trust that propelled Mike Tyson into becoming the heavyweight boxing champion never sought to develop his brainpower at the same level of proficiency.

They trained him to be a vicious savage inside the boxing ring with few social skills outside of the ring. He was trained to be a meal ticket, just as a horse trainer prepares a Kentucky Derby champion.

When they said how much they loved Mike and wanted the best for him, without preparing him to run his own business affairs, it was the same as saying, "I love my dog. We give him the best training and best kennels in the world."

The White slave master never worried about the slave's mind. Intellectual development of the slave was illegal and punishable by death. This was the basic breeding and conditioning process of Black males, and it has continued in the sports industry. When Black athletes excel in a particular sport, the language is altered to resemble the kind of communication reserved for specialized animal breeding. By contrast, this language is never used when big White males dominate a sport. George Mikan, star of the NBA in the early 1950s when it was dominated by White male basketball players, was never called a series of animal-connoted names. He was described as "a gentle giant."

Today, Black basketball stars are described as *thugs*, *criminals* and *muggers*. It is not unusual to hear or see White announcers describe a foul as a *mugging*. The mugging word goes back to the early 1970s' subway robberies in New York City. The mugging and mugger words came into national prominence as the news showed Black males robbing innocent victims in Central Park and on the subway. This description is rarely applied to professional hockey players or to White tennis stars or to race-car drivers even when they use deadly tricks on the raceway. The mugging word is related to other coded statements such as *playing alley ball tonight* or *street ball*. All of these words and phrases are references to race, community and background. These are not harmless words. It is part of the vocabulary and design to dehumanize successful Black people.

Ungrateful Athletes

This is a code term for an ungrateful *nigger* athlete. These people should be grateful because if not playing basketball, they would be robbing a corner convenience store or attempting to rape a White coed on campus. Unworthy and ungracious niggers forget that they were taken out of the bushes in Africa and given civilization. The ungrateful athletes phrase was pushed to the limit during the Major League baseball strike in 1994 and the NBA strike in 1998. High-performance baseball players like Barry Bonds, Ken Griffey, Jr., and Albert Belle, just to name a few, were ridiculed and blasted for being ungrateful, greedy, mentally deranged, arrogant and didn't care about the fans (the fans are the White males that pay to see Black males play ball) or the integrity of the game.

Black names and images were burned over the airwaves. Most of the White baseball players escaped the harsh anger of the White sports announcers, media people and sports public. The Black baseball players were made the visible scapegoat, and yet few if any were part of the bargaining team that made the decision to strike. This hidden racial feeling always comes to the surface about Black athletes. The media images of arrogant Black players help the owners gain the upper hand in the image game. The most unfavorable stories featured the Black baseball players. This helped to create the image that the Blacks were driving the strike because these brainless and clueless savages had gotten too big for their nigger britches. When Albert Belle and others returned to play ball the following season, they were the recipients of all kinds of verbal abuse and expletives. The White sports-talk industry showed little sympathy and sided with the White fans to condemn Albert Belle. The idea of an ungrateful nigger athlete did not end there. During the 1998 NBA strike, the Black basketball players were portrayed as being dumb, disinterested, incapable, greedy, arrogant and highly ungrateful.

The media was full of statements like *who really cares about the NBA anyway* or *"nobody watches the games until there are three minutes left in the game.* This is code language to play down the importance of the Black basketball star in the national psyche. In the 2000 Olympics in Sidney, Australia, the NBA players were called a *disgrace* for playing a close game with the all-white Lithuanian basketball team. When it is decoded, it means, "Look you Negroes, we pay you a ton of money to bounce a ball. This is what you were bred to do. How dare you lose to a second-rate group of White boys who will be scientists and doctors and only play basketball on the weekend."

Inner City Athletes

This is a term used to describe wild, savage and untamed young Black athletes. The racial code phrase "inner city" denotes a litany of racial images designed to imply that Black males are criminals, thugs, rapists, murderers, uncivilized and show backward behavior in any society. The inner city athlete is an undisciplined athlete who cannot follow coaching. They cannot read or write and is just in college to get to the NBA or NFL. The nigger jock from the inner city is the worst kind of athlete. He is not a Duke University Black athlete (which decoded means more civilized than his darker brother) and acts more like White boys on campus.

Inner City Youth

This is similar to the term inner city athletes. It is applied to all Black youth living in a certain physical location. When this term is used, it is designed to mean young savages, brutes, gang members, thieves, car jackers, drug dealers, uneducables, retards and upcoming rapists and gang bangers. This is the association with the so-called "hood" (which really means Black hoodlums and is a word Black people should stop using to describe their community). Inner city youth is used to stereotype and label young Black children and make them feel ashamed of their surroundings, family and community. They are automatically assumed to be the worst children on the planet because of where they live.

Proposition 42 Athletes

This was a short-lived phrase with a limited life span. The college entrance test was used to reduce the number of Black athletes on White college campuses.

Urban

This is a code word for Black people. The word urban in its original context was used to designate a geographical and social location. However, as Black people began to move into the central city and Whites began to leave, the urban word acquired a very strong racial orientation. It was used to separate Black areas from White areas. In the language of the back-to the-city movement of young Whites the word urban may take on a new racial meaning. In time this word could become associated with eager young White people ready to retake territory abandoned by their parents. However, for the present, the word urban still has strong Black connotations and direct racial meaning.

Urban Decay

These are the Black communities that fell victim to a policy of social neglect and disinvestment. These communities suffer from a lack of resources and are allowed to be over-run with crime, chemical poisoning, social maladies, drugs and other diseases.

Race Code Words

Urban Ills

This term refers to social problems in the Black community stimulated by White financial neglect. Ill means a disease or complications from ailments. It means that under a White system of supremacy, wherever Black people live will eventually become an environment with major social and economic problems.

Urban Blight

This term is also in the same class as the other concepts. The term blight is associated with plague or pestilence in the Black community.

Urban Renewal

This was a 1960-1970s term that when reinterpreted meant the removal of the Negro, or Black man, from the central city to be replaced with White people.

Urban Sprawl

This is a new code that means the niggers are coming. The expansion of city life is new. Little cities have been developed for years by majority White populations and have never been classified as urban areas. They were called suburban communities, which, when decoded, means White in order to distinguish them from Black communities.

As black people began to expand into the outer areas and geographical locations, the term urban, which has come to mean Black, is attached to the out-migration pattern. The sprawl word means to straggle, digress or stray. These are definitions designed to send hidden messages that the movement of Blacks into the sanctuaries of White people is wholly unaccepted.

Urban Legend

This is a code term for a lie or mistruth. In code language it means that some nigger has made up a lie. This phrase has gained great popularity and should be monitored very closely.

Uzi's

This code is applied to Black males. The word Uzi is attached to street violence and is also a code word for Black males.

RACE CODE WAR

Menace to Society

The phrase menace to society was used by FBI Director John Edgar Hoover to defame high-profile White crime figures such as Pretty Boy Floyd, John Dillinger and Bonnie and Clyde. In the 1980's this phrase was applied to Black males. This connection was popularized by the movie *"Menace to Society"* that showed dangerous Black youth senselessly murdering and destroying innocent people. This is one of the most dangerous terms ever devised. It is surely one of the tools used to set Black males up for concentration camps, prison or other institutions of racial containment. This means that Black males are under constant surveillance and deemed to be a threat to the order of White society. They are treated as suspects and criminals and judged to be guilty until proven innocent.

Blighted Areas

This refers to those areas where the majority of the population is Black.

Poverty Stricken

This term was originally used to define the living conditions of poor Whites. However, this has changed dramatically. The term is now reserved for the exclusive identification of Black people.

The term is interesting: how does poverty strike someone? Poverty is an economic condition brought on by purposeful neglect and exploitation.

New Prison Construction

Under the system of White supremacy, Black males are classified as criminals. And prisons are used to house criminals. The growth of the prison industry is largely driven by the rate of imprisonment of Blacks and other nonwhites. The record level of Blacks and other nonwhites imprisoned has fueled the abnormal growth of the crime industry in America.

Prison Reform

This is a code term for how to manage Black people in prison. It refers to the methods that work best for controlling and manipulating Black males in captivity.

Race Code Words

Convict or Felon

This is code for Black males. It is part of the criminalization of the Black male image in American society. The goal is to make Black males appear as inmates that are already guilty before they are tried. The Black male is convicted from the womb. He is classified as a useless eater and of little value.

Impoverished Community

This term has a similar meaning to poverty stricken. It was used largely to identify the poor White population. However, this has changed. Again this new language is now used to label Black communities as undesirable and hopeless. Similar language is used to justify all-White invasions of Africa and takeover attempts.

Da Hood

This is a very derogatory term that must be abandoned. The first thought that comes to mind is of a thug in a dark alley waiting to clobber and do harm to some innocent victim. A hooded person is considered someone who wants to hide his/her identity because he/she is involved in some dangerous and vicious activity.

Incorrigible Youth

This is code for Black youth who are disobedient, lawless, godless and forsaken ingrates.

Illiterate

This is code for Black and other nonwhite people in poor learning situations. The darker colored the people, the more the term is generally used to define their lack of intellectual development.
Black people are considered semi-literate slow learners.

The Illiteracy Rate

In reality this is a measurement of how well White supremacists are fooling Black people. If they can fool and deceive Blacks into engaging in destructive behaviors, refusing to be educated, it emboldens the effectiveness of other racist plans and polices.

RACE CODE WAR

Lazy, Dumb and Irresponsible

This set of codes has been used since the days of chattel slavery to define the behaviors of Black people. The post-slavery period featured a litany of eye-buzzing and moonshining darkies who were the poster children of the stereotyped image. This set of words has a long and storied history of race degradation and in the new millennium the meaning has not changed.

High Crime Areas

This is code for neighborhoods or areas where large numbers of Black people reside. This same label is applied if the neighborhood is turning from White to Black. During the 1960-1980 period when illegal drug use in the White community was well publicized, White communities were never classified as high-crime areas despite the incredible sale and use of high-powered, illegal drugs. While there were a number of drug busts, the larger White community was never painted with an ugly broad brush. The use of the code term high crime paints Black people as the worst offenders, a crime-loving population living in the most horrendous crime communities in the nation.

Fight Crime

This is a code phrase for locking up large numbers of Black males and decimating Black family relationships. Fight crime in its simplest explanation is the same as a declaration of war on Black people. The majority of the elements that produce crime in the Black community are exported there by calculating White supremacists. Drugs, weapons, alcohol, money, and so forth, have the greatest impact on the production of criminal behavior in the Black community. All of these commodities become traps and enticements that are produced and channeled into the Black neighborhood for a criminal purpose. Black people do not produce any of these products; however, they fall victim to an incorrect image of obtaining and using these commodities.

In the White supremacist lexicon, fighting crime is the same as waging war against Black males. Racist code doctrine lists Black males and crime as interchangeable or synonymous labels. The Black male under a coded racist system is the highest manifestation of a criminal. When the White politicians use the fight crime slogan or statement, they are telling majority White audiences that they will control niggers by getting tough and putting them away. One of the greatest abuses perpetuated under White racial domination is the criminalization of Black males.

From the date of his birth, the Black male is either a criminal prospect or athletic product. In the majority of cases he is a criminal. This is why so many Black males are falsely quoted as saying, "If I wasn't playing ball, I would be out robbing somebody."

Modern racism has ensured that even those who play ball or rap are still criminals. The connection of the rappers and athletes with criminal behavior has been well developed and glorified by the media. Sadly, this imaging process has been used for financial gain by the so-called Black media outlets, most of which are controlled by White money. In the end criminal behavior is encouraged and exalted. It is viewed as sexy, desirable and glamorous. This is the so-called bad boy syndrome.

The Black male instinctively knows that his choices move in this direction. He realizes that he is trapped and is being coded as product and packaged and imaged as a future criminal or an ungrateful athlete. Only in a special study or for a calculated political or financial purpose are Black males allowed to move in other directions. In the 2002 production of the Steven Spielberg motion picture "Minority Report" that starred Tom Cruise, the next step of the criminalization process was revealed. First, the term minority is a code for Black people. Black people have been labeled as minorities for many years, and the use of this word makes it clear as to what population is being targeted.

The city depicted in the movie is the nation's capital, Washington, D.C. It is a metropolis that has always been known as the chocolate city. The central theme of the movie is that the police force uses advanced technology that is designed to stop crime before it happens. It is the era of pre-crime prevention. The implications are staggering. It implies that the indigenous people that live in this city are born to commit crimes. The racial association should leave no doubt. However, there is an apparent effort to hide the racial link in the movie by using mostly White characters as the pre-criminals.

This strategy effectively covers the racially coded message. The fictional setting of Washington, D.C., a majority Black city, is a code for Black people and the crime connection. The message is that the city will only be cleaned up by arresting Black males before they commit criminal acts. Black males are born criminals so why wait for the act to occur. Why not reduce the probability and deter the situation before it happens. The city must be made safe for the White population that wants to move back into the area.

Get Tough on Crime

This term when decoded means getting tough on Black people and Black males in particular.

This code is designed to stimulate an attack on the stability of Black people and their living environments. An example of this was the launching of the chemical poisoning epidemic, or the flow of drugs against Black people, which was later called a war against crime.

Criminal

This word more than any other is directly connected to Black males. When a Black male walks into a room, a criminal has just entered the premises. This imaging leads to such activities as racial profiling which is one of the most recognized public manifestations of racial criminalization. Black males are now being tagged as future criminals and are called predators or super-predators. In the population-control psyche, the lowering of the birth rate in the Black community is defined as reducing crime. That is why the infant mortality rate among Black people here and abroad is still higher than among Whites.

Crime Ridden

This code implies that the Black community is hopelessly crime oriented and crime centered. It feeds the idea that the Black community is rotten to the core and full of criminals.

Crime Prone

This code says that Black males are naturally disposed to a life of criminal activity. The implication is that Black people are genetically endowed with criminal tendencies that cannot be altered no matter how much money is spent. These people are natural savages, murderers, rapists and useless eaters. They must be controlled through brain surgery or containment.

Race Code Words

Public Bus

This is a code phrase that means *niggers on the bus*. Public bus transportation is used by a great number by Black people in many cities for going to other parts of the city and to the suburbs. Public transportation is funded by federal and local tax initiatives in most communities. The county or region areas vote on the levy funding. This vote is often influenced by the concept that the busses carry Black people into their communities.

The public transportation system has developed a whole culture symbolized by the bus. This concept of linking of Black people to the bus started with the 1957 Montgomery Bus Boycott and the battle to end racial segregation. The next great linkage was the busing of children for so-called school desegregation in the mid-to late 1970s. The struggle was not over the color or size of the bus; it was over the color of who was on the bus. The same concept exists today with the voting and funding of bus levies. The bus once again is viewed as bringing poor Black people into White suburban areas.

Crime Ravaged

The term crime ravaged means a Black community overrun with criminals and trash. When the term crime ravaged area is used, it means a Black community. The word ravaged sounds like the word savage. This is no accidental word connection. This word is used frequently when dealing with AIDS in Africa. It brings to mind immediately the thought of savages tearing up a nation or a community. This term means to pillage and destroy a community with criminal activities. In this equation the purposeful economic neglect factor is omitted from the formula.

Crime in the Streets

This coded phrase is the same as saying all Black males commit crimes. It is both a racial and political concept that was fully developed in the 1970s. It means that niggers are running wild and are out of control like a pack of dogs in lustful, violent passion. The term crime in the streets means that every time a Black man is walking down the street, a crime is going to happen or has already been committed.

When Black males walk the streets, it is the same as a criminal or a criminal suspect walking down the street: in other words, a criminal.

91

This image has led to such concepts as walking Black, shopping Black and flying Black. When Black males are hanging around on the street, walking into a store, strolling through the shopping mall or to the ice cream parlor, in the minds of many Whites a criminal has just entered the premises and must be watched and checked for a possible theft or violent act.

This is very obvious by the way White people watch Blacks when they come into all White environments. Black males in particular are watched with a suspicious eye every step of the way. Any move they make is noted and recorded. This is why most Black males must be very careful when entering or even driving in White environments.

In stores Black people must realize that anytime they pick up an item to determine if they want to purchase it, they are under the watchful eye of the camera. Most White people will vehemently deny this fact. However, they cannot explain why it is that when a Black man enters a store or comes into a certain domain, the whole disposition changes. When Black people move into an area, the local stores take new precautions, such as selling gas through a glass-enclosed or bulletproof window or reducing the hours of store operation.

Crime in the streets is also used as a rallying cry to get greater resources to combat the imaginary threat of Black males. White people are fed stories of Black barbarian hordes invading their communities and raping the women. In many commercial advertisements in major White newspapers the image of the Black savage is subliminally embedded in the ad content. This is an illusion. History has no significant records of Black men raiding White communities and killing White females, elderly persons or children. The only historical note is to the extremely limited slave rebellions led by Nat Turner, Denmark Vessey and Gabriel Prosser.

Crime Prevention
This is code for keeping Black people under control. It means increasing the arrest of Black people to insure that they do not become threats to White society. It is very interesting that most crime prevention programs are in areas that are largely Black or have significant numbers of Black and White people living in the same area. The term crime has come to mean Black males. When put together with the word prevention, it means keeping the niggers from overrunning and invading White communities.

Race Code Words

Crime Rate(s)

This is the measurement of low-level crimes committed by Black and other nonwhite males. It is a racially based political counting method. It does not measure to any appreciable degree the so-called white-collar crimes. The media focuses on "low level" behavior such as petty burglaries, car thefts and the type of homicides committed by Black males. Crime rate means the number of low-level incidents committed by Black males. One way to determine when a community is undergoing racial transformation is to observe the number of businesses, especially gas stations, that force the consumer to pay through a security window after dark.

Street Crime

This is a point of reference for dealing with low value level transgressions committed by Black males. Unsavory offenses such as the open-air drug business, purse snatching, mugging, 7-11 convenience stores robberies or homicides usually over a twenty-dollar debt are emotional or dumb crimes. These do not require detail, planning, organization, technical competency or intelligence. These are the majority of crimes Black males are thought to take part in. Street crime is the opposite of the term white- collar crime. White- collar crime means "high line" professional sophisticated crime usually committed by white males. These crimes require planning, technical knowledge and detailed layout.

   This criminal activity might include illegal arms deals, massive stock swindles, insider trading and frauds, shipping illegal goods, forging expensive art treasures, nuclear theft, fencing stolen bearer bonds and high-price jewelry burglaries. Crimes with high residual value demand a network of money, power and connection. In movies like "Thief" with James Caan and "Heat" with Robert De Niro and Al Pacino, the differences between street crime and high-line crime were elaborated.

   In the 1995 movie "Heat," Al Pacino portrayed a LAPD (Los Angeles Police Department) detective. Pacino made a clear distinction between street crime and white-collar crime. When another detective asked if he were taking a murder and robbery case, he stated, "Does this look like gang bangers working the local seven-eleven to you?" Decoded, the statement reads, "Does this look like a nigger crime to you?" He also went on to say, "The m.o. shows they are good. They are technically proficient enough to go in on a prowl. So let's start looking for recent high-line burglaries that have mystified us." This is an unmistakable reference to the difference between White crime and street crime. This does not mean that Whites do not commit so-called street crimes or crimes of passion. They do commit these crimes; however, the image created is that these are crimes related to Black people.

Street Life

This code phrase is used to describe a low-level social lifestyle primarily experienced by Blacks and other nonwhites. This lifestyle is characterized by moving from one street corner to the next and engaging in random low-level criminal activity or socially destructive behavior. This lifestyle was glorified in the late 1960s to the mid 1980s in many derogatory films aimed to defame Black people.

War on Drugs

This is a code phrase for war on Black people. The number of Black males and females arrested for chemical abuse is evidence of the racial war on drugs. This war has consisted primarily of police raids on houses in the Black community. This has resulted in the arrest and conviction of Black males and females at astounding rates. It has created a generation of disenfranchised Black males with felony convictions rendering them unemployable and unable to vote. This rate of incarceration has produced so many dysfunctional families that children are raised without the income, guidance and presence of fathers and male role figures. It has also been used to justify the violation and erosion of personal freedoms and rights guaranteed by the U.S. Constitution. The driving and flying while Black racial profiling cases are a result of the war on drugs. According to most studies, the drug war should be conducted in the White suburbs. These studies reveal that the average drug merchant and user is White, male and lives in the suburbs.

Drugs

This is a code for Black male chemical dependency and abuse. When this word is used, it is in the context of "inner city drug use" or a CBS News "48 Hours" segment showing a Black victim of chemical dependency smoking a pipe of illegal chemicals or using a needle to shoot heroin into a vein. This word has been completely tied to the chemical dependency problems of Black people.

Drug Raids

This code is used to describe a police action in the Black community. The so-called drug raid rarely happens in the suburbs, where, according to most national reports, the bulk of the illegal drug trade is conducted. The drug raids in Black communities net little in terms of illegal chemicals and money.

Drug Infested

This is a new code-word combination. It is used to stereotype Black neighborhoods. It is a dynamic and explosive word combination that evokes visions of little brown and black creatures running amok. The intent of dropping these words on a community is to stigmatize the people with the stench of illegal drugs. The word "infested" insinuates a plague or disease.

This automatically connects with Whites because of the period in European history known as the Dark Ages. The history of Middle Ages Europe is replete with references to "red and black plagues" (the color connection is interesting; see the chapter on racial symbols). This term plays on the deep and ancient psychological fears of White people regarding the return of the Black Plague era. This enables the White collective to associate the plague with rodents and disease, and brown and black rodents with Brown and Black people. This is not the first time these associations have been made.

The color and persona of brown and black roaches have been attached to the cultural lifestyles of Black people on many occasions. The rodent extermination commercials probably more than any other effort help to make the connection between rodents and Black people. The television and radio commercials openly boast and celebrate the killing of little black and brown creatures. This is a subliminal reference to the extermination of Black and Brown people. It was during this same period, the late 1960s to mid 1970s, that White congressmen were laughing on the floor of the Congress about the size of rats and roaches in poor Southern and Northern Black households.

These commercials helped to bind the mental association between black and brown roaches and Black and Brown people. The words and images used in the commercials were more related to human warfare than to the extermination of household rodents. The commercial cartoons and marketing material showed rodents as armies of dark-skinned creatures raiding and mounting an attack on the food of innocent White households.

This attack on food symbolized the possible armed invasion of Blacks and other nonwhites into White communities. It was during this period that White people exploded into the suburbs and armed themselves to the teeth in preparation for the "great race war." In the game of deceptive racial warfare the number-one strategy objective is to cloak real meanings through symbol associations. This was also a time of race riots and the Vietnam War. These entanglements with two nonwhite groups (Asians and Africans) were portrayed as threats to maintaining White supremacy domination.

The name of one of the products, Black Flag, is worth noting in terms of its association with the extermination of black and brown creatures. The term drug infested conjures up the image of black and brown creatures running wild and unchecked through the neighborhood.

Heroin Addict
This code was associated with Black people during the nineteen sixties, but in the 1990s heroin use and addiction became mostly White.

AIDS Epidemic/ HIV Drug User
This code has come to mean Black people using drugs with needles and acquiring an incurable disease.

Drive-by Shooting
This term was originally associated with the Italian Mafia during the early part of the century in Chicago and New York. White gangsters would drive by in automobiles and shoot at unsuspecting rival gang targets. These cowardly murders or attempted murders were sensational and made to appear as glamorous and sexy deeds. Black males involved in unsavory activities that were readily available in many Black

neighborhoods in the late seventies and mid-eighties began to imitate these images, trying to justify them as glamorous. Today, this phrase is associated with young Black and Hispanic males.

Take Responsibility for Your Own Actions

This phrase arose from the White conservative movement as a reaction to the Black movement for justice. It also says that Whites do not want to be held accountable for the sins of the past and current. They want to forget that they are in control of the lives of Black people and therefore have no responsibility for their current condition. This is similar to asking slaves to take charge of their lives right after they are freed.

Crack

This word has become synonymous with Black people. When the word crack is uttered, the first image that pops into mind is that of a Black person. Crack is connected to African Americans like the words heroin or "junkie" were in the 1960s and 1970s. This word has been effectively combined with dramatic images of so-called dark drug raids in the Black community, the sale of drugs in "open air markets" on the street corner and courtrooms packed with Black faces contemplating long prison sentences. From the national news broadcasts to local evening news, Black people are the overwhelming majority of those visually linked to crack.

The majority of so-called "urban movies," and even gym shoe commercials, reinforce the association between the words crack, urban and Black. The Nike commercials are notorious for using urban playgrounds and subtle background scenes that imply drug sales and drug use. This is the political reason for the outcry over the issue of unequal sentencing for possession of cocaine and crack. Crack is Black drug use and cocaine is considered White drug use.

The White media, police departments, entertainment industry, courts and political infrastructure have made official the relationship between Black people and crack cocaine. This allowed the forces of White supremacy to evolve a whole glossary of words and visual image patterns that weld the mental connection. The end game is to hide the illegal drug use of White people by using Blacks as fall guys.

RACE CODE WAR

The emotional and mental association of Black and crack is so strong that even when presented with statistics contradicting the false images, most Whites and Blacks will still believe the image. The word crack is a racial symbol targeted to degrade the people and image of the Black community. This is deceptive because, according to the Human Rights Watch Report, White people use crack cocaine at nearly three times the rate of Black people.

Crack House

This is a racial code term for an inner city Black household where illegal drugs are bought, sold and consumed. The use of the words crack and house together is a new dynamic. This word combination did not appear until the mid-1980s. If these terms were used in 1970, it would have had no social or political meaning. It was only after the crack cocaine epidemic exploded out of Los Angeles, California, in the early 1980s, which was related to the Iran / Contra / CIA connection, that the word combination began to have relevant racial propaganda impact. The crack house is the place to buy, sell and use illegal drugs. This is an interesting word combination.

The "house" word is the symbol of a powerful, bonding and maternal forces. It evokes feelings of security, it is the center of existence and "the family line." The house is the spiritual infrastructure that binds people and community together in order to pass on the culture and the social lineage. The word crack means a fracture, fault line or small opening. Traditionally, the use of the word crack in reference to a house would be to point out that there is a crack in the door or the roof or the basement of the house. One might say that the house has a crack in the foundation or has many cracks in other areas. However, to use it in any other context with the word house did not fit with the explosion of the cooked cocaine epidemic, the word crack took on a new social and political meaning.

The word crack comes from the crackling sound made during the process of cooking cocaine. This process produces a drug known as crack cocaine. The two words joined together form a mental connection between the Black community and the drug culture. This is the rationale given by racists and non-thinking Black people as to why Black children

98

and Black youth identify with the language, dress styles, automobiles and music normally associated with people involved in gangs, drugs and violence. The protected existence of a crack house implies that these communities are natural breeding grounds for illegal drugs. In the late 1970s and mid-1980s this social belief was reinforced through the sounds of reggae music and the Rasta movement, symbolized by humongous brown dope cigars.

The racist used reggae to convince White people that drugs were endemic in Black communities. It is easy to sell drugs in the Black community because it is a natural part of their psyche. The people will have little or no resistance to it because it is something that is part of the very fabric of their amoral center of existence. In their communities, anything goes!

The term crack house was created to exclusively identify drugs with Black people. If this is not a true statement, what are the terms for drug houses in the White community? Where are the *coke or cocaine houses, marijuana or weed houses and crank houses*? The term crack house was designed purely as racial propaganda. There are thousands of White households in the cities, suburbs and rural areas where the sale and use of illegal drugs takes place. Racial labels are not attached to the entire social and cultural fabric of these communities. Their neighborhoods and family lines have not been besmirched by these horrible stigmas.

Crack Dealer

This is a code phrase for a Black person involved in the sale of illegal chemicals, a.k.a. drugs.
This term has come to represent a person in the community who is involved in the sale of drugs in the area.

Crack Addict

This code means a Black victim of a targeted and directed chemical-poisoning conspiracy.

Crack Head

This is code for a Black person destroyed by chemical poisoning. It is a very dangerous term that gained wide acceptance among Black people.

RACE CODE WAR

Cocaine
This code word has come to mean Black people. This word began as a reference to rich White drug users. However, with the coming of crack cocaine, the language and images have shifted. The cocaine abusers are now classified as Black.

Junkie
This is an old label from the nineteen fifties and sixties and evolves from the term "heroin junkie." This word is interesting because of the use of "junk" as the catch phrase. It was associated with Blacks with needles in their arms in some dark allies. The word junk is related to the word garbage that is related to the word trash.

Substance Abuser
This term is used to describe Black victims of crack cocaine and other chemical poisons.

Gangs
The use of this word began with the Italian and Jewish mobsters of the early 1900s. These were real gangs organized to gain economic and political power. They were involved in murderous and almost genocidal activities. Gangs controlled politicians, managed police departments, owned all the land in the area and enforced their rule of law. This is the real definition of a gang. Meyer Lansky was a gang member and Frank Costello was a gang member.

The NBA
The NBA stands for the National Basketball Association. In the racist's lexicon it stands for the National Black Association. At least 80% of the players in the league are Black athletes. In recent years the NBA has been pursuing efforts to bring in greater numbers of White, Latino and Asians. There are currently sixty foreign mostly White players in the league.

This is only the beginning. The 2002 NBA Division championship series between Sacramento and Los Angeles revealed the new racial strategy. The enshrouded purpose is to change the image of the NBA. To achieve this objective they have even traveled to a communist country to sign basketball players. The number one pick in

Race Code Words

the 2002 NBA Draft was a 7'6" player named Yao Ming who was from Communist China of all places!

The first big game showdown between Yao of the Houston Rockets and Shaquille O'Neal of the Los Angeles Lakers on Friday, January 17, 2003 generated great worldwide interest. The goal is to find players that can counter the awesome power of three-time champion Shaquille O'Neal (many racists refer to Shaq as a giant Black gorilla, Godzilla or *Shaqzilla* as one White sports commentator said). In other words they want to reduce or eliminate the Black male dominance of the game.

Regardless of these moves, all of the physical play and gamesmanship of the NBA are still tied to the performance, activity and style of the Black athletes. The highest paid and the most publicized stars in sports are the Black athletes in the NBA. College and professional basketball is a Black game. Black athletes are groomed to play basketball the same way horses are prepared to run in the Kentucky Derby. The little brown basketball and Black males and females are inseparable images. The affiliation with Black people and the game of basketball did not always exist. In the early 1950s the majority of the players in the NBA were White athletes.

During this era, the league played a "White style" of basketball that was by their own admission colorless, methodical, mechanical and lacked spontaneity. The Black basketball player did not make a big splash until the arrival of Bill Russell, K.C. Jones, Tom "Satch" Saunders, Wilt "The Stilt" Chamberlain, Elgin Baylor and Oscar "Big O" Robertson. The league then began to play a different style of professional basketball.

The conversion to a Black style was accelerated by the American Basketball Association (ABA). The ABA played a different style of basketball that was high-flying, open court and more entertaining. This kind of basketball was called street ball, or (decoded) *niggerball.* The ABA featured the high-wire act of the great superstar Julius "Dr. J" Erving. The ABA finally merged with the NBA, and a new kind of professional basketball came into being.

By the late 1970s, the NBA, with Kareem Abdul Jabbar, Willis Reed, Clyde Frazier and Earl "the Pearl" Monroe leading the way, was well on its way to becoming a Black-dominated sports league.

The dramatic and sudden change threatened the financial stability of the league. White viewers complained that they could no longer identify with the game. Television ratings and arena attendance dropped. The White superstars of yesteryear like Bob Cousy and Bob Petit were retired. Dave Cowen and Jerry West had played as long as their legs and bodies would allow. Right on cue, the great White gods sent forth a giant shaggy-haired guy from Indiana State University named Larry Bird.

This superstar was very tall with pinpoint shooting ability and legendary hustle. Bird had the physical appearance of a Viking warrior. He became an instant star, hero and superman to White basketball patrons and television viewers. His presence and especially in the city of Boston, revitalized the game. Bird brought large numbers of White people back into the arenas and in front of television screens. His arrival set the stage for a battle of racial supremacy on the hardwood floor. The game of basketball would become more than just a game of shooting, speed and team play. It would become the worldwide setting for a racial showdown.

The showdown would be against the Los Angeles Lakers and Ervin "Magic" Johnson. Fresh from their larger-than-life battle for the NCAA championship in 1979, the Magic and Bird duel pumped up the NBA in the 1980s. Larry Bird in a symbolic sense represented the White male and Magic Johnson, the Black male. The NBA reached a golden era (in decoded speech, it reached greater White audiences) with epic battles between the Black Los Angeles Lakers and the White Boston Celtics. White people identified with Bird and the Celtics and Black people connected with Magic, Jabbar and the Lakers. Larry Bird in the symbolic sense became the White knight that was sent to restore White pride and to defeat the "dark invaders."

The most recent NBA golden era began with the arrival of the ultra-chocolate-colored, almost super-human Michael Jordan. His brand of basketball was hard Black and extremely sensual and sexual. His deep black color, bald black head, long and extruding red tongue, sweating palms, huge hands, excessively long shorts that were a not-so-subtle inference of having to cover a bigger penis combined with gyrating aerial moves to drive White women to jump and cheer as if in a state of sexual frenzy. Dr. Frances Welsing points this out in her monumental work *The Isis Papers*. The big black hands and long arms extending to slam a big brown ball into white nets symbolizes a big black penis jamming into a white vagina. The long, extended arm and the ball cupped in the hand symbolically appear as an erect black penis. Jordan became a very potent black male phallic symbol. Jordan with his smooth black head looked like a walking black penis. He was the fulfillment of the White female's desire for deep, dark chocolate. This is why his demeanor on the court was so controlled and passive. He could not be viewed as a threat.

The moves to whitenized or to brighten-up the NBA is designed to *save the sport* from White disinterest. The idea of declining interest is based on the notion that White people are tired or a better word is angry at seeing Black males putting large brown balls through White nets for multi-million dollar paychecks. The idea that more White or near White players will generate **greater interest** means larger White audiences. Sports talk radio/television personalities have made this very clear when they use heavily coded phrases such as the new players play better *team ball, create greater excitement and interest* and they know the fundamentals of the game. All of these terms are intellectually related. Whereas coded phrases such as street ball, one on one and you only need to watch *the last two minutes of game* are used to convey the idea that watching Black males play is the same as seeing apes or a seven foot Godzilla with athletic ability.

The basketball games between Magic and Bird were reminiscent of the battles from the Star Wars and Godzilla movies. It is rather interesting that the first Star Wars movies came out during this period. One of the major themes from one of the most recent Star Wars movies, "The Phantom Menace," is to defeat the dark side. In the most recent version of the Godzilla movies, the monster mutated into hundreds of young Godzilla monsters. The baby monsters were dark skinned and seven-feet tall. In a chase scene set in Madison Square Garden, the home of the New York Knicks, a brief view depicted several seven-feet-tall baby Godzilla monsters chasing a group of frightened White people. As the monsters give chase, the White star throws a rack of basketballs to deter or slow them down. For a fleeting moment the bouncing balls touch the hands of the seven-foot Godzilla monsters. This has a subtle but very powerful emblematic meaning.

The scene was Madison Square Garden, home of the New York Knicks. At the time of the movie, most of the players on the Knicks were Black, and the star most representative of the team was a dark-skinned seven-foot sensation named Patrick Ewing. The symbolic racial connection between the dark-skinned Godzilla monster dribbling basketballs and Madison Square Garden, home of the Knicks, is inescapable. The final scenes in the movie show thousands of seven-foot Godzilla monsters being duplicated and taking over Madison Square Garden. In decoded language they were taking over New York, the financial capital, and if not stopped, would take over the rest of the White world. This was a thinly disguised code for comparing Black men to dark-colored monsters and to stopping the dark menace. There were two other (maybe more) noticeable examples linking the Godzilla monster and Black male athletes. NBA superstar Dennis Rodman was called Godzilla, further cementing the perceptual bond between the dark-skinned monsters and urban Black males.

Gang Member
This defines a misguided Black youth involved in low-level, unsavory street activity. This attempt at gang activity would be really laughable if the harm to their victims were not so real.

Gang Related
This code is like drug-related and it is a catch phrase for all Black youth issues. The term gang related is used to define all murders or other unsavory activities engaged in by Black male youth. The purpose of this term is to label young Black males as criminals and dangers to society.
It also codifies clothes, colors and sign language as gang based. In reality there is only one real gang and that is the gang of White supremacists who run the world.

Gang Violence
This is a term used to define Black male street-level activities that largely perpetrates violence on other Blacks.

Race Code Words

Gang Bangers
This term is also used to define a group of Black youth involved in sexual conquests or violent activity.

Gang Rape
This term is used to define the involvement of Black males in raping White females or White males in prison.

Forced Busing
This is a code phrase that evolved during the Nixon Administration. This term came to symbolize *a bus carrying Black children* to school in predominantly White areas. Forced busing became the mechanism to pressure Black children to interact in White learning environments. In decoded communication, the long school bus carried a breed of nonwhite savages, young rapists and culturally inferior offspring. With Black children in the classroom, subject matter would have to be tweaked and altered. The message of White domination would be endangered. Millions of White people fled the central city school districts and set-up new public and private education systems to protect and control the flow of information.

Desegregation
This is part of the coded busing language. In race code speech it means the break up of White learning environments. It is a threat to the social hegemony of White culture. It means Black boys with White girls and interracial offspring. It signals a new world order and race management systems.

Latchkey Kids
A code used to define inner city Black children that are left home alone. White conservatives in particular have a field day complaining about the wild inner city children with no parents, engaging in sex and creating social havoc.

Saturday Night Special
This was used to define the weapons that Black people used to rob and kill during the weekend.

In the 1970s the .22 caliber gun was considered a Black weapon. Saturday was the night that all Black people hit the town with wild parties and hot times. In decoded speech this term means Black people drinking, cussing, fighting and shooting.

Natives

This, more than any other term, has been used to define nonwhites in other areas of the world, especially Africa and darker Asia. The word gained popular use in movies in the 1950s. The natives meant blacks, Indians and very dark skinned Asian and/or Indians from India. The Tarzan books and motion pictures helped to institutionalize and attach this word to Black people. In White supremacist folklore it stands for savage and primitive people.

Troubled Area/Neighborhoods

This is code for an area in which the majority of the residents are Black people. The White supremacist will ensure that these areas remain destabilized and confused.

Troubled Kids

This is code for Black youth from inner city neighborhoods. It means also that these children are ill mannered, unkempt savages, violence prone and natural-born killers. They must be watched very closely for signs of disorder.

Dysfunctional Family

This is a code phrase to define Black families as incompetent and unable to function successfully. This term has all but devastated and debased the lives of millions of Black families.

Bitch

This is a very ugly code word for Black females. Unfortunately, it has become a word used by Black males to describe their relationships with females and incorrectly see Black females as untrustworthy, treacherous and more supportive of White males than of Black men. A bitch is a female dog. The nature of a dog suggests many things, ranging from lack of morals to viciousness to a nonstop baby-making machine. This connection of Black females to dogs began during slavery. The

Race Code Words

White master used Black women as breeders for his new slaves and for sexual frolic and perversion. The word bitch also suggests that the Black woman, particularly the darker-skinned variety, is not as feminine or as sexually attractive as the White female or very light-skinned Black female. It is rare even today to hear White females referred to as bitches. This designation is placed solely on Black women and is one of the most destructive and demeaning terms ever used to define a human being.

Ho
This is another code word for Black females. A ho refers to the opening of the vagina. It essentially means the Black female is a trick and a prostitute. She is good for only sexual purposes. It also implies that she is not worthy of attention, affection and commitment and should be used like an animal.

Violence Prone
This code phrase means that Black males are genetically predisposed to be violent, savage and sub-human. They are naturally uncivilized and all the money and social programs will not change their behavior. This is why political sayings such as *We can't keep throwing money at the problem* originated during the Reagan Administration. In this sentence the term "we" means White people, and the "problem" is Black people. This phrase means that it is a waste of money to try to upgrade these people because they are naturally inferior and are born violent and barbarian. They have limited intellectual and social development skills. The only way to handle them is to bleach the color out through the process of miscegenation, imprison the male population, thus reducing black-on-black reproduction, or selectively exterminate.

Troubled Youngsters
This has become a code designation for Black children. The word "troubled" implies that the individual is disturbed, deranged and emotionally unbalanced. This explains why so many Black children have been put on control drugs such as Ritalin. The word "troubled" also suggests that Black children are naturally afflicted from birth with an emotional, mental or social disorder or have a penchant for uncivilized behavior.

Rape/Rapists

This most horrendous sex act is linked to the definition of a Black male. The association of the word with Black males began during the period of chattel slavery. The White slave master concocted the notion that Black males were violent, lustful and undesirable creatures that craved sex with White females. According to the racist logic, White females did not want to be touched by the Black savage. The only way this could happen was if the Black male overpowered and forcefully took sex. The fear of Black male sexual and genetic superiority has been the driving force behind the rape accusation. The White fear was that Black males would use animal sexual instincts to overwhelm, influence and defile the White family's genetic pool, which would be defiled and corrupted by the inferior Black gene.

The act of sex would enable the Black male to gain control of the White female. The idea of sex with a Black male had to be painted in the most horrible and dehumanizing words. According to racist nonsense, the White female is the Lily of the Valley, the bright morning star, a pure white virgin untouched and unsoiled. In recent years White psychologists have suggested that rape is not as much a sexual act as it is the quest for male power over the female. This concept holds more truth for the White male than the Black male. Under the system of White domination, the White male holds the power; the act of rape is an expression of might. The Black male rape of White females is largely a part of the "get even" syndrome.

Thug

This code word has been linked to Black males for many years. In the nineteen seventies and eighties the term defined a hoodlum. A thug is a low-life character and a cheap criminal. He has no desire to go to school, to obey the rules and to cooperate with law. A thug is lower than a tramp or hobo. The tramp is dirty and has odor problems. This might be one of the reasons so many young Black males wear pants down below their butts and look unwashed. This is part of a tramp's outfit. The wearing of low pants is the same as telling White people (and some Black people) to kiss their ass. In the process they are also falling victim to the racist image of a low life. This is a racist image of a group of people without dignity or respect. On top of all this, he is not even considered a first-rate criminal. The thug is depicted as the worst kind of social varmint.

Race Code Words

The thug is a failed criminal who is relegated to low-bred and low-yield outlaw activity. The thug does not have the intellectual capacity for the white collar, high-line or high-end crime jobs. These are racial codes for the intelligent White criminals. A thug steals from small and defenseless people. He preys on old ladies, old men, low-income families and mom and pops grocery store owners and other weak victims. He lies in *the bush and the shadows* (two widely used code words to imply the evils of darkness and dark locations) to do his ugly deed. The word thug also suggests disorder and lawlessness. A thug must be locked up and never released into the general society. It is interesting that many young Black males fall into the image trap by identifying themselves as thugs and even going so far as to celebrate what they call *thug life.*

This is an extremely dangerous trend and it opens the floodgates of justification for more prisons, harsher jail sentences and greater social nullification. The racist can now openly label Black males as thugs, hoodlums and criminals and get away with it.

If Black people use these incriminating terms to define themselves, then Whites cannot be called racist when they do the same thing. What young Black people do not see or understand is the big racial picture. They do not know how the racist mind operates and do not understand how the racial word-trap works. Young Blacks think that the word thug is cool. They believe that it is swank to be a thug, except when your mother sees you in prison or when you try to get a job or are denied a student loan because of a felony record. They have unwittingly played into the hands of racists by helping them shape social legislation designed to lock Black people up. This is where race-based slogans, such as *clean up the streets,* come from, which when decoded means to rid the area of or minimize the number of Black males in a block, neighborhood, community or city.

Mugger

This word has a similar meaning to the term thug. A mugger is a small-time robber who sneaks up behind the victim to steal or remove some money or article. This term was popularized during the early 1980s when a White male shot a Black teenager during an alleged New York City subway robbery incident. A mugger is a small-time crook who robs to get immediate cash, jewelry or credit cards. He does not have the brains for a big job.

RACE CODE WAR

Mean Streets

This is a code term for a Black neighborhood. It means a community populated with Black troublemakers, prostitutes and hardened low-life individuals. How can a street be mean? Streets are paved concrete that have no personalities. So what is the hidden meaning of the word "mean" in this context? The meaning is that the people who live in these areas are extremely dangerous, filled with hate, nasty, morally decayed and corrupt. The term implies that they must be treated roughly because they are hard to handle, like tough and vicious mad dogs or black rhinos. This fits the profile that White supremacists want to establish. The often-heard saying *they put their lives on the line every day* is a direct code reference to the hazards of dealing with Black people on a daily basis.

In order to deal with these mad animals, the White supremacists must have the most sophisticated weaponry. They must posses the most inhuman firepower to stop these big, black Rodney King-size bucks from attacking and destroying. In order to patrol these mean streets, we must have military weapons because we are in a war zone. These drug dealers are better armed than we are. We need additional firepower to control the mean streets (decoded niggers). This is the rationale used to justify the purchase of massive weapons and arms for police and sheriffs' departments. Army manufacturers have drastically increased their sales to law-enforcement organizations.

The basis for the explosive growth in arms sales to local law enforcement agencies is the rabid fear of Black males. The hard data do not indicate that Black people are shooting White law enforcement officers. The real truth is that the White law enforcement officials are shooting and killing Black people. The mean street argument has been used for many years to explain why chemical trafficking has not been eliminated. This has also become a new excuse for increasing military maneuvers in preparation for so-called *urban warfare* in several cities across the nation.

Rough Neighborhood

This code phrase has a slightly different meaning from mean streets. The term rough neighborhood means a place of social discontentment and low achievement populated by ruffians. It is a neighborhood where it is not easy to live. Social relations are strained, and the people just can't get along. Everything is an uphill battle, with little cooperation and support for any action aimed at producing justice.

Race Code Words

Teenage Pregnancy

This is a code for young Black females. This word implies that young Black females are sex crazed with no moral restraint. They are totally irresponsible and have parents that are equally irresponsible. They are baby-making machines with a propensity for unbridled sex at an early age. It is the prostitution syndrome operating at an early age. In the early 1980s to mid-1990s teenage pregnancy was a powerful issue, and the primary focus was on the number of births per young Black female.

Zero Tolerance

This is a new code term that signifies the containment and control of young Black males. Zero tolerance views Black people as predators and enemies. The goal of the zero tolerance program and concept is to put the Black population under intense monitoring and restraint. This is why video cameras are placed on every corner in heavily Black populated areas.

Big Government

Historically speaking the word government connoted positive things. It meant authority, civilization and order. The battle between White people during the so-called revolutionary war was about the rights of the colonists to determine which group would be the first to expand White supremacy in an area populated by nonwhites. The objective was to achieve greater White self -determination, self-rule to develop a society where White men and women could thrive and preserve government.

The word government meant an advanced society or culture. In modern race propaganda
the combination of the words big and government has been demonized. Big government has come to symbolize a big black monster. They effectively tied the civil rights movement to the expansion or enlargement of government. Government is too big and should only be used for defense and smaller things. The church and social agencies should handle the problems of the "truly needy." This was a smoke screen to justify removing and/or downsizing critical programs that were benefiting Black people.

This term was used very effectively during the early eighties to rally hardcore Whites to oppose Black political advancement. For more than a quarter century, Black people used court rulings to gain employment opportunity, political representation, economic and education advancement, housing equality and other types of social progress. This angered many Whites who were caught by surprise when Blacks used White language to advance the Black cause. Whites began to see that their political process was being used against their own interests. Since they could no longer come out and say in brazen language "get them niggers off our backs," they used code language like "get the government off our backs."

Movies portrayed Whites as poor, oppressed people who had to deal with heartless and incompetent Black bureaucrats. This, of course, only intensified the anger and frustration of Whites who felt that they would have to enlist the aid of Black people to survive. By 1980 the anger meter was at the boiling point. So-called Black advancement had to be rolled back.

The strategy was to demonize government as a front for attacking Black people. The racial propagandist effectively separated the people from the government. There would be no government without people. It was a beautiful strategy. White people resented the tactic of using the law and the courts to force concessions to Black people. They began to scream, "Get the government off my back."

What they really meant was, "Get them niggers off my back." A myriad of phony cries of reverse discrimination oozed forward as a counter to stop the march of the civil rights movement. The smart White propagandist began to design the term big government as code to rally White sentiment against more advances and concessions. They fashioned an entire dialogue around the use of the word government. They said the government was too big, talked about cutting domestic spending and increasing military spending. The terms domestic spending and military spending symbolically represented the struggle between meeting the needs of White people and submitting to Black interests.

The big military budgets meant spending money on space travel, engineering, chemicals, transportation, electronics and so forth. The domestic side of the equation symbolized welfare, child nutrition, C.E.T.A, Model Cities and a host of other social programs that assisted Blacks in the war against hardcore racism. The term domestic spending became a code word for Black people and other nonwhites. These words were almost interchangeable during the heyday of the anti-big government campaign.

Race Code Words

This term was also used to demonize people on public assistance. The cry for welfare reform became synonymous with Black females. This became the biggest and most useful whipping horse used to stir up passions to cut big government. The military and intelligence budgets far outweighed spending on welfare. White people outnumbered Blacks on the welfare rolls. They were the primary beneficiaries of the big, fat government contracts, food stamps and agriculture opportunities.

Government Hand-Outs

This is code for giving Blacks more money. The biggest victims of the racial propaganda wars were people on welfare. The word hand-outs suggests that people don't want to work, are lazy and look for someone to give them something free of charge. A hand-out conjures up visions of bums standing in line to receive food even though they are able-bodied and capable of working. Government hand-outs evoke images of cheese lines full of leeches who don't have the will to do for themselves. In short, this term accomplished many propaganda goals. It established Black people as a marginal population who could be eliminated or even decimated.

Get Big Government Off Our Backs

When decoded this means *get the niggers off our backs*. Once we have decoded the word government in the modern lexicon, it is easy to see how this term has been manipulated to mean something completely different from the original concept. The word government, thanks to the superior efforts of White propagandists conjures a fire-breathing Black creature akin to Godzilla with huge destructive powers. It is inconceivable how a nonexistent symbol can become such a hated and feared reality. Government as single creature doesn't really exist. However, when associated with something to fear such as the black menace it takes on a new meaning. In this context the word government is used to hide the word nigger, which is what they really mean. Even those Black people who parrot these phrases have no real clue as to what they really mean. They simply repeat these slogans to gain favor with some White group.

Such slogans were parroted by politicians in the thirties, forties and fifties but did not have the menacing associations until used to assist Black people. Big government was viewed as the civil rights movement holding power over White people. Thus big government becomes a real enemy symbolized by such things as black ops, black bag jobs, black helicopters, men in black and so forth. These are the words in Western lore that attach color to evil deeds and to people of color. The thought is that these niggers are running everything and that Whites must get ready to regain their country even if it means racial warfare.

Throwing Money At The Problem

This is a code phrase used to oppose giving Black people any more money. In this approach we are never told what the problem is. In racist code logic money represents the power of White people. White people produce money and resources. The problem is Black people. The word problem indicates a source of vexation and menace that is troubling or difficult to deal with. In modern society the goal is to eliminate problems. We get rid of or reduce problems so that they do not remain "menaces to society," so why throw money at the problem when a better idea could be the "final solution." Remember, this is not so far fetched: when the Nazis wanted to dehumanize the Jews, they declared them to be a problem or nuisance to society. White supremacists are saying that they are tired of funding programs designed to upgrade Black people.

Essentially, they are saying that Blacks have inferior genes and therefore are a hopeless group of people and no amount of help can change that. So why waste any more tax dollars on "those people." The concept of throwing is also very interesting because throwing is an act of dispensing or getting rid of something. It appears as if there is no serious intent to address a situation because we are throwing something away. It appears that throwing money is wasteful.

If changing a situation were taken seriously, a more progressive word such as *investment* would have been used. The word investment implies that the problem has been given very careful consideration and that assigning resources to the effort would yield positive results. To throw something is regarded as an act of getting rid of it. It is akin to throwing something at the animals in the zoo. The act of throwing suggests that the people in question are not to be taken seriously. They are objects or things of little importance in the giant scheme of things;

they are just a throw-away population with little relevance and significance.

Behind the Eight Ball

This one is chock-full of hidden meanings. In the game of pool the eight ball is often the losing ball. The white ball is the operative ball. The game is played on a green surface that symbolizes land and earth. The colored balls stand for the manipulation and movement of colored people on the planet. The operative white ball must be the victor and the black ball the loser.

Prostitute / Hooker / Streetwalker

This is code for a Black female. Black prostitutes have been called hookers, whores, and prostitutes. Black women are called streetwalkers who solicit sexual business. Black females are portrayed as big-butt mamas, sleazy and dirty.

White prostitutes have been portrayed in the movies as call girls, bar girls or escort ladies under the guise of giving the trade "a little more class." The term call girl when decoded implies that the john, or client primarily initiates the sex. The word escort means a companion who goes on a date with a girlfriend, woman friend or man friend. The word hooker implies that the female or male is actively trying to pinch, rob and stab. All this language is related to forcing or conning an innocent victim into coerced, entrapped and illegal sexual activity. It is like invading the sea and enticing a fish into a trap that is a set-up. The word hooker gained national prominence as a sexual word on an ABC Sunday night movie in 1964 that depicted the struggle of Hispanic youth in New York City.

The word hooker has never been heavily identified with White female streetwalkers. It was linked with Hispanic and Black females. This is reflective of how Black females are still portrayed in the movies. They are portrayed as loud, trashy, hot and ready hoochie mamas and street-walkers. A classic illustration of this is a scene from Oliver Stone's movie *"JFK."* After interviewing a trashy-mouthed, White, hard-core racist, homosexual prisoner about his association with suspected presidential assassination associate Clay Shaw, New Orleans District Attorney Jim Garrison, played by actor Kevin Costner, says to his investigative assistant: " I always wondered why a woman has to have bad eyesight because she's a prostitute." In the very next scene a big-butt, dark-skinned Black female in a form-fitting and sparkling bright gold dress is standing on the corner near a restaurant entrance.

She is swaying her big butt back and forth in a suggestive manner as though trying to hook or to stimulate sexual business. The gold dress symbolizes money and the best sexual experience. As Garrison (Costner) gets out of the car and walks toward the restaurant, the woman approaches and asks Garrison if he remembers her from election night. He says yes and remembers that they sang a song with the words "you're the cream in my coffee". This is a very direct reference to racial integration, racial sexism and the desire of the Black female to have sex with a White male. On the surface this scene makes no sense until one looks a little deeper into the symbolism of the message.

The message was that Garrison had sex with Black females on a regular basis. There is and old saying in White supremacist lore that a White man is not a man until he has slept with a Black woman. The Black woman is symbolized as the highest, most rewarding and fulfilling sexual partner. In Arab lore every man that lives according to the faith is rewarded with a number of dark, brown-eyed Black women in heaven. Many White men still believe that sex with a Black woman makes them real men. This same sexual racism is also linked to sex between White women and Black men.

The *cream (crème) in your coffee* song contained very explicit lyrics. The *crème* is the White male Jim Garrison and the coffee is the sexual organ of a Black female. In essence it means that a White penis penetrates or enters a Black vagina either for money or for play. This is clearly a racial and sexual reference, and it is used as an age-old racist stereotype to tag Black women as hot, always ready for sex and symbols of prostitution. This scene accomplishes several objectives. First, it implants and reinforces the idea that Black women are hot creatures ready for sex at the drop of a hat. The second point is that they are far less valuable and far less virginal than White women, who would have been classified as call girls.

The words prostitute and Black females have become homogenized in White supremacy lore and even in films. The usual portrayal of Black people in films is disgraceful. In the 1970s Black females were often portrayed as hookers or ho's or bitches. Even in pornography movies in the year 2002 the Black females are labeled as Black bitches, Black ho's and Black hookers. In pornography titles it still is rare to see White women referred to as White hookers or hookers.

Illegitimate
This is a code for Black children born to Black parents. This word has been used for many years to discredit Black families and classify them as dysfunctional. In the mind of a White supremacist a nonwhite person is invalid and illegitimate. No Black individual can be a legitimate human as long as White supremacy exists.

Hackers
This is a new computer cyberspace term. It originally was applied to young White males who broke into computer systems. However, increasingly this term is being imaged with Black males, as in the movie "Mission Impossible." This is a derogatory term and therefore must have derogatory associations. It is a word to watch carefully.

Tax-Credit Housing
This is a code phrase for housing Black people. It identifies a new spin that allows White businessmen to get money to build largely Black developments in White suburbs.

Low Income (People, Area or Community)
This is code for Black people. The word low implies such things as insignificant, paltry, unimportant, depressed, vile, odious, dastardly, contemptible, despicable, corrupt, debased, debauched, sordid, abject, immoral, nasty and rotten. This term creates an instant derogatory mindset. *The term should be changed and never used to describe a group of people.* There are other words and terms such as livable-income group, livable-wage group, medium-livable income and constructive development area.

Loud Music
This term generally applies to Black music with loud stereo systems, blasting so loudly that the whole neighborhood can hear the music. The term means disorderly, unruly, riotous and profane.

RACE CODE WAR

The Projects
This is a code for poor Blacks. It means public housing communities. The public housing communities started as communities built for returning White war veterans and their families. In the mid-to late 1950s these began to change from White to Black communities. When the skin color of the residents changed, the labels for the community changed. These communities have been called hell, the pits and the slums. It has been said that nothing good comes out of public housing communities. The 1960s statement "I escaped from the ghetto," was based on images of public housing communities. The word project also connotes that people who live in these communities are dependent, low life, lazy, crazy, irresponsible, baby making machines and welfare recipients.

The Slums
This is another code term for the inner city. It was used in the nineteen fifties to define Black people living in large Midwestern and northern cities. This language was used extensively in federal government reports and urban renewal plans.

The Ghetto
Ghetto was originally tagged to Jews living in segregated areas of cities in Europe. It is now applied to Black people in major cities.

That's My Baby's Daddy
This is a new term developed and applied to young Black mothers and their relationships with the fathers of their children. This is another reference to the inner city and dysfunctional family propaganda.

Upward Mobility
This is a very interesting term that is used to appeal to the so-called Black middle-class.
It was designed to address the frustrations of Black people who expressed belief in the goodness of White supremacy. The term upward mobility means Black people trying to move up the social and economic ladder.

Blighted Area
This code phrase refers to Black neighborhoods. It means a bad area full of Black people and other nonwhites. This is a community

victimized through purposeful neglect. It is a community that is allowed to deteriorate and the people to suffer economic and social injustice.

Obesity
This has come to symbolize overweight, dark-skinned welfare recipients with large numbers of children.

Slow Learners
This term has always meant Black children in the classroom. They have been classified as slow, retarded and dysfunctional.

Lower Classroom Quality/ Lower Classroom Standards
This is code for clogging classrooms with an excess of Black children.

Classroom Discipline
This is a code term aimed at Black male students in the classroom. White females often fear large Black male children who are perceived as discipline problems. White teachers and some Black teachers ask for greater pay because they say it is hard to teach Black children, with special emphasis on teaching Black males.

Special Needs Population/Children
This is a new term for Black people. It means that Blacks need great assistance and support to achieve anything significant and are ignorant and incompetent. Their lives are crime filled and their children are discipline problems who need special attention.

Low Expectations
This term means Black people have low aims and no reason for existence. They are low-achieving people with little aspiration for greatness. Do not expect much from them, and do not give them much either. Just give them enough so they can continue to be the hewers of wood and diggers of the field. They are incapable of achieving greatness except in clown professions like sports and entertainment, never contributing to the growth and development of society.

Teacher Combat Pay
This term is code for dealing with Black students in urban school districts. White teachers view this as a war-like situation. This language

is not used in White school situations nor is extra pay in White school district contracts. Combat pay means White people want extra pay for taking physical or life-threatening risks for working with Black children. White supremacist teachers view Black students as little gremlins or little monsters. They also believe that these children have limited intellectual abilities, and therefore their real mission is to civilize the little savages. Under this concept, any White teacher willing to sacrifice her or his life by going into the jungle should be amply rewarded.

Homeless

This term has clearly become a word for Black people. When homeless people are shown on the street, the majority are Black men. If White men were seen as homeless, the political response to homelessness would be much more sympathetic. In the 1950s the disguise for homeless was the lovable hobo. The White comedian Red Skeleton popularized the White hobo and made it an adorable personality. The face of homeless became increasingly Black, and now homeless men are considered social parasites.

Teenage Unemployment Rate

This is another reference largely used to define Black males more than Whites. The numbers that get the most public attention pertain to the unemployment rate for Black males ages 16-22.

Hard-Core Unemployed/Unemployable

This describes Blacks who cannot be employed or are simply not employable. The hard-core unemployed are Blacks who are lazy, dumb and do not want to work. That is what this designation really means. It is a racist label attached to the victims of economic injustice.

Low-Proficiency Test Scores

This is another indicator of Black inferiority. It means that Blacks are not learning largely because they are inferior. Proficiency tests further prove that they are less capable than Whites and deserve inferior status. It also validates why White parents have to move to another school district or their children will be going to school with low-achieving and intellectually deficient Black children.

Race Code Words

Uneducable/ Special Education

Black children are unable to learn because they have genetic and cultural limitations. Therefore, they are special needs children and require special education. This code says that Black people are mentally backward and therefore are the natural inhabitants of special education programs. To send a White child to school with Black people guarantees an inferior education.

Socially Retarded

This is code for Black people, who are deemed slow in learning and social development.

School Discipline Problems

This is another code for Black school children. Whenever this term is used, realize that Whites are talking about Black children in urban, or so-called inner city, school districts.

In-School Suspension

This means Black children set-up in special detention classrooms for greater management and control. The effective majority of the students in in-school suspension programs are Black males. This is by design because the White supremacists have devised a school system that is structured to ensure Black dependency and Black failure. The public school system is designed to fail Black children and is not sensitive to the learning style of Black children. Author Jawanza Kunjufu documents the fourth grade failure syndrome. This means that Black children seem to lose interest with each grade there afterwards.

The classroom environment is not structured for high social interaction. It is a sterile environment more compatible with the temperament of the standard White personality. Social interaction dynamics are often viewed as being out of order, a state of chaos and hard to handle. Highly interactive students are called school discipline problems because they won't sit still. This does not take into account the myriad of social and family issues such as hunger, no electricity, no lunch money and chemical poisoning. The school system automatically brands these children as troublemakers, and this label follows them for many years.

121

RACE CODE WAR

Ritalin
This is code for Black children with emotional and hyperactivity problems. Ritalin is prescription medicine used for managing Black children in the classroom.

Lower the Pupil/Teacher Ratio/ Over-Crowded Classrooms
This is code to reduce the number of Black children in classrooms. Whites say that they cannot manage these Blacks and need combat pay.

Predator / Super Predator
In the highly successful motion picture "Predator," Arnold Swartzenegger led a group of highly trained combat specialists on a secret intelligence expedition. The mission was to hunt down and destroy the alien creatures that had landed on earth. The extraterrestrial was hard to trap and kill. He could strike without warning because of the ability to become invisible at will that left the audience in a quandary, wondering what the alien looked like. His facial features and color were cloaked until the final segments of the film. When his physical features were finally visible, they were quite revealing. The alien creature wore a hairstyle that resembled Rastafarian dreadlocks. He was dark skinned, had very thick lips and was at least seven feet tall with the movement and agility of a professional athlete. The predator's face and color were remarkably similar to the facial characteristics of an average Black male.

This movie was followed up by "Super Predator" which starred Black actor Danny Glover. In "Super Predator" any pretense at subtly connecting the alien beings to Black people went out the window. The opening scene of the movie was a gun battle between Black gangs in Los Angeles and the L.A.P.D. Danny Glover's role and presence in the film as a hard-fighting cop gave the film the cover needed to slip across several racial messages. Black males were portrayed as aliens, drug dealers, crazy and out of control, superstitious, voodoo-worshiping criminals. The physical image of the predator made a clear statement about racial identity. It left no doubt that the predator was a giant Jamaican or Rastafarian Black male. About the same time as the release of these two films, the connection of predators and predatory behavior to young Black males began to escalate. Media reports and news articles boldly talked about the evolution of the new young criminal class in the inner city. Black youth were being tagged as predators, or a new breed of criminals that could commit crimes without any hesitation, moral regret or social redemption. A sort of Black version of the Stanley Kubrick characters in "Clockwork Orange."

In 1996 a book called *Body Count: Moral Poverty and How to Win America's War Against Crime and Poverty* by William Bennett, John J. Dilulio and John P. Walters was highly touted in certain White circles. In this book the authors classify Black youth as super predators. The comments of John J. Dilulio are especially illuminating and should set off alarms. He calls Black youth a *ticking demographic crime bomb* that will soon explode. The word ticking means that something or someone is unpredictable and ready to go off at anytime. It requires that people be on guard at all times.

The word demographic is a code word for the targeted Black population in inner city areas. The word crime is a code word for Black male. The bomb word means gang warfare at a level that could put an entire metropolitan area under a siege similar to the opening scenes of the "Super Predator" movie. Dilulio shrewdly associates moral poverty with urban America while pretending sensitivity to the plight of Black youth. Listen to the sound of the code term "moral poverty." This is a very disturbing combination of words. What is moral poverty? Does this mean that the little Black savages are uncivilized, baby-making jungle bunnies? The horror reaped on the world by the brutal and barbaric behavior of White supremacy lends little credence to talk of morality.

The system of White supremacy has killed so many millions of nonwhite people that the real number of destroyed civilizations may be unknowable. If this scenario is to be believed, what are implications for Black people? The implications are not good. The conversation of racists would go something like this: "Why invest in a people or community that is breeding a criminal class. Why not simply destroy them because they are morally decayed and mentally bankrupted. Don't waste good money and resources. It's like throwing good money after bad."

Savage

This code word is borrowed from "Tarzan" novels which were later made into a series of movies. Black men were portrayed and labeled as savages. The term savage implies that the individuals are barbarian, brutes, beasts and cannibalistic. A savage is the lowest form of

123

uncivilized and backward man. Black men have been labeled savages by White supremacy for more than 500 years. This word is being quietly associated with the events in Africa. White news commentators frequently use sayings such as "savage beating," "a savage war," "savage killing" or "savage condition." It is a subtle association of savage to Black-related conditions and situations. More and more White commentators feel comfortable enough to use this word and related terms such as Dark Continent, primitive and backward. This word must be watched very carefully as its acceptance without challenge signals the beginning of a return to hardcore supremacy.

Endangered Species
This is a recent term that has been applied to Black males. It is designed to portray Black males as a hopeless lot in danger of becoming extinct.

Primitive
This word has double-edged meaning. It really means the prototype, but it has been used to paint Black people as illiterate, backward barbarians.

Public Assistance/Welfare
This code is used in the White political arena to denigrate and defile Black females. This is one of the most powerful and useful political code terms devised. It has become one of the crudest weapons used to classify and destroy generations of Black people. The labeling process is so effective that Black people regurgitate this language without understanding the social ramifications.

Welfare Cheats
This is a code phrase for Black females that means Blacks steal and cheat taxpayer's money and live disrespectful lifestyles.

Welfare Reform
This code means let's get Black people off the public rolls. The language is clear and direct. It was part of the rallying cry of White conservatives from the era of the Reagan administration. This wording was also used by the Clinton administration to cut welfare spending and reduce welfare rolls.

Race Code Words

Welfare Recipients
More than any other political code, this term has come to mean Black females. It is also used to demonize Black females.

Welfare Bums
This is a code term for Black males who do not work and want a social safety net hand-out.

Food Stamps
This is a code phrase for Black families. In some counties poor Black families were put on display because they had to stand in line to cash their public assistance checks and redeem the food stamp vouchers.

Under-Privileged
This is a code for Black people living in poverty or in a materially deficient social condition.

Failed Schools
This is a universal code term for Black schools or Black-dominated education systems. White supremacists consider any control by Black people over any public school program the same as a failed school or failed education system.

Socially Deprived
This is older code for Black people who have limited exposure to White people. This concept postulates that the greater the exposure to Whiteness, the more a child can improve his or her backward state of existence.

Socially Disadvantaged
This code term means that Black people are in an inferior position in the social order.

These and many other code words that are not listed are used regularly on the job and in political campaign commercials, marketing strategies, government proposals, television and radio nightly news reports, talk shows, classrooms, business meetings and police reports. This does not mean that every person that uses these terms is a racist or perpetuates racism. Many Black and White people use these words out of habit or without having a full understanding of their powerful and crushing impact. Words define the image, and in the modern world image is everything! Language implants images, symbols and words into the mindset. The manipulative power of racial code wording and imaging is awesome.

RACE CODE WORD MEANINGS

The modern race game can be changed. White and Black people must comprehend what they are doing when words that are identified as racial code language are continuously used in the normal social lexicon. It is extremely important that each individual using these words clearly understands what they mean and how they are connected to racist thinking.

In our highly coded cultural environment words in particular must be surgically precise. If it is determined that a word is racially derogatory, the statement(s) should be restated without the use of any language that has racial connotations. The goal is to remove all racist/color-coded embeds and implications from normal social dialogue. The new non-racist wordings must be repeated in private and public social settings so that they gain verbal, psychological and sociological validity. The following are identified code words and terms with the real meanings attached. The list shows what a racist really means when he/she uses these phrases.

Code Word or Term	Decoded Racist Meaning
Abortion	nonwhite population control
Affirmative Action	Black tokenism
Aids Epidemic	over-sexed Negroes
Athletic Ability	animal or horse-like nigger creatures
Athletics	nigger jocks
At Risk	Black males
At Risk Youth	Black male youth
Birth Control	reduce nonwhite population growth
Bitch	Black female
Blighted Area	Black communities
Civil Rights	Negro concessions
Crack	niggers doing drugs
Crack Addict	Black drug user
Crack Dealers	Black males selling drugs

Race Code Words

Crackhead	Black druggie
Crack House	Black drug den
Crime in the Streets	Black male on the street
Crime Prevention	lock more niggers up
Crime Prone	Black people are born criminals
Crime Rate	measurement of Black crime
Crime Ravaged	communities destroyed by Black people
Crime Ridden	areas where Black people live
Criminal(s)	Black males
Da Hood	dangerous and wild areas
Desegregation	forcing some White people to live with Black people
Diversity	modern method of racial management
Drive –By Shooting	Black gang banging
Drugs	Black males
Drug Addicts	Black males/females
Drug Dealer	young Black male
Drug Infested	Black neighborhoods
Drug Raid	catching niggers using drugs
Drug Related	Black people killing each other for drugs
Drug Runners	Black males on bicycles
Drug User	Black male/female
Drug Zone	Black residential areas
Dysfunctional Family	Black families
Endangered Species	reduce the Black male population
Far-Flung Suburbs	new White safe havens
Female Heads of Households	nigger women in charge
Fight Crime	contain Black males
Food Stamps	nigger stamps
Forced Busing	going to school with niggers
Gangs	Black male youth
Gang Bang	Black male youth sex orgies
Gang Member	Black male
Gang Rape	Black males having sex with White females
Gang Related	Black male youth crime
Gang Violence	Black savagery
Government Housing Tax Credit	reservation program for Black females
Government Program	Black pacification plans
Hardcore Unemployed	Black males
Heroin Addict	Black males/females
High Blood Pressure Population	Black males
High Crime	Black males in the area

RACE CODE WAR

High Crime Area	the number of Black males in the area
HIV Drug User	Black drug addict
Ho	Black female
Homeless	groups of Black males
Housing Projects	places where large groups of poor niggers live
Illiterates	untrained Black people
Impoverished	poor Negroes
Inner City	wild, untamed and criminal Black people
Inner City Athletes	criminal Black athletes
Inner City Youth	wild untamed and crime-prone young Black people
In School Suspension	racial management of Black students
Irresponsible People	niggers who need to be taken care of
Junkie	Black dope user
Latchkey Kids	wandering untamed Black children
Lazy Dumb and Irresponsible	stupid Negroes
Loss of Property Value	too many Black people living in the area
Loud Music	that nigger music
Low Expectations	Black people are naturally mentally inferior
Low Income	Black people
Low Proficiency Test	Black students are unable to comprehend
Lower Classroom Quality	too many Black children in the classroom
Lower Pupil-Teacher Ratio	reduce the number of Black children teachers
Mean Streets	Black neighborhoods
Menace to Society	Black males who need to be locked up
Mental Lapse	Black people have less brain capacity
Minorities	less than or inferior to White
Mother Fucker	Black male
Mugging	Negroes robbing on the streets
Multi- Cultural	let a few of them in the door
NBA	National Black Association or Nigger Ball
Association	New Prison ready to lock up more Black males
Obesity	big Black females
Old Suburbs	let the Negroes have it; we are leaving
Overcrowded Classrooms	too many Black children
Predators	young Black males
People Selling Drugs	low-level Black peddlers
Poverty	Black people economically dependent
Poverty Areas	areas designed for Black people
Primitive	Black and nonwhite people
Poverty Stricken	purposely suppressed areas
Proposition 42	keep down the number of Black athletes

Race Code Words

Public Assistance	paying for loud-mouth Black females
Quotas	guaranteed number of niggers or too many niggers in the house
Race Card	racial con game, or you niggers are paranoid
Reverse Discrimination	stop Black progress
Rape	normal Black male sexual behavior
Rapists	Black male sexual predators/stalkers
Ritalin	crazy Black children
Rough Neighborhood	Black community
Roach Infested Housing	Black households
Saturday Night Special	niggers with cheap guns
Savage	Black people here and abroad
School Desegregation	forcing Black people into our schools
School Discipline	Black males
Selling Drugs	Black male dope peddlers
Slum Areas	Black neighborhoods
Slum Districts	Black residential areas
Slum Dwellers	Black people
Social Disinvestment	putting money into Black neighborhoods
Socially Deprived	keep Black people behind
Socially Disadvantaged	keep Black people behind
Socially Retarded	keep Black people dummy-downed
Special Education	Black students are naturally mentally inferior
Special Needs Children	Black children moving into suburban areas
Special Needs Population	Black people
Street Life	niggers on the street
Street Crime	Black males on the street
Substance Abusers	Black males and females
Suburban Sprawl	run farther and faster because the niggers are coming
Super Predators	young Black males
Take Responsibility	don't blame the White man for your problems
Teacher Combat Pay	extra money for working with these nigger children
Teenage Pregnancy	young Black females
Teenage Unemployment	young Black males
That's My Baby's Daddy	baby-making young Black males
The Ghetto	all Black neighborhoods
Them People	Black people
This Guy's a Stud	nigger is an animal or horse
Those People	Black people
Thug	young nigger male criminal
Troubled Areas	Black communities

Troubled Kids	very young Black children
Troubled Neighborhood	Black neighborhood
Troubled Youngsters	teenage Black males
Two-Fers	Black females
Uneducable	young Black children
Under-Privileged	keep Black people in an inferior state
Unemployable	Black males yield minimum productivity
Ungrateful Athletes	nigger jocks
Upward Mobility	let some of them rise above the rest
Urban	Black people
Urban Blight	poor Black communities
Urban Decay	Black people live in the area in great numbers
Urban Decline	Black people are taking over the area
Urban Ills	Black people are natural problems
Urban Legend	telling nigger lies
Urban Renewal	retake areas populated by Black people
Urban Riots	Black people out of control
Urban Sprawl	the niggers are coming/the nigger problem is spreading
Uzi's	Negroes with dangerous weapons
War on Drugs	war on Black people
Welfare	lazy Black females having babies
Welfare Bums	lazy Black males/females having babies
Welfare Recipient	Black female
Welfare Reform	kick the niggers off the dole/put them to work
Violence Prone	Black males are born criminals
Zero Tolerance	contain Black males at all levels

CORRECT WORDS to COUNTER CODE LANGUAGE

When a code word is identified, it must be decoded so that the exact meaning is discovered. The truth in a racially coded social environment is often hidden behind a wall of deception so that a false perception emerges. For example, if a coded statement says "urban dwellers sell drugs," while this is a partially accurate assertion, the major question is where do the "urban dwellers" get the drugs? And what is meant by the word urban?

Who controls the flow of drugs and makes the really big money? Without the flow of drugs urban dwellers or, decoded, Black people would not be able to sell or buy drugs. One thing is clear: Black people do not control or direct the flow of drugs here or abroad. When describing any social problem affecting Black people, the words that are used must tell the whole truth.

The objective is to eliminate the deception by countering the resulting confusion with clarity. The words used must define the problem in a correct manner and with consistent terms so that it leave no doubts about the who, what and why of any given situation.

To do this, language must cut through the fat and get straight to the bone. Words have to be used with such surgical accuracy that confusion is minimized and clarity is maximized. Purposely misdirected or disjointed words and sentences that say nothing are misleading and more confusing than clarifying. The success of the race-code word game is based on deception and confusion. This is one of the reasons why the White supremacist continuously shifts and redefines the problems impacting Black people.

One day the Black problem is economic disenfranchisement and the next hour it will shift to political apathy while tomorrow it will be moral deterioration. The lack of a consistent, precise, accurate and truthful definition of the problems affecting Black people has lead to great confusion. This, of course, is part of the language strategy to hide racism in plain sight by defusing coherent counter-racist thinking. The racist uses words that redefine the problem in a hundred different ways.

The purpose is to confuse and to defuse the development of a sound-thinking pattern and to create enough perceptual and mental distance to visually be detached from the problem. Black people are thus led further away from a clear identification of the forces that they are up against. The problem must always be defined in clear, exact and precise language that establishes the whole truth about the situation, event or incident.

The root cause of all of the problems facing Black people is White supremacy domination. Black people are wholly dependent and totally controlled by White domination. All of the social, political and economic situations are a direct result of living under White domination for 400-plus years. The preceding list contains correct statements. Correct and exact language is discouraged, condemned, rerouted and labeled as racist.

Clearing the Air
It is not sufficient to identify race-code words. There must be effective counter or correct words in the language that clarify or expose the whole

situation. Without correct words in the language, race-code words become accepted in the modern social lexicon. The use of correct words puts the spotlight on the real perpetrators and identifies the behavior and deeds of the racists as the real problem. Instead of addressing this situation, words are used as a weapon to duck the responsibility of producing justice.

When racial code words are used in dialogue, political speeches or everyday conversation, an individual can respond by clarifying the statement with a response utterance that begins with "Oh, you mean." This is the beginning of a response designed to correct a racially coded statement. The following is a short list of examples of how to use correct words that expose the real meaning of code words. The objective is to force the real meaning out into the open so that racist intent or direction is revealed.

Racial Code Words   Precise Words That Tell the Truth

When This Is Said	Oh, You Mean...
Abortion	nonwhite population management
At risk	Black male destruction
Civil rights	Black people asking for justice
Minority	marginal or disposable population
Reverse discrimination	stop the advancement of Black people
Diversity	the illusion of inclusion
Two-fers	Black female utilization
Loss and/or decline in property value	Black people have less value
Social disinvestment	do not spend any more money on Black people
Race card	minimizing the impact of racism
Athletic ability	animalization of Black males
This guy's a stud	the sexual breeding of Black males
Urban decay	problems resulting from purposeful disinvestments
Urban riots	ineffective response to racial injustice
Poverty stricken	results of racial and economic injustice
New prison construction	racial containment facilities
Impoverished community	areas victimized by racial and economic injustice
Da hood	areas where criminal injustice is allowed to exist

Race Code Words

Inner city	purposely neglected areas
Inner city youth	products of racial degradation
Illiterate	racial miseducation
The illiteracy rate	the level of racial miseducation
High crime area (s)	where injustice is allowed to exist
Crime	injustice against Black people
Crime ridden	injustice allowed to exist in certain areas
Crime prone	justification for racial injustice
Crime ravaged areas	areas where injustice is allowed to exist
Crime rate(s)	the level of injustice allowed to exist
Street crime	product of racial injustice
Street life/the streets	prison recruitment locations
War on drugs	war on Black people
Drugs	race chemicals
Drug raids	deceptive responses to fool victims of racial chemicalization
Drug infested	racial chemicalization
Drug related	race chemical victimization
Drug dealer	low-level race chemical peddler
Drug addict	victim of race chemicalization
Drug zone	areas where race chemicals are allowed to exist
Drug runner(s)	low-level race chemical peddlers
Selling drugs	race chemical peddling
Heroin addict	victim of race chemicals
AIDS epidemic	purposeful and targeted genocide
Take responsibility	diversion for racist injustice
Crack	racially labeled chemicals
Crack house(s)	protected race / chemical outlets
Crack dealer	low-level race / chemical peddler
Crack addict / Crackhead	victim of racial chemicalization
Gangs	ineffective imitations of organized racist violence
Gang related	acts that imitate racist-organized violence
Gang violence	victims victimizing other victims
Gang bang	incorrect response to racist injustice
Saturday night specials	permitted weapons of criminal injustice
Troubled area	areas of purposeful neglect
Troubled kids	children without racial justice
Bitch	purposeful racial / sexual degradation
Ho	purposeful programmed prostitution
Violence prone	justification for racial injustice

RACE CODE WAR

Troubled youngsters	products of racial domination
Sex abuser(s)	incorrect response to racist injustice / victims abusing other victims
Rape/rapist	incorrect response to racist injustice / victims abusing other victims
Thug	product of racial domination
Mugging	incorrect response to racial injustice
Mean streets	level of injustice allowed to exist
Teenage pregnancy	product of racial and sexual injustice
Zero tolerance	containment of Black males
Government programs	inadequate recompense for racial injustice
Low income	economic and racial injustice
Loud music	programmed racial chaos
Housing projects	purposeful racially dysfunctional areas
The slums/slum areas	purposely neglected areas
The ghetto	purposely racially neglected area
That's my baby's daddy	incorrect response to ineffective relationships
Upward mobility	trying to gain material efficiencies or racial con game
Obesity	incorrect bodily reaction to racial pressure
Slow learners	misunderstanding White supremacy
Lower classroom quality	racial injustice in education
Classroom discipline	miseducation justification
Special needs children	racially abused Black children
Low Expectation	purposeful racial degradation
Teacher combat pay	racists pretending to be under siege / miseducation justification
Unemployable	victim of economic and racial injustice / product of racial domination
Homeless	victim of racial and economic injustice / product of racial domination
Teenage unemployment rate	purposeful racial criminalization
Hardcore unemployed	racial criminalization / product of racial domination
Low proficiency test scores	purposeful racial inferiorization
Uneducable	destruction of racial self-esteem
Special education	purposeful racial stereotyping
Overcrowded classrooms	encouragement of learning disabilities based on race
School Discipline problems	allowance of pre-criminal behavior
In-school suspensions	ineffective response to racial miseducation

134

Race Code Words

Lower the pupil-teacher ratio	racial miseducation justification
Predators	racial criminalization
Super predators	increasing racial criminalization
Savage(s)	purposeful racial degradation
Endangered species	purposeful racial annihilation
Primitive	purposeful racial degradation
Public assistance	purposeful racial minimization
Welfare	purposeful racial degradation / dependency
Welfare reform	purposeful racial destabilization
Welfare recipient	purposeful racially degraded dependent
Food stamps	public racial degradation
Under-privileged	purposeful racial backwardness
Socially deprived	purposely disadvantaged
Socially disadvantaged	purposeful backwardness
Underclass	purposely neglected racial population

SELECTED CODE WORDS THAT SIGNIFY for WHITE PEOPLE

The following is a list of some of the most frequently used code words that mean White people, things and places.

Man

This often-used term means White male or White man. In White cultural society there are thousands of movies, sociological textbooks, religious writings, social magazines, historical quotations, books, videos and illustrations that have titles and references to the word man. Statements like *man and his environment, God and man, man and nature, man cannot live by bread alone* are part of millions of direct references to the White man. In each one of these references the word man always directly or indirectly refers to a white male. The effective majority of physical and visual examples or artistic illustrations of man are still of White men. When a reference is made to men other than White males, they are described and defined by color, race or ethnic background. This is done to demonstrate that while there are other branches of human males, they are not the "man" in the word man. This is also done to define other men in the world as outside a White frame of reference. A frame of reference means that all interpretation is made from a certain point of view. In the context of a White frame of reference it means that

White people, white things and white places are at the center of the universe and everything else in the universe must evolve around Whiteness. It keeps the focus on White people and creates a deep belief in the idea that white is right. White people are the best, should be in charge, will do the right thing and are always on the side of what is good and just. It also establishes deep sensitivity to White problems, White suffering and White progress in the mindset of Black people. Their minds are trained to identify with Whiteness over blackness. Many Black people will readily believe what the White news media says about a Black individual before they will believe what the Black person says. They are connected to a strong almost unbreakable belief in the White is right syndrome.

Thus, when a frame of reference is applied to the word man, it is clear that man is viewed from the perspective of a White man. If the use of the word man were intended as a universal definition without regard to race, creed or color, nonwhite males would not be defined by a reference to their color or race. Other males are classified as Black men, Chinese men, Arabs and so forth.

In the majority of books, videos, movies, etc., nonwhite men are defined by race and color. A Black male in particular is never defined simply as a man over in the corner. He is defined as the Black man in the corner or that Black guy in the corner. Another reason for the color-based definition is to establish color supremacy. The White man is superior to the Black man, Brown man, Red man and Yellow man. The third purpose is to establish the White worldview, the White frame of reference as the standard for the world.

In this way all men regardless of race/color would have to look up to and be judged based on their conversion to or degree of acceptance of Whiteness. The next reason is to declare which man is the "man" and who is in charge. Why? Because White supremacy ensures that the standard of all humanity is based on the superiority of Whiteness. All other colors are subordinate to the color of Whiteness. The entire world is displayed, written about, talked about and viewed through the eyes and minds of White people.

The goal is to force all nonwhites to think and believe in the supremacy of Whiteness. All people in the known universe must meet the White standard of approval. Under this concept, *the Man is the highest state of humankind. And the concept of White man is the highest stage of masculine development.* This is the reason why millions

Race Code Words

of fictional novel pages, thousands of movie scripts and tens of thousands of magazines never describe the color of the White male character. It is taken for granted that the White man is simply Man, or the standard by which all men are evaluated. They never say *"this White man"* or *"that White man"*. *He is described as a man in the corner not a Black man in the corner. If nonwhite, the man in the corner must be a Black or a Chinese or an Indian in the corner. The White man must always be the standard of manhood and humanity.*

EXAMPLES OF THE USE OF THE WORD MAN

Statements	Decoded Meanings
Man and his world	White man and his world
Man and God	White man and God
Mankind	White male variety
Human	White man
God created man	God created the White man
God created man in his own image	God created the White man in his own White image
Man's inhumanity toward man	White people fighting each other
Man shall not live by bread alone	White men must develop spiritually

The Man

This reference is from the 1960s era. It means White power and White control. The man has the juice and force. Therefore he is the Man.

Woman

This term, like the word man, means White female. All other females will be defined by their color except the White woman. Whenever the women's movement says women, it means White women. When Black women or women of color are discussed, they are not called women; they are called Black women and defined by a color reference. The racist will say that the Black women in the women's movement want to be called by a color reference.

This may be true because they were not and are not considered as women. They were and still are classified as Black women. This means that they are inferior and less valuable. Despite the loud rhetoric and false claims, there are hundreds of thousands of examples and references to the standardization of White females as women.

RACE CODE WAR

When Black women are included, there is usually some subtle or overt reference to race or color. It is rare, just as in the case of Black males, for Black women to be defined simply as women. Under the system of White supremacy, this cannot be allowed on any grand level. There may be some exceptions, such as Oprah Winfrey; however this is a special exception and is used to get the claim of racism and/or racial exclusion off their backs.

In the everyday context of thousands of books, videos, movies, educational illustrations, Internet web sites and so forth, the depiction of Black women as Black women and not simply as women is pronounced. Under the concept of White supremacy, a Black woman is not considered a woman; she is considered a Black girl, Black female or Black woman. The only women in the ideology of Whiteness are White women.

Some References to the Word Woman

Statements	Decoded meaning
The women's movement	White women's movement
Woman's right to choose	White Women have rights over their own bodies
Women's studies	The study of White women first and others second
Women's vote	White women voters
Suburban moms	White women with families
Middleclass women	Educated White women
Rich women	White women with money
Discrimination against women	White females complaining of discrimination
Equal pay for equal work	White females paving the way to move up
Working moms	White females working
Women managers	White women in charge

WHITE FEMALE CODES USED IN RACIAL CONTEXT

Woman
Middle-aged White female

Women
White female population

Women's Liberation
White females of all ages and generations

Race Code Words

Beautiful Woman
Individual White female

Most Beautiful Woman in the World
White female

Most Beautiful Women in the World
White or near-white females

Pretty Woman
White or near-white female

Pretty Brunette
White female with dark hair

Redhead
White female

Sexpot
White female

Hotties
White females, usually blonde

Bombshell
Blonde White female

Buxom
Large-breasted White female

Blonde
Light-haired White female

Blonde Bombshell
Light haired white sexual female

Blonde and Beautiful
White female

RACE CODE WAR

<u>Blondes Have More Fun</u>
Amorous saying about White females

<u>Boobs and Broads</u>
Sexually active White females

<u>Glamorous, Charming and Intelligent</u>
White, rich and famous females

<u>California Girls</u>
Suntanned White females usually imaged as blondes

<u>Beach Bunnies</u>
Young White females

<u>Chicks</u>
An expression used in the 1940s to the late 1970s

<u>First Lady</u>
Middle-aged White female

<u>Suburban Wife</u>
Young to middle-aged White female

<u>Doll</u>
Heavily made -up, perky and dumb, sexually appealing White female

<u>Toots</u>
Sexual endearment for White females used in 1920s to late 1960s

<u>Feminine</u>
White female

<u>Babe(s)</u>
Term for White females used in the 1920s to 1969; reborn with the television series "<u>Bay Watch Babes</u>"

<u>Porn Stars</u>
White females, even though the number of Black females is growing

Race Code Words

White females as a group, despite their claims, have not had to see their men hunted down like wild animals, lynched and castrated and their babies snatched from them at birth and sold never to be seen again. The whole population of White females has not been degraded and described as animals, subhuman, whores and prostitutes. White females have had to deal with some imaging issues such as being used as sex objects by their men. However, much of this sexual imaging has been with their consent. There have not been enough legal charges hurled against white men because of the images that they have created. White female were not forcefully sold into posing nude or posing on top of a car wearing a tight dress. This was voluntary and considered desirable and respectable work. They were not sold and dragged like animals into slavery. The women's liberation struggle has never been about the elimination of White supremacy domination. Their argument with their men has been about their desire to gain equality with White men. White females have been praised as the smartest, most beautiful, glamorous, desirable, industrious and best mothers on the planet.

If she is a White supremacist, her argument would be that she can improve her role and move from being a junior partner to achieving senior partner status in the business of White supremacy domination. She wants to run the White-oriented giant corporations, educational systems and government institutions that routinely oppress Black females. Her leadership in these giant financial, industrial, commercial and technological corporations has not diminished the oppressive nature of White supremacy domination.

Her presence in many instances has added to the nature of deception. She has not been ready and willing to massively invest resources and funds into eliminating the conditions of so-called ghettos. Rather she has become an aggressive mouthpiece and seeks to justify the continued and purposeful neglect and ghettoization of environments where large numbers of Black people reside.

The White female has had to endure her share of struggle and pain. White Irish, Polish, Italian and Hispanic females have had to bite their tongues and hold their peace while waiting to be accepted by other Whites into the larger White collective. However, the whole race of White females has never been imaged, labeled, classified and treated as ugly loud-mouthed bitches, welfare queens and whores. This is not to suggest that White females have not had to deal with social stigmas. Certainly, many of the poor White women in geographical areas such as West Virginia and Kentucky have had to fight for their dignity and family income. However, these social and political struggles and issues were part of the fight for entry into or acceptance from the larger White collective.

White women do not seek an end to White supremacy domination or racial injustice. They want greater concessions, greater acceptance and greater recognition of their social plight from their White brethren. The White female has not demonstrated a great effort to hold the White male accountable for hundreds of years of racial injustice. She has only sought to maximize her benefits and participation in the system. She uses hard-won counter-racist gains, such as affirmative action programs, to advance her family income and social stability.

Black and Red females are still left in the dusk bringing up the rear. The White supremacist female has greatly benefited from the work of the White supremacist male. She is his partner, bedmate and soul supporter. The women's liberation movement was and is a very deceptive *racial movement*. When their activist language is decoded, what they really want is to provide greater options for White women. Whenever the questions of other women are brought into the fray, they are separated and labeled quickly as issues dealing with Black women or women of color. However, the issues dealing with so-called women of color always languish on the back burner.

Authority
This is an old code word for White man in charge. It is linked with the supremacy of White people and their superior position. This term more than any other means White and in charge.

Expert
This is another code word for White people. This means that White people are the smartest and know more about most things than any other group in the world. They are the source of knowledge and are best suited to answer any question and solve any issue.

Race Code Words

Baby Boomers
This term means middle-aged White people. It is designed to measure the progress of White people at a certain point in time.

Normally Peaceful Community
This term is used when an incident happens in a predominantly White community. The goal is to deflect derogatory images. The normal course of events is to insure that Black people are the real varmints and their communities are where the criminals reside.

Sources
This term is used by White media types to define White expertise on a hidden or background level. A source is the beginning and control of knowledge.

Red Blooded American
This is a classic code term for White supremacy. It means a White male. The phrase red-blooded means hot or passionate. All blood is red so the term red bloodied is an oxymoron. Red is associated with concepts like passion, mania and heat. A red-blooded American is an aggressive personality. The red-blooded American takes control of the situation. It is a form of manifest destiny that means that God Almighty has ordained them to be in charge and in control. A red-blooded American believes in the ideas of democratization, which that means effective racial management. He or she will defend these ideas to the death.

Advisors
This is another word used to define White males. An advisor is considered a smart and in-charge kind of individual. Under White code thinking, this description fits the image of a White individual.

Official
This is another standard word that means White man. It is the standard by which all things are measured and weighed. Things do not become accepted as valid without a White person's sign-off at some level. It doesn't matter what rank or position the Black individual holds; a White supremacist will always seek to challenge the authenticity of his or her words and will look for a White person to confirm or credit the statement. This happens to Black people at all levels of society.

Under the conditions of white supremacy the lowest ranking White individual feels that he or she can challenge the highest positioned Black individual. The White supremacist believes that the Black individual is sitting in a White seat and is there to serve the White interest. He or she is a dressed-up servant with bells and whistles. Black people cannot validate anything on their own. They are always suspect, and their motives are always attacked. When a White man walks through the door, he walks through with credibility that is based on his Whiteness. The White man must work hard to prove himself unworthy. And even then there are many who come to his aid and defense, as witnessed in the 1998 impeachment trial of President Bill Clinton. Despite the lies and cover-ups, Bill Clinton was given the benefit of the doubt. Under White supremacy, a White man is always given the benefit of the doubt based on his Whiteness.

Whiteness is a badge of honor, validity and correctness. A White man's words are the law and his actions are accepted as legitimate. Under the doctrine of White supremacy, White men are innocent before guilty. The reverse is true for Black males.

Quiet Area/Normally Peaceful Community

This is code for the suburbs. The term area means an area where White people live in dominant numbers. The White supremacist has created the impression that they are peace-loving, quiet and civilized people. The image is of a White picket fence, which when decoded means White and protected area with friendly people. In reality many White supremacists who live in these communities fly around the world and engage in actions that oppress, suppress, destabilize and destroy Black people.

Their actions create and sustain violence in Black dominant environments. They create unstable conditions in the nonwhite environment, then go home and relax in quiet and peaceful surroundings. The facade is that of peace and quiet. In reality those communities harbor deadly White supremacists who continue to work on projects, secret operations, plans and so forth that lead to the exploitation, destruction and degradation of Black people. They pose as civilized, wonderful people—the salt of the earth—while they wreak havoc and destruction all over the world.

Race Code Words

Affluent

This is another code for White people. White people are the richest and most powerful people in the world. They regularly show off their riches for the world to see. From the incredible wealth of such places as Boca Raton, Florida, to the old showcases of glamorous wealth in Hollywood, California White people have been showing off their riches to the poor nonwhite world for centuries. They brag about being well off while two-thirds of the colored world lives in squalor and poverty.

Nonwhite people are leaving their homelands in record numbers trying to reach the lands of White people in Europe, Australia and North America. These nonwhites come out of their breeding grounds into the citadels of direct White power to get more income and a better life. They believe that just being close to the power and wealth of White people automatically means a better life. Why? Because they believe that White people are superior, better and of highest value.

Rich

This word means White or a desire to be White like. Rich and White are interchangeable words. White and powerful are interchangeable. White and smart are interchangeable. This is part of the White supremacist indoctrination. The words rich and affluent have the same powerful meanings. The effective majority of the world's population believes that White people are rich and powerful. They believe that they have more value as human beings than any other group of people in the universe.

Rich really means to have greater value and to have your civilization ranked higher than any other. The world's currency is based on the performance of the money system designed and controlled by White people. A very large percentage of Black people who accumulate a lot of money get it from some relationship with White people. The majority of the wealthiest Black people did not get rich interacting with other Black people. There is no independent, organized and self-sustaining Black political system or economy.

The talents, intellect and skills of Black people are exploited to create wealth for White people both here and on the African continent. The recording and music industry where, according to news reports, Black people are supposed to be the most independent is heavily dominated and controlled by White money interests. Black-owned radio stations heavily depend on White revenue to survive and stay in business. In sports White people pay Black athletes big money to play on their teams. In the motion picture industry, high-profile Black actors are paid to appear in White-produced movies. The hard-hitting, high-powered, high-flying and high-profiled Black athletes are on salary. In the world of regular business, powerful White money interests subsidize some "minority business operations."

This is the meaning of minority set-a-sides, which, when decoded, mean handouts. It means that White people have budgeted a small sum of their revenue as a sort of donation or hush money in order to appear to be assisting some Black business. Without this assistance, many of these businesses would not survive. Black people do not own and control independent wealth. They are heavily subsidized by White-controlled dollars. Their money is recycled back into the hands of White money interests.

The Man
Some people would say that this code word originated with Black people in the 1960s. However, that would not be correct. Black males have always been classified as boys. White males have always been identified as men. Manhood symbolizes power and strength. Boyhood is a state of dependency, immaturity and powerlessness.

Miss Ann
This means a White female in charge. The image of Miss Ann is the desire of far too many White-educated Black women. Miss Ann was accorded special privileges simply by being White and female.

Mister Charlie
This is another term for White male. Mister Charlie is a term that was used to identify the White man during the 1960s.

Glamorous
This word has been associated with White females for many years. Today it is still associated with White females. The standard for glamour and beauty is White and blonde. Despite all of the fuss over one or two dark-skinned Black models, the highest standard of beauty and glamour

Race Code Words

remains White and blonde. The most glamorous Black females are usually the ones who most resemble White women.

The Silent Majority

This code term was developed during the Nixon Administration to speak to and rally White people. It was designed to communicate, using a term that appears on the surface to be nonracial.

Code words are designed for special audiences, where it is clear to whom the message is directed. Today the term silent majority is rephrased as "working families."

Vice president Al Gore used this term repeatedly during his acceptance speech at the 2000 Democratic National Convention in Los Angeles, California. He repeatedly said, as if in a hypnotic trance, "I will fight, I will fight" for working families.

This coded phrase was repeated over and over by many speakers during the convention. When this message is decoded, it means White families. Al Gore's message was that he would fight to preserve White values of domination, the White family, White workers and the White nation and would serve as a White president if elected. His rating numbers jumped once he calmed fears that he would not give away the store to Black people.

Middleclass

This word always means White people. It has been used to describe the effective majority of White people. When White leaders want to send a codified message, they use a calling-card phrase like middle-class. It cements communication with the average White individual.

The Black Panther Party used the term middleclass when they tried to communicate with large numbers of White people. The middleclass is considered as the salt (White) of the earth, the unmovable army of righteousness and the backbone of White imperialism. The middleclass has fought the biggest wars for domination all over the planet. They hold the line of White supremacy thought, behavior, actions and speech on a daily basis. The wide use of middle-class jargon has given many Black people the illusion that they are included.

This is an inaccurate reading. The language of the middle-class it is not an inclusive term. Class has very little to do with income level. If the issue were simply the measurement of income, the class word would never have to be invoked. Class is used because it has a White pedigree and bloodline implications. It is these issues that establish class. Words such as lineage, decent, heritage and birthright are the real determinants of class. It was revealed recently in several publications that many of the presidents of the United States were able to trace their bloodlines and pedigrees.

One of the conditions for suitability to high office is that pedigree and bloodline are preferred over income. Most presidents have not been exceedingly rich before taking office. According to most respected biographies of former president Bill Clinton, he grew up dirt poor in the state of Arkansas. This did not keep Clinton or Jimmy Carter, another White southern boy of humble origin, from obtaining the most powerful political position in the world. It was bloodline and pedigree that opened the magical door. There is an effort by some Black people to be recognized as part of the bloodline of White people like former president Thomas Jefferson. This bloodline claim is regarded as frayed by many White "experts." Jefferson defenders say that if it occurred, it was during a time of sexual weakness more than Jefferson's plan to extend his bloodline.

This does not mean that someday a Black individual will not be placed into the presidential seat. However, it is a safe bet that he/she will have a traceable bloodline and pedigree to certain White people, i.e., Colin Powell or his son Michael (the New York-based *Village Voice* newspaper speculated that the very light-skinned Michael Powell was on a track to become the first "Black" president). Black people in general are considered a non-class. They may have income but not class. They do not have an acceptable pedigree that is traceable and untainted. The pedigree and bloodline were destroyed because of uncontrollable racist crossbreeding during chattel slavery. The middle-class word is a call to reassure nervous White people that White privilege, pedigree and bloodline will be protected and continued.

Far-Flung Suburbs

This is a new term for newly created, White-dominated neighborhoods. These neighborhoods are the new relocation areas for Whites wanting to get farther away from Black people. Black people have started to invade the old suburbs. The term old suburb is code language for the invasion of Black people. When White people see Black people move in, sooner or later the majority will pack up their bags and move out.

Race Code Words

The desire not to live next to Black people is driving the creation of unnecessary new White communities. The public relations cover story is designed to show that the reason for construction of new homes is that people want new and larger houses. Why? The average size of White families certainly has not grown. As a matter of fact, the White population is growing at a lower rate all over the world.

Soccer Moms

This is a code phrase for White females. This term is part of the new code-war vocabulary that evolves daily. This term was developed by the White political establishment to focus on White women and make White people the center of attention. The objective is to keep the focus on the needs of White people so that all racial populations will focus on meeting their needs.

Suburban and Suburbia

This is code for White people, White community, White neighborhoods and wonderful White life.

House in the Suburbs

This is the American Dream. Most of the symbols of fulfillment revolve around having a home in the suburbs. The home in the suburbs means that an individual has truly arrived. The house in the suburbs means the fulfillment of the White American aspiration. For some Black people living in the suburbs next to good White people is the promised land.

Sun Tan

This is code for White people trying to be Black people without carrying the label of racial inferiority. Sun tanning is a way for White people to get more vividness in their skin tone. This is a way of fulfilling a well-documented desire to have more color. They are trying to be darker in color without having the drawback of being classified as Black.

Red Head

This refers to White females with reddish-tinged and reddish-colored hair. The redhead is second only to the blonde as the hottest and most desirable White woman. It is very interesting that in the White supremacy system the color of hair is used to define the value of a woman. The whitest woman has the highest value in White supremacy folklore.

Blonde

This is code for White female. The word blonde immediately conjures up images of Jean Harlow, Marilyn Monroe, Jayne Mansfield, Farrah Fawcett and many other White females. The White female is still considered the highest standard of beauty in the world. The blonde is the most beautiful White woman.

Every woman in the world whether she admits it or not desires to be blonde. The concept of White supremacy is that Whiteness is superior, prettier and far more desirable. A blonde White female is considered the most beautiful goddess in White supremacy culture and folklore. The saying that blondes have more fun is heard all over the world. Black people from former NBA star Dennis Rodman, tennis star Serena Williams, to everyday Black females adopted the idea that blonde was more beautiful.

Black people spend millions of dollars each year attempting to look whiter with blonde-dyed hair, blue-eyed contact lenses and surgery to reduce lips, buttocks and nose sizes. The idea that blonde is beautiful is central to the theme that White is beautiful. In 2003, despite all claims to the contrary, the blonde woman was still the dominant standard of beauty.

Brunette

This is code for the third tier of White females. Brunette, black or brown means more than hair color to the majority of White females. The brunette is considered the meat and potatoes woman. She is the standard White woman and has less esthetic value in the White supremacist idiom.

Most Desirable Types of White Women

Blonde
Redhead
Brunett

Gay

This is code for White male homosexuals. The gay word has great propaganda value. The word "homosexual" had been greatly demonized in the battle against the religious White conservatives. The leaders of

Race Code Words

the White homosexual movement needed to change the language in order to move the debate in a more favorable direction. The use of the gay word as a replacement for homosexuality was a real stroke of genius.

This redefined the image and playing field. It described homosexuals as innocent, happy and fun loving. According to dictionaries, the word gay means cheering, beaming, radiant, glistening and glowing. This replacement word helped to marginalize the opposition to where it is today. Who could be opposed to someone that is beaming, happy and wonderful? The use of the gay word subtly recruits and seductively attracts individuals to the lifestyle. Most people want a life full of fun, enjoyment and fascinating experiences. Who wants to be worried and troubled? The gay word made the homosexual lifestyle appear to be exciting, innocent and harmless. The marketing strategy was beautiful. It said, "We are wonderful, fun-loving people. We always smile and treat other people with dignity and kindness. Why do you want to bring harm to a non-violent, peace- loving people who just want to be left alone?" This was an excellent propaganda ploy. To dumb Joe Six Pack, gay people were not the same as those rabid, morally degenerate homosexuals.

Many people forget that before the White homosexual or anti-sexual movement, the definition of the word gay had no relationship to sexual orientation. With the coming of the AIDS virus, the luster of the White homosexual lifestyle vanished. However, the White homosexual movement fought back with an effective sexual media campaign. In the year 2003 the public relations crusade has been so effective that a large percentage of people consider this anti-sexual behavior and lifestyle as normal. They even have a flag that symbolizes white sexual nationalism and individualism. Flags are used to establish territory.

Some experts have even predicted that within the next 50 years homosexuality will be considered as the normal state of existence. Whew! The power of words can change the whole landscape. On the other side of the tracks, Black males in that life are called Black homosexuals or Black gays. In the national debate on gay issues Black gays are not the chief spokespersons. They are rarely referred to simply as gay or homosexual. The Black homosexuals are generally defined first by race or color and then by sexual orientation.

151

The Black gay, or homosexual, is considered a pathetic and isolated creature by White gay racists. This is not the same for the White gay who is considered refined, intellectual, rich and powerful. White gayness has value. The so-called revitalization of materially deficient Black communities is based on White homosexuals choosing to relocate into the areas. It is the Whiteness that gives it value and worth.

The Militia Movement
Meaning: less powerful Whites who are organizing to fight higher powered White people for the right to manage the nonwhite populations.

White Christmas
This is code for a religious holiday for White people.

White Christmas Symbols
White Jesus
White Santa Claus
White Santa helpers
White snow
White North Pole

Snow Covered
This means white, pure, pristine, virginal, unsullied, unsoiled, unspoiled, spotless, unstained and perfect. This is the idea behind the statement of the snow- capped Rockies.

White Collar/Professional
This is a reference that means White people and competency. This term is similar to the word middleclass. It is used to communicate with White people. The use of the collar word has a slave and criminal connotation. In the early development of the middleclass many White people appeared to be very robotic in behavior and speech. IBM was the classic example of the white-collar syndrome. IBM demanded that employees wear the symbolic white shirt.

The white shirt signified Whiteness, purity, cleanliness and superiority. Black people who worked at places like IBM during this era were psychologically impacted by the symbol of the white collar. It replaced the slave chain collar. It had the same impact. They were trained to give up their Blackness and to act and look like White people. The corporate word was used to hide this indoctrination.

White Collar Crime
A code for the smart crimes that only White people can commit. This is a highly sophisticated crime that requires intelligence, smart planning, imaginative methods and brilliant tactics. This is not a street or (decoded) nigger crime. The Whites that commit nigger street crimes are considered *white trash* and as dumb as niggers.

Jesus Christ
This is the image of the White male as God.

Upscale / Trendy
This code word is used to define usually younger Whites who are trying to get more acceptance in the White world and more income. They are the fashion setters and leaders of new thinking at a certain level of White interaction. The alternative code for this lifestyle is jet setters.

Mainstream
This code word means the White community and White people. The term Black community means non-mainstream or nonwhite. No activity, service or resource is considered legitimate or validly mainstream until it has the White community's acceptance and blessing.

Heady / Intelligent
This code word gained wide use first in the sports context. The purpose was to separate the White athlete from the Black athlete. The Black athlete has athletic ability, and the White athlete is a heady ballplayer that relies on intelligence. The term *blue-collar kind of guy* is also code for White athletes.

Modern
This is a code word for White social development and civilization.

Revitalization
This word is a code for White people coming back to live or capture the business in an area largely inhabited by Black and other nonwhite people. The word revitalization means to regenerate or to repopulate

the area with people of a different genetic make-up. This code is often interchangeable with the gentrification word.

Most of the revitalization is based on the resettlement of a White population back into an area largely abandoned and left to Black people. Rarely are revitalization programs designed to economically benefit Black populations. Far too many "revitalized" neighborhoods wind up being special districts for the resettlement of White gays and other affluent White groups.

Liberals /Conservatives

These are code words for groups of White supremacists who have developed a cultivated technique for dealing with Black people. The word liberal is associated with many good things. It indicates tolerance, open-mindedness, free-thinking, open handedness, generosity, and big heartedness. The word alone is powerful enough to attract individuals. Who wouldn't want to belong to a group of people that have these qualities? The word liberal also has a distinct political meaning. In political rhetoric it is considered left wing. The uniting of political philosophies to "wings" brings about an immediate perceptual association with birds or flying. One of the cornerstone symbols of white domination is the big bird called the eagle. The eagle is a big-eyed, smart predator that surveys the entire landscape and then calmly waits out its prey.

The intended prey is lulled into thinking that the eagle is not interested and is harmless. However, that is part of its game of deception. The eagle has every intention of attacking its target. The prey will never know when and where the eagle will strike. The same eagle has both a left wing and a right wing. Both wings are part of a predatory creature that seeks to devour its victim. The left wing, or liberals, have done much to derail, mislead and deceive Black people.

This assessment is based on the history of White liberalism and its relationship to Black people. Liberals have never pushed for the dismantlement of the world-wide system of White domination. At best, the efforts have produced a piecemeal level of set-a-sides that Black people are supposed to be grateful for and contented with. The liberals want to control Black people in a less harsh/rigid and yet far more deceptive manner. This is part of the yo-yo effect or bouncing back and forth between the confusion of the left wing and right wing while in reality both sides are the White-wing.

Race Code Words

One side points a finger at the other to explain why the degrading social and economic conditions of Black people have not changed. The left blames the right and the right blames the left. Each side recruits pathetic Black spokespersons to spout the party line in return for money and fame. On the surface it appears that the liberals and conservatives are hostile enemies. This is a good game. In the final analysis they play the same game of containment and control. The liberal versus conservative con game never allows Black people to be certain about the validity or the existence of racism.

The liberal does more to confuse Black people than the conservative. The liberal is a real magician. He blurs the image of the White supremacist. With a liberal around, it is hard to see the antics of the racist in clear focus. His words, gestures and public appearances are acts of very great deception.

He wants diversity and to have a few rich Black people at the pool party. He will even allow or encourage a Black male to date or to marry one of his daughters. However, this behavior has nothing to do with the attainment of real power. The right wing will at least indicate that they are for maintaining the existing structure of racial domination. The liberal will mislead and purposely delude black people into believing they are against the system. The inconsistency of the left and the right messages are painful and confusing. The one consistent dynamic is that the pattern of domination does not change.

Conservative is code for White people who want to conserve the existing racial order of things. The conservative in the political sense is the partner of the liberal in the game of confusion. What are these people talking about when they say that they are conservatives? What are they trying to conserve? The only thing that can be conserved is the existing social construct of White domination.

Soft on Crime

This is code for a White man or woman who is afraid to deal or get tough with Black males.

White politicians often accuse their opponents of not wanting to incarcerate larger number of Black males. If the opposing candidate is Black, it is said that he or she will not deal with their people in any aggressive plan to imprison more of them. In the racist lexicon the word crime means Black males.

OTHER SELECTED RACE CODE WORDS
The following are short descriptions of current and past racial code expressions

The Bell Curve
Black people are dumb and genetically inferior

Forced Busing
Pressured to go to school with dumb niggers

Busing to Achieve Racial Balance
Bring more Black people to the school

Integration
Let some of them come in the door

Segregation
Keep them out and stay away from them or they will get your daughter and your son

Piece of the Pie
A term for giving Black people an illusion of Black capitalism

Level Playing Field
White families have a net worth 11 times that of black families and will inherit 10 trillion in assets, with this gap there is no level field.

Fair Housing
Be careful about how discrimination is practiced

A Piece of the Action
Illusion of economic inclusion to keep them in their own neighborhood

Race Code Words

Enterprise Zones
Set a side some land and pretend that Black people will develop it for you

Law and Order
Keep Black males under tighter control or get these niggers under control

Pygmy Mentality
Nigger dumb

Militant
Angry, menacing and dangerous Black males.

Renew America
Get greater and Whiter control

Immigration
More nonwhites teeming at the border

Undesirable Parasites
Niggers living off White people

Dumb Women
Black and nonwhite females

School-Yard Violence
Young niggers carrying guns to school

After-School Programs
Pacification of black youth

Midnight Basketball
Use sports to calm these people down

WORD BOMBS

Explosive language devices used to degrade and besmirch targeted racial populations

Word bombs are highly inflammatory racial code words. The word bomb acts as an explosive that detonates inside the mindset upon verbal or written contact. Word bombs produce intense emotional derogatory reactions toward targeted racial individuals, populations, groups and communities. Left unchecked, unchallenged and uncorrected, word bomb labels become hard to remove social stains.

Word bombs are used to label a racially targeted population in the worst way possible. The word bomb operates in the mindset in the same way an aerial bomb does in its destructive impact. Aerial bombs are demons-of-death devices that blow up and destroy on physical contact. The purpose is to kill humans, animals and plants and to obliterate everything material within its path with extreme prejudice. The aerial bomb is one of the most destructive devices ever known to mankind.

The word bomb has the same impact except it uses words to inflict immeasurable psychological, perceptual and social damage. Word bombs are dropped in the media, education system, politics and other areas of life. These highly inflammatory racial code words are often attached to images, music and symbols that are used as racial propaganda.

Word bombs are dropped most frequently in television newscasts, cable television documentaries, public television programs, radio talk shows, newspaper articles, books, audio cassettes, music compact discs, commercial advertisements, billboards, Internet web sites, movies, television shows, motion pictures, videos and other forms of modern communication.

It is not unusual to hear broadcasters in the media describe Black communities as *mean streets, rough neighborhoods and high-crime areas*. These kinds of words have an explosive impact on the image of people who live in that neighborhood. The entire community is labeled criminal regardless of the population's occupations, religious beliefs or family backgrounds.

Race Code Words

In this society, where most people only know each other from interaction in the workplace or through the media, the image is extremely important.

The effective majority of Black people and White people even in the new century still do not reside in the same communities. The majority of Black people and White people are still physically separated. They have no real way of knowing each other except through words and images in the media. These words and images are embedded in the mind so that people carry them everywhere they go.

Word bombs are indispensable weapons in modern racism. Racial code words can be difficult to decode at the conscious level. They are used as hidden and subtle persuaders to penetrate the mental and emotional terrain of the perceptual experience and subconscious mind. The soft racial code word slips in the back door of the subconscious mind undetected. Black people are not trained to understand how a White supremacist really thinks and are deceived very easily.

The horrid tales and legacy of KKK racial terrorism are well known and established. In the real White world they are the least effective and the most exposed White supremacists. Black people have been skillfully manipulated into believing that White supremacy applies only to a small number of redneck, tobacco-chewing and horse-manure-smelling misfits.

When the term White supremacy is used in the media, whether on television or over the radio, a finger points or a voice gestures toward a white-hooded creature riding a white horse and burning a white cross while spreading terror throughout the land. This is a skillful manipulation of images and words designed to cloak the real racists. The most effective White supremacists go about their work on a daily basis largely undetected and unnoticed.

All individual and group behavior is evaluated by words and images. When different racial groups interact at supermarkets, shopping malls or entertainment events, the interpretations of these interactions are based on embedded words and images.

If the word or image is of criminals, thugs, big-butt mamas, gang-bangers and rapists, the social treatment system will be based on those conceptualizations. This is why White women literally clutch their purses when shopping around or walking by Black males. This outdated belief is based on words that are backed up by thousands of

159

visual depictions casting Black males as thieves. When White people drive through African American neighborhoods, their car doors are often locked.

White males seem to hold their women closer or call to their children to come closer when Black males pass them on the street or are seen in the plaza or mall. This is because many of them believe in the words that pronounce Black males as rapists or thugs. This paranoid perception is far from reality. Blacks have no strong historical record of raiding White communities beyond the one or two slave revolts led by Nat Turner or Denmark Vessey 150 years ago.

Black people have never mounted an offensive campaign to wage war against White people and burn, rape and pillage their neighborhoods. As a matter of historical record, the reverse is true. White supremacists have inflicted pain and suffering on Black people for hundreds of years. Somehow this history of oppression is conveniently forgotten. Black people should fear riding through any White community, based on the historical record of lynching and murder. Derogatory racial words enable White people to believe that Blacks are evil, dangerous and crime ridden. Some of them even believe that Black people are planning to conduct a race war in their communities. Millions of White people in rural and suburban communities are armed to the teeth and some are still actively preparing for a race war. This racial fear is also reflected in the loud calls for fighting crime, which when decoded mean incarcerating Black males. In their fear of a Black race war they disregard the most salient race-crime statistics. These statistics reveal that only a small number of Whites are the criminal victims of Blacks. Most of the crimes committed against White people are by White people.

The irrational fear of and belief in the inferiority of Black people leads to their substandard treatment in all areas of life from common things such as the delivery of basic city services, such as picking up the trash, to equal police protection, receiving justice from the legal system and receiving a quality education. If a population is perceived as criminals, they will be treated as criminals. Crimes exist in the White community and so does illegal drug use.

The White race is not besmirched because a few people engage in illegal drug activities. In 1970 White college youth were the most publicly recognized users of illegal drugs. The language was quite different when describing the drug epidemic on White college campuses. The terms used were *students experimenting with drugs* and *turn on and tune out*. The language was designed to extol the high virtues of experimentation and intellectualize drug use. Even as late as 1986, during the rhetoric of the "just say no" anti-drug Reagan Administration, the language was still embedded with appreciation for the smartness and intellectualism of the White drug dealers. In the book *Doctor Dealer* by Mark Bowden, 1986, the cover of the paperback version describes the major character:

> **To the world Larry Lavin was a successful young dentist, skillful businessman, and dedicated family man. In reality, he was the mastermind of a sixty million-a-year cocaine empire, the biggest drug operation in Philadelphia's history.**

There are several words that play subtly on one's mental perception of Mr. Lavin. The term "mastermind" implies smart, intellectual and genius. This is a strange choice of words. All chemical peddlers have some degree of intelligence, yet when Blacks are dealing illegal chemicals, the terms are some of the harshest known to humanity. The other words used to describe Mr. Lavin are equally interesting: *dedicated family man* and *skilled businessman*. While the author was attempting to make a comparison between Lavin's two different lifestyles, his use of certain words has a powerful influence on the perception of Mr. Lavin's character. He is subtly portrayed as a decent man who just happens to get caught in the cruel drug business. The hype on the back cover design shows that Mr. Lavin's participation in illegal chemical peddling was somehow "glamorous" and "ultra posh." In reality there was nothing glamorous about what he was doing. Simply put, Mr. Lavin was a criminal peddler of illegal chemicals. This is part of the spin put out to play down the criminal activity of White people.

Whites can be engaged in the same crimes as Blacks yet be perceived as different. Disparaging words are applied so frequently to characterize illegal activities in the Black community that it is very difficult to think of other terms when referring to these neighborhoods.

RACE CODE WAR

The derogatory racial language barrage is so piercing that even the people who live in the communities use the language to describe where they live. They do not understand the kind of economic, political and image damage that is inflicted on their community when they use derogatory language to define their surroundings.

They think that using these words will get the attention of White people so that the problem can be corrected. However, this only plays into the hands of the crafty White supremacist. They will allow Blacks plenty of media time to use words that describe their living environments as *drug or crime-infested communities*. However, Black people do not stop to think about the power of words. They just believe that some phrase is the latest thing and therefore will make them appear to be intelligent and hip.

This is why so many young and naive Black children go before the television cameras and say things like, "well, if I wasn't involved in playing basketball, I would be out on the streets selling drugs or involved in other crimes." As if the only option in life is to exist as a criminal or as a professional athlete. The unsuspecting black individual does not have a real clue about the kind of social damage these statements have on the value of a community.

What is a crime-infested community? If 50 people in a community of 5,000 are using illegal drugs, does that mean the entire community is drug-infested? What is the numerical or percentage threshold for drug infestation in an area? Is the infestation level 10, 20, 30 or 40 percent of the population of a defined geographical area? The role of the media is to get the story correct. To besmirch an entire community for the behavior of a few unsavory characters is getting the story incorrect and purposely spreading a lie. This allows a racist to use cover when they want to degrade Black people. They will say, "I am not a racist because I use these words. The people who live in the community use the same language." They know damn well where the language and concept originated and how it has been inserted into the daily dialogue. This is the power of the word bomb. It is infectious and very destructive.

The media are so involved with implanting derogatory messages regarding the African American community that many do not give it a second thought. As a matter of fact, they see it as their duty to gloss over reporting the truth. If they wanted to tell the truth, the show would be about how these communities evolved into this social condition. They would do extensive reports detailing how racism coupled with financial neglect, purposeful disinvestments and political rip-offs hurt the people in these communities. There is no real attempt to tell the truth. What they want to do is implant a negative image of the people in order to justify their mental abuse and social containment. The real vision of the black community becomes completely blurred with a distorted social reality. This is part of the explosive power of the word bomb to degrade, destabilize, devalue and destroy the self- esteem and public perception of targeted Black populations.

Word bombs are dropped during word war raids. Word war raids are large-scale derogatory language bombardments against targeted Black populations and their living environments. Word raids are designed like military warfare to be used like aerial bombing raids, where hundreds of explosive devices are dropped to inflict maximum physical destruction. Word raids act in a slightly different manner. They are large-scale bombardments of word bombs dropped strategically on a concentrated racial population or social environment. The goal is to establish an immediately unfavorable image of a racial population or area. When White populations want to relocate to an area that is populated by Black people, different language is used to describe the area changes. They will rename and redefine the area and create a different impression of it. Dropping word bombs will stop and new, more positive words will appear.

Word raids destroy the image of a racial population and the people's living environment. Word raids are conducted in television news shows, movies, political speeches, Internet web site pages, radio broadcasts and newspaper and magazine columns.

The barrage of word bombs sets-off derogatory mental and emotional responses against targeted racial populations and their living environments. These atrocious word raids happen without any counter-offensive from the targeted racial population. The lack of response gives validity and the sound of truth to the racial accusations. What is said, written or musically is taken for granted as the truth. These forms of racial communication are designed to stereotype populations for years, decades and even centuries.

It takes years to repair the image damage and destruction done by the word bombs during word raids. Word bombs are based on racial myths, cultural myths and inaccurate racial historical presentations. These racial labels often originate from White supremacists who work for think tanks, academic institutions, political parties, political consultant agencies, government agencies, military leaders, media outlets, real estate companies and so forth. The word bomb creates suspicion, fear, disgust, hate, anger, dread and hostility.

The word bomb paints a highly charged emotional and derogatory racial opinion about an individual, group or environment. It antagonizes and polarizes racial groups and populations by spreading and feeding on the worst racial fears. Word bombs are crafted to inflame the beliefs racial groups have accumulated about each other through years of mental conditioning.

One derogatory word shrewdly combined with another deprecatory word can wipe out any positive images of populations and their living environments. These words used over and over again with unfavorable visual images form a racial point of view that becomes established and embellished.

This racial point of view becomes institutionalized in the national culture and is reflected in social interaction. These well-crafted explosive language devices can drastically lower and ruin property values, increase crime rates and cause social instability. Residents in the area are afraid and want to move, their children believe what the word bombs say and resort to anti-social behavior and the adults feel ashamed of where they live.

Examples of Some Frequently Used Word Bombs

Crime-Infested Area

Drug Infestation

High-Crime Area

Race Code Words

Crack-Infested Neighborhood

Troubled Neighborhood

Savage or Savage Instincts

Poverty Stricken

Darkest or Deepest Africa

Gang Bang Area

Aunt Jemima

Political Ineptitude

Mismanagement

Declining Population

Uncivilized Behavior

Warring Tribes

Black Africa

Natives

Pagan

Dark Continent

Menace to Society
There are certain racial words that effectively recall deeply implanted feelings, fears and beliefs. If these words are not countered effectively,

they can take on a life force and become real obstacles. Racial codes word slip across quiet messages while word bombs are explosive.

When the word bombs are accepted in the national lexicon it is a signal that social change is about to happen. When the language is quietly hardened, the hardening of the social political structure is close behind. The levels of coded race words determine in which direction the White supremacists plan to move. If the language is soft race code, it means that a more skillful game of deception is being employed or is required.

The language will be coded in such a way that the victim feels that the program or activity is designed to benefit him and his people. For example, if the racist wants to move back into a predominantly Black area, they will use softer racial code words to convey their intentions about living together and improving the community. For a while it will appear that this is the case. Then the community will start to change, with Black people slipping out and White people easing in. Ten years later the community has completely changed from Black to White. The language used to describe the community will also change.

Under the concept of white supremacy white people have and hold value. Their presence and residence in a neighborhood allow a community to hold its value. When a reverse racial immigration pattern is underway the following codes are mentioned:

Diverse area
Mixed-income housing
Neighborhood revitalization
Blended neighborhoods
New town in town
New urbanism

These words promise a quality of life with improvements in property value and greater social acceptance. It is a signal that the racial composition of an area that was once Black is about to become White. Who could be against the revitalization of a broken down

Race Code Words

community? This kind of soft racial code language reduces the natural resistance to those who not long ago said that these areas were "drug infested" and not fit for human habitation.

Soft racial code language is used when a very sensitive operation is underway that requires the greatest level of deceptive skills. These kind soft word campaigns are run in so-called Third World countries to get the people to cooperate with birth control plans or opening up economic markets.

Soft code words were used to fool Black people during the years of the anti-poverty programs. Terms such as *model cities, affirmative action, urban renewal, equal employment opportunity, minority enterprise and citizen participation* created an impression of positive change. However, the real change of self-reliance was never realized. The anti-poverty program ran strong and was designed to neutralize the Black revolution, Black resistance, Black rebellion, Black self- development and Black economic independence.

The soft race code word operation was spun backward with the election of Ronald Reagan. When the Reagan Administration came into office, soft racial code words became harder. The purpose was to change the direction because the racist neutralization operation had achieved its objectives.

This happened almost overnight. The new language was *the truly needy, trickle down theory, reduce the deficit, cut domestic spending, get big government off our backs, stop reverse discrimination and get government out of the way.* The coded language had hardened, with tougher action such as massive budget cuts in social programs targeted toward Blacks and other nonwhites. In race code word terms big government was portrayed as Black people getting special social programs, welfare and tax breaks. The terms *cut domestic spending* and *boost defense spending* meant reduce nigger programs. And that is what they did. The hard race code war swing lasted for about 12 years from 1980-1992 until the election of Bill Clinton. The language had to change because George Bush, the former president, had declared that a new world order existed. Was this a code word for rearranging White domination?

RACE CODE WAR

WORD BOMBS DISGUISED AS SPORTS TALK

One of the newest ways to destroy Black male images is through sports talk. The boom of the sports talk show format makes it easier for racist males to let out their hostilities, frustrations and bad blood toward Black males. It is done most frequently in a manner designed to hide this race-based objective. All too often White male broadcasters have become very adept at using racial code words. Often Black males are labeled as having athletic ability while if White athletes make the same play it is *a heady play* or he is *a cerebral kind of guy.* This is why White broadcasters have difficult times interviewing modern Black athletes. They do not understand how their racially based mindset impacts on how they see Black people. This is notably different when Black interviewers such as "NFL Today" host and former great Deion Saunders or ESPN "SportsCenter" anchor Stuart Scott do the interview.

Far too many White male broadcasters still see Black males as horses and mules and use language such as athletic ability to reflect the perception of a dumb male endowed like an animal. These race biases often boil over into very hostile reactions when Blacks infract the law. Consider the reaction to the NBA Philadelphia 76ers' star Allen Iverson's incident surrounding his wife or the car incident involving NFL Minnesota Vikings' wide receiver Randy Moss, who was charged with possession of marijuana in his car after pushing a traffic cop with it. While both of these incidents are wrong and cannot be justified, the spin of White radio talk hosts was that both of these Black males were the worst human beings on the planet.

There are many other incidents concerning Black athletes that bring out the hidden or often cloaked attitudes. For example, the baseball strikes of 1994, the antics of former NBA superstars Dennis Rodman and J.R. Rider, the attitude of major league baseball stars Barry Bonds and Albert Bell, heavyweight boxer Mike Tyson and many more. The White talk show hosts often make Black men the butt of their rage. White callers openly use language that under ordinary situations would be considered racist talk. However, under the glitz of sports they are able to slide messages to each other without being labeled racist.

During the baseball strike in 1994, the Black baseball players took the brunt of the heaviest and angriest criticism even though the baseball players in the bargaining unit were all White. White baseball players cut the deals and called for the strike. Black players were blamed or served as scapegoats for White frustration. They were labeled ungrateful athletes, which is a code term for arrogant niggers.

Many White callers said that if these inner-city Black athletes were not playing baseball they would be robbing banks, mugging people on the streets, digging ditches or picking up garbage in an alley. Sadly, too many Black athletes are so money hungry with so little understanding of the power of an image that they will allow a White publicist to talk them into perpetrating all kinds of derogatory imagery.

They unwittingly play into the hands of racists who develop images that are akin to the old Southern race imaging practices of Watermelon Joe. Chicago Bulls' Star Dennis Rodman put on a wedding dress to stage an artificial marriage. He posed as a female bride dressed in white, which, in the White supremacist marriage context, is the racial symbol of purity and virginity. In reality it appears that Rodman has plenty of women, including White women, to go around. He played this role to get more money and attention and did not understand or care about the long- term image consequences of this kind of behavior. Millions of Black and White people see these powerful images and believe that Black men are sexual predators, perverts and freaks. They take the opportunity to poke fun and make jokes about the stupidity of Black males.

Former Heisman Trophy winner Ricky Williams posed with former New Orleans Saints head football coach Mike Ditka in a White bridal grown. Mike Ditka was the male groom and Ricky Williams was the female bride. Ditka did not wear the dress. He understood the power of images. The same thing happened to New York Knicks' star Larry Johnson when he put on a dress to portray the role of granny. Black male movie star Martin Lawrence dressed as an elderly, overweight Black female in the degrading "Big Mama" movie. Flip Wilson dressed as a woman when he portrayed Geraldine in the 1970s, and Eddie Murphy cross-dressed in the "Nutty Professor" and "The Klumps movies". This perpetuates the image of Black men as less than real men.

Cross-dressing is part of the Ru Paul transvestite's syndrome. The objective of the White supremacist is to get the most talented and physically gifted and masculine-looking Black males into women's clothing. The objective is to emasculate the image of Black men. The record rise of Black male transvestitism is a testament to the effectiveness of these images. Most of the prison movies, such as HBO's "Oz," feature Black men as the worst kind of deviate homosexuals.

The sports talk show format under the guise of discussing sports and allowing the listener to let off steam allows for a sea load of word bombs against Black males. In nine out of every ten complaints about major sports such as baseball, football and basketball the bad boys and no-goods are the Black athletes. In professional football the image of Black athletes is as criminals and sex-crazed miniature King Kongs who love to chase blonde White females.

The case of the NBA New York Knick's superstar Latrell Sprewell choking his coach P.J. Carlesimo, coach of the NBA Golden State Warriors, created a violent reaction all around the world. The thought of a big Black man with his hands around a White man's neck sparked tons of racist outrage and was full of racial symbolism. It touched a racial nerve with millions of White males.

Sprewell's giant hands around the neck of the former Seton Hall University basketball coach symbolized Black men getting a stranglehold on the White master and overthrowing White supremacy. His hands around the throat of a White coach, who decoded symbolized White authority and control, sent a troubling message to most White males, many of whom turned red with anger when even discussing the issue.

This incident far exceeded just a disagreement between a coach and a disagreeable superstar. After all, (at Texas Tech University) former Indiana University basketball coach Bobby Knight squeezed necks on a regular basis, and yet the uproar over his misdeeds was quite different. It had more to do with his embarrassing and out-of-control behavior.

The sports talk shows went crazy over the Sprewell choking incident. They called Sprewell an animal and degenerate thug. They found him guilty before innocent. In racial symbolic language it meant how dare a Black man put his big Black hands around the neck of the White master? The NBA commissioner suspended him and he lost millions of dollars in the 1997-98 season. This at the same time that White player Tom Chambers of the Phoenix Suns wasn't suspended for punching a Phoenix assistant coach a few weeks before the Sprewell incident.

This regrettable incident symbolized a Black uprising in the White mindset. It symbolized a possible revolt in the slave quarters, the coming of a Nat Turner slave rebellion in the white conscience. It also could mean discontent among the highly prized and spoon-fed Black bucks. After all, haven't we given these animals a wonderful life? Aren't they satisfied? These niggers seem to have forgotten that they are no more than prize racehorses in the racist mindset.

Basketball is a running game with half-clothed Black men racing up and down a wooden court jamming a big brown ball into white nets. It's just the same as the Kentucky Derby, The Preakness and Belmont Stakes. Black men are Black bucks who are bred as basketball players to run up and down the court just like trained horses.

Most of the race horses are dark brown to black. To date there have not been a great number of white horses with winning records in the super-rich-high-stake horse races. Most of the great athletes in football and basketball are dark brown to black. How many times have Black men in sports been compared to bucks and horses in a stable?

HBO boxing commentator Larry Merchant has on many boxing telecasts described Black male boxers as belonging to a stable or as being stablemates. Sprewell's choking of his coach represented the rise of the Black menace threat. If he did it and got away with it, how many more Black men would believe they could squeeze White men's necks, which means destroying White authority, and get away with it.

How many more Black men would believe that they do not have to submit to White authority, domination and control. If this incident were not correctly understood, how many more would get out of the box, be out of control and containment. The most physically endowed bucks might rise up to overthrow White supremacy.

This thought provoked wild fear and anger into the mindset of the White male collective. The niggers are coming to attack the men, women and children. These nigger bucks will not follow authority and the rules' which decoded mean White domination, White male leadership and White control. Under the guise of sports talk, Black men have been attacked and defiled as animals, savages, thugs, hoods and arrogant criminals.

RACE CODE WAR

Selected Examples of Sports Talk Word Bombs

Term/Word	Meaning
He is a real beast	He is a wild animal
Training stable	Black boxers
He is a stud	He is an animal
He is a head case	He is mentally underdeveloped
He is a problem child	He is emotionally and mentally backwards
He is nothing but an athlete	He cannot think
He is a thoroughbred	high genetically bred animal for sports
He is a stallion/real horse	high genetically bred animal for sports
Inner city athlete	predisposed to be a criminal
Disgrace to the game	black athletes
No respect for the game	black athletes
He is a jock	dumb athlete

CHAPTER FOUR
HIDDEN RACIAL IMAGES in the MOVIES

RACIAL IMAGING

According to *Webster's New Collegiate Dictionary,* an image is a popular conception of a person, institution or nation through the media. It is also a mental conception held in common by members of a group and is symbolic of a basic attitude and orientation. In other words, images are commonly held perceptual and psychological conceptions of people and places that have verbal, written or symbolic translations.

When visualizations are attached to certain words or symbols or placed subliminally inside other images it is part of the purposeful development of a visual or verbal depiction to achieve a specific propaganda result. One of the most devastating forms of mass communication imaging is the practice of racial imaging. Racial imaging is the use of visual, verbal and color characterizations and conceptualizations in a derogatory manner to denigrate a targeted racial population. Racial imaging is a destructive and demeaning practice. It is used to produce positive/superior or derogatory/inferior images. Therefore it is a racist practice. The development of an approach to redress the effects of racially based derogatory images is a corrective process and therefore not racist.

The so-called "WAR ON DRUGS" has produced some of the seediest practices of racial imaging. In reality it is a war against Black males. In this war Black males have been imaged as the enemy of the state. The mass media has fashioned crack cocaine to be a Black problem. The White-dominated law-enforcement system has aided and supported this view through large-scale surveillance and excessive arrests of Black people. The linkage between crack cocaine and Black people is now so commonplace that the habit is considered part of the natural lifestyle of most Black people. Even so, most national and local research studies indicate that the largest users of crack cocaine are White males.

A Human Rights Watch report in a June 8, 2000, revealed that since 1984, under the cover of the War on Drugs, the greatest mass imprisonment of Black people since chattel slavery has taken place. Much of this has been driven by the deformation of Black male images. The greatest irony is that Black people have applauded and supported the massive lockup. Calling them thugs, hoods and criminals, the fearful images of violent Black drug dealers have proliferated all over the world. More than 1.4 million Black males in North America have been incarcerated, alienated from their family base and denied the right of political empowerment because of felony disenfranchisement.

According to the Human Rights report, White people use illegal drugs such as crack cocaine nearly five times as much as Black people. Still, Black males are imprisoned in some states up to 57 times more often than White males for drug offenses. Based on their rate of drug usage, the war on drugs and drug raids should be carried out mainly in White communities.

The mass media imaging of Black males as the sellers, buyers and users of crack cocaine laid the groundwork for race-based practices such as racial profiling. These false images are repeated millions of times and are firmly embedded in the psyche of the intended audiences. These are not accidental images. They have been so embedded in the media that many White people think that all Black males are thugs and hoods. This is why it is so easy for politicians to get away with saying that they are fighting crime. It is curious that fighting crime rarely involves exposing the crooked activities of some White people.

Fighting crime activities were never carried out against the Russian Mafia despite the fact that they stole billions of dollars and laundered it through some of the biggest banks in New York City. The crime wave, fighting crime and crime in the street tags were at no time used to describe the outright theft of billions of dollars.

This kind of systematic imaging establishes the image of a degraded population that does not have to be treated with dignity and respect and casts its the male population as a breed of criminals. And it feeds the growth of such oppressive racially based industries as the prison-industrial complex. It is also used as the justification for purposeful economic disinvestments in many Black neighborhoods. Why would a good investor spend money in a community full of thugs, gang bangers, criminals and rapists? That is the same as throwing money away.

When voters do approve ballot initiatives for more spending, it is for more prisons, police, surveillance cameras on telephone poles and helicopters that buzz around late at night.

Systematic racial imaging has become the new form of slavery identification.

Hidden Racial Images in the Movies

Racial images also determine how other nonwhite populations view Black people. Transplanted inhabitants from areas like China, Korea, India, Palestine, Iraq, Iran and India are told that Black people are lazy, thieves and crooks.

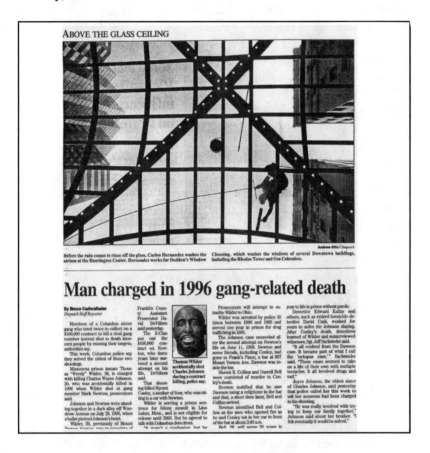

ABOVE THE GLASS CEILING

Andrew Otto / *Dispatch*

Before the rain comes to rinse off the glass, Carlos Hernandez washes the atrium at the Huntington Center. Hernandez works for Dedden's Window Cleaning, which washes the windows of several Downtown buildings, including the Rhodes Tower and One Columbus.

Man charged in 1996 gang-related death

The design in the picture in upper left corner looks like a black X. The X has been associated with such things as the Black Muslims, Malcolm X, brand X meaning inferior or X rated as in sleazy and disgraceful. Was it sheer coincidence that a picture with a black X would be placed on the same page with a derogatory story about a black male? Think about it!

They are told that Black women are prostitutes and welfare queens. These kinds of false images determine how they treat Black people within their own neighborhoods. The real tragedy is that young Black people have adopted these images as a sign of status and success. They have joined in the rush to glorify images that are designed to destroy Black people here and abroad. For minor chump change they have bought into the glorification of thuggery and criminality and wear it as if it were a badge of honor.

Young Blacks have been spoon fed a diet of Italian Mafia movies that prompt them into ineffective attempts to emulate the White gangster life. White corporations eagerly spend lots of "mad loot" to buy advertisements in Black youth-oriented magazines that feature some of the worst visual images of Black people since the days of ante-bellum Southern culture.

Black Entertainment Television (BET) is probably the most watched black oriented cable television channel. Robert Johnson, the Black BET majority stockholder sold the media company to Viacom, a giant White controlled media conglomerate on January 23, 2001. In December 2002 Viacom announced that it was canceling three of BET news and information shows including BET Tonight with Ed Gordon, Lead Story and Teen Summit. This follows the cancellation of other popular BET information shows including Our Voices with Bev Smith, BET Weekend and BET Tonight with Tavis Smiley. This effectively wipes out any national television medium for constructive Black oriented information, discussion and news. These BET shows were eliminated while at the same time Black people were being fed a steady diet of sexually degrading bump and grind music videos, gossip and comedy shows. The symbolic message is that Black people do not deserve to be informed –"they're animals anyway so let them lose their souls!"

The racist rationale is that Black people are only good at running the football or running against animals in Fox Network specials like Man Versus Beast. This January 2003 Fox Network program featured a Black male named Steve Crawford whose nickname is Cheetah Man running against a giraffe and a zebra! This very racist event called back memories of the humiliation of the great track star Jesse Owens running against a horse. There is hope on the horizon. In January 2003 Radio One, a Black-owned media company with 66 radio stations in 22 cities, announced that they were teaming with the giant Comcast cable service to launch a Black cable network. They are promising a whole new format geared toward quality news and information. Hopefully this will provide a much-needed media outlet for issues related to Black political development and economic empowerment.

Hidden Racial Images in the Movies

RACIAL IMAGING: THE GOOD and BAD

Racial imaging connects ideas of good and bad to colors and words that are associated with black and white and light and dark. Derogatory, or bad, images are placed in the framework of darkness or Negroid behavior. The bad image is always dark or dressed in dark clothes or has dark hair or some other very noticeable dark feature. In racial imaging the color black is a negative.

The word negative is close in spelling to Negro. Both words begin with the *neg* spelling and sound. N*eg* is often a racist substitute for the word Negro. It is also used in other derogatory or sexual words such as negation, neglect, negligence, negligible and negligees, which are usually worn at night or in the darkness. It doesn't take a great mental leap to connect the *neg* spelling to issues of color and race.

The majority of words that begin with *neg* indicate something unfavorable. In a racially charged environment the perception is that all *neg* word beginnings are associated to Negroes and are negative. The word negative also becomes a racially embedded substitute for Negro, African American, African, Black, Sudra and so on.

The notion of good guys and bad guys is so deeply embedded in the mind that it is virtually impossible to dissociate bad and negative from dark or black; good from god; and god from white. The greatest number of visual images portraying good and bad are white and black. The impact of the five-hundred-year-old brainwashing is immeasurable. In the process, Black people have all but given up their traditional forms of religious worship and beliefs and now bow to a White image of God. It is through this form of worship that Black people have gained an emotional attachment to White thought, White culture and White history.

GOOD GUY	BAD GUY
White Hat	Black Cat
White Horse	Black Horse
White Knight	Black Knight
White Tornado	Dark Tornado
White Tiger	Black Panther
White Castle	Dark Castle
White Robe	Black Robe
Silver Sword	Black Sword
Silver Streak	Black Streak

RACE CODE WAR

Good Side	Dark Side
White Saddle	Black Saddle
White Lie	Black Lie
White Baggies	Black Trash Baggies
White Teeth	Dark-Stained Teeth
Clear Face	Dark Face
Bright Student	Bad Student
Good Student	Badly Behaved Student

This section will analyze several feature length motion pictures in order to demonstrate how race and color-coded images are used. The selected pictures were chosen because they are effective illustrations of race and coded images in the movies.

"BARBERSHOP": IMAGES of DISRESPECT

The big controversy that surrounded the movie "Barber Shop" missed many of the subtle racial messages that flowed even from the minds of some of the Black writers. All motion pictures are symbols and codes of communication. No scenes, colors, background people, lighting tints or scripted lines are there by accident. If it is in the film, it is designed to send a message or to shape an image. While much was made over the political statements about civil rights, Black leaders, Rodney King, O.J. Simpson, reparations and other issues, the ingrained color and race issues passed right past the radar screen. While some of these scripted words and comments are sad and regrettable, they are symptoms and reflections of the modern day racial disconnection of Black people to their history here and abroad.

Black-oriented motion pictures are mirror reflections of the general confusion about race and color. There are some powerful and meaningful interactions. One of the most thoughtful scenes is the interaction between Eddie and Calvin outside the barbershop. Calvin has to admit to Eddie that he has sold the shop to Lester Wallace. The lines in this scene about developing Black people are the best in the movie. "Barbershop" had mixed racial and color messages and often the derogatory lines overwhelmed the solid passages, and most of the movie left a trail of belittling images of racial disrespect in the name of *"well its real. That's how they talk in the barbershops."*

Hidden Racial Images in the Movies

The Uproar

The movie starred popular rapper and actor Ice Cube and comedian Cedric the Entertainer. According to the concept of the movie, the barbershop is supposed to be a place of social protection where a Black male can feel free to express his style and real thinking. Most of the uproar was based on the scripted statements made by Cedric about Rosa Parks, Dr. Martin Luther King, Jr., Jesse Jackson and the Civil Rights movement. Cedric played the role of Eddie, the elder barber. It is interesting that most of the so-called disrespectful statements came from the older barber.

Many of his most objectionable statements were made during some of the most compelling scenes in the movie, and because of the way it was set-up, the viewer had to focus on the words and behavioral antics of Cedric. As Eddie stood in the middle of the room, he grabbed center stage at the same time the camera angle was shooting up at him. Most of the barbers and customers except Ice Cube and Calvin (he was situated like a deacon in the Baptist church) and Rick, the light-skinned barber, were physically positioned below or behind Eddie in an instruction— -receiving manner.

When Eddie made his harshest statements, Rick stood on his left side in a resistant body-language pose. This meant that Rick was not buying what Eddie was saying. However, the majority of the barbers and customers looked up to Eddie and gave his words credibility. When he was questioned about his views, the camera angle was from his face downward to the people who were sitting in the seats. This angle reduced the importance of their arguments against Eddie. In essence they were the naive students and he was the brainy professor.

Eddie's character in this scene and in the movie was that of a powerful authority figure, and he was the center of attention much like a preacher in the pulpit or a judge in the courtroom.

His speaking style and vocal cadence were like a preacher in the Baptist church. His shop apron signified the robe that ministers and courtroom judges normally wear. The robe is a powerful religious symbol that indicates holiness and righteousness.

In the imaging context and speaking style, the robe and camera angles were designed to give his words/thoughts greater weight, importance, reverence and validity. This is the reason that scripted and unchallenged statements such as *Black people can't have nothing; you know this neighborhood is getting worse every day, see, this is why you can't have an honest business in the ghetto; and all Rosa Parks did was sit her black ass down* leave a powerful racial impression. These statements should have had an effective or counter-response from a credible individual in the movie. The weak response from the older man and emotional retorts of the barbers simply didn't cut it. To allow these kinds of statements to go unanswered cements beliefs that Black people are hopeless and that the fighters in the race struggle did nothing and their sacrifices were largely unimportant.

The Color Code in Full Effect
Black-oriented motion pictures have a defined way of communicating color and racial messages. There are many movie examples that have perpetuated the ingrained color stereotypes of Black people. Melvin Van Peebles in the 1998 film documentary "Classified X" examined the issue of the color code as far back as the days of legendary Black filmmakers such as Oscar Micheaux, whose film career spanned the years from 1919-1948. Even in many of those early Black films, Van Peebles revealed that the color code was in full effect.

One of the more recent examples of color-coding was the 1978 motion picture "The Wiz" that starred Diana Ross and Michael Jackson. This picture was a take-off on the Broadway musical featuring Stephanie Mills and the 1939 "Wizard of Oz" with Judy Garland. In the 1939 version the Wicked Witch of the West was dressed in black and wore a black hat. This was a color code that signaled that she was the evil witch. The good witch was dressed in white and light clothing and wore a white head crown to indicate that she was angelic and good. In *The Wiz* the same kind of color code existed. The good witch was light skinned; she wore light clothes and had a higher-pitched voice. The evil witch was darker skinned with a big nose and thick lips and was overweight. The subjects in her kingdom were also dark or black and unpleasant appearing.

The same is true of the movie *"Barbershop"*, except that it is far more subtle and deceptive to the point of almost being unnoticeable. The good characters, Ice Cube and his wife, are tan to light-brown skinned. The good barber, Rick, is light skinned, and he is the innocent victim of the two darker-skinned criminals.

In one scene near the end of the picture it is obvious how the subtle color code reinforces color bias among Black people. Ice Cube and Rick are caught inside the crooked Lester Wallace's illegal chop shop. The setting is very dark, implying evil, and on one side are the two lighter-skinned good guys and on the other side are the two darker-skinned crooks. The loan shark, Lester Wallace, played by Keith David is darker skinned and his so-called bodyguard, more a servant and idiot than a protector, is very dark skinned.

There are many degrading dark-skinned characters in the film. Eddie the barber is dark skinned. The suspicious car dealer, the banker that says no to Calvin, the Black female flirting with the male from Pakistan and the large red-shirted Black male who goes up and down the stairs when the criminals are trying to move the stolen ATM are all dark or darker skinned. The snooty/educated barber named Jimmy is dark skinned and he is portrayed as a veiled racist.

In the end he apologizes to the White barber while Calvin looks on with smiling approval. The two leading criminals in the film are dark-skinned idiots and buffoons. The loud-mouthed female manager of the property banging at the door of one of the ATM robbers is dark skinned. The big-mouthed gossiping beauty shop owner next door is very large and dark skinned. The cheating Black male who is the love interest of the lighter-skin-toned female barber, is darker skinned, too.

The majority of the roles that were comical, loud mouthed, crooked or outright buffoonish were played by darker-skinned Black people. This is no accident but a reflection of an embedded color code that says black or dark is inferior. The practice of color coding is so ingrained that most Black people do not pick-up on it and do not understand how it contributes to why Black people still believe that dark and black are ugly, stupid, buffoonish and evil.

The White Barber
The White barber is the first chair in the barbershop, which symbolizes that he is number one.
He is cast as a harmless, likeable and somewhat dim fellow who wouldn't hurt a fly. His looks, hair cut, clothing, voice, use of language and mannerisms are symbols of racial adaptation.
He mixes in so well that Eddie forgets that the White barber is in the shop when he says, "I wouldn't say this in front of White people." To intimate that he doesn't belong in the Black barbershop among Black people would be the same as saying Eddie was a racist.

It is interesting that while professing a love for Blackness Eddie displays a ton of racial arrogance right in front of a room full of Black males and is allowed to get away with it! He says to the dark-skinned educated Black barber named Jimmy that he really wants to be like him or to be White. He even goes so far as to call Jimmy, *cheese toast,* which when decoded means a White mind in a Black body. The cheese is yellow or light and the toast is dark. Statements such as *he's toast* have very deep racial meanings. It means that one is in trouble because he has become darker.

The White barber feels so secure that he even brags that he is Blacker than one of the darkest-skinned males in the cast. This kind of open racist hostility could only happen in a black movie. The males in this movie are powerless and defenseless. The White barber is allowed to say or do anything he wants and it is all right with the Black males. This is the height of racial degradation and disrespect because it says that someone is so good that he can come into your sanctuary, defile your women and eventually takeover your operation or run your nation.

The appearance of the White male within a Black cultural setting also indicates that a new racial penetration is about to commence. It is a message about the beginning stages of taking over another Black-dominated service industry. The intrusion into a Black-dominated setting is a symbol of what has happened to Black people for thousands of years.

The predator innocently camps along the banks of the happy village and acts very friendly. He interacts with females and through them gets the approval and acceptance of the males. He adapts the ways and some of the movements of Black people in order to neatly fit in. His main goal is to learn what they are doing and to eventually destroy or take it over.

The White barber even acknowledges his goal when he says that one day he could own a Black barbershop. When this is decoded it means that Whites are going to take over this industry also. Next, Whites will take over the Black beauty shop. Large White corporations such as Revlon have made dramatic in-roads into the Black female hair care industry. This predatory relationship has happened repeatedly in Black history (Dr. Chancellor Williams in his monumental work, *The Destruction of Black Civilization* describes the predatory process).

The White barber's hidden aim is to take over one of the last bastions of independent Black ownership. This has already happened to the Black hair care business, the Black insurance companies, the numbers/gambling industry, the Black funeral home business, the Black newspaper business and a host of other service industries once dominated by Black people.

This is validated by detailed scenes showing his expertise in cutting Black hair. *These are the only scenes that actually show hair being cut.* What is the message here? White people can cut Black hair as good as Black people so why go to a Black barbershop?

This scene also has a deep religious/ political symbolism. In the Holy Bible the secret of mighty Sampson's strength is in his hair. When his hair is cut, he loses power. The cutting of hair implies Jimmy's loss of power. His relatively strong Black nationalist perspective is discredited and his resolve to oppose the historical predator is weakened as his hair is cut.

Africa and Reparations

The use of a buffoonish cartoon character to play the role of the Black man from Africa was an insult to the connection and relationship of Black people to the motherland.

His character symbolized Africa, the motherland. Rick mannerisms were subtly homosexual, and he was called degrading names by other Black people. The African was accorded no respect and his presence was largely comical, buffoonish and irrelevant. Rick even engages in a fight with another Black man as if to underscore the rift between Black people here and in Africa.

His character reflects how Black people feel about their African heritage and how they relate to the modern-day motherland. White people with German heritage do not crack jokes and poke fun at or about their historical lineage. In this movie Africa is symbolized and treated as a big joke. This treatment of Africa blurs the connection between the motherland and Black people in America. This is also reflected in how the issue of reparations is treated in the movie.

"Barbershop" is one of the first Black movies to take on the question of reparations. Judging from the script, it is clear that the movie writers and producers do not favor the idea. Not one of the characters speaks clearly in favor of the idea of reparations for slavery. The emphasis is on getting some money and not on the significance of chattel slavery and what it has done to the development of Black people here and abroad.

This is a very dangerous message. There are no movies where Jewish or Japanese Americans are against reparations for the evil deeds that were committed against their people. The references to affirmative action and welfare are done in a joking manner too, calling them *respirations*. This says that the idea of reparations is a joke and should not be taken seriously. However, the writers do not deal with reparations for Jewish people in the same way. They make sure that it is treated with reverence and deference. Rick refers to the Jews as Holocaust survivors with great respect. There are no jokes in this movie about the suffering of Jews under Nazi rule. However, the issue of reparations is treated as a prank and a wild dream.

To date, no Jewish individuals or groups have opposed reparations from the powerful and rich Swiss bankers. The Jews do not treat the issue of Jewish reparations as a joke or wild dream.
No group of people or foreign population on this earth has suffered more than Black people under White supremacy domination. In the Congo alone during the rule of Belgium's King Leopold there were as many as 10-15 million Black people killed, maimed and slaughtered. In the same region, since 1999 more than 3.5 million Black people have been killed.

During the horrific Middle Passages slave ship crossings from Africa, Black people were lost by the millions. Their land was stolen, Black people were/are stripped of their identity, the family structure was destroyed and the people branded as property. Yet Blacks in this film scoff and put down the idea of reparations. It is portrayed as a ludicrous idea with no substance or merit.

This is one of the dangerous aspects of the movie. It is designed to send a message that says *whatever you niggers went through is irrelevant. After all, you can handle it because you are savages and animals. You niggers have enough and should be happy that you have what you have!*

There should have been a credible character like Calvin arguing why reparations are necessary. Rick shuts down the debate by saying that reparations are unnecessary because Black people in the United States are some of the richest Negroes on the planet and that there is *plenty of opportunity.* He uses the word *restraint* to indicate that Black people do not need to be compensated for 350 years of racial abuse.

Hidden Racial Images in the Movies

Who Is the Real Ho?

One of the most disgraceful statements comes at the very end of the movie. In the midst of joy and happiness in the barbershop, Eddie's closing remark, "Dr. King was a ho" is said in a comedic fashion to reduce the resistance to this kind of racially degrading remark. The message is that Dr. King was a sexual degenerate and that in honor of his birthday everyone should "get your freak on" or, in this era of AIDS, have freaky sex all day long as a fitting tribute.

This was truly one of the most sickening references. Dr. Martin Luther King was killed at the early age of 39 fighting for freedom and justice for Black people. He took a bullet in his head because he would not back down against the raging power of hardcore White supremacy. He stood against the forces of racism, faced character assassination, bomb threats, assassination attempts, death threats to his family and yet this brave soldier fought on. To belittle a man that gave his life so that others might have a better life is a *despicable act* and is simply unforgivable. This is the same as a Jewish American making a major motion picture that praises Nazi leader Hitler and calls former Israeli Prime Minister Golda Meir a harlot or former Prime Minister Rabin a sexual pervert. It would be an unthinkable act of dishonor and disrespect. To use a movie to transmit such a degrading message is the crowning achievement of modern racism. The final thought left with the public is that Dr. King was a sexual pervert. The writers of the movie used Eddie, the eldest barber and one of the movie's most credible characters, to make this disgusting statement.

Eddie talked about how young Black people *"have no sense of history."* Cedric the Entertainer and others have grown very famous and rich because of the sacrifices of men and women like Dr. King, Rosa Parks and others. It seems as though they have no understanding or sense of the importance of history when they gladly say such lines. To add insult to injury, they even had the nerve to tour the country peddling this film as some kind of great and new concept in Black motion pictures. This is a new level of *confusion* and Dr. King is not and never has been the ho!

Despite protests against the disparaging remarks made by comedian Cedric the Entertainer about Dr. Martin Luther King in the movie Barbershop, the NAACP still chose him to host its March 2003 Image Awards Show at the Universal Amphitheatre in Los Angeles, California. I commend Rosa Parks for refusing to attend. The new NAACP attempted to do a balancing act between the money and glamour of Hollywood and the remnants of the civil rights movement. What is the meaning of the word image to the leadership of such organizations as the NAACP? Does it mean that anything goes, "just show me the money?" It is a sad day when the most treasured icons of a racial group can be so easily trampled on and the offenders are financially rewarded and uplifted, extolled and admired. This sends a message to the world that Black people really do not understand the power of images. No other racial population on this earth would allow such blatant disrespect and disregard to its most sacred images and symbols.

"MONSTER'S BALL"

The movie "Monsters Ball" starred Halle Berry, one of the most talented actresses in the motion picture industry. She received an Academy Award in 2002 for her portrayal of a befuddled and self-destructive Black female. This movie was very effective at using racial symbolism to convey racial messages and to maintain cultural stereotypes. This was supposed be a story about how two tragic figures from different racial and cultural backgrounds found security and comfort in each other's arms and the effect it had on their ideas about racial and human relations. Her role in this kind of movie is very disconcerting to many Black people.

Why would an actress at her level of talent appear in a motion picture like this? Why was she given more accolades for a performance that was of far less value than her roles in "Losing Isaiah" or as Dorothy Dandridge? This role had no real value-or did it? The lead character played by Berry was a confused and highly misdirected Black female. This role symbolized the image of the Black female who cannot develop an effective relationship with any Black male.

Monsters, Nothing But Monsters

Under the concept of White supremacy, Black males are considered beasts and monsters.

They are big like horses and dumb like donkeys. All of Berry's Black relationships are either with or produced by monsters because as long she chooses mates from the Black community, she gets nothing but monsters. Her son's father (Sean "Pi Diddy" Combs) is a monster and a convicted murderer. He is on death row and is eventually executed in the early part of the movie. The execution symbolizes the inherent

Hidden Racial Images in the Movies

criminal nature and brief life expectancy of the Black male. The message is: do not hitch your wagon to Black males because they are criminals, unstable, unreliable and will not be there to take care of you.

In this movie the father and the son, or both generations of Black males are hopeless, dysfunctional and short-lived. This symbolizes the destruction of generations of Black men. It is a subtle yet powerful message. The message is that it is better to kill or die than to reproduce more Black males. It is a blessing to get rid of as many as possible because all of them are maladjusted beings that threaten the social order. The death of the father and the son in the movie symbolizes the wiping out of Black male genes. There would be no son or daughter to give birth to a family of new monsters. The notion that Black males are monsters is a deep part of the White supremacist's mindset and social construct. The word monster in the movie really means Black males. White males in particular often refer to Black male athletes with the racially coded phrase *he's a real beast!* This wording is a not so subtle, linking Black males with beasts and monsters. Thus, monster's ball is a code for rescuing the Black female from the clutches of these monsters. The message is very clear and it says *even a low-life racist is better for the Black female than a Black male.*

The Big Fat Son
Berry's son is a greedy, big fat gluttonous child that tragically dies early in the film. The child is dramatically overweight, which means that he has no control over his eating habits. Berry verbally abuses and derides the child often for not being able to control his consumption. The symbolism of food in this movie is very interesting. The consumption of food is an oral and pleasurable act and has sexual connotations. There are countless allusions from the world of art and fashion design that draw strong correlations between food, eating and sex. The bonding word among the worlds of eat, food and sex is the word oral. This is a sexual label.

The act of overeating symbolizes an oversexed individual, a glutton with no scruples, morals or limitations on what he would do. In many motion pictures fat individuals, especially in biblical pictures, are always imaged as greedy, rich and sexually immoral characters. The association implies that a male who is a food addict will eventually become a sex addict. He has eaten so much food that his large size cannot attract enough women to satisfy his unchecked cravings.

187

In the process he will become a sexual masturbator, he will pay prostitutes for sex or he will get them by hook or crook. Does the symbolism of fat and greedy imply that her son has a hidden sexual problem or that he is a sexual deviant on the way to becoming a pervert or maybe even a rapist? In the symbolic world a fat man has special problems getting the girl. Very few movies feature the fat guy as the leading man. He is often the victim of laughter and ridicule and is left behind. This feeling of rejection stimulates a deep resentment for women. He might blame his mother for being fat and being without a woman. In essence the child in this movie is a monster in the making. It is better to destroy the child than allow it to destroy mankind.

Sleeping with the Enemy

On the other side of the fence is an avowed White supremacist who literally hates Black people. The father of the White supremacist is an old-line, hardcore White supremacist. The son is supposedly a far more tolerant individual but in the end proves to be very weak, confused and mentally ill. The son eventually shoots himself to death in front of his father. Common sense would dictate that if an individual really did not like the views of his/her parents, he could easily catch a bus out of town. The suicidal killing is supposed to symbolize the son's rejection of hardcore White supremacy. Rather than live in a racist world or become a racist he chooses to die a violent death. However, another message comes through loud and clear. *The inference is that because he chooses not to be a White supremacist, he is weak and mentally deranged and deserves to die.*

He is a race traitor. While the father deep down loves his son, he knows that he is not able to carry the torch. In the hardcore racial context, the message is that the weak gene has to be destroyed. This new liberal, or ultra-radical, was putting the continuation of White supremacy domination in serious jeopardy. Son or not, he had to go. However, the father is given an opportunity to have another, hopefully male, child.

He does what most White supremacists have done from the days of chattel slavery and has sex with a Black woman. They see Black females as their property, and whenever they want sexual congress or sexual access they are entitled to have it. The hero's involvement with the Black woman does not contradict the behavior of a White supremacist despite what the movie tries to impart. This behavior is very consistent with the history of Black and White relationships in this area of the

Hidden Racial Images in the Movies

world. The worst racist on the block will be secretly involved with a number of Black females.

The heroine's interaction with the White male at a time of severe desperation means that Black men have nearly destroyed her before the White savior once again comes to the rescue. In the symbolic world, sleeping with her indicates that he wishes to get her pregnant to compensate for the tragic loss of his son. However, this time around he might be able to reduce the monster genes that are inherit in the Black bloodline. This falls right into line with the softcore White supremacist's view that the way to eliminate the Black monster gene is to breed it out.

There are other hardcore White supremacists who vehemently fear Black and White unions because once hit with the Black gene, they believe it is impossible to breed it out.

In the end the Black female will not produce any more identifiable Black males because she is having sex with a White male. This is now a popular theme in White motion pictures: to show the union of White males and light-skinned Black females. In the racist mind the outcome would be a mulatto class more devoted to the idea of being White than Black. This would be preferable to a weak White male who could not carry forth the work of racial salvation. This White male insertion only furthers the disruption and confusion among Black people. Sleeping with an avowed enemy of her race indicates that she has high levels of weakness, childlike behavior, stupidity and confusion.

The White male insertion only contributes to the level of confusion and misdirection. It also implies that she sees herself as really belonging to him. Despite her attempts to go the other way, her blood call is to the White side. As the film ends, the message is clear that the future of Black females is to be with White males. This is another subtle attack on Black unity and stability. This movie glorifies the symbolism and idea that being a racial traitor is the patriotic thing to do.

TRAINING DAY

For the movie *Training Day* screen star Denzel Washington won the 2002 Academy Award for best actor by playing the role of an extremely corrupt police detective in the Narcotics Division of the Los Angeles Police Department (LAPD). He was denied the Oscar for his most honorable work as the great Malcolm X. His portrayal of Malcolm was Denzel's finest hour and greatest acting performance. His character in

Training Day was so vile, corrupt and unredeemable that in the end he was gunned down like Sonny Corleone in the death scene of the movie The Godfather (as shown in the theater version).

Training Day is a modern-day version of the old-style Western and Tarzan movies rolled into one. The Western and Tarzan films were racial conquest movies. Tarzan was pure White supremacy domination. He ruled over Africa and was king of the "black natives."

The word Western as a movie genre has very little to do with a geographical location. If it were only a geographical location, there would have been movies designated as Eastern or Northern movies. The two movie genres that made any reference to geographical designations were Old South and Westerns. In both genres these geographical locations were code words for racial domination.

The Old South movies such as *Gone With The Wind* emphasized the enslavement and domination of Black people. The thousands of Western movies symbolized the harshest element of hardcore racial domination. In decoded language the word Western is a racial term that means White supremacist culture, White domination, genocide against Red people and stealing valuable lands and resources. This is why the image of John Wayne is so powerful and long lasting in the White supremacist frame of reference. Wayne embodied the very idea of the White conqueror and imperialist engaged in the practice of manifest destiny.

The racial symbolism of the movie *Training Day* jumps out from the photo on the marketing poster and video/DVD box. The photo shows a stalking Washington with his upper torso angled to the left. His hand on the left side of his body is in his pocket, his head is slightly tilted to the left and his left eye is peering like a big black panther eyeing his target. Both of the men's heads in the photo are turned to the left. This is designed to transmit leftist or so-called radical ideas. Turning to the left also implies going in the wrong direction or, if it is a police officer, it means engaging in corruption.

The politically correct direction is to the *right* or the *conservative* side. If the photo had shown the men turning toward the right, it would have signalled that they were the "good guys." The White male in the background shows that he is only looking to his left, and he has not made a body move toward the left. His posture signals that he is not a political leftist or a radical. He is a right wing conservative law-and-order man. The photo also indicates that he is very leery of Mr. Washington.

Hidden Racial Images in the Movies

Denzel's body language in the photo gives the impression that he is stalking in the jungle. His slightly hunched over posture and long arms look like those of a big black gorilla. He is wearing a black cap, gold earring, black leather jacket, dark shirt and pants with gold jewelry, a slightly obscured cross and a police badge hanging from his neck. From a distance or with squinted eyes the photo looks like a gorilla brooding and moving in the jungle. Denzel's black leather jacket has the same color and texture as the belly and hands of a costume-party gorilla suit. His entire outfit except for his tee-shirt is black or very dark (white tee-shirt implies that underneath he is a sell-out to Black people). His outfit and mode of transportation (the surveillance car is black) personifies the classic use of racial colors to send a signal that Blackness is evil and corrupt.

The black cap on his skull has the subliminal look of a gorilla's head. This visual image is interlaced with the title of the movie. When the video box is turned upside down, it reads like so-called gang writing and signals on abandoned storefronts and houses in many communities. The movie title automatically triggers the idea of taming wild animals. The training word is most often associated with animals in a cage, on the loose, on a chain or in the zoo. The training word implies obedience to the master. Dogs, cats and animals are trained while human beings are educated and cultivated. The movie title has deep racial implications. It connotes that living environments that are heavily populated by Black people are like the jungles of Africa.

This means that these communities are wild, hot, dangerous and uncivilized. The role of the police officer or law authority is to contain the animals in the jungle in order to keep them from ruining civilization. This theme has been used in a number of motion pictures. One of the most glaring examples is a line from the movie "Prince of the City." Actor Treat Williams, who plays a corrupt narcotics detective, indicates to federal investigators dealing with police corruption in New York City that they are the only barriers "to them and the jungle", which decoded means keeping the animals from overrunning civilization. The only time the animal is allowed out of the jungle is when he/she has been trained to be obedient to the master.

This thinking was borne out by "the gorillas in the midst" statement of White police officers in connection with the Rodney King beating in Los Angeles The concept of the "training day" was to instruct the White rookie cop on how to deal with the Black community or, in decoded language, the gorillas in the zoo. In one of Denzel's lines he says, "King Kong ain't got nothing on me!" as he stands near his black car after a losing showdown with the White rookie cop. This is a very strong and powerful evocation of the name of King Kong, making it very clear that Denzel's character is a gorilla of the same name.

THE ROOKIE'S DAY
The hero of Training Day is a White rookie cop named Jake, played effectively by actor Ethan Hawke. In a close-up shot from one of the early scenes in the movie his manhood is symbolically confirmed by the angle from which he picks up a gun lying on the table. As he picks up the gun, it looks as if it were connected to his body near the front pelvis area. It becomes a penis symbol. The White rookie cop is the symbol of goodness, purity and honesty. In the first incident of the day of training he watches a drug deal take place in what appears to be an Hispanic community.

The White rookie cop is appalled by the way Denzel handles the young White drug users. He calls them "college kids," which decoded means "smart White genetic material," "good White kids" or " White untouchables." While he does his job, he does not want them to be arrested or handled improperly. In the decoded context it means that these young White people are not the real criminals; they are just college kids having a little fun.

The real criminals are these niggers on the street, or, decoded, gorillas in the jungle. Near the end of the film, Jake has had enough of Denzel's corruption. After escaping death at the hands of the Mexican gangs, decoded Mexican banditos, he gets on a bus headed home toward safety. But his commitment to justice will not let him stay on the bus. The bus is a symbol of the stagecoach in the old Western movies. The stagecoach is where life and death decisions are made. He gets off the bus because he has decided to deal with the dark menace to society. He walks alone down the darkened streets in a scene that symbolizes both the wilds of Africa, as in the jungle, and Dodge City in the Wild West. He must now demonstrate the courage to stand alone and face down this scourge of the earth. The gallant White hero has come to settle the score with the bad guy. He walks alone, as there are no other human beings in sight in this full-angle shot. This setting is the classic Western formula for the get-out-of-town-before- sundown showdown.

He is a tall-in-the-saddle, strong and silent White male like Gary Cooper in "High Noon," James Arness in "*Gunsmoke*" and big

Hidden Racial Images in the Movies

John Wayne facing down the bad men dressed in black. The rookie is the modern *"High Nooner"* who has come to catch the bad Black guy. It is his solemn duty to rid the White society of this unholy dark menace and keep it safe from the wilds of the jungle. As the rookie strolls defiantly down the neighborhood streets, he holds a big, black revolver on his hip. In a close-up shot the gun appears as if it were an extension of his body, like a penis. The gun is long and thick, which when decoded means that his penis is long and that he is a big and whole man. As he walks down the streets, he is confronted by a group of armed lookout men who yell to him about what they want in their neighborhood. In the symbolic world the rookie has entered an Indian reservation or a jungle village.

The lookouts are the same as those hidden in the background in old Indian movies. The armed lookouts are never shown in any clarity, and they never cause the hero to break his stride. He never responds to their questions because he doesn't have to answer. He is the Man. The earlier scene in the movie where the gun was placed in the middle of his frontal hip area made the idea of manhood and fatherhood very clear. He is the Lone Ranger riding into the Red Man's stronghold to capture a crazy, mad Indian and implement the White man's justice. When the rookie reaches the house where Denzel is located, he is met at the door by two or three tough-looking Black males. The lead Black male has a glistening Cross around his neck and is smoking a thin, brown cigar, which decoded means he has a small penis or no balls to stand up to Jake. Despite all of his gangster ways and bravado, Denzel needs a savior. When Jake tells them that he is there to take care of Denzel, they stand aside to let him walk through like Moses parting the waters of the Red Sea.

Jake is the symbolic White man and he cannot be denied entry to any location on this earth. No Black man can ever stand in his way. As they step aside to allow the rookie to move toward the door, the Black male's white glistening Cross shines strongly in the night. The glistening white cross means that he is a disciple of the white Jesus. In his mind the White rookie is the promised one. He is the savior/ messiah that they have been looking for to do battle with the black devil.

The rookie is so good that he even convinces Denzel's little innocent son to betray father in favor of a complete stranger. This racial message that means that a Black son-or the future of the race-should turn against his Black father and pledge his belief in and loyalty to the

White man. It means that from the earliest age possible, the Black child should be programmed to trust and select the leadership of White men, White leadership and White domination over Black men/women, Black leadership and Black development.

At the end of the movie, "the savior" gives the people the courage to defy the devil, Denzel. In the process they choose the White over the Black man. Denzel's ungodliness is used to justify this act of racial treason. The White man is right and good, the Black man is wrong and evil. There are no Black male roles in this movie that are redeemable or positive. The Black males are cast as members of gangs, corrupt cops, a wheelchair-bound drug dealer and racial turncoats.

This movie sends a damaging and recurring racial message that Black males are no good and have no credibility while the White man is always righteous and correct. The awarding of an Oscar to Denzel for this role says *We shall reward and glamorize those Black male and female actors and actresses if they play the most degrading roles.*

THE BIRDS

Birds are among nature's most lovable creatures and, like many other things, have been used to symbolize color and race in the movies. Often in literature, speeches and real-life examples, many items from eggplants to raisins have been used as background props and surrogates to send social messages. The pedigree, color and type of birds can set off many feelings about things as varied as death and bad luck.

The birds that are used to trigger these kinds of emotions in White-supremacy folklore are the darkest birds such as crows, ravens and blackbirds. These are the birds that movie directors use most frequently to represent themes of terror, horror, death, darkness and Blackness.

One of the most notable examples is from the motion picture *The Birds* directed by Alfred Hitchcock. This clever terror film is a tale about how different species of birds unite and begin to terrorize, in fact, declare war against humanity. The bird coalition is led by crows and blackbirds.

In the decoded racial context, the birds represent a racial population. In the symbolic sense, the blackbirds, crows and ravens represent Black people. This is revealed in the dialogue in the restaurant scene after the birds have attacked a school filled with children. In the restaurant scene several characters hold an impromptu discussion about the bird situation.

Hidden Racial Images in the Movies

An older, mannish or lesbian-appearing White female anthropologist named Mrs. Bundy attempts to allay the fears of the people gathered in the eatery. Her psychoanalysis about the intelligence of blackbirds and black crows is quite revealing. Upon closer inspection of the scripted conversation, it is quite clear that the birds are an implicit stand-in for some other concern.

Mrs. Bundy says, I hardly think that either species (crow or blackbird) would have significant intelligence to launch a mass attack. Their brain pans are not big enough." It is clear here that the birds have come to represent a targeted human population. This language has been used many times to describe the intelligence and capabilities of Black people. In coded language the words species and race are interchangeable. To talk about species in creatures is in racial code the same as talking about race to describe the diversity of mankind. When the film speech is decoded, it would read as follows: "I hardly think that either crows or blackbirds would have sufficient brainpower to organize or launch a massive attack against us."

The restaurant scene features a frustrated White male in a hat and business suit who had just walked into the restaurant and ordered a drink. While consuming his beverage, he makes some startling yet very provocative comments. He responds to a conversation about how the birds had overrun a captain's boat by saying, "The captain should have shot them. They are all just scavengers anyway, most birds are. Get yourselves some guns and wipe them off the face of the earth." The businessman appears to be conservative and angry. His use of the word scavengers is quite telling. The word scavenger is very similar to the spelling of savages. It is close enough to make the connection in the coded context. It is so close that the script had to cover itself by saying most birds are scavengers. This is designed to shield the real meaning. His statement urging people to get a gun and shoot these "savages" dovetails with the widespread belief that Black people might overrun the suburbs and therefore White people should get guns and be prepared. When his statements are decoded, they read as follows: "captain should have shot all of them. They are all just savages anyway, most of these black niggers are. Get yourselves some guns and wipe them niggers off the face of the earth."

As the conversation continues the exchange between the lead female character and Mrs. Bundy heats up. Mrs. Bundy very arrogantly disputes the claims of birds flocking together to attack humans. She says, "I have never known birds of different species to flock together. The very concept is unimaginable. Why, if that happened we wouldn't have a chance. How could we hope to fight them?" That is a heavily coded message. This was 1963 and the fight for racial and social integration was very intense and in full public view. The notion of racial integration sent shivers down the spines of many White people. The old White female was saying that Black and White people could never live together. They are not of the same breed. When this message is decoded it says the following: "I have never known people of different races to live together. The very concept is inconceivable. Why, if that happened we wouldn't have a chance. How could we hope to fight them in alliance with some White traitors."

Mrs. Bundy is not talking about birds. She is really using the dialogue to conceal the racially coded conversation. What they are really talking about is the fear of the rise of Black people. This coded conversation is a discussion about how White-dominated civilization could be overrun by these furious, uncompromising black creatures.

The older White woman has an advanced knowledge of the nature of different birds. Her posture and language indicate that the birds represent different groups, or so-called tribes, of dark and Black people in various locations around the world. She appears to be an anthropologist who has studied how different groups of Black people might react. She is trying to convince the townsfolk how good the control and domination training have been and that these Black people, or blackbirds, are so dumb and docile that they could not get out of control.

One of the most chilling and memorable scenes of the movie is the gathering of hundreds of black birds that sit on power lines and gather in increasing numbers on the playground in order to prepare for an attack. From a racial communications standpoint, this symbolizes the growing threat of the dark menace sitting at the banks of the White establishment and moving in on the White domain. During this same period, suburban growth began to explode as White people began their exodus from the central city.

The location of the movie is on an island near San Francisco Bay where the terror of white seagulls would have been as equally believable. The film does use white or lighter-colored seagulls in some of the scenes. However, to create terror and fear and establish danger, it uses the looming presence of the blackbirds and crows. Why not use seagulls or white birds and let them gather in increasing numbers on the playground?

The color white would not have established the idea of terror and threat in the mindset of White people. The use of crows, ravens and blackbirds allows the movie to skillfully play on the theme of the dark menace and the mounting racial fear and paranoia of the predominantly White audience. The paranoia starts at the beginning of the movie. Blackbirds are shown flying around in a forbidding and hostile attack formation.

This scene sets the psychological stage for holy terror. One of the main female characters is a dark-haired, lovesick teacher who is killed by blackbirds. The women and children are attacked at the school building by blackbirds. The lead blonde female character is nearly killed, with the blackbirds leading the assault. The message is that the blackbirds, not the seagulls, are the clear and present danger.

When decoded this means Black people are a clear and present lurking danger. This film was released in 1963, and the blackbirds symbolized the angry, swarming Black masses rising up against the power of White domination. During this period urban Black communities were stirring in rebellion. It was a very volatile period. The March on Washington occurred in 1963, and one year later, in 1964 Harlem, NY, exploded in a bloody rebellion. In 1965 the Watts area in Los Angeles went up in flames and Malcolm X was killed. In 1966 Stokley Carmichael (Kwame Toure) called for Black power and the African continent was already in the midst of a very powerful political revolution.

In this kind of highly charged atmosphere of Black ascension, it would be very difficult not to perceive that blackbirds terrorizing White people is, in fact, sending subtle color and racial messages. The producers and directors of the film were quite aware of the political risks of sending overt racial messages. If only blackbirds attacked White people, it would be too obvious and the hidden message might be exposed. To conceal some of the color and racial themes, an array of different-colored birds was employed. However, in *The Birds* the most dangerous and frightful attacks come from the blackbirds.

Using blackbirds and crows to symbolize Black people has occurred in other racial contexts. In the Walt Disney movie *Dumbo*, the crows represent Black people. In Britain during the mid-sixties, there was an issue concerning shipping dock workers, so-called illegal Black workers, back to their native homes. The White dock workers complained that these workers were illegal immigrants and were illegitimately taking their jobs. The British government shipped many of these Black workers home. This turned out to be a racial powder keg. On the day that some of the Black and dark-skinned workers were to be exported, the White dock workers gathered to see them leave and sang the tune "Bye Bye Blackbird."

Symbolic warnings proliferate in the movie *The Birds*, where in 1963 attacking blackbirds symbolizes the coming great Black wave about to sweep over and maybe overwhelm a White-dominated and controlled planet. The big, black birds terrorize the youth, or future, of White people. Hitchcock accurately predicts the rise of the Black masses by using the black crows and blackbirds as symbols of the gathering storm of angry Black people who would overrun Whites if they are not united and prepared.

The black birds that decoded mean Black people are used to strike terror into the mind of White people. This movie was released at the height of the civil rights movement in America and independence struggles in Africa. There were even lines in the movie that made direct reference to the nature of the blackbirds in a social context that only the most illiterate moviegoers would not have been able to decode. In this instance the word association between blackbird and Black people is again unmistakable.

BATMAN: THE DARK KNIGHT

The Batman character first appeared in May, 1939, during the height of the Western economic depression, when the fear of starvation and death fueled a greater fear of the dark peril.

The coming war against the Yellow peril and Nazi war machine (dressed in black) would follow in less than three years. When the meaning is decoded Batman should be called Blackman. The body of Batman is wrapped in darkness and blackness from the top of his head to the bottom of his feet. The Batmobile is black, his working office is black and his body suit from head to toe is black.

Batman's weapons are black, his rope is black and the bat plane is black. According to the authors of DC Comics from their web site's " Secret Files: Batman Text," the character of Batman grew out of a fear of dark streets and urban (decoded Black) crime:

> *Though regarded by many Gothamites as an urban legend built on superstition and fear of the city's darkened streets, Bruce Wayne knows all too well that the Batman is cold, hard   reality of his own fabrication. Since his parents' untimely death in Gotham's "Crime Alley," Wayne has spent his life in pursuit of physical and mental perfection in order to wage unrelenting war on crime.*

The war on crime means, in symbolic connotation, a war on dark and Black people. All of Batman's regalia suggest that he perceives Blackness, darkness and crime as one and the same. He is called the Dark Knight, which when decoded means a Black character fighting the dark evil, or fire with fire. To become a successful crime fighter, Batman believes that he must wear dark clothes to camouflage himself among dark people and dark criminal surroundings. Batman is regarded as the Dark Knight from the darkened streets. Every aspect of his life and being is shrouded in darkness.

What does this symbolism really mean? The Batman character is also part of a contradictory image and desire to be or to worship a Black hero. For many years Batman provided millions of young White males an opportunity to fulfill these dreams. Like Elvis Presley, Batman or Blackman, enabled millions of people to deal with their distorted fantasies about Blackness and color. The Batman character was different from Superman. The Superman character symbolized all of the White American virtues.

The Clark Kent character originated from Smallville, USA, or when decoded, the suburban area. He represents the middleclass suburban White boy. Bruce Wayne's character comes from traditional family wealth in New York City. Both comic book characters lost their parents as children. But Bruce Wayne's character is just the opposite of Superman's.

RACE CODE WAR

Bruce Wayne is a White male with the power to clean up the problems of the dark peril. He is rich, powerful and politically connected. He also harbors a deep desire to be a Black man. He has a deep fascination with darkness and a deeper fascination with Blackness. In the daytime he is the perfect White male and does all the good White things. He has all of the authoritative White boy credentials. He is unattached, influential and highly cultured. He is the idealization of the perfect, powerful White male. However, like Superman, he is a master deceiver. He goes to great lengths to protect a lie. He is the master of deception and illusion. He wears a huge black mask to conceal his face and identity. This means that he is trying not to reveal his true identity or real intentions because he is a deceiver of people. It also means that he can freely engage in the wonderfulness of Blackness and, at the same time, serve as a watchdog of Black people. A man who is dedicated to the implementation of justice has no reason to practice deception.

Criminals engage in acts of deception and underhanded dealings. Crime fighters behaving in a deceptive manner raise questions about their real intentions. The line is blurred between crime fighting and benefiting from the crime that is allowed to exist. The Batman suit is designed to give him a powerfully muscled dark or black body. This is very similar to bodybuilders, who try to get as dark as possible in order to look better in bodybuilding competition. This is probably why Black males regularly win these titles: they are naturally endowed with color. It is also similar to the ancient Greeks, who used the Black male body form of Ethiopians and Egyptians as models for their sculptures. They adorned the bodies with Greek heads to achieve the look of powerfully built Black men.

Thus, Batman can live out his great desire for color and Black power. The strange obsession and association between the desire for Blackness and the hate of it have stumped and confused millions of Black people. When Batman's character goes into action at night he becomes a Black man. He operates according to what he calls the code of the streets or, decoded, the jungle.

The association of the Batman character with darkness, the night and urban power are interesting. He operates a lot like the fictional White character Tarzan in a fictional Black environment called the jungle. Except that he is in the city, which when decoded means the Black jungle.

Hidden Racial Images in the Movies

Batman's role is to safeguard Gotham City and patrol the urban communities to arrest criminals dressed in black clothes who symbolize Black men. The choice of the title of Batman's urban environment, Gotham City, is also interesting. The word Gotham is associated with the word gothic. According to *Webster's New Collegiate Dictionary*, one of the meanings of the word gothic is: "relating to a style of fiction characterized by the use of desolate or remote settings and macabre, mysterious or violent incidents." Other word associations with the term gothic are darkness and blackness. Some modern White high school and college students affect the gothic look, which means dressing in black with black hair and black make-up topped off with a pale white face. The producers of the Batman movies created a dark city called Gotham in New York where crime takes place.

Gotham City decoded means Harlem. It means crime in the Black city. All crime takes place in Gotham City, aka Harlem. *The sound of the two words Harlem and Gotham is very similar. Both of the words include the spelling of the word ham, which means in religious code a Black male as in the Holy Bible. The words gothic and ham are coded terms that refer to Blackness. The word Harlem sounds close to the words harem and harlot or woman of the street, whore, pimp and crime.*

The only thing close to a dark city in New York in the White mindset is the community of Harlem. This area of New York City is home to thousands of Black people. Batman's real job is to control criminals dressed in black, which decoded means Black males in Harlem. The criminals, while played by White actors, are dressed in black clothes in Batman movies and in the mid-1960s television series. Gotham in the symbolic perception represents Harlem.

The majority of the criminals confronted by Batman wear dark clothing. This means that they are dark characters. This also symbolically represents the criminal as a dark and/or Black man who carries out crime in the city. Black people, more than any other group, are associated with crime in the city.

The Batman comic strip was used as far back as the 1940s to quell the fears of White people regarding the growing Black presence in Harlem and other big cities. Batman, the rich super-hero, was on the case. He was big daddy with big bucks and could determine how much economic and social development would take place in Harlem. Bruce Wayne was on the case, and he could handle the niggers, talk their talk and bring them to heel. The Batman character was, indeed, different from the Superman character.

Even in the early nineteen forties the cartoon characters still symbolized Black men as criminals as well as White males who, when they acted Black, instantly became criminals. The White male has always appropriated the symbols associated with Blackness as symbols of power. The black car, the black and dark suit, the black hat, black shoes and socks, black cell phones, black ink pens and black beepers are some of the symbols of Black power. This is no accident. Deep within the mind of the racist, he or she fears Blackness, and this fear is expressed through reverence for black color.

This constitutes the confusion: the White supremacist loves and hates Blackness at the same time. While blackness is a symbol for all things evil, it is also used as a symbol of power and prestige. The desire of the White supremacist to attain color is embedded in his fear and respect for Blackness; in other words, this state of confusion over Blackness sends mixed messages to Black people. Batman's character echoes the life of bats. He lives in a cave and operates in the darkness of the night. The bat's character has been linked for years with vampires (another dark creature who operates at night and sucks blood, or, decoded, is a Black parasite and bloodsucker on society) and other such ghoulish creatures.

MOBY DICK: THE MOVIE and the GREAT WHITE WHALE

What is the mystery of the 1956 movie version of the Herman Melville novel entitled *Moby Dick?* Was it simply a movie about a Captain Ahab (played by actor Gregory Peck) who was haunted by a large white whale or is there a hidden meaning? In the movie version, Moby Dick was called the great white whale.

Why is the story about a big white whale? The standard explanation given is that the author lived by the sea and heard rumors of a large white whale. Would this whale have attracted so much attention if he had been a darker-colored whale? What was the rationale for whitening-up the whale?

Was it a white coded message? In the film version Moby Dick was accorded a godlike status and was considered the most powerful whale in the ocean. He was portrayed as greater than all of the dark-colored whales combined. The darker-colored whales were easy to capture, which of course implied that they had less intelligence and less value.

The colored whales presented no special challenges or problems. They could be caught by the tons and they made the whaling expeditions very profitable. However, Captain Ahab had a big thing for the big white whale. He would often sacrifice the profitability of the easy catches so that he could stay in pursuit of the elusive Moby Dick. In Ahab's way of thinking, the great white whale had far more economic value than a shipload of colored whales. This elevation or devaluation of people and things based on lightness or darkness of color is a consistent theme in the fantasy and ideology of racism.

THE HUNT for WHITE DICK

Captain Ahab's hunt for the white whale was based on his need for revenge, mental and spiritual obsession and his desire to be made a whole man. Ahab believed that he was less than a whole man because of the loss of his leg. In the motion picture, his peg leg had a white covering. This was designed to show that his manhood had been destroyed. His objective was to capture the whale and thus garner many things, including his phallus. He had lost his leg, symbolically his phallus, in previous attempts to capture Moby Dick. The white whale had in effect taken away his "dick."

The old seaman believed that he could only be made whole in the symbolic context by the fortifying powers of the great white male sperm whale. This is why at the end of the movie he drowns while attempting to kill Moby Dick. His quest to compensate for the loss of his phallus is never realized. The creator of the Moby Dick character was Herman Melville, who was rumored to be a homosexual. Could he have created Captain Ahab because he was fascinated with white penises? If he were a homosexual, he would have spent his life pursuing sexual satisfaction from males.

Was *Moby Dick* a racially and sexually coded story about his own sexual frustrations? Was he in search of a big white penis in his neighborhood? The word whale is very close in spelling and in sound to the word male. In the world of racial symbolism, Moby Dick, the great white whale, is a metaphor for Dick, the great White male. Even the physical features of the whale in the movie version resemble that of a white penis. The intense association between the white whale, a White male and homosexuality is clear.

(A quick note. Those White people engaged in the practice of White supremacy have exhibited a relentless and restless desire to search for things in nature that are not naturally white.

They look for and glorify the great white shark, white gorilla, white monkey, white bats, a white elephant, a white horse, white tiger and so forth.)

In addition to being the whitest whale, Moby is considered the most intelligent. The movie version skillfully depicts the white whale as being able to outmaneuver any ship, virtually impossible to kill and even harder to capture.

The unmistakable inference is that because he is a white whale, he possesses a greater gift of intelligence, instinct and toughness. He presents a far more demanding challenge than do the colored whales in the sea. In essence Moby Dick is the superior whale. The name Moby Dick, in fact, carries a modern-day sexual innuendo.

The word dick has become a slang expression for the male sexual organ. At the time of the writing of *Moby Dick*, it is difficult to conclude that dick was a slang term for penis. However, it is clear that in 1956 dick was a known word for the male genitals. The whale in the movie resembles a giant white phallus splashing inside a wet vagina, and when the color of the whale is factored into the analysis, it clearly has racial sexual meanings.

The giant white phallus symbol is part of the need to have the biggest and most fertile sexual organ in the world. The phallus symbol means virility, maleness, masculinity, superiority, power and domination. The story *Moby Dick* was created to glorify the dominance and power of the white sexual organ and the being that brings it forth.

In terms of body function, the penis is the instrument that releases the sperm. And the big white creature is, indeed, a sperm whale. The word sperm triggers sexual thinking and sexual responses. Sperm is carried in the semen that is ejaculated into the vagina to begin the process of procreation. Going further, the word semen sounds like the word seaman! The connections between the words whale, male, sperm, semen and seaman are not accidental. The word associations and symbolism go like this:

Seaman means semen
The Sperm whale means male sperm
White sperm whale means white male ejaculation

Hidden Racial Images in the Movies

Therefore, the connections between the author's rumored homosexuality and his preoccupation with the words seaman, semen, sperm, white whales and white males are not coincidental.

THE GREAT WHITE GOD

In the motion picture, Moby Dick has godlike powers and rules the seas. This message is reinforced in the movie with the words of the little Black dancing boy on the ship. The little Black boy says that Moby Dick "ain't no whale but a great white god." The reference to an image of a White god is interesting. When this concept is decoded, it means that the white whale, or White male, rules the earth. This immediately indicates that the white whale symbolizes more than just a big animal in the water. It is a White male god. The penis in conjunction with the wet vagina has the power to produce life and is part of the worship of sex as practiced in ancient fertility cults. In racist thinking, the products that come from the union of White sperm and White egg are superior and godlike.

The products that come from the union of nonwhite people are little more than garbage and trash. The movie uses a little Black male child to marvel at the wonders of the powerful white whale. The use of the little Black boy signifies several things. The little Black boy represents the economical and political underdevelopment of Black males. The White supremacist compensates for his feeling of sexual inadequacy by using symbols of power related to racial masculinity and manhood. He uses these symbols in subtle yet powerful references that portray Black men as little boys.

The racial/ sexual theme has been repeated over and over again in thousands of writings, books, movies, plays and so forth. The constant desire is to belittle Black males and blow up White male as the standard of manhood. Black males are still called boys because they do not have real economic, political and military power. This group/ race of people because of inferiority and backwardness must worship at the altar of the White god forever. The white whale represents the White male as a god that must be praised and worshiped like the slave must worship the master. The Black boy also symbolizes the childlike mentality of Black males. The movie portrays the Black male characters as spooked, scared, superstitious, easy to influence, voodoo-oriented and primitive.

THE POWER of the WATER

The water has great sexual significance in the symbolism of Moby Dick. In some symbolic interpretations it means fertility or sexuality. The phallus has three primary functions: to procreate, produce sexual gratification and release bodily waste in liquid form called urine. Water is a fertility symbol and it is reasonable to conclude that the author was making reference to reproduction as well as destruction of life.

In the racial context water means that the White supremacist has roamed the seas and the land ceaselessly in an attempt to plant his seed in every nonwhite female. He has roamed the world debasing other cultures, raping other women, depopulating other societies and implanting through rape his genetic seed to repopulate in his image. Was this Herman Melville's way of saying that this activity needed to be brought under control? Why would he create and/or embellish the story of a large white phallus symbol roaming the seas unregulated and uncontrolled? When the sea is decoded, it means the whole universe. The White supremacist could go anywhere in an unregulated manner with no accountability to nonwhite populations. Was this the author's way of expressing his conscious awareness of the White supremacist's plunder, murder and abuse of people without any restraints anywhere on the planet?

According to Hans Biedermann in the book *Dictionary of Symbols* the whale is, at least in Christian belief, a symbol of the resurrection of the dead. Was Melville trying to resurrect the White male or trying to destroy White males? In the movie Ahab stuck a dark-colored harpoon into Moby Dick over and over again while cursing him as a demon and evil force. What was he trying to tell us? Another interesting connection is between the words great and white. Moby Dick was called a great white whale. The connection between great and white is profound. A modern example of this is the use of the word greater in connection with the suburbs. The suburbs, or areas with majority White populations, are called the Greater area, for example, Greater Los Angeles, Greater Columbus, Greater Boston and so on. The word greater implies bigger, better, more desirable, more rewarding, supreme, superb and the best.

STAR WARS: DEFEAT THE DARK SIDE

In the Western World's vocabulary the term dark side has a highly derogatory meaning. The phrase *the dark side* has become a popular and accepted saying. The expression represents such things as terror,

Hidden Racial Images in the Movies

horror, bad morals, ugly things, depressing matters and personal demons. In the racial context it has a much deeper significance. This is part of a racially loaded and coded lexicon that has gained a new acceptance along with the growing usage of other dark-based prefix words. Dark has become the subtle replacement for the word black.

Too many people were becoming aware of the derogatory uses of the word black so the word dark had to be temporarily exchanged to cover its racist purpose. This was the hidden meaning of the Republican presidential campaign in the year 2000. During the Bob Jones University flap between George Bush and John McCain, the real question on the table was who was the real White man? They were looking for a real White man to defeat the dark side.

If there is a dark side, then there must be a light side. What is the light side? Is the light side the good side? Which group represents the light side? It is very clear that the term light side is close in spelling and sound to the term white side.

The word light is close in spelling and in meaning to the word white. The reverse message of *defeat the dark side* is *win with the light or white side.* When this phrase is used, it is a clarion call about matters of race. Where did this obsession with darkness and blackness begin? According to the great historian, J.A. Rogers writing in, *Sex and Race* and *Nature Knows No Color Line,* the ancient people of Europe associated darkness with harmful, evil or bad things. They feared the coming of the night. The darkness of night and dark colors were overwhelming and created a sense of deep insecurity and fear. The fear of the night and darkness is extremely powerful in the White mindset. This is largely a European psychological response to the fear of color domination. It is one of the subtle reasons why Europeans try to light up the night. They claim it is to see better and, of course, this reason certainly has validity.

However, there is a strong desire to neutralize the color of the night in order to manage the fear of darkness. There are fears that dark and Black men are moving about hidden in the night, desiring to rape, pillage and destroy White society. There is also a great desire to have sexual contact with color. This theme has been depicted in pages of romance literature where the darkness or blackness of the night is portrayed as sexual, sensual, mysterious, desirable and powerful. Teasing statements such as *tall, dark and handsome* reflect sexual attractiveness and the desire to engage in sex at night.

207

RACE CODE WAR

There is a strong association between sexual pleasure and midnight, symbolically the blackest hour of the night. Darkness and blackness seem to establish fear and at the same time free the sexual inhibitions of the White mindset. Yet, even in the modern era the debasement of blackness as ugly, bad, sinful and evil continues. In the present day the most evil or degraded things in the European mentality and mythology are associated with dark or blackness. This affects every area of life in Eurocentric cultural behavior. Sex is called smut and dirty. Smut and dirt are dark or black colored. Promiscuous women are often called *sluts,* which when decoded means smut. A slut is a tarnished or defiled woman. The first three letters of the word tarnished spell tar. And the word tar is associated with blackness and darkness.

THE DARK INVADER

Do the "Star Wars" epics symbolize race war? Are the creators warning of a day when color would again rule the world and create a showdown for supremacy? Were they preparing the top White minds for the coming race war? Why would the term dark side have so much power and be repeated so often in so many contexts at the beginning of a new century if it were not a warning sign, *look you better get ready because these people are coming to destroy you.*

One of the highly publicized themes of one of the most recent "Star Wars" movies was to *defeat the dark side.* This slogan was heard on radio and television commercials, and appeared on posters in world-famous hamburger restaurants and in many speeches.

The most memorable of the early "Stars Wars" characters is still Darth Vader. He is shaped like a phallus and strongly resembles a black penis. *Darth Vader, or decoded Dark Invader,* is a physical threat to a White-ruled planet. The dark invader is a recurring notion in many fantasy motion pictures. The dark invader is either dark skinned, dressed in dark or lives in a darkened environment. When decoded, the meaning of the dark invader is that dark-skinned people are invading or threatening to invade traditional White homelands. In the present day many White people feel under siege by what they perceive as the onslaught of dark immigrants and the perceived economic progress and new arrogance of Black people. Therefore, they are subliminally calling for a big roll back. They want the dark side defeated and brought under control. In every facet of life the users of symbolism have the power to

208

Hidden Racial Images in the Movies

deliver covert and overt messages. In movies such as "The Birds" and "Star Wars" symbols are used to send strong racial messages that otherwise would be decoded, diffused and exposed very quickly. Yet the theme of one of the latest movies "Star Wars: The Phantom Menace" is *defeat the dark side, or when decoded, defeat the Black side.* The opposite message is victory for the White or light side.

If color is not associated with the ideas of good and evil, then why not say *defeat the light side or defeat the white side?* The characters of the "Star Wars" movies symbolize the pieces of the Black/White race war. The Darth Vader character is the Black evil villain. His body is shaped like a jet-black penis. Darth Vader is a threat to destroy the kingdom, or civilization, which decoded means White civilization. The war is between Darth Vader and Luke Skywalker, who is attempting to defend and save his queen, or White civilization.

It is the dark invader invading White civilization and attempting to destroy White society with his powerful Black sperm. When this is decoded, it exposes a story of annihilation generated by the power of Black sperm that is based in the Black penis. The early "Star Wars" movies are about the dark invaders attempting White annihilation.

When this distinction began to become rather obvious, the products began to change the characters by showing that the dark invader was in reality a White male hidden in a dark outfit. However, by that time the damage was done. The image was already established firmly in the popular mind. These early versions of the "Star Wars" movies are considered classics and will be replayed for many years. The disclosure of the White male in the black suit is irrelevant. The mighty voice of Black actor James Earl Jones, his walk and superior acting ability combined to establish the Black Darth Vader as the Dark Invader.

Even in the title, "Star Wars," the color hint is embedded. When the first letter in the spelling of star is removed it changes to the word tar. The word tar is associated with smut, and it means to blacken, discolor or give a black mark. The word tar is clearly associated with the color black, the tar baby and tar on a street's surface. The real title could just as easily read "Tar Wars," which when decoded means race war, or Black versus White.

These kinds of messages will gain momentum as population shifts continue in Europe, New Zealand, Canada and the United States.

RACE CODE WAR

The fear of a Black planet will rally the White supremacists to look at several options for managing population growth. The options are:

A. Reduce the nonwhite population through disease, poverty, wars, famine and genocide

B. Increase the White population through fertility and cloning programs

C. Go to war with the largest nonwhite populations before they can reach maximum power levels

D. Establish colonies on other planets and leave earth as a deserted wasteland

The subtle color conflict is one of the reasons why "Star Wars" has had such great appeal. It is also one of the reasons why, in addition to making money, technological and business corporations were encouraged to give their workers time off to see the first showings of the movie. The vast majority of young technical workers were either White or near White, with a White mental frame of reference. Did someone want this group to read and heed the message and discuss the concepts in code in order to understand the meaning without confusion? It is much harder under the current assault on the system to get the proper message out and across. In the old days it was very easy.

Then schools were segregated and the hard-line curriculum was rarely challenged. However, such games as inclusion and diversity have made the messages more challenging to deliver. The seed was planted twenty-some years ago in the original "Stars Wars" motion picture. Black people now constitute some of the top movie stars, mayors, television talk show hosts, airline owners, government officials and so forth. At the rate they are going, they will take over and run Whites in the near future.

That is why Black males in America must be incarcerated and Black people in Africa must be destroyed. Black men must be locked up so that they cannot proliferate or destroy the White race with mixed-race colored babies. This is why White-controlled drug manufacturing corporations refuse to reduce the price of AIDS drugs and refused to send many of their employees to the 13th international AIDS conference in Durban, South Africa. In the past these same drug corporations sent large delegations to the AIDS conferences. Yet in the year 2000 they decided that it was a security risk to go to Africa. Their reasons were based on the fear of White women being raped and getting the AIDS virus.

This is racism at its worst, a throwback to the thinking of Dark Continent times, when Black men were presented as sex-crazed apes

Hidden Racial Images in the Movies

lusting after blonde White women. A rape has never been reported at any AIDS conferences in the past 12 years, so why fear this happening in Africa. Furthermore, security for the Durban AIDS conference was the best ever.

There were no problems or reported incidents at the conference other than street demonstrations against the lack of effective drugs to fight AIDS.

PLANET of the APES

Probably no other depiction of White domination in the movies is more profound, dramatic and illustrative than the "Planet of the Apes" movies. The 2001 version is a slick update of the original 1976 production. The original movie featured actors Charlton Heston and Roddy McDowell. This motion picture clearly depicts the level of racial hierarchies and social demarcations. It is very revealing that Michael Clarke, a very big, heavy, muscular, dark-skinned Black male actor with broad facial features, plays the role of the big, black gorilla military leader in the 2001 version. This is about as direct as it comes to making the connection between black gorillas and Black males. This is the King Kong syndrome revisited. The differences in the colors of the apes are used to symbolize levels of superiority, intelligence and savagery. At the top of this mythical movie social ladder is the lightest color group in the ape family.

The light-skinned orangutans are portrayed as the wisest and greatest of men in the society. In this movie the orangutan is the powerful, learned and wealthy ruling class. He is the lawmaker, entrepreneur and controller of the order of things. His counsel is deemed superior, and he is the intellectual father of the society. The second level of the hierarchy is the chimpanzee. Roddy McDowell is the leader of the chimpanzees.

In this film the chimp body parts most visible on the screen are the hands and face. These are the areas of the chimpanzee that are the lightest. The chimp's character is more human than a monkey's. They are fully clothed and this makes their bodies appear whiter than is normal for chimpanzees. The chimpanzees symbolize the masses of White people, or the White middleclass. The hardworking, red-bloodied White male and female who White propaganda describes as the salt of the earth. This group espouses the virtues of decent, clean living, hard work, religious principles, family values, respect, dignity and the love of country, that is, old-fashioned patriotism.

211

On the third rung of the ladder and in the lowest social position are the gorillas. To no one's surprise, the gorillas are the Black people. However, in reality Black people do not have armies that rule over White people. Since the apes are from Africa, the armies symbolize the military juntas on that continent. The gorillas represent brutes, savages, dummies, murderers and barbarians.

The gorillas were the least admired and most feared, and they symbolize the classic notion of the dark menace. This film is the classic depiction of the social color hierarchy in White supremacy literature and lore. This movie is a very clear illustration of how symbolism can be used to perpetuate racist thinking and hidden race-based concepts. The gorillas are depicted as the biggest threat to peace and order, used as stooges to protect White society.

The leader of the gorillas is a brutal militaristic dictator, an Idi Amin type of character who firmly believes in the power of brute force and the institution of slavery. The gorillas are the brutal savage enforcers of a slave system. It is interesting how the victims of racism and slavery are now the brutal defenders of this unjust system. This movie is very deceptive. The black gorillas are cast as the brutal enforcers of a slave system who capture and brutalize of other living species, including human beings.

"SUPERMAN"

The 1950's hit television series "Superman" was based on the DC Comics popular character. "Superman" used words, images and symbols very effectively. The character of Superman was one of the greatest symbols of the power of White male supremacy. His purpose was to promote truth, justice and the American Way. Millions of young White male children identified with this display of White power. They often quoted the words, "faster than a speeding bullet, more powerful than a locomotive, able to leap tall buildings in a single bound." The social impact of these words and symbols on the youthful imagination of White males was staggering.

Millions of young White would-be super-studs imagined themselves to be more super than Superman. Years later thousands of these White dreamers became space engineers and designed spacecrafts and other super-mechanical devices to fulfill their dreams. Superman means superior man or supreme man. The Superman character is a White male with super powers. He is considered a supreme male power.

Hidden Racial Images in the Movies

The symbol of Superman is the symbol of White superiority. His character was designed to portray the same kind of public power management and mannerism as the governments of White-dominated environments. The Superman character engages in deception, the same as a racist who uses deception to mislead millions of nonwhite victims. The Superman fable is the classic story of how the White supremacist male character uses deception to dominate people and control the planet. Superman is a model of what the White male supremacist should be. It is similar to the Nazi propaganda of the superior Aryan.

Superman is a musclebound, tall White male who is clothed in red boots, with red briefs covering his genital area, symbolizing his hot sexual passion. He sports a big red "S" across his chest and wears blue tights, symbolizing the American Way. The colors of his costume, red and blue, are the same colors as the flag of the most powerful White-dominated nation. The color red stands for red-blooded, the blue color means the domination of every human being under the Earth's blue skies and, of course, his facial whiteness stands for the White man and woman.

"Superman" episodes had many dazzling special effects besides their entertainment value. What do these super skills really mean? Among his many abilities, those that deserve special attention are the ability to fly, super speed and strength and X-ray vision. What do the super abilities symbolize? First, the ability to fly symbolizes superior air power. The dazzling speed is the swiftness of the mighty war machine, the incredible strength of the military and technological, economic and political power. Third, the X-ray vision is the spying apparatus and advanced communications technology of the intelligence agencies. Superman has the power to see everything, which is the symbol of the All Seeing Eye.

To hide his real personality and intentions, he takes on a disguise that is the exact opposite of his true identity. Clark Kent is the classic White male supremacist characterization that is used in thousands of racially deceptive scenarios. Clark's character is drawn as a timid, absent-minded gentleman who would not hurt a fly.

This is a highly refined and rehearsed image contrived to hide the brutal character and nature of a racist. When racists first appeared on the shores of nonwhite people, they posed as non-threatening, benevolent characters in search of spices and trade. They said they came "in peace" to Africa, often posing as Christian missionaries before the commencement of the horrendous chattel slave trade. The Clark Kent character is the classic persona mask of racist deception.

The Clark Kent character is designed to gain the trust of the unsuspecting target with well-designed acts of deception. The character is portrayed as harmless while all the time Clark plots the demise of intended victims. The purpose of the Clark Kent character is to get the victim to let his guard down and forget that underneath the smooth, soft demeanor is a raging power with a single purpose: to dominate, control and contain. In the modern era this character portrayal is duplicated millions of times and it is called "doing business." The creators of Superman smartly chose not to give the character blond hair. They correctly understood that this would have been too close to the Nazi concept of the super Aryan. To be a credible character, Superman could not appear as an overt White racial domination figure.

BLACK MEN and MONSTERS

The moguls in the entertainment industry have fostered the belief that television and movies are harmless forms of wonderful amusement. Nothing could be further from the truth! Movies and television contain some of the most sophisticated propaganda ever devised to manipulate and influence masses of unsuspecting people. When powerful political or economic forces want to influence mass behavior and social attitudes, they use the mediums of television and film.
No one escapes the power of the message.

Movies and television shows are replayed countless times in many formats. From the big and little screen to cable, closed circuit, pay for view, video cassettes, CD-ROM, DVD and foreign markets—sooner or later everyone will see the message. The scripts from movies and television frequently rewrite history, reinterpret existing social conditions or give clues as to what is planned for the future.

This is one of the reasons why there is so much calamity and uneasiness surrounding the release of movies like "JFK," "Nixon" and "Amistad." The big, wide screen with its larger-than-life impact has a powerful influence and profound effect on the believability factor. Motion picture and television studios often employ psychologists to analyze and study the impact of movie/television images, symbols and messages. Television and film producers and directors are highly trained individuals who know how to use code words, subliminal symbols and targeted images to effectively communicate social, economic, class, cultural, racial, sexual and political messages.

Hidden Racial Images in the Movies

They understand the importance and power of every scene and line in a script. That is the reason why every line and scene is rehearsed repeatedly and reviewed for content and impact. The camera lens, the tint of the picture, the sound track—all are designed to transmit social messages that leave lasting impressions. Too many people get caught up in the planned emotional moments of a movie and they do not perceive or understand how the hidden messages are transmitted. They do not understand, for example, how *barely audible sounds* are smoothly tucked underneath the overt music in scenes designed to sway emotions and implant new thoughts.

Another example of this is the way tobacco companies use the motion picture industry to influence young people to smoke cigarettes. In the last few years there has been a slew of motion pictures that feature major actors and actresses smoking cigarettes. Notwithstanding the scandals, congressional hearings, legal cases and dire health warnings about cigarette smoking the movie moguls in Hollywood still produce movies that openly and unashamedly promote the consumption of such a deadly product. The reason for this is quite simple.

Many motion picture producers receive financial backing from the tobacco industry. The high cost of motion picture development has caused many executive producers to sell-out their ideals in return for badly needed revenue for motion picture production. The tobacco industry gets to advertise smoking on the big screen and in return they provide financing for the motion picture producers. Much of this advertising has been aimed at the minds of young people. The tobacco industry knows that the effective majority of movie patrons are between ages 12 and 35. This industry survives by addicting smokers at an early age and keeping them addicted for many years.

The power and influence of movie and television messages, code words and symbols are unparalleled. The motion picture industry must be held accountable for years of blatant and subliminal racial imaging and depictions of Black people. The individuals who control and influence the motion picture industry have been among the greatest perpetrators of derogatory cinema images of Black people. They have made an industry out of using some of the worst images imaginable to portray Black people. In the last few years there have been a host of derogatory Black male images in the movies, from the direct depiction of the urban gangster to monster flicks that thinly disguise the association of evil with darkness and Blackness. With all of the money spent on the production of motion pictures, there are no movies about the real events of Black history other than during chattel slavery times or the civil rights movement.

What is missing are important historical epics that bring to the big screen the role of Black people in ancient Ethiopia, Egypt, Spain, ruled for 700 years by Moors, the huge empire of mighty Songhai, the founding of North and South America, ancient Europe, China, India and Australia. There are hundreds of movies that depict European history, such as "The Ten Commandants" and "Braveheart." The list is endless. The majority of these movies convey very positive and successful aspects of the history of White people. These movies are extremely effective in informing millions of people about Western history.

Sadly, movies such as "New Jack City," "Boyz in the Hood," "Menace to Society," "On Any Given Sunday," "The Green Mile" and "The Krumps" do very little to improve the image of Black people. Yet, these kinds of movies are always going to be in demand in the motion picture industry. These movies maintain the racial imaging and derogatory depictions of Black people. Motion pictures like *"Die, Darkman, Die," "Alien Resurrection," "Spawn," "Godzilla and Mighty Joe Young," "Signs," "Minority Report," etc.,* play on the fears of the dark menace by associating the idea of the monster with the perceived image and characteristics of Black males. Is this the reason why so many movie monsters have dark or black complexions?

Many of the most popular movie monsters have the same physical characteristics. They are dark or black and have large nostrils, thick lips, nappy to kinky hair and broad noses. The following chart exemplifies this:

POPULAR MONSTERS	COLOR RANGE
Godzilla	Dark to Black
Mighty Rodan	Dark to Black
King Kong	Dark to Black
Mighty Joe Young	Dark to Black
Dracula	Dark to Black Hair and Clothes
Werewolf	Dark Brown
The Predators	Dark to Black
The Alien	Dark to Black
The Birds	Dark to Black
Creature from the Black Lagoon	Dark to Black
The Gremlins	Brown to Black
Signs	Dark to Black
Eight-Legged Monster	Dark to Black

Hidden Racial Images in the Movies

The monster's dark color and broad facial features have a purposeful and uncanny resemblance to the facial looks of the original dark-skinned Black males who were first brought to America as chattel slaves. These facial features have been manipulated in Southern racial characterizations and have been made to look ugly. They have been connected to the look of a monster. Black males have been imaged as monsters in White society. The monster movies take this derogatory imaging to the next level and make dark color, full noses, thick lips and dark skin a fearsome sight to behold. This depiction of the monster as a Black male creates a mental association of all Black males as monsters.

Motion picture monsters do not exist so directors have had to create a look and physical model. The monster's physical looks have to be based on some existing human population, social characteristics or social condition in order for the audience to connect with the story line. The objective is to scare the largely White audiences, and what better way than to use the group that has been portrayed as the scariest population in America. What group is more feared than dark-skinned Black males? They have become the scapegoats for all economic and social problems and failures. The motion picture industry has often catered to these fears to make tons of money and redirect White anger and hostility.

No wonder school children poke fun at people with very dark skin, kinky hair, thick lips and broad noses. These children have been conditioned through watching thousands of hours of horror movies to believe that people with these features look and act like monsters. Could this be the reason why so many school teachers refer to little Black male children as little monsters and menaces to society?

Even young Black males are now calling each other monsters. This is a result of the social conditioning that images Black males as terror-based monsters. The two "Gremlin" movies are examples of how the imaging of a monster works. From a communications standpoint, this film appears to be a family-oriented and harmless movie. But a closer examination from a racial context reveals some very disturbing messages. These movies were made in the late 1980s at the height of a Reagan Administration that had strong racial overtones.

In the "Gremlin" movies the good Gremlin is lightest-colored one with the white furry look. This Gremlin is considered a nice, fuzzy and lovable creature. When the Gremlins become evil, they change color. When they become very dark, they are violently destructive and kill people. Why do the Gremlins become evil and destructive as they become darker? Why aren't the light-colored Gremlins portrayed as the evil ones?

Why are the majority of the major and most well known monsters dark or shrouded in black? Why do most villains in the White culture dress in black or have dark shadows? Is there a hidden message in all of these images that connect darkness and blackness to evil? The "Gremlin" movies went so far as to caricature the images of some well-known Black personalities. This allowed the audience to make a mental connection between the Gremlins and Black people.

For example, in one of the scenes from the original "Gremlin" movie there is a dark-skinned Gremlin drinking at a bar, and he appears to look like Sammy Davis, Jr. In several scenes the dark-colored Gremlins dance and spin in a manner that resembles break- dancing, which was very popular in Black communities during the 1980s. The break-dancing, dark Gremlin is an obvious reference to Black youth break-dancing in Black communities. Is this a coincidence? It was not so long ago that movie producers turned dark-colored raisins into Black musical entertainers. Further, when the word gremlins is anagrammed, one of the spellings is "negrs." This is a near spelling of the word Negroes! The bad Gremlins are dark to black, they break-dance, play cards, get drunk and high, and fight with what look like Saturday night specials. All of these derogatory behaviors were attributed to Black people in the late 1970s and early to mid-1980s.

Are the movies about the social consequences of allowing Black people to move into the pristine, snow-White suburban neighborhoods with all the calamities that would bring? It is easy to get the impression from motion pictures that monster and Black are synonymous. In the "Alien" series the monsters are also very dark to black in color. In the newest installment of this series, "Alien Resurrection," the dark-skinned humans and the evil black colored monsters are eliminated. At the end of the movie, the only survivors left to build a new life are the four White characters.

The title of the movie "Die, Darkman, Die is also troublesome. This title sends a very stark message no matter how much the movie tries to portray Darkman as some kind of hero. What if the picture were entitled "Die, Whiteman, Die" or "Die, Lightman, Die"? The public would then be a little more curious as to the real meaning of the title.

The movie "Die, Darkman, Die" was advertised over and over again on mainstream television. During the advertising period, not a word of social protest regarding the title of this movie was ever heard.

Hidden Racial Images in the Movies

In the summer of 1998 another blockbuster *"Godzilla"* movie was released. The original monster was extremely violent, huge, dark and/ or black in color and given to tearing up cities. The new monster is also violent, big, black and intent on destroying New York City. The advertising theme for the new movie was "size does matter." Could this have been a not-so-subtle reference to the age-old myth about the size of Black male genitals and sexuality? One of the most telling scenes from this "Godzilla" movie is the scene that shows about five, seven-foot Godzilla monsters chasing the lead White male and female characters around Madison Square Garden.

To keep the monsters at bay during the chase, the White male turns over a bale full of basketballs. For a freeze-frame moment, the Godzilla monsters appear to have basketballs in or near their paws or hands almost in a dribbling motion. What is the connection here? Are the seven-foot Godzilla monsters being connected with the seven-foot tall Black basketball players who play in Madison Square Garden? A few months later, a television commercial featured NBA and Toronto Raptors superstar Vince Carter playing basketball against a Godzilla-like creature! Again there is the more-than-subtle connection between Black men and dark-colored monsters. When these kinds of messages are played out on the social level, it comes out like this: "We've got these Black gangs and thugs [remember the "gorillas in the midst" statement made by the Los Angeles police officer while beating Rodney King] roaming the streets with powerful rapid-fire weapons, wreaking havoc and making it unsafe in American cities. We need more and bigger prisons and greater firepower to stop them."

As a matter of record, there is a huge-selling book entitled *Monster* about a Black Los Angeles gang member and gang life in the about a Black superhero. Why is "Spawn" imaged as a disfigured and deformed creature? Why is he killed and cast down into hell with a dark Satan? His sidekick in hell is an extremely treacherous "doo-doo smelling varmint." Back on earth, Spawn's best buddy is a White male who betrays him and marries his Black wife, and they have an interracial child. This would never happen to a White superhero like Superman.

In the summer of 1999 theaters featured another remake of "Mighty Joe Young" which was originally made in the 1930s. This is the same period of history when Black males were openly called apes and were hired to play ape roles. King Kong and Mighty Joe Young are interchangeable characters designed to link the movie apes to the behavior of Black males.

This is achieved by giving **King Kong and Mighty Joe Young** human characteristics yet subliminally linking the apes' behavior and very dark, menacing presence with the racial image of Black males. The apes are dumb, lazy, prone to violence, physically powerful and oversexed, with insatiable desire for blonde White women.

Other classic examples of racist movies is the *Predator* series. In both the *Predator* movies all the aliens are dark and very tall, like Black professional basketball players. They wear dreadlocks and have thick, full features. In *Predator Two*, the Danny Glover version, the movie opens with the L.A. police fighting inner-city gangs (code words for Black youth). Is it just a passing coincidence that young Black males are now being called predators and super predators? This kind of depiction is not limited to the monster movies.

Films like *Jackie Brown* and *Midnight in the Garden of Good and Evil* also depict Black males and females in less than glittering images. Every Black individual character in the movie "Midnight in the Garden of Good and Evil," from the stinky voodoo woman and the older man walking an invisible dog to the transvestite is the worst kind of racial image and depiction ever shown on a movie screen. Even in the scenes about African American high society, the young Black males and females are trashed. They are called whores and sluts by the transvestite stripper!

In Jackie Brown there are three major black male characters. Two of the characters are drugs and weapon dealers and the third is a big inarticulate manchild. All three of the males are untrustworthy, violent, childlike, really stupid and subservient. The Jackie Brown (Pam Grier) character is a Black female who can no longer be trusted, at least not by a Black male.

The major Black male character, O'Dell Robbie, played by Samuel Jackson, uses the word *nigger* regularly in open conversation with the White characters as if the word is standard English used routinely by White people. It's worth noting, however, that none of the White characters in the movie ever uses the word nigger. In the end Jackie Brown sets-up the lecherous O'Dell Robbie. To accomplish this, she entrusts two White male policemen to help her entrap the Black male. Her closest ally is the White bail bondsman who appears to fall in love with her. She eventually builds a trusting and almost loving relationship with the kind, understanding, faithful and smart White bail bondsman. Movies are extremely powerful imaging devices and must be controlled.

Hidden Racial Images in the Movies

The imaging of Black males as monsters must be studied very carefully to understand the very powerful social and political ramifications.

"KING KONG"

The persistent theme of the big Black male raping the White female is at the heart of the White supremacist culture of racial imaging and symbolism. One of the most dramatic symbols used to illustrate this theme is the big black ape, or big black gorilla. Many movies and social depictions have been used to develop images that portray Black males as big monsters. However, one of the most brazen images is the linking of an entire race of males to apes and gorillas.

Among the most memorable illustrations is King Kong. When the terms king and kong are decoded, they mean ding and dong. The dong term means a big penis, and ding means dim-witted or without intelligence. It is the same as saying the ape is a big black nigger with a big dick and no brains. The Black stud syndrome all over again. No other image has been laid at the feet of Black males more than that of having oversized, horse-like genitals and no brainpower.

The most blatant symbolism of King Kong is of the darkest-skinned Black male with a big penis who desires to rape or have sex with the blonde White female. In the minds and perceptions of some racists the concepts of rape and White females having sex with Black males are identical. The "King Kong" movies are part of a tradition that has unashamedly portrayed Black males as animals and wild beasts. The racial message of the "King Kong" movies is that Black males worship White and near-White females whom they believe are the most desirable and superior females in the world and they would do anything to have a White female.

Black men are little more than large wild animals with children's minds who think with their penises and not with their brains. The King Dong image fits the racial fantasies and racial stereotypes of Black males that exist in the minds of many people. In the 1976 version of "King Kong," when the leading White male character discovers that the blonde female was with Kong, he makes a very strange comment about the giant ape's possible intentions with the woman. He wonders aloud if the 50-foot giant gorilla might have sexual desires for the tiny blonde White woman.

This suggestion about the sexual desires or intentions of a giant ape has little to do with the actual King Kong character. Even the most

This is a depiction from King Kong advertisements promoting the 1933 movie. In this scene he is terrorizing the streets of New York City. The giant *dark male* menace from the *dark* continent of Africa is carrying a delirious and half-naked (implying that she was raped and kidnapped) blonde white female.

Hidden Racial Images in the Movies

This illustration is one of the most glaring examples of the symbolic linking of black males to monsters. This is an interesting comparison with the 1933 **King Kong** movie advertisement and the year 2000 **Got Milk** promotion with NBA star **Kevin Garnett**. The shots are remarkably similar. Each character has intense rampaging eyes, wide-open mouth, dark skin or color and both have an African connection. The tall buildings in the GOT Milk ad were even similar to the ones depicted in the 1933 Kong advertisement. Accidental? Don't bet the house on it! This is also like some of the scenes in **Godzilla 1998** of the giant *dark menace* terrorizing New York City. In the 1998 movie a number of seven feet tall Godzilla monsters had basketballs in or near their hands during a chase scene in Madison Square Garden. The video promotion of the heavyweight championship fight between Lennox Lewis and Michael Grant in April 2000 fight played on the King Kong vs. Godzilla theme showing the two men stalking the city towering like dark giant monsters over the tops of buildings. NBA star Vince Carter made a Gatorade commercial that pitted him in a one on one game against a Godzilla looking creature under the cover of *Vince Carter vs. Jurassic Park*.

ILLUSTRATION PHOTO CREDITS
King Kong -RKO Pictures
Kevin Garnett Got Milk -National Diary Association
Godzilla - BBC News and TOHO CO., LTD.

racist mind would understand that Kong could not possibly have sex with the tiny female. It would be physically impossible. So what is the purpose of such a ludicrous statement in this movie? The racial message associates the King Kong character with the Ding Dong character, that is, the wild, sexually-starved Black male with the big penis.

To underscore this sexual theme, a long, black, oily log is slid across the top of the fort to lock the door of the compound where the natives live. The log symbolizes a long black phallus sliding down the vaginal shaft of a female. The idea of the female having sexual intercourse with or being raped by Ding Dong is thus subliminally implanted. This scene also implies that Kong has been coming to this location regularly for sex with a number of hot, animal-like Black females. This theme is consistent with the racist idea of the black, dumb, crazed ape with big rolling eyes and a big erection.

This sex-crazed image is further instilled by the camera shots of Kong's eyes as he first approaches the blonde White female in distress. His eyes were wild and deranged. This gives further substance to the absurd allegation that Kong has a sexual desire for this little White female who is no bigger than the size of his hand.

At the heart of the King Kong creation is the belief that Black males are rapists and sexual molesters. If given a chance, they will use their oversized genitals to impregnate White females. This movie reinforces the belief that Black males are a constant threat to rape White women and thus dilute the White genetic pool. This also showcases another side of racist perversion, which is the fascination of many racists with watching Black males have sex with White females. In a racist mind, it is the same thing as watching an ape or wild beast have sex with his woman. The phenomenal rise of animal sex is tied to this kind of racist perversion.

The King Dong character plays on this very bizarre desire: the image of a well-hung black ape copulating with a virgin White female. This is a strong reference in racial code to bestiality. This also feeds the lie that Black men are sex-crazed and sex-starved beasts who are obsessed with the beauty and sexuality of White females. According to this big lie, the Black male would pass over more than ten Black women just to have one white woman. This idea is made very clear in the "King Kong" movie when the chief of the "wild natives" offers the White captain six Black females in exchange for the one blonde White female.

Hidden Racial Images in the Movies

The chief reasons that King Kong would be pleased and would really love to have the White female. Kong would value her as his highest and greatest offering. The chief believes that Kong would treasure and value this woman far more than the Black females he was prepared to offer. In the chief's mind one blonde White female is worth far more than six or more Black females. He probably would offer more if he had more females on hand. The chief believes that the blonde White woman is far more desirable and superior to his Black women. In the world of racial symbolism, the chief and King Kong are both examples of wild, primitive, dark, savage beasts.

The only symbolic difference between the chief and Kong is size. The chief believes the White female is more beautiful; he therefore concludes that Kong would react the same way. The chief has to believe this White woman is superior. There could be no other reason for his offering of six or more Black females for one blonde White woman. The White males turn down the chief's offer without hesitation or second thought. This whole scene sends a chilling racial message: Black females, especially the darker- skinned variety, are the most savage, inferior, undesirable and in no way equal to the value of a White woman. The racial degradation of the dark-skinned Black female is alive and well. The message says that the White woman is so valuable that no nonwhite woman can compare or even come close to her level of value, superiority and greatness. Under the basic concept of White supremacy, the White woman is the most valued, beautiful and desirable and is the highest stage of womanhood. She is the queen, the embodiment of goodness and motherhood. In racist lore the Black woman is inferior, loud-mouthed, a bitch, non-feminine and a prostitute. So long as these kinds of hardcore racial images exist, Black females can never be equal to White females. This low grading devaluation of the Black woman—especially dark-skinned Black woman—is part of the racist desire to degrade her and at the same time his desire to have sex with Black females in a dark (notice the word dark again) alley. The racist does not value the Black female as anything more than a whore. He will sneak around, have sex on the workplace desktop or solicit Black females who sell sex on the corner in the dark of night. This desire to have sex with Black females is part of the sexual rites of manhood for many White males. There is a belief among them that they are not real men unless they have sex with a Black woman who is, according to racist sexual lore, a wild, sex- crazed animal.

225

The White supremacist wants to portray Black men and women as sub-animals, sexual freaks and hot bitches and will use many venues to achieve that goal. The capture, enslavement and display of Kong, decoded, means the capture of Black slaves and their transport to the New World. Black people were similarly captured, enslaved and sold or put on display. The placing of Kong in the bottom of a huge ship to transport him from a mythical racist African setting is the same as putting slaves in the holds of the old coffin vessels.

Kong's futile attempt to fight the racists by climbing up the tallest building in New York City represents his attempt to attack the power of White supremacy as symbolized by the male phallus. It is interesting that he is finally slain atop the then tallest white building in the world, the Empire State Building. This symbolizes Kong's failed attempt to overtake the White male by destroying his ability to reproduce White children. The White male phallus represents the sperm and germ cell of White civilization. In the racist symbolic sense, Kong wants control of White society and White females and therefore has to be destroyed. Again, the threat of the dark menace rears its head. The "King Kong" characters are among the many racial symbols designed to depict black males and Black females in a derogatory manner.

What Must Be Done to Address Racial Images in the Movies

Black movie roles with Black actors and Black-oriented scripts must communicate messages/ visions about Black people becoming self-reliant and overcoming White supremacy domination. Where are the motion pictures that portray Black people in the present and in the future living and developing without White domination? Where are the movies that project Black people in powerful command and control positions that they developed, organized and brought to fruition?

The media is a propaganda and public relations tool to be used to create well-balanced and correct images. The perpetuation of images that continue to feed racial stereotypes must be stopped. One way to stop these images is through awareness and taking action based on understanding how these negative images affect social relations between Black and White people. Study the role and image of Black people in both big and little motion pictures. Pay attention to everything, including such things as the background setting, camera angles and set colors.

When a Black individual appears on screen, watch very closely for any overt or subtle references to color or race. These references, clues or codes are used to send a racial message beneath the radar screen.

Hidden Racial Images in the Movies

There may not be a line in the script that uses the Negro or African American or some other direct racial word. However, if a racist is involved in making or writing the movie, they will find some way to communicate a racist message using a code word or a racial symbol.

A racist can use many things to trigger racist reactions, thoughts and behaviors. For example, a White actress could make a racial reference by talking about a big snowfall in a movie, with the line, "Look at the beautiful white stuff falling from the sky." The falling snow might be beautiful; however, this line can and often does contain a double or hidden color/racial meaning. Or a Black actor could remark, "Oh those bananas are so dark", and if there is no other reference to race in the movie, bet your bottom dollar that this statement is a racial color code message. The "bananas are so dark" statement is a message about Black sexuality.

On the surface both of the above comments sound innocent and unattached to anything racial. However, beware: this is where the trap is set. Any color-based word such as white, black, dark or light must be carefully understood when it is used in a motion picture. This is because it is the modern way to get in a race message without being exposed.

The "White stuff" reference could be a racial trigger term designed to establish a certain reaction to the way the Black character is acting in the movie. The actor may be acting like he or she is in control of the White people in the movie. The words are placed there to give the White viewer a coded reassurance that they are in control regardless of what the Black character says or portrays. In most cases when a Black person is in a movie with White people, there will be some subtle, covert or overt reference to race and color. When a color code word is used, watch how it is used, who uses it, what the camera focuses on when the word is said and what is the reaction.

SELECTED BLACK MOVIES and TELEVISION SERIES to WATCH and STUDY

There are many Black-oriented movies that have constructive or educational themes. The selected list below indicates those motion pictures that have attempted in some fashion to address the problems created by racism. There are others that could have been included in this list, which show examples of what to look for. While most of these efforts do not answer every question or solve all of the issues, they represent an approach or attempt to expose the situation, and they show Black people unifying to solve their own problems.

RACE CODE WAR

ANTWONE FISHER - 2003

This is about a young dark skin Black male trying to deal with his feelings of anger and abandonment. He is raised as a foster child and was sexually, physically, and psychologically abused. The early childhood sexual abuse issues of Black males are rarely if ever depicted on the big screen. Far too many Black males have been abused as children and have not received counseling to deal with hidden histories of mistreatment.

The movie used symbolism such as Fisher's visions of food, farm fields, the huge dinner tables (as seen from the eyes of a child), the Sunday family gatherings and the touching/ holding of hands in an effective manner. These were symbols of mental health, healing, and bonding.

The most powerful scene was the opening of the doors to the hidden living room to reveal a council of elders. When this is decoded it means the opening of the gates of heaven where the ancestors live. The dreamlike scenes between Fisher and the dark skin matriarch seated at the table symbolized the return of the lost and stolen black man to the motherland.

The most troubling part of the movie was the color-coding of the dark skin individual as the bad guys (except for the dark skin matriarch). We just can't seem to get past this color-coded issue even in positive movies. The mother that abandoned him, the abusive foster parent, the female child molester, Fisher's father and Denzel's insensitive father were all darker skin individuals. Many of the most positive characters including Fisher's girlfriend, Denzel's wife and his newly discovered female cousin were all lighter skin. Despite this issue this is a very effective, spiritual and moving motion picture.

ALL POWER to the PEOPLE- 1997

This is one of the better documentaries about what happened to independent efforts to unify and develop Black people. This piece focuses on the dismantlement of the Black Panther Party. It clarifies many misconceptions about who did what to whom.

BABY BOY –2001

This movie highlights the emasculation of Black males. The systematic raising of Black males to be "boys" is addressed in an effective manner.

Hidden Racial Images in the Movies

BAMBOOZLED - 2000
Effectively deals with how Black people are purposefully encouraged and manipulated into playing roles of Black buffoons and racial stereotypes. It also exposes the use of some racial and color code words.

BELLY - 1998
This is a very intriguing and controversial movie about the way in which Black males are used and recruited to sell drugs and to participate in drug and Black political assassinations.
It implicates the hidden powers behind who and what really runs the drug empire.

BERNIE MAC SHOW- 2003
The Bernie Mac Show is a let down. It has so many flaws that on the surface many of the roles are similar to those of the big-eyed darkies so prevalent in 20th century films. However, there is a subtle yet effective lesson in the script that says an individual can be Black and function in a White world without losing awareness of self.

This series should be studied carefully to understand the modern portrayal of Black images in White settings.

BUCK and the PREACHER -1971
One of the first pictures to deal with Third World and nonwhite coalition building.

CLASSIFIED X -1998
Melvin Van Peebles does an outstanding job in exposing how racial images have been used to degrade and manipulate Black people. Highly recommended!

CLAUDINE -1974
This movie illustrates how Black families and Black people can pull together despite conflict and solve problems without the assistance of or reliance on White people.

CRY FREEDOM -1987
One of the first significant stories about apartheid in South Africa. It centers on the struggle of Steve Biko, who probably was one of the greatest and most under-appreciated voices in the anti-apartheid movement.

RACE CODE WAR

COSBY SHOW -1985
This series broke new ground in an effort to present a new image of Black life. The unfortunate part is that it was a comedy and not a serious drama and that it gave the impression that the race problem had been solved since the Black people in the sitcom were doing so well. However, despite these drawbacks, the Cosby Show was able to slip through many important clues about how Black people can manipulate the system to their advantage.

CRY the BELOVED COUNTRY -1959
This is one of the first motion pictures to expose the conditions of apartheid in South Africa.

DAUGHTERS of the DUST -1991
The story focuses primarily on the women descended from the slaves who have preserved many of the traditions, beliefs and languages of African ancestors. Only the matriarch, an 88-year-old mystic, refuses to leave the island for Northern /urban life. She stays in order to preserve her spiritual connection to mother Africa. This is a must see movie.

DROP SQUAD –1995
 A very interesting movie that specifically addresses the problems associated with so-called Uncle Tomism, sell-outs and cultural disconnections in the Black community. At least it raises the issue and offers an approach.

DEEP COVER - 1992
This movie exposes the powers that be and manipulation behind drug proliferation in the Black community.

DO the RIGHT THING -1989
A very good movie that exposes the explosive nature of benevolent racial domination within Black communities.

FINAL COMEDOWN-1972
This movie attempts to address the question of what would happen if the black community were to engage in a violent and protracted arms war against the White community.

Hidden Racial Images in the Movies

GET on the BUS -1996
The first and only major motion picture to date to deal specifically with issues related to the historic 1995 Million Man March in Washington, DC.

GLORY - 1989
This is one of the few films to show the pivotal role of black soldiers in the Civil War.

HOLLYWOOD SHUFFLE -1987
This is one of the first movies to address how Black people are co-opted by the White-dominated media to play degrading Black roles. The movie took a strong position against playing degrading roles that sustain deplorable images.

JUNGLE FEVER -1991
One of the first motion pictures to examine racial integration relationships from a thoughtful Black viewpoint. It deals with the problems and deep racial issues associated with miscegenation. It also adds additional exposure of the impact that the chemical epidemic has on the Black community.

LIBERTY STANDS STILL –2002
The story is about how an invisible sniper with a covert operations background uses modern technology to hold the female co-owner of the world's largest gun manufacturing company hostage in order to kill her husband in retaliation for the death of his daughter. This movie reveals how guns and drugs are proliferated in the Black community. The sniper is played by Wesley Snipes. It is rather interesting that the last name of Wesley Snipes is very close to the spelling of the word sniper (Snipes and sniper). This is more than a coincidence. Black males are increasingly coded as snipers and covert killers.

The timing of this film's release is even more disturbing given the tragic and senseless deaths and nationwide headlines surrounding the capture of John Muhammad and John Malvo in the Washington, DC, area for the murders of ten innocent people during October, 2002. Under no circumstances can or should innocent lives be taken for any purpose. However, this horrible series of crimes brought out the use of many coded words and phrases. For example, the crime-solving tip—white van—when decoded means White man.

This tip, in addition to the racial profiling of the sniper as a White male, was the reason why white vans with White men were being stopped. The use of the Bushmaster .223 to perform the killings is also revealing. Why use the Bushmaster weapon at the time of a Bush presidency? Does the term Bushmaster have a subtle or coded meaning? Could this mean, in reverse order or in word association, Master Bush? The arrest of the two Black males as the snipers happened during the time of a strategic election for control of the U.S. House and Senate.

The vote in the mid-term congressional elections of 2002 was clearly on racial grounds. The sweeping Republican victory was attributed to a large White voter turnout that in no small part was spurred on by the revelation that a dark menace was stalking and killing people in the White community. In decoded language it meant that White people and communities were again under siege, even though a number of the murder victims were Black and nonwhite.

LUMUMBA-2001
This is a must see-motion picture that depicts the short but explosive political career of the great Patrice Lumumba.

MALCOLM X -1992
A monumental effort in portraying the life of one of our greatest Black men. While there is too much attention given to certain elements of his life and not enough to Malcolm's struggle to unite Black people here and abroad, it still contains enough nuggets of information to expand awareness.

MISSISSIPPI MASALA- 1991
This movie attempts to bridge the gap between Black people here and Black people and dark-skinned people in India. Very few black people know that there are millions of Black people in India and Pakistan. Here is a broad effort to show that Black people exist all over the world and must begin to see their commonality despite custom and language differences. It is only the major movie to date that has attempted to address this issue.

Hidden Racial Images in the Movies

NOTHING BUT A MAN -1964
Presents a very moving portrait of the struggle against hardcore racism in the South and the ability of Black men and women to work together to solve their problems in spite of the ugliness of racial domination.

PANTHER –1995
An excellent movie about who and what was behind the destruction of the Black Panther Party. A must-see movie.

PUTNEY SWOPE - 1969
The first major motion picture to address the issue of Black people gaining and using power in the corporate-controlled environment, this film exposes the myriad of racial games played to keep and regain control.

RAISIN in the SUN - 1961
This is one of the movies that looks at the issues of racial integration from the perspective of ordinary Black people. It deals with their fears, struggles and desires relative to interacting with White people in a racist and hostile social environment.

ROSEWOOD -1997
This movie raises awareness about the hidden impact of violence and raw racial supremacy. It reveals the existence of Black-dominated and relatively self- sufficient cities with independent financial, educational and housing systems. It shows how white supremacists use any pretext to destroy efforts to build Black independence.

RIVER NIGER -1976
Shows how Black families are welded and held together despite being set-up and surrounded by sell-outs. It reveals the level of secret penetration into the Black community.

SANKOFA -1993
This is one of the best motion pictures to address the many historical inaccuracies surrounding the slave revolts here and abroad.

SCHOOL DAZE -1987
The first and only major motion picture to openly address the color-code issue in the Black community. It is a very important picture that must be understood.

RACE CODE WAR

SOUL FOOD- 1997
The strength of the Black family to overcome great obstacles is not talked about or portrayed enough. The "Showtime" series is interesting though not as penetrating as the movie.

SOUNDER- 1972
This movie displays the strength, dignity and character of Black people living under the harshest and most oppressive racial conditions in the Deep South. This seems to be a forgotten lesson in some quarters of our community.

THE GREATEST-1977
Portrays the astounding power of a Black man who believes in himself, makes sacrifices and commits to achieving a specific goal. This is a Black man who has no doubts about who he is and what he can achieve.

THE LONG SHIPS -1964
The only major movie to connect Black people with the ancient Moors who dominated Spain and Europe during the Middle Ages. While the ending of the movie is typically racist, the historical connection between Black people and the Moors is powerful and binding.

THE MAN -1972
This is the first movie to pose the question: what if there were a Black president of the United States. What would he do and whom would he serve?

UP AGAINST THE WALL-1991
Directed by Ron O'Neal, produced by Jawanza Kunjufu, and starring Marla Gibbs and Salli Richardson. This positive movie promotes Black family values, and addresses negative peer pressure, teen sexuality, and drug abuse.

THE WIZ-1978
The color codes here are very interesting as are some of the subtle messages about racism.

WAITING to EXHALE -1995
This movie is one of the more civil attempts to address the critical issue of Black male/female relationships. At least this movie presents redeemable Black men and holds Black women equally accountable for making constructive changes in their lives.

CHAPTER FIVE

RACIAL SYMBOLS

A racial symbol is any material thing, visual object or an individual, place and event that are used to deceive and maintain the domination of a targeted racial population. A racist will use symbols to trigger a thought, speech, or action that has a racial objective. For example, Black elected officials are often used as racial symbols of progress. This is magnified even more when it is the first time a Black individual has been elected, selected or appointed to a certain political position. This kind of representation is known as the first Negro syndrome which is racial symbolism at its finest.

The racial symbolism that is portrayed as a racial gain is in many cases after careful scrutiny nothing more than part of a racial shell game. Racial symbolism does change the material living conditions and the dependency state of the effective majority of Black people. What it does change is the material living condition of the individual who is used as a symbol. Racial symbolism must not be used as a substitute for racial justice.

If racial domination were being dismantled there would be no need to use symbols or to use glorification ceremonies such as the first Negro syndrome. If racism were being truly disassembled, the correct response to the advancement of a black individual would be, *"we are truly ashamed that it took so long for this event to occur. We are sad that because of our racial discrimination and injustice we have caused your people so much harm and developmental delay. This is only the beginning and we will work harder every day to correct all of the racial problems that we have created.*

The first Negro syndrome becomes nothing more than a celebration of three hundred years of evil by using racial symbols and racial propaganda to cover it up. The symbols cannot change the reality of the continued evils of inferior housing, education, and economic underdevelopment. The use of racial symbols signifies a desire to continue divert attention away from the real issue. The only symbolism that works is when the ghetto and inner cities are eliminated and Black people are totally self-sufficient.

In a racist mind many things can be used as racial symbols. Large animals such as black horses have often been used as racial symbols and they are subtly linked with the images of Black males. Black professional football players are called beasts and studs. Black professional prizefighters are labeled as stable mates. Both are code words for the animalization of Black males.

Horses are also used as color-coded symbol. The shiny black appearance has often been compared to the oily dark skin of Black people. Dark colored raising were transformed in 1987 into soul singers that sung popular Motown recordings such as *Heard It Through The Grapevine.*

RACIAL and COLOR SYMBOLS

Item	Symbolic Meaning
Black Shoes	Shiny Dark Negroes
Black Garbage Cans	Black Trash
Black Garbage Bags	Black Trash
Black Gym Shoes	Toughest Shoes
Black Cleats	Rugged Shoes
Black Stick Shift	Black Phallus
Black Horse	Black Power
Black Cow	Black Female
Black Cat	Trouble
Black Dog	Mean Dog
Blackbird	Evil
Black Car	Sex
Black House	Wicked Castle
Black Bugs	Pestilence
Black Roaches	Filth
Black Flies	Nasty
Black Boots	Sex and Power
Black Socks	Coolness and Playboy
Black Panties	Ready
Black Bras	Hot and Sexy
Black Stockings	Beautiful Legs
Black Bag	Danger/Business/Espionage

Racial Symbols

Black Wallet	Money
Black Book	Women/Stud
Black Rhino	Power and Virility
Black Bull	Potent
Black Airplane	Spy/ Mysterious
Black Shorts	Sexy Body
Black Hat	Bad Guy or Authority
Black Dress	Slim and Sexy
Black Bear	Peril
Black Bow Tie	Special Event
Black Gloves	Crook
White Ball	Power
White Box	Surprise
White Fence	Family and Stability
White Knight	Good Warrior
White Shirt	Upright
White Sugar	Sweetness
White Salt	Spicy
White Bread	Staff of Life
White Paper	Intellectual
White Sale	Reduced
White Shoe	Top Notch
White Boat	Luxury
White Pearl	Rich
White Sand	Beautiful
White Hot	Aphrodisiac
White Chocolate	Integration
White Cat	White Female
White Dog	White Male
White Head	Brain
White Panties	Virgin
White Sheets	Sleeping
White Walls	Clean
White Washing Machine	Clean
White Horse	The Leader/Champion
White Gorilla	Freak
White Bird	White Female
White Purse	Church Lady
White Necklace	Married Female
White (Polar) Bear	Friendly

"THOSE BIG, BLACK, UGLY THINGS"

In a racist social infrastructure many items take on a racist meaning and purpose. The following story is an excellent example of how an object that is designed for a special use becomes part of racial code talk and the racial agenda. The case in particular is the story that happened around 1985 in the city of Columbus, Ohio. It is the strange story of 360-gallon trash containers. The Columbus City Council and the Mayor's office were embroiled in a political controversy over the implementation of a new trash-collection system. At the core of the issue was the replacement of the existing metal garbage cans with new and larger trash containers in the backyard. The city staff convened several community meetings in both Black and White neighborhoods to hear concerns regarding the new system. Some residents and community organizations bitterly complained because they were upset about no longer being able to use the old-fashioned metal cans.

The major issue was that large numbers of residents would have to take the trash out at night into the alley and put it in the new, huge 360-gallon trash receptacle. Most of the complaints came from White females who imagined all sorts of evil emanating from the large, black trash container. Many of these concerns had the ring of legitimacy and would not have garnered special attention except for the fact that they kept referring to the color of the 360-gallon trash containers. They made this a real issue.

The color or size of the trash containers did not surface as a major issue or concern in the meetings held in the Black community. The majority of the containers were black in color, rotund in physical appearance and close to six feet in height. In the dark of the night some of the White females intimated that the containers resembled large, dark beings. Many of the White respondents made constant reference to the size and, most importantly, to the color of the containers. They kept referring to the containers as *"those big, black, ugly things."*

Why was the color of a trash container such an issue? Would it have made a difference if the trash containers were white, silver or yellow? What was the nature of this strange fear, and why did it create so much turmoil in the installation of a more efficient trash-collection system? Was it because each large, black trash container symbolized in the White mindset a large, dark man lurking in the dark shadows? To many of the women, the trash container top looked like the head of a large, black phallus. When decoded this symbolized a big Black man with a big black phallus waiting in the bushes to rape the White female.

In the White supremacist lexicon, the word rape has become a code word for black male. The distorted belief that all Black men want to rape White women goes all the way back to the dreadful days of chattel slavery. In order to terrify and instill fear in the mind of the average White person, the Black men were labeled as beastly and lustful sexual predators with huge horse-like genitals. White females in particular were instructed to stay away from the Black savages. White men were told to implement laws that severely punished the Black men who violated the scared code of behavior. The core belief in this view has not abated in the racist mindset. There are countless examples of Western World memorabilia and historical documents that point to this continuing fear. Among the most powerful, enduring and larger-than-life examples are monster movies like "King Kong," "Mighty Joe Young and Godzilla", which play to the deep fears associated with the dark menace.

That is how a racist mindset associates the color of a thing or object with a race of people. "Those big, black, ugly things" were big, phallic-shaped Black men waiting in the alley to commit crimes against White people and rape White females. Let's explore this a little deeper. Is it an accident that so many large trash containers are black-phallus shaped objects? Look around and observe the trash containers that are black or dark brown in color, from office trash containers to the large trash receptacles in backyards. A large percentage of trash containers today are dark colored, either black or dark brown. This is not to discount some of the more feminine-looking trash containers. And in some cities the trash containers are metal and silver colored. Still, in the present day, the majority of trash containers are black or very dark brown. Why are trash containers dark or black in color? Have the words trash and black become synonymous terms? In his revealing book **Dictionary of Symbolism,** *Hans Biedermann says that black in Europe is a color with negative associations. He cites phrases such as* **black man, a house in shadows, and a dark snake** *as examples. Words and symbolic meanings are carried over from one generation to the next despite physical geographical differences.*

RACE CODE WAR

The word black in Europe has the same connotation as it does in most White-dominant cultures. In the White supremacist world the word black is generally synonymous with trash, dirt and filth. While this is not true in all situations, in general, it is true enough to conclude that it is not random or accidental. What is the real message? The message is that whatever comes out of a black penis is trash. The historical treatment of Black people gives birth to this conclusion. White racists have treated Black people like trash and disposable items for almost 400 years. From South Africa to South America Blacks have been and remain on the bottom, classified as useless eaters, etc.

The historical record is replete with evidence of maltreatment and mistreatment. The most glaring and enduring example is, of course, the slave trade. Chattel slavery by some estimates killed between 35 and 100 million Black people during the middle passage. This is a testament to and proof positive of the suffering of beings who originated from Black genetic stock. It indicates that the Black individual is considered garbage, and there is plenty of history to validate this statement. The trash receptacles are a constant reminder that Black people are symbols of trash.

RED, WHITE and BLUE

Red, white and blue have coded color and racial meanings. The colors red, white and blue are the symbolic representation of White imperialism, domination and power over the past 500 years. The deep affiliation with and reaffirmation of the red, white and blue were brought on by the horrible attack on the World Trade Center on Tuesday, September 11, 2001. This increased the visibility, association with and symbolic meanings of these colors. *(Innocent people, no matter what race or color, should never be victimized because of murderous terrorist plots of revenge. The taking or massacre of innocent lives is totally unacceptable anywhere on the planet.)*

When supremacists perceive themselves as under siege (such as by massive immigration) or under physical attack, they use the red, white and blue symbolism to send racial, political and military messages. The red, white and blue colors awaken the inner core of the White mindset to the threat of the dark menace and the need to fight for the survival of the race. When threatened, race and color symbolism take front stage as part of the counter-offensive.

Racial Symbols

The rallying cry is against the darkest evil. The threat is called the *darkest day in history, dark threats of violence, dark terror or the dark side*. All of these racial and color references reawaken the fear of the dark menace within the White collective. The use of racial and color symbolism has even motivated and reconnected many of those young generation X White people who had declared separation from the concept of the White supremacism. Thousands, maybe millions, of generation X young White adults have purchased new lethal weapons and gas masks and are advocating war or signing up to fight. This is because they do not understand the power of the implanted color symbols, such as red, white and blue. Embeds are mental, emotional and spiritually implanted concepts.

When required, signals can be sent about impending danger or annihilation from dark-skinned or Black populations. The implanted embed uses racial and color symbolism to connect darkness and Blackness with danger and evil. The embedding process is so effective that many people do not consciously recognize the power until triggered by an incident or situation.

There are hundreds of fiction and non-fiction movies made by White producers and books written by White authors warning of impending attacks against White people by the coded dark menace. These warnings signal the White mindset to get ready for coming battles. This kind of evil color imaging begins at birth and continues until death. The tragic incident of September 11, 2001, formalized the fight against the dark menace.

Red, white and blue serve as one of the most powerful triggering devices to rally the racial and cultural survival responses. Color embeds are implanted in the social order in many formats. Among the most effective are the symbols of red, white and blue, which send messages of racial solidarity that reaffirm White power and invincibility. This is the affirmation that was used to establish racial solidarity.

The red, white and blue are also the same colors that spread White supremacy imperialism. From the red, white and blue of the British, also nicknamed the Redcoats during the Revolutionary War, to the red, white and blue of Australia, these color combinations were spread while conquering the nonwhite world. The most famous examples of red, white and blue are the national flags. The flag symbolizes people, groups, corporations and ideas. Saluting the flag means that one agrees with and supports the ideas and concepts that it represents. It also means that you give allegiance to the things it symbolizes or represents.

Pledging allegiance to a flag doesn't just apply to a nation, state or city. There are thousands of corporations that have flags, flag symbols or emblems. The employees of the corporation pledge allegiance to the corporate mission, goals and objectives. This is done the moment they are employed and agree to the mission and purpose of the corporation.

This allegiance is constantly reinforced through commercials, advertisements, pep rallies, United Way campaigns, corporate outings, etc. When the employees wear tee-shirts, jackets and uniforms bearing corporate flags and emblems, they bind themselves to the corporation and to its symbols and purposes. These color combinations and symbols are selected with great care and purpose. It is part of a massive ongoing propaganda and indoctrination process. In our racial and social order there are millions of social, commercial, religious and cultural things that are red, white and blue.

Many corporate commercial colors are based in red, white and blue, including logos and trademarks such as the circle trademark of Pepsi Cola. An equal number of commercial products and services are based in related color combinations of blue and white or red and white. The red-blue or red-white combinations carry the same symbolic and political meanings that are attached to red, white and blue. This is part of a massive propaganda campaign based on colorization. Red, white and blue are emotionally, spiritually, psychically and psychologically linked to the ideas of God, race and country. However, red, white and blue have different historical meanings for Black people and White people. For Black people, the red, white and blue symbolizes enslavement and degradation.

These are the official colors of a slave-holding nation, population and generation. These color combinations hung high on the slave ships operated by barbaric slavers who tortured and enslaved millions of Black people. The Confederate and Union flags were both red, white and blue. The designs were different, but the colors had basically the same meaning of White domination. The choice was between Union domination, which could be benevolent but required greater dependence, or Confederate domination, which was harsher and yet more progressive in terms of economic independence.

Racial Symbols

Black people were told by each side to pledge allegiance to one or the other of these flags. Red, white and blue have deep spiritual meaning for millions of White people all over the world who have a deep emotional connection to the red, white and blue because they are inseparable from their historical mission of accumulating power and control. Each color represents an important spiritual, emotional, psychological and cultural connection. It is a psychic driving force that propels White people to dominate.

The emotional attachment to red, white and blue is inextricably bound to an emotional attachment to White supremacy domination. Black people are equally attached to the emotional meaning of red, white and blue. Black people in White-dominated nations believe that they are an abandoned people. They do not believe that the Black people in Africa want them to live there. This is why so many claim America as their ancestral homeland.

They are quick to point out how Africans do not like Black people in the United States and other areas of the world. They have been fed the same lies everywhere to divide and conquer. They have been groomed to have mental and emotional attachments to White supremacy domination.

Any color combination that is close to or resembles red, white and blue triggers the racial ideas associated with these colors. The meanings that are attached to red, white and blue individually are automatically reassigned and subliminally transferred to the other two colors. The most visible and recognized manifestation of red, white and blue is the flag, often called Old Glory, that represents the United States.

The colors of the flag have been explained in various ways. One of the most used explanations is that the red stands for valor, zeal and fervency; the white stands for hope purity, cleanliness of life, and rectitude of conduct; and the blue stands for the color of heaven, reverence to God, loyalty, sincerity, justice and truth. These Masonic-style explanations are used to deflect the hidden meanings of red, white and blue.

It has been widely reported that the symbolism of the flag was interpreted by the Father of Our Country, President George Washington in the following manner: "we take the stars from heaven, the red from our mother country, separating it by white stripes thus showing that we

243

have separated from her, and the white stripes shall go down to posterity representing liberty." This was a slave-holding and White-dominated nation, where Black people were considered 3/5 of a person. They had no human, political or social rights and were not factored into the equation of the construction of a nation.

In this kind of highly racist environment President Washington could have only been making references to the development of White people and a white nation. Some of the coded phrases in Washington's statements include the following: "White stripes shall go down to posterity representing liberty." The word posterity means the offspring of one progenitor multiplied to the furthest generations. It is the planting of the seed that grows and multiplies. This was a signal that the new frontier called the United States would be a White-developed and controlled domain.

The descendants, or those who will be in control, shall be White and will remain so for generations to come. His use of the phrase "color red from the mother country" was designed to symbolize the connection of blood or the same gene pool as those of White people in Great Britain and Europe. This coded reference also means that the Americans have the same bloodline and pedigree and commitment to the expansion of White supremacy domination. After all, they were also White people and from the same good stock as other Whites from the mother country.

The use of the word mother is very revealing. It means parent, origin of birth, genealogy, bloodline, pedigree, descent, ancestry and so forth. It is a code word used to establish biological, cultural, spiritual and family connections. It is a deep-bonding term that basically unites rather than divides. It says that we are brothers and sisters, and we have the same family language, traditions, customs and roots. We are one, united group of people, despite our squabbles and geographical distances.

White people in America are the long-distance cousins, brothers, sisters, nieces and nephews of White people in the British Empire. The series of battles between the British and Americans was misnamed the Revolutionary War. It was in reality a prolonged, violent family feud that somehow involved their cousins over how to divide up the new spoils of the Western World.

Washington's reference to the stars from heaven implies that the colonies' later-renamed states were intended for White people as White settlements. The stars are white, symbolizing Whiteness as being godlike or celestial. This also symbolizes the divinity or divine mission of White people to rule over the beasts of the earth. His reference to "separation by white stripes *thus showing that we have separated from her"* means the branching off and expansion of the White collective. It is akin to leaving home or the womb of the mother to go out into the world, like branches growing outward but still remaining part of the whole tree. This expansion would be achieved by establishing another domain of White power apart from yet still part of the existing White collective. The stripes symbolize the expansion of the White collective to control all corners of the earth. White power never really divided, it only expanded into additional components in order to grow stronger. This was part of the expansion of White supremacy domination.

The colors of the flag could have been any combination—green, gray, brown or yellow. However, red, white and blue have significant and important racial and color meaning. When decoded, it is clear that the color red stands for being red blooded and belonging to the same gene pool. This identity is often reflected in such sayings as red-blooded American, Frenchmen or Englishman and is a very common phrase that is often used to describe the bonding of White manhood.

The color white clearly stands for White people. Among the three colors, white is the most important. It is used subtly in the American flag by placing the stripes or bars in the middle so that it serves as the glue that bonds the red and blue. The white also stands for all of the racial symbolism associated with Whiteness. White represents White male, White female, White children, White family, White nation, White house, white picket fence, white socks, white milk, white bread, white teeth, white gloves, white suits, white cars, white mansions and all of the other objects of whiteness in this area of the world. It is the color white that makes the red and blue important.

In the racial and color context the blue color means blue skies. When decoded it means that everything under the blue skies, i.e., the land, air and sea, will be under White supremacy domination. Red, white and blue when decoded are part of the color symbols of white supremacy domination. A significant number of White populations and White-dominated geographical areas use red, white and blue or red and white. When red, white and blue are used for any purpose, the symbols must always be examined or audited for possible overt or covert racial content and color meaning. The following is a selected list of the national colors of White dominant populations that use red, white and blue or related color combinations such as red and white or blue and white.

NATION	COLORS
United States	Red, White and Blue
Great Britain	Red, White and Blue
Australia	Red White and Blue
France	Red, White and Blue
Netherlands	Red, White and Blue
Yugoslavia	Red, White and Blue
Paraguay	Red, White and Blue
Russia	Red, White and Blue
Austria	Red and White
Czech Republic	Red, White and Blue
Norway	Red, White and Blue
New Zealand	Red, White and Blue
Croatia	Red, White and Blue
Scotland	Red, White and Blue
Luxembourg	Red, White and Blue
Switzerland	Red and White
Iceland	Red, White and Blue
Slovenia	Red, White and Blue
Canada	Red and White

THE CONFEDERATE FLAG

The Confederate flag is the most dominant symbol of White Southern culture. Notwithstanding, it represents one of the most reprehensible symbols for Black people in North America. It is similar to Jewish people looking at the Nazi Swastika and saluting and pledging allegiance. This is what the Confederate flag represents in the Black perceptual experience and mindset. Jewish people will not allow one Nazi flag to be sold in any major store in North America. The Jewish Anti-Defamation League would raise holy hell and be ready to go to war. The Confederate flag is a symbol that is as devastating as the Nazi flag. Yet the Confederate flag is sold in many stores in the United States without any protest, political sanctions or economic repercussions.

The genocide in Nazi Germany that killed millions of Jewish people in Europe lasted over a 12-year period. The Confederate flag symbolizes the horror of chattel slavery from *1619 to 1865*. This was a period of 246 years. During this 246-year period, 150 million Black people were lost, murdered, butchered, drowned and destroyed during and after the Middle Passages, the most horrible voyages in recorded history. The Middle Passage was just the beginning of the horror. What followed on the White plantations was even more inhuman and barbaric. An untold number of Black people were killed and destroyed.

Many Black people have not recovered from effects of those horrid days. Still, in the present day, the Confederate flag is sold as a commodity and is accorded tacit acceptance in the north as well as in the South. The Confederate flag design is sold in many variations on items such as wallpaper, bumper stickers, cups, coffee mugs, lunch boxes, toy cars, writing pens, shopping bags and wrapping paper.

This racist flag stands for the death of millions of Black people destroyed during hundreds of years of slavery. The Passages themselves were the voyages from Africa to the Americas, Canada, Europe and the Caribbean that brutally uprooted and transplanted millions of Black people into slavery. The Confederate flag stands for the brutal rape of Black women and horrible relocation to a strange, cold land. It stands for the loss of a collective memory of a once united people. The Confederate flag triggers all the things that Black people pretend do not exist. After all the illusion of racial camaraderie is gone, one of the greatest symbols of racism flies free and unabated without any sanction or penalty. These flags are legally produced and sold all over the country.

There is no prohibition on the production and public display of the Confederate flag. The Nazi Flag while not outlawed in America is banned in France, Germany, Italy, Hungary and it is politically prohibited in the nation of Israel. In America it is political, economical or social suicide to wave or sport a Nazi Flag on the back of a car or in an office building. Only hardcore and overt racists engage in this behavior. Yet it is okay to have or wave a Confederate flag on a car, bumper sticker, television commercial, racing cars, cans of tobacco and so forth. There are millions of small hand-held flags manufactured, sold and waved every year in the nation.

RACE CODE WAR

The continued manufacturing and selling of the design of this flag means that Black people do not matter and are still slaves in the minds of White supremacists. This is similar to the sports symbols that are used to poke fun at the Red man and woman. The names and heads of Native Americans are on baseball caps, tee-shirts, football and basketball jerseys and so forth. *For example:*

Chicago Blackhawks
Atlanta Braves
Cleveland Indians
Cincinnati Reds
Washington Redskins
St. John's Redmen (now called Red Storm)

What's in a name? Everything.

The *racial conquering mentality* dictates that the nonwhite victim once destroyed or subdued must be degraded and made a laughing stock or used for money making and entertainment purposes. Active degradation or stirring up feelings of degradation are never out of the racist's mind. The Confederate flag is an accepted and protected racial symbol. The Confederate flag signals White supremacy and it is alive and well and has not faded. Racism has realigned itself and become more deceptive. It triggers racial emotions, racial pride and racial solidarity. It is a quiet and yet very drastic *racial reminder* of the days of hardcore racial domination. It is also an inaudible yet potent reminder of the days of Black subhuman status and classification as property, beasts, rapists and monsters.

The Confederate flag represents White Southern culture just like the big white mansions, which are also symbols of racist oppression. They are the local regional copycats of the big White House in Washington. These big white houses are manifestations and representations of oppressive racist culture. The plantations were miniature colonies that reflected the domination of White supremacy over the nonwhite world. During this era, the British Empire was the greatest power in the world. World domination had not been transferred to the United States.

Racial Symbols

The plantation had among other things big white or very light-colored houses, and these units represented a White heaven, the place to go when the slave died. The racist belief was that the Black would remain a slave forever. The white house represented the royalty, such as the White king, queen, princess and prince. The symbol of the white picket-fenced house is part of the idealized image of the great American dream. Each American was trained to have a little white house to live in and to remember his purpose and focus his direction on White supremacy domination. The white house with the white picket fence is one of the most *racially dynamic* symbols in society. *The normal, quiet picket-fenced white house is a subliminal and constant racial reminder of the idea of the big White plantation. White houses all over the country are racial embeds that trigger ideas associated with Southern slavery and hardcore White supremacy domination.*

The Confederate flag triggers all of the antebellum *racial ideas and concepts*. It keeps the concept of slavery alive in the minds of Black and White people and in most cases without many of them understanding the full ramifications. The mindset of the hardcore White supremacists is very informative. Rather than give up the brutal, barbaric and genocidal system of slavery, the southerners went to war. They lost thousands of their youth and kin to maintain the most horrible system of dehumanization and injustice the world has ever known. They despised and disregarded Black people so much that they would rather fight, kill and be killed by their White brethren than change an outdated, inhumane system. This is deep. Yet they have the nerve to wave this flag symbol of raw, naked, horrible racism in the face of Black people.

Racists become inflamed when Black people will not allow the kind of abuse practiced under the brutal racial management system. The White supremacist gets angry when not allowed to continue to abuse and deceive. This is part of the sport of White domination. Yet the flag symbol of outright White supremacy domination is sold without sanction or political repercussions.

What this means is that as long as the Confederate flag is allowed to exist, the slave legacy will still live. Slavery and nigger will be synonymous. The flag says it all. Every time the flag is seen, it is a subtle yet overt reminder that Black people must be watched, controlled and kept underneath the pile—even murdered if required. The real purpose of racial symbols is to trigger racial, physical, and emotional responses and be a constant reminder of how things must be. When the flag waves on a pole, hangs on the rear bumper of a car or is for sale in a store, it carries the following meanings:

RACIAL MEANINGS of the CONFEDERATE FLAG
Chattel Slavery of Black People
Black Servitude
Murder and Genocide of Black People
Destruction of the Black Family
Whippings, Beatings, Lynching of Black People
Sub- Humanization of Black People
Dumb, Stupid Darkies
Sexual Rape of Black Women and Men
Mental Rape of Black People
Physical Degradation of Blackness
Rape of Mother Africa
Nigger Jokes and Public Humiliation
Spiritual Debasement
Mental Genocide
Emasculation of the Black Man
The Klu Klux Klan
Cross Burnings
Welfare
Discrimination
Economic Rape

THE CLOWN
What is the meaning of the clown in White culture? Is it just a creature to laugh at or to poke fun at? What is the role of the clown in Western society? What are the symbols of the clown? What is the purpose of a clown, and how does it fit into the concept of racial domination? The modern day clown in White supremacist folklore is a character with big, nappy hair in the style of an Afro, a really big nose, large behind, large mouth, big eyes and great big feet. These are the physical characteristics that have been linked to Black people in myriad jokes and racist banter.

There are historical products with pictures of enlarged and distorted Black facial features. This is a way to openly poke fun at

Racial Symbols

Black features and the way Blacks look without being called a racist. If this is not true, why are the features of the clown considered gross distortions and yet are the subject of great laughter?

Why doesn't the clown have small eyes, small nose and thin lips? Why not poke fun at these features? The clown symbolizes Black people and poking fun disguises racism as good clean family fun. When an innocent Black child laughs at a clown, he or she is in truth laughing at the image of Black people. This is disguised by painting the clown white to give the impression that it has nothing to do with race. The colorization has a dual purpose. It tells those Whites who look or act like a clown that they are stupid and physically ugly. They are visually ugly because they then look like niggers.

That is also why most Black people are thought of as comical or as clowns. It is common to hear Black men referred to as clowns and buffoons. There is a real mental and social association with the concept of a clown and Black males. The large, nappy hair means unruly, wild and savage; those with kinky hair are unmanageable and inferior. It also means that the people who have this kind of hair are viewed as clowns, inferiors and dangerous. This is the kind of humiliation the Jews went through in Nazi Germany. One of the most talked about physical characteristics was the Jewish nappy or kinky hair. The closeness of the Jewish hair to that of the nigger apes was what Nazi leader Adolph Hitler took as a clear sign of racial and mental inferiority.

Hitler believed that this genetic trait must be destroyed to avert the possibility of it affecting the superior White gene. He concluded that this genetic trait was a sign of inferiority and of nigger intrusion into the bloodline. The hair of Black people has been the subject of so much ridicule that many have attempted to change their hair.

Blacks have fried, dyed, curled, straightened and even burned their hair in an attempt to change nappy hair to straight hair. This behavior is also reflected in the wearing of wigs that can be blonde, auburn or other colors. Only in the 1960s did this trend change to any appreciable degree with the Afro wig. And as fast as this trend appeared, it disappeared. The new fashion of long dreadlocks appears to be gaining some acceptability in certain circles. However, it is still a minority of Black females who wear this style due to their belief that black hair is ugly and inferior.

RACE CODE WAR

The same is true with other physical characteristics of the clown, such as the large nose. The large nose is clearly a trait that has been historically associated with Black people. Even though there are White people with large noses, this trait is not associated with them as a primary physical characteristic. The large, wide flat noses of Black people have been the butts of many jokes. The issue of the large Black nose came into question again with the revelation that the world's greatest pop performer, Michael Jackson, had his nose completely reshaped and recolored. His apparent disgust for his natural facial features was apparently so great that he completely changed his whole physical appearance. He altered his skin color, hair, nose, lips and eyes. Legendary soul performer Patti Labelle in a striking interview on the Oprah Winfrey Show said, " I had that sucker cut off," a direct reference to her big Black nose. Her apparent goal is to look more European or White.

This is because the noses of Black people have been maligned and called undesirable and unattractive. The laughable image and distorted vision of the clown with its big nose subtly reinforces this belief. The big feet of the clown subtly refer to the big feet of Black males. This also has been for years a racial stereotype: that Black males have big feet, large hands and oversized penises.

The size of Black men's feet has been stuff that racial folklore has been made of for hundreds of years. The feet of Black males have been the subject of millions of White jokes and ugly racist lampooning. The hidden meaning attached is the notion that Black males have "big dicks." This racial stereotype still persists even in the new century. The clown with big "feet" is part of the Southern concept of the big, dumb, black servant with big feet and bug eyes moving and talking slowly while scratching his head like the Lightening character in the television series "Kingfish."

Former NBA superstar Bob Lanier was a Negro poster boy because of his 20-plus shoe size. White sports announcers on television would often crack jokes about the size of his feet under the pretext of having fun. However, this gave credibility to the racist notion of niggers with big feet. This has also been done with other Black basketball and football players in reference to the size of their hands and feet. It was common in the sports media to hear comments about the size of the hands of basketball superstar Michael Jordan. The notion of Blacks' big feet is firmly embedded in the white consciousness.

Racial Symbols

The inflated lips of the clown is also an important facial characteristic. The clown's big lips are a clear message that these features are unsuitable, ugly and should be avoided. In this culture people with big lips are considered ugly. When has a dark-skinned Black woman with big lips ever won a major beauty contest? Big lips have been the stuff of jokes for many years. Black people have been abused, lambasted and made the laughingstock in horrible racial jokes. Probably, with the exception of the eyes, the lips have been the subject of most cartoons, derogatory images and humiliating laughter.

Lip reduction surgery among Black people has reached historical levels. The number of Blacks who hate and even talk about big lips is legion. No other physical feature has been the subject of as much laughter or talked about more than the lips. Such jokes get more laughs when told by Black comedians to Black audiences than the White clown gets by accenting big lips and spreading bright red lipstick over vast areas to simulate large lips.

Black people with big lips are taunted, laughed at and made to look undesirable. It was not unusual to hear Black females poke fun and laugh at characters like JJ on the CBS television series "Good Times." Comments that stood out were references to his big lips or *"them big liver lips."* This again is part of the strange paradox of racism. The lip enhancement industry is doing a booming business because White females want to have bigger lips.

The clown also pokes fun at the buttocks. Most clowns have large behinds that emphasize the unattractiveness and funny look of large *derrieres.* However, this has been a harder sell, especially among Black males. This cultural trait is hard to destroy. However, there has been some progress even in this area. Many Black females are engaged in counseling, medical help and physical exercise in efforts to live with or lose their large behinds.

They have been told that big butts are undesirable. Many Black women have had nervous breakdowns and mental problems because they wanted smaller behinds and a more acceptable, or White, look. Many of them have spent countless hours in the exercise room hoping to reduce the butt or have endured surgery to remove parts of their posteriors.

The media and the movies in particular feed us a diet of skinny White females. These women often have no discernable behinds and appear to be as much male as female. Black women have been called hot, and many are considered physical anomalies because of the size of their buttocks. The clown represents an effort to poke fun and to establish the behind of the White female as the standard for all females. This is another attack on the physical and mental being of Black people.

THE SLAVE

The symbol of the slave in White supremacist folklore is a Black person. Black people and Black history are the most dramatic symbols of human enslavement. The color black has been largely degraded and demonized in White folklore and culture. In the majority of instances where this word is used, there are visual or verbal references to Black people here or abroad. This association and these symbols even go beyond the tales of the bondage of the Jewish children in biblical stories. The whole concept and idea of slaves, bondage and servitude are wrapped around the enslavement of Black people in the Western Hemisphere.

In the modern White world just the mention of the word slave automatically denotes black people and not Jews despite the many biblical legends. Slavery existed for thousands of years in many parts of the world. Slavery did not begin with the enslavement of Black people. *The ancient Romans enslaved the White British; the Arabs enslaved Turkish women; and the Chinese enslaved the Tibetans.* There are many kinds of enslavement. During the early part of the 20th century, trafficking in White female prostitution was called White slavery. The term White slavery clearly denotes the difference between regular slavery that is Black and a special kind of unusual enslavement. White slavery means that White females have been forced into servitude and bondage against their will.

The connection of words like slavery to a specific color is part of the color and racial indoctrination. The goal is to establish a mindset that equates the color black with slaves and relegates Black people, regardless of their present social condition, to slave status. In the concept of Whiteness, peace and freedom are associated with white birds or white doves. Enslavement and slavery are also connected to such things as terror, blackness and darkness. One of the dreaded symbols of enslavement and repression in the White world was the *black-suited, black-booted SS* in Nazi Germany. Wearing black with red emblems was designed to strike terror in the hearts of those opposed to Nazism in Germany.

The association of black to slavery has had carryover impact even within other areas of White culture. For example, those working in professions that are associated with servants and servitude are usually dressed in black. The traditional colors of the professional servants like butlers and maids are still basic black. Some may argue that this is because if food spills on the outfits it does not show up as easily. And this argument does have some merit. However, it loses credibility when it is viewed in a racial color context. The words Black, slave, and servant in White supremacist culture and mindset are interchangeable terms. The wearing of black as in the traditional dress of the maid and butler symbolizes servitude and obedience. If not, why not wear brown, blue, white or red? The servant relationship also exalts the employer to the status of a controller.

That is why many maids in areas like England refer to the woman of the house as the mistress. Many catering companies, when serving very powerful customers, will dress their employees in black servant outfits. This attachment to black and servitude spills over into traditional White religion. In traditional religion the church minister is supposed to be a servant of God and the servant of the people. The traditional dress for a minister is a black or dark suit or black robe. The Catholic priest and nun who commit to living a life of service, servitude and sacrifice dress in black suits, jackets and dresses. The nun and priest are supposed to be the servants of God and mankind.

A Christian minister or priest who wears bright colors is considered disloyal to his role of servitude and sacrifice as the humble servant of the Lord. A counter argument could be made that the color black in the priest and nun's attire is to express the values that are associated with being conservative and maintaining social stability. And this argument would have some merit if all things were equal and the systematic degradation of certain racial groups and colors did not exist.

All things good or bad that are related to the idea of slavery, servants or servitude is symbolized by the wearing of black. This association extends to every facet of life in White supremacist culture. In politics the highest elected official in the land is the President of the United States. He or she is considered an elected public servant. The President rides around in a long, black car and is attired in mostly dark suits. The dark colors also have very interesting connotations. The black color is a symbol of power and status in the White world. The black tie and evening dress are considered the highest and finest style. Marriage for men requires a black suit or black tuxedo while women are married in white, which means purity. It is indeed a paradox and strange juxtaposition. However, despite the contradictions, overwhelmingly blackness is derogatory and symbolizes such things as slavery, servitude and evil.

THE DOMINATRIX

Another very powerful and glaring example of the symbolic connection of Blackness to slavery and servitude is the sexual practice of the *Dominatrix,* tradition and ritual of racial domination. This sexual domination practice uses color and subtle race symbols in plain sight. The practitioners of this form of sexual gratification unashamedly use language, color, sex and race codes to express domination and control. In this bizarre behavior the use of dark colors and dark references are direct and blatant expressions of color domination. In the practice of this kind of sexual domination, which is often referred to as bondage or *sado-masochism,* in magazines, movies and real life interactions, the *Dominatrix,* or Mistress of Bondage, is the dominant individual.

She is the female equivalent of the master and must be served and strictly obeyed. The Dominatrix is usually dressed in a black or a dark-colored outfit. She administers justice, training, obedience and punishment to the slave. The slaves are taught in these roles to obey the Mistress, or *Dominatrix.*

In some movies and magazines red outfits are worn, but in the practice of S&M and bondage the dominant color is black. Most of the major paraphernalia used in the rituals for punishment, discipline and pleasure are black or dark colored. The rubber suits worn by the *Dominatrix* are black and sometimes red. The rubber gloves are usually black. The black rubber suits appear to be very shiny and sensual looking. It makes the female wearer appear heavier with a bigger butt. Bigger bones and bigger behinds are generally attributes associated with Black females. The shiny rubber suit gives a more identifiable black, oily look. Dark Black people have a shiny, oily skin that is highly reflective in the sunlight. This has historical and present day relevancy. Many Black males earned their income shining white men's shoes with, in most cases, black polish because most of the shoes worn by males were the color black (get the connection).

Shining shoes is/was part of the Black—White male power relationship. The Black male had to look up or keep his head down while the White male sat or stood on top and looked down. At one time Black people were called "shines". The *Dominatrix'* rubber suit gives a very shiny look, which that adds to the impression that the individual wearing the suit is a Black man or Black woman. The boots and shoes are black. The full or partial facial mask is black or red. When dressed in full regalia, the *Dominatrix* is symbolically a Black woman. In the S&M

world, many of the Dominatrixes are larger women. The whole range of color associations in the practice of S&M and bondage is very revealing.

The two groups of people who have suffered the most under White domination are the Black and Red people. In the world of slavery and bondage, the two dominant colors are black and red. These are the two colors that are most associated with slavery, bondage, pain, humiliation, servitude, degradation and genocide. It is also interesting that in sexual domination games the White male or female will allow the entirely black-dressed *Dominatrix* to apply pain and humiliation to their bodies while they worship her black shiny body.

It gives the impression that a Black female is punishing them for the years of injustice. This is probably why Black females are hired to act as Mistresses in sexual domination games. An increasing number of Dominatrix women are big-butt, Black females. The color fantasy sometimes spills over into a need for real life *very black* women to administer abuse and humiliation. Is this desire a deep reflection of a guilty conscience that for centuries has enjoyed a racially superior status because of the degradation and abuse heaped on Black and Red people? Are these Whites acting out a secret desire to be dominated, spit on and urinated on by people of color? Is there a deep fear of Black domination, and are these games played out to alleviate those trepidations? This is why there are many magazines that feature the deep fantasies of White males being dominated by Black females or females dressed in hard, black colors. The White female in black is the dark Dominatrix.

SELECTED BLACK-COLORED
S&M and BONDAGE PARAPHERNALIA

Dildo
Whip
Corset
Clamps
Rubber Suit
Rubber Facial Mask
Rubber Boots
Shoes
Stockings
High Heels
Spikes

Rubber Gloves
Gold
Chains
Skirts
Dresses
Bracelets
Plastic Gloves
Belts
Pants
Panties
Briefs
Bra
Fetish Wear
Latex Wear
Collars
Feather Boas

SELECTED S&M LANGUAGE
Hand Spanking
Whipping
Paddling
Restrictive Bondage
Corporal Discipline
CBT and Verbal Abuse
Cross-dressing Training
Boots and Fetish Worship
Foot Slaves
Rope Art
Abductions
Voyeurism
Sadomasochism
Asphyxiation
Deprivations
Kidnapping
Burning
Tantric Rites
Nurse Role Playing
Female Supremacism
Submission
Discipline

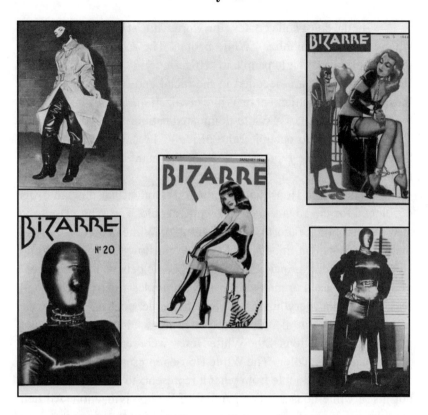

The Dominatrix plays a game on sexual domination. The most popular colors used in this game of sexual power, slavery and submission are black and red. These are also the two colors that evoke the greatest emotional responses in white supremacist cultures. It is also the colors of the most abused racial populations under white racial domination. This is one example of how color-coding is used to send messages and establish values that often are associated with race.

THE WHITE HOUSE

One of the most enduring symbols of power and domination in the Western World is the White House. No other color symbol of domination is as blatant or as large. The White House is the symbol of the political and economic dominion of White civilization. What does the white in White House really mean? Is it just a color or does it have much deeper meaning?

In the color code context the word white stands for whiteness, which decoded symbolizes White people. The second word, house, means a place for White people to settle.

When both words are decoded in the racial and color code context, they mean White settlement or White civilization. The White House is the spiritual symbol of a White-dominated nation.

The men who have occupied the office of President of the United States are symbolic representations of the male head of the White family.

The White House is a symbolic reminder that this land was developed for the advancement of white people. The White House is also a symbol of the most powerful group of White people. All of the major decisions that impact the White world flow through the White House. The effective majority of White people believe in the concept of a White House. For many this symbol provides a sense of calm and reassurance that everything is all right and under control.

Many White people would have tremendous emotional and psychological reactions if the White House were renamed or if it were painted a different color. The White House represents something very different to White people from what it represents to Black people. It is not just a white house, it is a symbol of White civilization. All hell would break loose if someone or some group tried to change the color and name of the White House. This would be like removing the White collective's security and stability blanket.

The White House to most White people means their house and home. It is no accident that the number of white houses far outnumber any other color of houses in the nation. Each White family in the symbolic sense has some identity with the idea of a White House. This is illustrated in many popular cultural sayings and images. One of the most popular cultural symbols *is getting married and living in a white house or a house with a white picket fence.* Changing of the name to the Black House or Red House would imply to many White people that they are no longer in control and in charge.

The color code that is associated with the house or home communicates a strong sense of comfort and racial identity and stability as a base of operations. This symbol is very important in

Racial Symbols

preparing succeeding generations to maintain control of the social order. The home is the smallest unit of the nation and is the most powerful transmitter of values, thoughts and behavior. The transmission of values and the social development of children take place in the home. The home is extremely important to the continued evolution of the nation.

In order to achieve smooth transitions and continuity, the home environment must be solid and reasonably free of derogatory social situations. With a stable and nurturing environment, the human mind, body and soul will develop to its highest capacity. When there is chaos and disorder, the minds and behavior of children will reflect that environment. For the majority of White females, the home is a place to nest, to settle, to reproduce and to raise a family. She must have all of the symbolic and psychological trappings to effectively convey the message of the history, development, survival and future of the race. The White House is the mother of all houses in the nation. It is one of the most powerful and dynamic symbols of Whiteness.

THE WHITE JESUS and GOD

The Christian faith is a magnificent religious belief system. This is the faith that I grew up with and continue to believe. However, like many other things under White supremacy domination, this great and mighty faith has been racialized and colorized. The symbol of Jesus has been promoted all over the world to foster racial identity and establish racial propaganda that depicts him as a White male. In White religious tradition God is White. The only begotten Son is a White male. The Virgin Mary is White. The three most important figures of the Christian faith are recognized throughout the world as White people.

What color was Jesus? If He were to walk down a main street in America, would we know Him by His looks? If He lived on earth, He would have to have had an ethnic identity. What did His hair, lips and nose look like? Did He look like the actor Robert Redford, a blond White male; Wesley Snipes, a dark-skinned Black male actor; the Latino singer Ricky Martin, the comedian Milton Berle, a Jewish male, or an Arab political leader?

This is the most popular image of Jesus. Despite acceptable evidence that Jesus was most likely a dark to very dark skinned man the old whitenized images continue to proliferate. Notice also in the picture with the black couple how the male hands crosses with the female to form an X pattern. Is there a hidden message?

In 1999 there was a great controversy, which stirred the passion of a White nation, surrounding the depiction of the Holy Virgin Mary in the Brooklyn Museum of Art. It stirred so much controversy that Rudolph Giuliani, Mayor of the City of New York, attempted to freeze millions of dollars in museum funding because the exhibit called "Holy Virgin" was a dung-decorated portrait of a Black Virgin Mary. The depiction had the Virgin wrapped in elephant dung with alleged pornographic cutouts, which many people, especially White people, believed were offensive, sickening and disgusting. But beneath all the turmoil was the fact that the artist had chosen to portray the Virgin Mary as a Black female.

If the Virgin Mary were allowed to be Black, the offspring, Jesus, would be Black too. A depiction of Jesus as a Black man raised eyebrows in a painting called the "Jesus of the People" that was

Racial Symbols

published in the *National Catholic Reporter*. This depiction of Jesus caused the editor of the publication to predict that the era of the blond, blue-eyed Jesus was over. Maybe.

Hundreds of thousands of churches, businesses and schools have entrenched images of Jesus as a White male. Billions of dollars have been spent to perpetuate the image of White male godliness. The white supremacists have published millions of Sunday school booklets, billboards, movies, videos, video games, church fans, church bracelets and rings, posters, religious bumper stickers, newspapers, magazines, prayer cloths, candles, church hymn books, bibles, church paintings, church murals, choir robes, training and teaching materials and large pictures on church walls perpetuating this image of Jesus as a White male, and it has been drummed into the minds of people around the world.

Ask any child or adult whether Black, White, Asian, Latino or Indian what Jesus looked like and—/even in 2003—at least 90 percent will point to the picture of a White male. If the color of a man doesn't matter, why have White supremacists spent billions of dollars to perpetuate the image of Jesus as a White male? Color does matter.

What are the power and impact of this kind of White imaging of Jesus on the psyche of White, Black and other people? If Jesus were a White male, then White men in the symbolic sense become the image of God. The White male embodies all that is good, wonderful, clean and holy. Angels are depicted as White, heaven is a white place and, most importantly, Jesus is White. The nemesis of Jesus is the devil. The devil is always painted as a dark creature with dark clothes, dark hair and evil traits that are codified as Black. God is White and God is good.

The concept of goodness is associated with race and color. For example, the old gospel saying states, *yes, he will wash you whiter than snow*. Goodness, God and Whiteness have become synonymous terms. Badness is associated with Blackness, hell, darkness, evil and the devil.

The White symbol is powerfully attached to the emotions of the true believer because prayer is a very intimate and spiritually binding act. It is the bonding process of the faith to the believer. The mind attaches the emotions to the symbol. Since no one has actually seen God, the mind must develop some symbol of who God is. The mind is bombarded with millions of pictures, paintings, photos and emotional attachments that depict God in a White context, and the human mind has no other believable frame of reference.

RACE CODE WAR

The believer prays to the symbol that is believed to be a valid representation of God. The people who closest resemble the White image of Jesus will be viewed as the closest connection to God. God is White and the devil is Black; therefore, White is good and Black is bad and evil.

This very simple theme is one of the most effective racial symbols ever devised. It establishes a clear sense of good and bad based on color. The symbolism of the white Jesus establishes the white male as a god on earth. It is hard to go against what a god says. Gods are all seeing, all knowing, all wise and would never do anything wrong or misleading. To go against a god is to seal your fate in hell and darkness for eternity.

Messages are implanted in Black and White minds from childhood, and even in the modern world there are few Bibles or other Christian images featuring Jesus as anything other than a White male. Black and White people have been so conditioned to accept this image that they will destroy any serious effort to take down the picture of the White Jesus. They will say that it doesn't matter what color Jesus was and will accuse the advocate for change of being racist and having a color hang-up. Black and White people have shared their most intimate, emotional and venerating moments with Jesus.

People believe that Jesus is a personal savior and the giver of eternal life. And they count on Him to fight their battles. That is the most ironic and probably the most confusing part.

They believe that the same White man whom they believe is God and Jesus will do the right thing and set them free. Emotional confusion can run wild because it is extremely hard to question anyone worshipped as God. This is why Black people will believe a White man or White woman before they will a Black man or woman.

Many Black people have been conditioned to believe in the goodness and godliness of White people. Most will never openly admit to this. They will say that even to suggest such nonsense is stupid and without validity. The behavior of Black people with some few exceptions proves this beyond a doubt. Deep in the minds of Black people is the unshakable belief that if the White man says so, it must be true. The belief in Whites as gods helps to give them unprecedented credibility among Black people. No other race of people would entrust their destiny to another that has committed such atrocities, destruction, deception and death against them all over the world. Yet, the strong and silent worship of the White male image of Jesus keeps the confusion intact. *When confusion rules order takes control.* Prayer is a total mental, spiritual and emotional engagement that requires total surrender and submission. Words like *master* or statements such as, *choose you this day whom you shall serve* or *do you need a "personal savior?"* Seal the deal.

When decoded such statements reveal that people are powerless to solve their own problems. These quiet yet effective associations play on one's mental correlation with the slave master's terminology. Whitenized biblical symbolism is subliminally incorporated into the mind and emotions so that the association with the slave master is maintained through the language of the religion. The slave wants to be free from the White oppressor while at the same instant praying to a White male image of God for justice and freedom.

This emotional contradiction heightens the confusion that produces misdirection and disorientation. That is why even the slightest hint at resistance against Whiteness sends many Black people cowering and running for cover. They cannot bring themselves to oppose, hurt or defy this incorrect image of a White God. Simultaneously, the Black man is cast as the devil. The devil is dark, menacing and lives in the dark bottomless pit with no sunshine. The equation is *black man + evil = the devil.* Unfortunately there is no real concept of a Black Jesus. Any pictures of a Black Jesus changes each and every week. There is no consistent picture of a Black Jesus that can be sold or marketed as a counter or challenge to the White male image.

The White male Jesus is used to personify the idea of male perfection. His straight hair is perfect. This is consistent with the notion that White hair is good hair. His skin color is the perfect color, which means that it is white or near white. His eyes are blue, which means they are the perfect color. This is the racist image of the perfect male, which is the image of a White man.

This perfect male does not commit a sin or engage in extramarital relationships. The White image of Jesus is invented to be the ultimate prize for a female. Every woman is made to desire and have a White Jesus kind of man. This whitenized racial imagery should not be associated or confused with real belief in the Christian faith. This grand falsification creates the notion that God is white and the Devil is Black. God is God and it has nothing to do with the color codes of race.

RACE CODE WAR

WHAT MUST BE DONE

The faith should be worshipped without references to race or color. This can be achieved in either two ways. Remove all of the racial references and pictures that portray Europeanized versions of the Christian faith. Or establish a consistent Black male image of the Christ figure, with a Black Bible as the study guide so that God can be worshipped in an image that reflects the people doing the worshipping. The Black image should be displayed equally with the White in all White churches, Bibles and on the movie screen.

This is, of course, not the ideal solution. However, we cannot ever say that race and color have nothing to do with Jesus or God so long as a White male image of Jesus is hanging from the church rafters, shown on the stained windows and is the only Christ image in the Bible. Jesus Christ did not live in Europe. The whitenized version has been used to redirect the faith for racial, political and economic purposes. The Black version may offer some compensation for the years of White indoctrination. It may help some Black people to believe in themselves as a people. To believe in one-self and to see oneself as a reflection of God changes how people believe and behave.

THE WHITENIZED CROSS

Another powerful symbol is the old rugged cross. It is the most highly recognized symbol of the supreme sacrifice and resurrection of the Lamb of God. The cross symbolizes crucifixion and resurrection of Jesus Christ. According the book *Dictionary of Symbols by Hans Biedermann as Translated by James Hulbert:*
"The cross is most universal of the simple symbolic figures. The familiar Christian symbolism of the cross refers to the means of Christ execution, an instrument of excessive cruelty that, however, through the resurrection, came to symbolize eternal life."
In the early Christian era many of the symbolic depictions of the cross were as rugged dark brown or dark wooden tree colored structures. In the modern era the depiction of the cross has been changed to a whiter and smoother looking object. The most prolific symbol of the cross is the white cross.

What does the white cross mean? To the Klu Klux Klan the unveiled the white cross symbolized the uniting of the four corners of the white nation under a white god.

266

Racial Symbols

The cross is white redemption, resurrection and the salvation of white people.

The meaning of the cross is very different for black and white people that believe in and practice racial supremacy. For white people that believe in and practice white supremacy it is seen as a symbol of white eternity, white dominance, white nationalism or the bonding of the white race. For black people the cross is seen as a symbol of transformation into non-racist existence.

The rugged cross means struggling thru a strife and pain filled life that can be overcome with a strong belief and faith in another continuation of life that is based on truth, justice and righteousness.

The darker cross symbolize the ending of racial oppression and being under the yoke of white supremacy domination. When the discussions about sin and evil abound the only point of reference is to the world as it currently is. The world as we know it is dominated by racial and color supremacy, therefore, the meaning of leaving this world for a better place is the same as being freed of racial and color domination. The cross means that with struggle and perseverance we shall overcome the evils issues of race and color discrimination. Black people relate to the darker cross that is more symbolic of blackness and the culture of struggle and freedom from oppression than of dominance.

The streets are paved with gold means that everybody will be equal and enough food, clothing and shelter to go around there will be no lying, stealing and killing in that holy place. All of our troubles and worries will be over. Black people visualized a different heaven free of racial domination with a benevolent and righteous God.

The new white cross is too smooth and silky and it gives the impression that there never was a struggle. This does not jive with the emotional meanings of the old rugged cross to black people. The old cross means that there was and still is a deep burden to bear in life. The white cross portends that racism and other ugly barriers did not and do not now exist and that life is smooth without all of the rugged racial, color and social edges of the dark cross. This is a false portrayal because it omits the greatest barrier to freedom and justice and that is racism and colorism.

DETERGENT

The idea of getting whites whiter has been pushed for many years in hundreds of television laundry detergent advertisements. Most of the largest selling washing soap products contain granules of little white grains that claim to fight the most reprehensible form of color which is that something called dirt. It interesting that white granules would be used to fight the evils and dangers associated with darkness and color.

Some recent soap products have attempted to counter this perception by mixing up the colors of the granules. However, the great majority of dry soap products are still light or white. And more importantly the propaganda that is used to sell these soap products still use words that have double meanings that can easily be construed to have racial and color meaning.

Far too many of these slogans or washing instructions send double messages that portend to be about the washing of clothes but are more like messages about the mixing or social/ sexual interaction of racial and color populations. Is the act of washing clothes being used as a cover to send a race and color message? Many of the terms used in soap washing ads act like trigger words that immediately conjure up other ideas, feelings and reactions about the issue of race or color. When items like bleach are added to the dialogue it transmits an even clearer color and racial messages. Without a doubt the words bleaching or bleach have double meaning. In the clothes washing world bleaching has different role that it does in the racial and color process. In the clothes washing context bleaching is supposed to get clothes cleaner by getting at the harder to reach dirt. The word bleach or bleaching has another meaning that can be easily converted to a racial or color context. The word bleach or bleaching triggers a racial and color meaning. For example, one of the meanings for the word bleach amongst black populations has always been the bleaching cream that have been sold in the black communities for many years.

Skin bleaching is viewed as a means to help some dark skin black people to feel better by getting lighter colored skin or whitening-up. In the white communities bleaching means to remove darkness. The bleaching process has been used to breed or bleed out dark skin as in Nazi Germany or in ancient India. In both cases the objective was to bleach out color. In the language of racial miscegenation bleaching is a process of wiping out color thru interbreeding, intermarriage or sexual relations the act of bleaching means to remove skin pigmentation thru decolorization. It is very interesting how easy language with a different purpose can be transferred into a coded racial or color message.

Racial Symbols

The subtle yet powerful overlap of words like bleaching or color mixing can used very effectively to send color and racial messages under the cover of talking about something else like washing clothes. When one hears the message that says, do not mix colors or do not mix whites or lights with colors, it sends a double message that in a highly charged color and racial social order can be interpreted within a racial context.

On the back of many of the boxes, cartons or containers are instructions on how to wash white and colored clothes. The instructions make certain references about the dangers of mixing of colors. The words read more like warnings about race and color mixing than about the washing of clothes. According to the instructions on the back of the boxes or containers of the washing of colored clothes in cold water is design to keep colors from affecting the colors of other clothes in the wash.

The mixing of white and colored clothes in the same wash is in most cases a *no-no*. *If white and colored clothes are washed together and washed in warm water, the colored clothes tend to bleed into the white clothes. The word bleeding sends a double race and color - coded message.* In decoded racial and color language it means that racial integration will impact the purity of the bloodline. The surface or cover message is about how to wash clothes so that the material is not ruined. That is a good cover to send a racial and color-coded message.

The other not so detectable beneath the surface message sends a race and color communication about the dangers of color and race mixing. Is this a fear of the power of black genetic material and its ability to be the dominant gene? Notice the use of the word bleed in this commonly used statement about mixing colors in a washing machine. The word bleed comes from the word blood.

According to Webster's New Collegiate Dictionary, one definition of blood is *human stock or lineage and persons related through common descent.* Blood is also a fluid that circulates in the heart, arteries, capillaries and veins of a vertebrate animal carrying nourishment and oxygen and bringing away waste products from all parts of the body. Bleeding is the *emitting or loss of blood*. The process of bleeding in a racial context means to drop semen into another bloodstream. When a fabric bleeds into a material it dramatically alters

269

the colors of the other cloth and in the racial/color context the same thing occurs. The racial stock is dramatically altered.

This is what happens when black people enter the bloodstream of white people or vice versa. It dramatically alters the color and upsets the lineage. It creates a genetically altered human being. This baby is neither white nor black. The final definition of how this individual will be classified will depend on the existing racial and political environment.

It is safe to conclude that most of the soapbox commercials are marketed for women. These commercials are aired during the daytime most frequently during the airing of the so-called Soap Box Operas and talk shows that are aimed primarily at female audiences. Women are the carriers of the seed of the next generation (*gen-er-ra-tion*).

The double meaning messages are design to alert women of the dangers of fooling around with other racial populations. It is a subtle yet effective method that the white supremacist uses to protects his flank while working because in the back of his mind he may unsure of his woman. He is terrified by the notion that when the cats are away the mouse will play. The commercial messages act as a *mental chastity belt*. The message is clear leave them alone. A racist would say these people are dangerous to the perpetuation our racial lineage.

The double meanings of the words that are embedded in the commercials shrewdly instill racial nation building themes. Slick and undetectable that encourages females to get their *whites even whiter cleaner or to wash whites and coloreds separately*. The messages are very slick but are some the best examples of how common everyday products can carry other messages that have a hidden and different purpose.

BAR SOAP

Some of the greatest selling bar soap products in history are *Ivory Soap, Dove and Jergens*.

The names' Ivory and Dove have come to denote cleanliness as whiteness. The word white implies that an object or thing is clean, pure and perfect. Ivory soap has been the standard of bar soap for many years. Even today with anti-bacterial soap, the largest selling hand soaps are still colored white. Until recently most bar soap was white. Even one of the biggest selling colored bars is named after a white ethnic group. This bar is called *Irish Spring*.

The washing of the body with a white bar of soap has the effect of symbolically white washing the body. *The washing of the very dark or black body with a white bar of soap is a form of psychological and physical bleaching. In the racial and color context, this is an act of trying to wash away blackness and install more whiteness in the body.* The white soap lathered upon the dark or black face and body is a way for black people to subconsciously believe that they are getting closer to being white and more accepted socially. The white bar is cleaning away the dark dirt and making the body whiter and purer and the cleaner the whiter and the more passable. This bathing or showering process occurs billions of times each day without black or white people having a clue as to the subtle racial color meaning.

If the color of the bar soap has no relevancy then why aren't some of the bar soap products black? There are few if any major bar soap products that are black. Some are mixed colors and from gold, light blue or light greenish colors. However, none are black. Bar soap is a very intimate product. It goes into the most sensitive and sexual parts of the body.

When a black individual trust the use of a white bar of soap in his or her most private parts, it means that they have symbolically allowed whiteness to invade their most secret and precious areas. It establishes a deep and trusting mental and emotional attachment to whiteness at the most basic and primal level. To allow any substance or chemical product into a body orifice is evidence of a very trusting relationship. The user trusts it to make them better because they believe it causes them to be cleaner and more acceptable to society.

Black people have a triple whammy. They use it to get clean, to wash away dirt and to restore the hope of social acceptance. For women soap has even greater attachment than men. Women spend billions of dollars to buy different colors and fragrant of soap products. They link soap with ideas of romance, luxury and sensuality. They bathe their children with white colored soaps like Ivory that continues the subtle whitenization process.

The female has an even greater mental, chemical, emotional, sensual and sexual attachment to soap. The impact of bar soap is probably greater on her than the male counterpart. She is more sensitive to body odors, smell and the social dynamics attached to it. The social order place a greater importance and unequal burden on the cleanliness of the female. She must smell good, wear clean clothes and keep a clean-living environment.

The attachment of the color of a bar of soap to transmit a racial/color message is almost unfathomable. Very few people would suspect that a bar of soap could have hidden racial and color messages that help to reinforce white supremacy. This use of bar soap also capitalizes on the whole notion of good and bad. In the racial and color context the white bar of soap is considered the cleanest and it takes away the most dark dirt from the body. The washing of the body with black soap called *African Summer* would symbolize in a color and racial context that black, clean and pure also have synonymous meanings. The association of white with clean is deeply ingrained in the social order and is manifested in the color symbols of such things as bar soap. This is a powerful method to communicate a racial and color message, because most people miss the very subtle association.

ADVANCE WHITENING: TOOTHPASTE

The most recent marketing push in the toothpaste industry is the concept of whitening. The big rush in on to increase the whitening of teeth and the whiter the better. It is back door method to send new racial messages. In the modern racial construct, these messages have to be transmitted in more hidden and decoded methods. The timing of the rush for the greater whitening of teeth is very interesting. This commercial push is happening at a time when white people feel under great siege by the growth and infiltration of nonwhites within their domain. Whites are being told daily that sooner or later they will become a minority and that infidel minorities or nonwhites will decimate their ranks.

Hardcore white supremacists regularly preach that the day of white genocide is coming. They hollow over and over that white people must unite to defeat the dark side or perish. To survive they must drive the black devils into the sea. Many of the new toothpaste products give interesting race and color messages. Arm and Hammer has toothpaste literally called *Advance White.* This is a clear color-coded message about the progress of the collective white population. The message is to

272

Racial Symbols

advance white people and all that they stand for. The word advance means to *accelerate the growth or progress.* This is a very effective way of sending an open message. It is called hiding the message in plain sight.

These products are on the supermarket shelves and are seen by millions of white, black, brown, yellow and red people. *During the fall of the year 2002 a new Advance White commercial talked about a whitening guide. This was a coded reference for the classification of white, how to become whiter and what the new standards are for whitenization. Of course this was done under the guise of getting whiter teeth.*

This message also encourages the nonwhite groups to support and push white advancement. Toothpaste has a pleasant almost sweet taste. It is a very intimate product. It is very oral substance and invades one of the most scared parts of the body, the mouth. Only the most trusted things can enter the mouth. Items such as water, food and medicine are allowed in the mouth. Anything else can be dangerous and life threatening. Toothpaste is trusted not to harm, maim or kill.

Therefore, the concepts and the subtle messages are accepted at the most trusting levels of the mind. An intimate relationship is established with toothpaste. It sweetens the breath, makes teeth appear without food substances clinging in between. It gives greater confidence that it will enhance social acceptance. In modern society so-called stingy breath is socially unacceptable and unbearable in terms of its odor. The subtle messages that are associated with toothpaste and whitening cling deep into the psyche and perceptual experience. Another toothpaste is called *Close-Up Whitening.* On the cover of the toothpaste box is a picture of three smiling white people, one male and two females, and a smiling black female. The black female is attempting to draw close to the white female that is within touching and caressing distance of each other. Standing over top is a smiling white male.

The ad implies that whitening is the thing to do. That in order to be accepted and to be better the black female must attempt to become as white as possible. The black female can do this by having white friends, accepting white ideas, believing that white is always right and by having sex with white guys hovering above and around. Get close enough some whiteness will rub off.

SEX in a BOTTLE

The Pepsi and Coke bottle used to be compared to the figure of a black woman. During the early years of Pepsi and its rival Coca Cola, was sold in pop bottles. This was before the cans; plastic bottles and cartoons became a popular consumer item. The old Pepsi and Coke bottles were shaped like a female. The content inside the bottle was a very dark liquid substance called soda, pop or beverage drink. The dark liquid combined with a shapely bottle gave the impression of the curve of a female body. To be more precisely it gave the impression of a dark or black female body. Black females have often been referred to as being shaped like a bottle of coke. Today, the round can and plastic bottles have replaced the female figure.

Today, the round can and plastic bottles have replaced the female figure.

However, the color of the substance has not changed. The desire to consume the dark colored substance is greater than ever. The sale of Coke, Pepsi, Diet Rite Cola and other dark colored beverages are much greater than Seven-Up, Mountain Dew and other combined.

The consumption of this very dark substance was in effect taking a black potion into the body. In a racial and color context it meant the digestion of color. White people have consumed billions of tons of dark colored products from soft drinks to chocolate. Soft drinks have little

Racial Symbols

to no effective nutritional value, yet products such as Coke and Pepsi sell billions of units each year. What is the allure?

Some say that it is because of the addictive nature of the substance itself. Some cola soft drink products have been rumored to contain highly addictive drugs such as cocaine. However, in the racial and color context the desire for the product is based on the desire of many whites to consume blackness within their system. It has the subliminal impact of creating color. It has the reverse affect of washing with white soap.

It allows many white people to act out getting greater skin color thru the digestion of a magic color potion. In the old witchcraft images the female demon is dressed in dark and is always brewing up a special intoxicated formula. This brew is always a dark and sexual substance. It is often an intoxicant such gin, beer, wine or rum which are all dark colored substances. The dark colored substances symbolize power, mystery and sex.

This is one of the subtle attractions of Coke and Pepsi, it represents the power of sexual energy and for males the notion of virility. The subliminal message in the visual marketing packages of some of the soft drinks is a blue devil or a demon character that is barely visible to the discerning eye. This hidden message connotes a feeling of power, energy and invulnerability.

GANG-BANGING: SYMBOLS of the SET-UP
The set-up is a controlled game designed to trap and maintain
Black people in inferior and destructive behaviors

Black people do not have real gangs that control real territory. The so-called areas that these gangs call their territory are the neighborhoods where injustice, crime, drugs and mayhem are allowed to exist. They dare not cross over the border and bring into the White suburban communities open-air drug markets, loud music and drive-by shootings. They know that they would be crushed immediately.

These so-called Black gangs are desperate groups of Black males engaging in ineffective responses to racism by playing dangerous games of life and death that are centered around self-destructive activities. They are involved in distributing quantities of destructive drugs in their own communities to their own people while shooting, maiming and killing each other with guns they do not manufacture. They prey on helpless and defenseless people. They do not fight armed and well-organized people. They are engaged in insane activities that help to destroy the lives of their own people, many of whom are their mothers, sisters and brothers.

These gangs do not own and control multi-billion-dollar banks to launder trillions of dollars. They do not control huge, organized fleets of planes, trucks and ships to transfer drugs. In reality these so-called gang bangers are little more than minor leaguers who try to live out hardcore gang fantasies that have been placed in their minds from childhood.

They learned these images from watching hours of television, movies and videos that showed white people engaging in drive-by shootings and killing people. They try to imitate this behavior without understanding the social and racial consequences. They have no clue as to the origins of these kinds of destructive images, words, thoughts and symbols. In these movies, White people kill people without remorse or any sense of humanity. It is almost as if the people killed were not humans.

In the worldview of the White supremacist human life is highly expendable. Wanton disregard and insensitivity to human life are an integral part of the violence and power so pervasive in White supremacist culture. Derogatory images and disregard for human life are imitated at the crudest level by highly untrained, undisciplined and undeveloped young Black male minds. The Black gangsters emulate the worst behavioral aspects of White gangsters, yet they do not take on the best parts which, are associated with community control and development. The Black gangster does not seem to understand that if the base of his community is destroyed, his base of power will evaporate. The first rule is to keep the home community strong, free of drugs and horrible devastation. The Black gang banger and the gangster lifestyle have been glorified in the White media. It is considered as an acceptable and fashionable lifestyle.

Along the way, White entrepreneurs have made an economic windfall reaping billions of dollars from the so-called gangster culture. They sell millions of copies of rap CDs, low-cut jeans, gold chains, underwear, bandanas, shoes, eyeglasses, jewelry and so forth. These so-called gang bangers are in reality nothing more than punks and cowards. They are punks and cowards because they pick on and prey on defenseless Black people. If these Black youth were really gangsters, they would have real control over industries, shipping docks, towering skyscrapers and control major business districts, and they would control hundreds of politicians. These are the characteristics of a real gang. If they were a real gang, they would go after power. They would take on the Mafia, the international bankers, multinational businesses, corrupt politicians and the massive intelligence superstructure.

These are the worst gangsters in history! The so-called Black gangsters never use their ill-gotten weapons to raid White supremacist communities, yet they would, without real thought or hesitation, destroy and leave trails of blood and devastation in their own communities. The Mafia is a real gang. They control resources, politicians, whole sections of the federal military budget and state government departments, and they own factories.

If the Black gangsters were a real gang, they would build their communities with the so-called ill-gotten loot instead of helping to destroy it with the insane drug trade. They would have the power to keep drugs out of their mothers' community. If they sold drugs, which they should not, it would only be in non-Black communities. If they were really good imitators of real gangs, they would do exactly what the Mafia did: economically enhance and build up their community and homeland. The scene from the 1972 movie classic "The Godfather" underscores this when one of the Mafia Dons, speaking at an organized crime commission meeting designed to broker the peace, makes a startling comment regarding the drug trade, He says, speaking of drugs, *"I don't want it near schools. In our comminutes keep the drugs among the colored, the darkies._They are animals anyway so let them lose their souls.*" This is power! The Black youth engaged in the gangster lifestyle are engaged in self-destructive activities and incredibly stupid behavior.

THE SYMBOLS of SEDUCTION

Youth are seduced into this gangster lifestyle through the symbols of wealth, power, sex, invincibility, virility, freedom, arrogance and lack of strong male guidance, stable families, unified and developed comminutes, moral foundations and principles, lack of power in the Black community and lack of an understanding of White supremacy. Black children are easy prey for White supremacist influence and direction.

The name of the set -up and/or operation is called gangster or gang banging. The symbols of a set-up include caches of jewelry, the bandana, head scarf, earrings, cell phones, droopy pants, cap turned backward, rap music, the forty-ounce liquor, gold, silver, rings, gold chains, money and flashing cash, palatial homes, jet planes, shining cars, the gun sometimes known as an Uzi or a glock nine and the most powerful weapon of all, words. All of these items are produced for and targeted purposely toward Black people.

These powerful and highly addictive symbols lead to a fast, short and deadly life. The most powerful symbol is gold. It symbolizes royalty and power. It is a magic potion. The religious traditions of Black people, especially in the Western World, are inundated with notions of the streets of heaven being paved with gold.

The association between God and gold is powerful stuff. Gold is an everlasting substance that guarantees eternal life and has godlike powers. The gold says that I am king of the earth and must be treated with respect. The gold has social transformation powers. Black males fight over gold chains. If asked about the mental association, they will say that is not true. They will probably respond that they just wear gold because it looks good.

A lot of material resources look good, but gold above all is the superior substance with the supreme and magic powers that mean kingliness and royalty. It unlocks the door to the secret temple that leads from boyhood to manhood. It is part of the rites of passage. This has a deep, unconscious meaning. The gold chain becomes a substitute for the real gold of Fort Knox.

In White supremacist lore, Black men are more concerned with looking good (which when decoded means still trying to prove to White people that they are somebody) than quietly amassing collective economic

Racial Symbols

power. Black people flash gold to show White people that they are not slaves, beggars and socially incapacitated. Gold rings also symbolize eternity. These symbols implant the idea within the deep recesses of the mind of the young gangster, that he is unbreakable and immortal.

The flashing of cash symbolizes that one has an abundance of wealth and resources. For the materially successful Black, the large home in the suburbs symbolizes equality with White people. He is no longer a dumb nigger who has to live in materially inferior conditions. He is now a man of honor. The economically successful gang bangers never use their ill-gotten millions of dollars to physically redevelop Black communities. They will move out of the community and seek to live among White people in the suburbs. And they will never allow chaos to exist in their new, mostly White environments.

However, they set up and run chemical houses that contribute to the existing chaos and desolation in the Black community. The big cars symbolize virility and sexual strength. In street thinking, "He is a man who is able to provide. He is the big dog. The bandana means loyalty. He is part of a family or a soul-tight crew. He is willing to be cast as an identified member of a gang even if it costs him his life."The scarf cap that covers the head and ties in the back re-creates the image of a pirate. A pirate is a bad guy, thief, robber, outlaw, criminal and scoundrel. It is part of the imaging and symbolizing of the Black male as a born criminal. In the old black-and-white movies the pirates wore the same kind of headscarf complete with an earring. The Black males who innocently emulate this look, believing that it is a fashion statement, are unknowingly being imaged as thugs, criminals and hoods.

Gangster rap music lays the groundwork for the expansion of this lifestyle. It validates the Black male criminal image in the minds of impressionable young White males. This also means that as these young White males mature and assume their rightful place in the social structure, they will believe that Black males are natural, dangerous criminals who must be locked up. They will vote for the candidate who will fight crime.

In Western society it is normal for young males to identify with tough criminal or rebellious figures. More than eighty years ago, it was Al Capone, John Milliner and Bonnie and Clyde. In the 1950s young White males were called rebels without a cause and identified with the tough young White males on motorcycles, wearing black caps and black leather outfits. During the hippie generation, White males rebelled against their parents and spouted slogans such as *tune in and drop out* and words like *generation gap* and *revolution.*

However, once they understood and accepted their role, they became the standard bearers for the maintenance of social order. They became the prosecuting attorneys, judges and sheriffs who incarcerate bad guys. These symbols serve as social compensations for a powerless existence. The symbols have the power to intoxicate the believers into a frenzied, altered state.

This is why it is so hard to convince young Black people to abandon the destructive lifestyle and move in a positive and constructive direction. The power of theses symbols is similar to the way young Indian braves and warriors on the American plains felt before going into battle against the United States Cavalry.

Young Blacks feel vengeance, infallibility and invincibility. They feel that they can beat the game and not get caught, and they are ready to die to prove it even though they know how many individuals have crashed and burned in the process. It doesn't matter because symbols have created a highly distorted mindset. They live the way they want to, do whatever the large sums of cash will produce, be with any woman they choose and go anywhere they wish.

They feel larger than the people around them because they view others as dumb and weak and see this as a way to achieve their own objectives. They have no respect for the shirt-and-tie way of life. This is why they can display so much disrespect, disdain and disregard. They say to the older Black male and female, if money is the thing, *"shit, I've smoked yo' old ass already."*

These material symbols have become part of the big set-up. What is the big set-up? The big set-up is the use of material and symbolic inducements to entrap, incarcerate and eliminate millions of young Black males. These intoxicating symbols are used to image and glorify a destructive lifestyle as wonderful. The big set-up is designed to trap Black males at an early age through the symbols of manhood, power, big money, eternal life, royalty, unequaled adventure, unlimited excitement, unbridled sex and intrigue.

The young Black males live under the direct glare of White supremacy indoctrination. They have no real image alternative, counter-thinking or cultural shield to protect them from the most addictive racial propaganda system in the known world. Black people in North America do not identify with or speak a separate language, nor do they have strong cultural remembrances that enable them to withstand the barrages of propaganda.

The racial propaganda of White ideas, White values, White glamour and standards of social progress have decimated the idea of Blackness as a cultural, social, political, intellectual, historical bonding process. The first objective of a racial propaganda system is to establish a program of indoctrination to get young Blacks to see Blackness as an *acceptable* derogatory lifestyle. This is achieved through glamorization of this corrupt lifestyle by television, movies, videos, the Internet and computer war games. It is achieved by the disconnection and destruction of real Black history, supplanting it with the glorification of nonsense. The only history that is permitted at a mass level is the slave or social protest history. This history is so embarrassing and limited that most Black males would rather not know the story.

The second objective is to establish and reinforce symbols and value systems that encourage the devaluation of Black life. The greatest symbol here is the dollar bill. The dollar bill is flashed before their eyes, a symbol of great riches, fabulous lifestyle and wonderful existence. They have been conditioned to believe that having many dollar bills is far more valuable than a human life. Getting money becomes the reason for living. Without money an individual has no value and is worthless.

They have been taught that it is perfectly acceptable and expected to get money through illegal and violent means. They have been trained to believe it is all right to use, terrorize and even kill powerless Black people to get their money. This is made easy by the use of hypnotic music and derogatory language that devalues and debases Black people.

This devaluation is reflected in the use of words such as *nigga*, *bitch* and *ho bitch* as standard dialogue in the presence of older black females and White people. This is a grand departure from the recent past, when Black males would not use curse words in the presence of older Black women. And they never used the word nigger in front of White people. The recording companies have encouraged and financed this kind of racial debasement. They rationalize and say, "Hell, if they call themselves niggers, they cannot accuse us of racism. These niggers are dumber than we thought." *White supremacists do not develop and promote music or other products that knowingly glorify the devaluation and debasement of their own race. They know better.*

Yet the White supremacist will encourage, underwrite, sponsor and exploit the debasement and devaluation of Black people. They will pay Black males/females millions of dollars to degrade themselves and their race.

The third objective is to incorporate in the minds of Blacks involved in the gang banging lifestyle the belief that other Black people are the enemy. Redirecting the target from fighting White injustice to fighting other Black people is a classic work of art. The purpose is to convince young Blacks to believe that other Black people are responsible for the existence of the horrendous social conditions. They are conditioned to believe that Black people have abandoned them and do not care whether they live or die. These young Blacks grow up to hate and disrespect other Black people. They are encouraged to believe that to get what they want, Black people, or niggas, that stand in their way must be eliminated.

White supremacist training teaches Black people that other Black people are the enemy. They are trained to believe that other Black people in another part of town have control of things and territories that they want. The subliminal billboards, commercials, music videos and magazine covers repeat this central theme: the Black male is the enemy. He has Uzi's, glock nines and other weapons of destruction. The Black male above all must be killed because he is the enemy. Young Blacks involved in gang banging have been programmed like zombies to kill and debase each other. They believe without question that Black people, or niggas, are dispensable, lowlife snakes that deserve to be killed because they are menaces to society. Do society a favor and kill a nigga. After all, nothing will happen when you kill a nigga. They understand that Black life has no value under White supremacy. They have watched with great indifference the destruction of millions of Black people.

The genocide of millions of Black people in Rwanda, the Congo and other locations on the African continent was hardly mentioned above a whisper even in the Black media (black-formatted radio, cable television, newspapers). Therefore, who cares if a nigger dies? They heard reports during the 13th annual AIDS conference in Durban, South Africa, that up to 60 million Black people would die in less than five years from the AIDS virus, and no major Black person seemed to care. They surmised from this information that Black life is highly expendable.

These young, untrained, uncultured Black minds never think about challenging the really dominant force in their lives: White supremacy. They have been programmed to respect the symbols of White supremacy. They have been taught to admire, fear and respect White people. They may not admit this, and as a matter of record they will say

Racial Symbols

that they hate "White people." However, the facts and their behavior show that the opposite is true.

They have been conditioned to hate Black people. That is why they kill Black people. They believe that White people are the ultimate and most feared people and power on earth. They do not disrupt White businesses or White society. They know better. They clearly understand the social and personal consequences of that kind of action. The following are general examples of Black self- hate language and symbols.

SELF-HATE LANGUAGE	DECODED MEANINGS
Niggers and Niggas Ain't Shit	Die, Nigger, Die
Them Nigggas	The Enemy
My Nigga	My Friend
Fuck You, Bitch	You Ain't Shit
Bitch Nigga	Lowlife
Bitch Ho Nigga	Lowlife No Good
Nigga Bitch	No Good Woman
Ho Bitch	Low Grade Female
Blow Them Niggas Away	Kill Black People
Funky Bitch	No Good Women
Get That Money Bitch	Bring Me the Money, Ho or Sell That Dope
Count That Money Nigga	Bring Me My Drug Money
Take a Nigga Down	Kill the Nigger Now
Slut	Women Don't Deserve Respect
Nigger and Flies	Black People Are No Good
Motherfucker and Motherfucka	No Good Nigger
Cant Trust Them Niggers and Niggas	Be Careful When Dealing With Niggers
Fuck Them Niggas Up	Destroy These Black People
Something about That Nigga	Take Care of the Problem
Hardcore	Dangerous to Other Blacks
Roughneck	Fights with Other Blacks
What's Up, Dog?	What's Up, Lowlife Trick
Nigga	No Good Black Trick
Bitch	No Good Black Female

SYMBOLS of the SET-UP

SYMBOLS	SOCIAL MEANING
Gold	Everlasting Life
Silver	Wealth/Dollar Signs
Cash	Get Money Now
Jewelry	Kingly, Royalty

283

Fast Cars	Power/Masculinity
Homes	Stability and Strength
Droopy Pants	Kick My Ass White Man and Bitch Ho Niggas
A Cap Turned Backward	You Can't Tell Me Anything Because You Ain't Done Nothing
Forty-Ounce Malt Liquor	Sexual Prowess and Immunity
Uzi	I'm Invincible, Motherfucka
Glock Nine	I've Got the Equalizer
The Bandana	I Belong to a Family
Hood	I Am Unseen and Unknowable
Very Low Haircut	Efficient Manipulator
Bald	Smooth, Quick, Slick Hustler
Afro	Racial Identification and Rebellion
Loud Music	Shut Up, Nigga, I'm Talking
Bouncing Cars	Look At Me, I'm Important
Earring	Brotherhood

These and other words and symbols of debasement and devaluation have been made acceptable and have become standard language in some Black communities. And some justify it by saying, "Well, this is our Black culture," and other horrible nonsense. Young Black minds do not understand the extremely powerful impact and social ramifications. They look to make money to get out of the poverty trap or to bring attention to their social plight. However, the White supremacist will use all of these innocent and sincere desires for change against Black people. These symbols are flashed over and over again in the movies, the music videos and the words of songs that prominently feature in dazzling array such words as nigger, motherfucker, motherfucka, fuck you, bitch, ho bitch, bitch nigger, my nigger, my nigga, suck my dick or jimmy, hands on the nine, get money and so forth. The gang banging lifestyle feeds the image of young Blacks as dangerous criminals.

BLACK MEN and HORSES
The creation of a racial symbols that portray the Black male as an animal are consistent with the ideas of Hitler and fit all of the ugliest racial stereotypes of wild savages and beasts. The animalization of Black males has been going on for many years. One of the more recent examples appeared in the 1995 movie "Nixon."

Racial Symbols

The most symbolic illustration featured a scene and dialogue between Nixon and FBI Director J. Edgar Hoover as they walk together down a race track. Hoover comments about the "degenerate Dr. King." In the next scene he is attempting to pet a black horse that is foaming at the mouth and is wildly rejecting Hoover's touch. The horse seems to fear Hoover and shows emotional instability. The symbolic meaning of this scene is very important.

The black horse symbolizes Dr. King, or Black males. The foaming at the mouth implies that he has a disease like HIV AIDS and is an immoral deviant. The wild behavior means that the Black male is out of control, dangerous, hostile and must be corralled and controlled or exterminated. The scene uses symbolism to give dual meanings to and make subtle connections between the black horse and Black male. The "Nixon" movie was not made to especially appeal to Black audiences, yet it showed scenes that associated words about Black males with scenes of horses and wild beasts.

This same kind of association between Black males and horses was made in the movie "The Godfather." During a scene at a horse stable owned by a movie mogul, the Godfather's attorney, Tom Hagen, played by actor Robert Duvall, tries to persuade the mogul to give the Godfather's godson, a Frank Sinatra-type character, a prime role in an upcoming motion picture. As they stand in the horse stable, the mogul shows off his black horse to Tom Hagen. He calls his black horse Khartoum. Khartoum is the capital city of Sudan, a nation of Black people on the African continent.

The Sudanese people are some of the darkest-skinned people on the planet. In the scene a Black man named Tony is the handler of Khartoum. An immediate subliminal connection is made between the Black male handler and the black horse. The horse and male are black. The black Male's name is Tony or, decoded, pony. The black horse is named after a Black city called Khartoum in the Sudan, a Black nation on a Black continent called Africa. Would the same message come through if the horse handler were a White man, the horse pure white and he was named after the city Berlin, Germany, located in Europe?

This association is also connected with the practice of bestiality. Women in countries like Germany, Sweden, France and the Netherlands have been featured in pornographic movies that depict oral and vaginal sex, often with dark black horses. From the angle of many of the shots in these gross movies, it often appears as if the women are having sex with Black males. White supremacists conquer and break horses in the same way they have broken Black men to be used for sport, amusement and domination.

Racists glorify Black males as the greatest sprinters who run the same kind of short-distance speed races favored by the owners of prized horses. They are called the greatest *running backs* in football and have been compared to running horses. In White supremacist sexual lore Black male genitals have been compared in size to those of horses, with statements such as *"that nigger is hung like a horse."* Note the subliminal connection between the word race and the act of running.

In *"The Godfather"* movie the studio mogul says that he would not race the black horse but would put him out for stud service. This statement and scene have powerful racial implications. During chattel slavery, Black males were raced against each other and were sold as studs to breed other slaves. The era of this particular movie scene was between 1944 and 1950. This would have been after Jesse Owens' earth- shattering performance at the 1936 Olympics held in Berlin, Germany. Jesse was still considered one of the most famous athletes in the world. It was during this era that Jesse Owens raced against a horse, symbolizing two animals running against each other.

One of the most dramatic scenes in *"The Godfather"* occurs when the head of the black horse is seen in the bed of the movie mogul. This symbolizes more than the Mafia's power and credo. It symbolizes cutting off the head and mind of Khari over in Africa, or the Black man, through the flow of heroin and other drugs into the black communities. This message is reinforced in a harder and more crass scene showing a big commission meeting of Mafia leaders. During a tense roundtable discussion dealing with how the illegal drug trade would be operated, one of the Mafia chieftains makes the following comment: *"In our city we would keep the drugs in with the coloreds, the darkies. They are animals anyway so let them lose their souls."* Notice the hard connection between Black people and animals.

Such associations seem never ending. For example, in professional boxing language Black boxers have *trainers,* and if they box out of the same gym they are called *stablemates*. The reference to stablemates is often heard during HBO and Showtime boxing shows. HBO boxing commentator Larry Merchant often refers to Black boxers as stablemates or horses. In professional and college football Black males are often called studs, a not so subtle allusion to the breeding of powerful stallions. Even the civil rights leaders of the 1960s fell victim to the such racial comparisons.

Racial Symbols

During the sixties they used a popular refrain that stated "a man cannot ride your back unless it is broke." Or they would say "White folks are on my back" or "riding my back." This was a direct reference to the practice of riding. There are only a small number of mammals that can be ridden. This includes the elephant and the camel. The elephant and camel are not in plentiful supply in the Western World. Therefore, the next best animal is the horse. After watching White men tame and ride thousands of horses in the Wild West, civil rights leaders came to associate riding with horses or mules. Horse riding requires sitting on the back of the horse. In White supremacist folklore Black men are considered big horses. The racial association is clear. Black males have become world famous athletes for running track or racing against other males.

ELVIS PRESLEY

The Elvis Presley phenomenon has had a tremendous racial impact on White culture. This phenomenon has a deep Black foundation. Blackness is the basis of the Presley dynamic. It is the worship of a Black man in white skin. Presley was an outlet for the deep frustration of White females who desired to worship and be with Black males and for White males who secretly desired to be like Black males. Elvis Presley gave them open license to express these desires without associating with Blackness. Elvis symbolized the White man's desire to escape his deadness, sterility and lack of soul. Elvis Presley's verbal style, walk and hair were Black.

He kept a dark tan—the darker the better—and he loved wearing black clothes and black shoes. He copied Black music and tried to imitate Black dance movements in his show routines. He literally bathed himself in the whole scope of Blackness. His early and most important musical influences and entertainment styles came from Black people like Bo Diddley. He could sell the Black style in a safe manner. He could enable White people to satisfy their great hunger and endless desire for dark chocolate, darkness, black night sex, black garters, black panties, black stockings, black cars and so forth. White people have a tremendous fixation and extremely deep obsession with Darkness and Blackness.

Whites have a love-hate relationship with deep, dark color. They want to be darker in color, as witness their incessant desire to suntan. They think black is sexual, as witness their purchase of black panties, black dildos, black stockings and black high-heel shoes. Elvis came along at a time when the word integration was a code for breaking up the hard rule of White supremacy. The thought of receiving Blackness directly from Black people was too overwhelming a force to reckon with. The White handlers were very fearful of the power of Black sound, movement and soul.

Racists feared that Blackness would have a powerful effect on many young White people. Too much exposure to the power of Blackness could warp the White psyche and create great confusion among young untrained minds. It sends messages of confusion about Whiteness. The Columbine High School murders were an example of young White men receiving confused messages. They thought that White supremacy was supposed to be implemented in a hardcore fashion, and their confusion led to the desire to control Black people as in the old days. They felt that Black was too bold and dominating and therefore must be destroyed. Youth is always impatient, moving before the word is given. They wanted racial warfare now to save the White race. Racial supremacists also tried to understand why other Whites went along with the refinement. They decided that these Whites were traitors to the race and must be destroyed. Thus, the old White supremacist's worst fears about the power of Blackness were realized. Elvis came along to satisfy the desire to touch velvety Black skin, hear Black sounds and rhythms and see Black movement. However, White leaders had to maintain Blackness at a certain distance in order to control the powerful influences of Blackness on the White psyche.

Elvis was not the first or last example of a Black man in white skin. Other Black surrogates include Frank Sinatra who tried to emulate the Black cool jazz style, Paul Whiteman and Benny Goodman who tried to steal the black jazz style, the Beatles who admitted copying Black culture and John Lennon who admitted the same in an article in *Jet Magazine*. The list is endless, even down to today with such groups as Eminem, the Beastie Boys, The Backstreet Boys and N'Synch imitating Black sound and stage movement. However, no one ever symbolized Blackness in white skin like Elvis Presley. The existence of Presley allowed White males to act like Black men without being called niggers. They could worship the Black god (in the form of a White surrogate).

White youth emulated Elvis instead of the dynamic Jackie Wilson, James Brown or Little Richard. Elvis was a White racial symbol that enabled many White people to explore Blackness without losing Whiteness. With Elvis, they could very easily satisfy their secret desire to be Black.

CHAPTER SIX

COLOR CODE WAR

According to *Webster's New Collegiate Dictionary,* definitions of the word color range from "a phenomenon of light" to "a visual perception that enables one to differentiate otherwise identical objects" to *"skin pigmentation other than white characteristics of race."* Color is the visible perception that permits humans to determine differences within such categories as flowers, birds, dogs, cats and humans. In nature all colors and hues are equal in value and each serves a particular purpose. The purpose is different in accordance with the nature of a thing.

The Creator did not qualify which things by virtue of color were inferior and superior. Colors create beautiful variety in the universe and make life more enjoyable, abundant and wonderful. All colors support each other in a dynamic blend of spectacular universal harmony. Only the human species has interpreted and organized differences based on color. People terrified and obsessed with it assign certain values and meanings to individuals, populations, things and places on the basis of color. Color has been codified, racialized and politicized and has become a major tool of racial warfare. The value of life and the quality of life are determined by color of skin, hair, eyes and even the color of a neighborhood. In the color code war the highest social value is given to the whitest or near whitest population, thing or place. Social value is different from economic value. In terms of social value, Black people with big money and economic abundance are still not as valuable as White people with middle-income dollars.

The concept of social value under white supremacy is based on the collective image of a group or population. An individual within a group may do well or be perceived as acceptable. However, if their racial group is imaged as thieves, dope dealers and inferiors, the individual would still be thought of as abnormal within their original group. But because of their original gene pool, traces of inferiority would still be in their bloodline. In a race/color-based society they still cannot escape the fact that they are from a certain population. Despite their ability to advance and to be recognized, their value is permanently linked to the value of the collective body no matter how hard they try to escape.

In comparison to White people, Black people have far less social value. This is one of the reasons why so many White businesses leave an area even when Black people with good incomes move in. Regardless of income or education, the Black population is viewed as having little intrinsic value other than what is given to them by White people. And in the White supremacist mindset Whiteness is the number-one value. This colorization formula ensures that so-called White neighborhoods in the majority of cases will have higher social value, which translates into economic/political value, simply because of the color of the skin of the residents. The value of property is determined by the color of the people and not the property. Wherever people of color reside, that is the most important factor in determining value.

The color code war's oldest catch phrase still has power: *If you are white, you are all right. If you are yellow, you're mellow. If you are brown, stick around. If you are black, get back.* The language has many derogatory references to dark and black and just as many laudatory associations to the light and bright words. The language must be decolorized to the extent feasible and effective. A social system based on thoughts, words, policies and practices that establish the inferiorization and superiorization of colors is inherently discriminatory and racist.

Examples of Color Code War Messages.

WHITE ITEMS	**RACIAL/COLOR CODE MESSAGE**
White Face Bowls	Cleanliness is godliness / washes away black dirt/ sins
White Bathtubs	Cleanliness is next to godliness / washes away black body dirt /sins
White Toilets	Cleaning away the dark waste from the body
White Toilet Tissue	Use to wipe away black enemies from the body
White Diapers	Whiteness is the first Form Of Social/Individual Protection And Comfort
White Tampons/ Kotex	Whiteness Is Safe, Protective, Comforting And Virtuousness

Color Code War

White Crackers/ Saltines	Whiteness Is Safe, Protective, Comforting And Virtuousness
White Napkins	Whiteness Is Cleanliness
White Socks	White Cleanliness
Computers	White And Light Equals Knowledge And Power
Whitenizing Toothpaste	The Whiter The Purer, Cleaner And More Desirable
Mother's/White Milk	Whiteness Is The Really Pure Substance Of Life
White Dinner Plates	Good clean food
White Turkey Meat	White meat is sacred, holy, pure, full of blessings and grace
Old-Style Nurse Uniform	Whiteness is healing, caring and protective
White Rocket Ships	White phallus, sexual, explosive and with reproductive power
White Space Station	Whiteness is home and the bases of life
White Detergent	Whiteness can wash away the black stains
White House	The highest individual symbol of the White nation
White Cars	The best cars
White Envelopes	Licking the white penis/vagina. The act of using the tongue to wet and stick
Blonde Hair	The best and most desirable hair
White Soap	Totally clean; washes away all the dirt
White Hat	The good guy, the winner and the best and most important person
White refrigerator	A colder climate in Western White environments
White Cross	The symbol of White power and sacred strength
White Paint	The closest thing to having a white body
White Handkerchiefs	To wipe away the black
White Shoes	Heavenly feet
White Enriched Bread	White people are the staff and substance of life
White Refined Sugar	White civilization is better and angelic
White Enriched Flour	Becoming White and rich is the real substance of life
White Eggs	The most nutritious protein
White Cotton Balls	White is clean and healthy
White Q-Tips	White is clean and healthy
White Sheets	Cleanliness is next to godliness, which is next to whiteness
White Shirts and Collars	White collective and privileged class
White Nurse Stockings	Clean and pure and therefore a Clara Barton figure
White Underwear	Control and support of genitals
White Chef Uniform	Clean food
White Horse	White powder or cocaine and/or White power establishment

White Surgical Gown	Clean and purely professional
White Plantation Houses	The White nation over Black people
White Tablecloths	Clean and good food
White Salad Dressing / Mayonnaise	Dressed up and civilized
White Robe	Pure and holy

DARK/ BLACK ITEMS	**RACIAL/ COLOR MESSAGES**
Black cars	Black penises
Black shoes	Power associated with black genitals
Black boots	Power associated with black genitals
Black garbage cans	Shaped like black penises to indicate the sperm produced is garbage
Black garbage baggies	Shaped like vaginal opening to indicate that whatever comes out is garbage
Black suits	To give color to white people
Black ties	Black phallus symbols
Black hat	Black male
Black pen	Ancient knowledge that the black man is your daddy
Black cat	Black luck because of black people
Black leather	Black sexual power

Sayings such as *dark forces* are color-coded messages that translate into racially coded messages. Color words are used to attach value to people, places or things, i.e., good or ugly. A murderer does not have to be described as a dark character with a shadowy background. He or she can be described simply as unsavory and untrustworthy, an unsafe person to be around, a murderer or a taker of life. There is no need to add a descriptive color word to the depiction. Another example of this language behavior is the phrase a *black day.* There is no such thing as a black day. If a black day exists then there must be a white day.

Colors do not exist in a vacuum. What is a white day and how does it differ from a black day? Are white days good and black days bad? People have become so conditioned to believing and accepting the subtleness of derogatory language regarding Black people that this language is hardly given a second thought. The term black day is a misnomer. The very word day implies that the sun is shining. It can be

Color Code War

obscured when a tornado, thunderstorm or other threatening weather is on the horizon, but the sun is still shining.

The following list of widely used expressions show examples of color sayings followed by counter-color sayings: The "Do Not Say" column means that these expressions should not be used to define conditions or characters that are unjust. Do not use a color word to define or explain a derogatory situation. The expressions in the "Decoded Racist Meaning" column show what is really meant when the pejorative terms are used in the current climate of racial communications.

A. The suggestions in the "Do Say" column offer non-racist and non-color-coded statements. These statements give the correct expression to use about situations or people that are engaged in unsavory or non-constructive activities. These should be used except in situations where a specific race or color code war activity must be identified and revealed. Then it is proper to define the activity as a color or race code war operation. The purpose is to expose and root out the color and racial code war activity of the individual or population.

B. The expressions in the "Do Say" column allow for the description of positive or derogatory events, people, places and things without applying a color or racial attachment. That is, unless it is a specific race or color code war based activity. Then it is proper to define the activity as a color or race code war operation. The purpose is to expose and root out the color and racial code war activity of the individual or population.

C. The expressions in the "Do Say" column will provide an alternative way to describe unpleasant or incorrect people, locations, things and events without attaching color words to them. Color words should only be used to objectively describe or define colors. For example, (an object might be greenish orange, reddish blue or gray. Color words should never be used to describe such things as days, hours, locations, problems or happy situations.

RACE CODE WAR

DO NOT SAY	DECODED RACIST MEANING	DO SAY
Defeat the dark side	Control and contain the Black menace	Eliminate injustice
The dark force	The Black menace	Eliminate Injustice
The black knight	The evil warrior	Incorrect individual
The white knight	The good king/warrior	Correct behavior
White lie	Innocent playful story	A lie is a lie
Black lie	Dangerous story	A lie is a lie
Dark personality	Acts like a dangerous nigger	Untruthful character
I had a nightmare	Dark and evil are synonymous	Disturbing dreams
This is a nightmare	Bad events are synonymous with darkness	This is a disturbing situation
Dark Continent	Land of the Black savages	Africa, home of the world's history
Blackmail	Black criminal	Incorrect and deceptive
Dark and evil	Black male or acts like Black male	Injustice
Tarnish	Blackened and darkened up	Ineffective
Black, dark and ugly	All niggered up	Incorrect circumstances
Dirty motherfucka	Dark, Black and no good individual	Untrustworthy
Dirt-cheap	Black is cheap/ dark has no value	Affordable-priced smut and pornography
That girl is a slut	Prostitution equals Black female	Unsavory/incorrect reputation
Darkened streets	Nigger side of town	Vulnerable area
He's a dirty dog	Acts like a lowlife nigger	Unworthy character
You dirty motherfucker	Lowlife equals nigger	Incorrect individual
Shadowy figure	Dark equals danger and uncertainty	Inconspicuous individual
This is a gloomy day	It's a black and dark day	Difficult or unproductive period
It's a dark day	Black equals wicked day	Difficult or unproductive period
It's dreary outside	Black and depressing	Displeasing weather
There's a brighter day	Whiter and wonderful life ahead	Productive period of time
Bright and cheerful	White or White-acting and happy	Constructive attitude
Fair-minded	White minded	Balanced perspective
Fair and honest	White equals truthful	Truth, justice and correctness
Fair decision	White and determined	Just and balanced ruling
Lighten up	White equals advancement	Improved temperament

Color Code War

Lighthearted	White equals good/compassion	Treat people correctly
Thief in the night	Dishonesty equals darkness	Incorrect individual
Blackguard	Black equals rogue	White supremacists
Black cat	Black equals bad luck	Victim of racism
Singing the blues	Dark equals depression	Don't feel well
I'm feeling blue today	Dark day and depressed	Don't feel well today
Brown nosing	Colored equals cowardice	Going along to get along
The blues	Dark equals depression	Rough time

COLOR CODE WAR on BEAUTY

The struggle between light and dark is the ultimate color code war. The existence of a society based on White supremacy means the words that describe light and dark take on significant racial and color implications. In decoded language it is the battle of White versus Black. Light and dark have become the racial and color-coded symbols and are far more than just innocent descriptions of color, visibility or levels of illumination.

Light and dark express such things as notions of superior and inferior, good and bad. The most dramatic example of this usage are the notions of what is beautiful and what is ugly. Here, issues of race and color are expressed in a more blatant manner. The cultural stereotype related to issues of physical appearance is probably where racism has done its greatest damage. Millions of Black women of all shades of color have suffered untold horror, degradation and misery from being told for centuries that they were ugly, beastlike and totally undesirable. The blackest female with traditional broad facial and body features has had to bear the heaviest burden in terms being called unattractive. Under the concept of modern racism, the first criterion for determining the beauty of an individual or a thing is its color.

It is not the only variable although it is the most important, especially as it relates to judgment of feminine beauty. The record on this is very clear and leaves little room for disagreement. The overwhelming majority of the winners of major national or international beauty contests have been White or, if Black, very light or high-brown skin color with keener features and straight hair. As the percentage of light and tan-skinned Black females increased, the more they were considered as possible beauty candidates.

RACE CODE WAR

In 1983 Vanessa Williams, the first Black woman to win the title of Miss America, was a light-skinned Black female. After she was dethroned in 1984 while a college student for posing nude in *Penthouse* magazine, her replacement was another light-skinned Black female. The 2002 Miss America was another Black female from Illinois named Erika Herald who looks like a White female with a deep tan. The most sensual and alluring Black women under the concept of White supremacy domination are still the light, tan and light brown Black women. Never has an extremely dark-skinned Black female with broad features, large buttocks and short nappy hair won the beauty contest.

Every standard and measurement of beauty in Western civilization begins with color and then proceeds from there. The cult of colorism with its inherent discriminatory values has impacted how people see beauty. In the year 2003, despite all claims to the contrary, color is still the number-one factor in determining what is beautiful or ugly. The standardization of the White female as the most beautiful woman in the world has been based primarily on skin color. The color of her skin greatly increases her chances of winning the big prize. Whiteness or lightness of skin has enabled her for the last four hundred years to be called the most beautiful woman in the world.

IF YOU'RE YELLOW YOU MIGHT BE MELLOW
In the White supremacy mindset Whiteness of skin is considered one of the highest and most important standards of beauty. This factor combined with keen or straight facial features is a sure-fire recipe for victory. The closer one is to looking or being White, the better the chances of being classified as beautiful. The acceptability and classification of beauty of Black females have always been based on color. The list of White media-appointed beautiful Black women is rife with lighter-skinned females.

The examples are numerous from Lena Horne, Dorothy Dandridge, Jayne Kennedy and Freda Payne to Tina Turner. The lighter skin color is what they have in common. As Black women become lighter in skin color, they are considered prettier or better looking. Therefore, some of the derogatory language and verbal descriptions used to poke fun change slightly. The lighter-skinned Black female through no fault of her own, is the first one in the door, and she is still portrayed by the White-dominated media as the most beautiful and acceptable of Black females.

Color Code War

Even in the year 2003 the highest profiled Black beauty is the light-skinned, mixed-race actress Halle Berry. The most sensual and alluring Black women under the concept of White supremacy domination are still the lightest. This is an indisputable fact no matter how hard black people and white people try to dispel it.

The light-skinned Black female, however, is not one step above the dark-skinned Black female. While being told that she is the prettiest, she is still imaged in a racist/sexist manner as a hot female with an unlimited and perverted sexual drive. The Academy Award-winning and degrading performance of Halle Berry in the motion picture "Monster's Ball" is very clear evidence that the image of Black females, regardless of skin tone, has not dramatically changed.

The Black woman is still called a bitch and a baby-making machine who is dumb and backward and solely responsible for the welfare state and for the existence of inner-city baby colonies. When a Black male calls a Black woman, regardless of her skin tone, a bitch, it sends a cold and dangerous chill down her spine. This word in addition to being a racist term is also a degrading *color trigger word* that immediately causes her to psychically envision years of slavery, rape, toiling for Miss Ann, brutality, hate, scorn, disrespect and feeling like a non-class non-citizen. It also conjures up the feelings of being used as a sexual outhouse, feeling like nothing more than sexual dog meat for any man willing to stop by or drop a dime on the table. When she is called a bitch, it reminds her that she has been viewed and treated like an unprotected woman left to be devoured by the male wolves of any race who want a taste.

This racial debasement is connected to her racial identification, and the sexual branding adds to her feelings of worthlessness. Under this racist and sexist scenario, she is considered to have lower sexual morals than her White female counterpart. In reality her lighter color buys her nothing except anger from darker-skinned females. She is often viewed as arrogant and acting superior. She can be used to drive a color wedge between Black people. The racist will taunt her physical appearance as superior to that of the dark-skinned, broad-featured Black female. She has to walk a very thin line between using her looks to excel in life and not flaunting her appearance so that she does not seem to be acting superior because of her physical closeness to White females.

RACE CODE WAR

IF YOU'RE REAL BLACK, GET WAY BACK

It is extremely rare or it has never happened that Black people have in this area of the world chosen as their national standard of female beauty women that look like the late Esther Rolle, Shirley Chisolm, Sarah Vaughan, Esther Phillips, Whoopi Goldberg or Nina Simone. None of these darker-skinned, broad-featured women are never held up as examples of great Black beauty. And even if she has an acceptable look and is dark skinned, most Black people will describe the more African-looking woman in the following manner: *"She is black or dark, but she is still pretty."* These kinds of statements imply that the color black or being very dark is a real impediment to being beautiful. It is the same as saying that despite her dark skin, she has overcome this obstacle by having acceptable facial features and straight hair. Even during the heyday of Black and proud beauty contests, the majority of the winners were not the blackest of the Black females.

For the few years between 1967 and 1969 dark-skinned females were chosen as centerpieces of Black beauty. This was during the heady days of Black awareness. However this *"choice of color"* did not last long. Shortly after, in 1972, around time the whitenized Super Fly look emerged the preference for light and tan began a strong resurgence. It was the light tan or brown skinned black female with the big Afro who became the poster child of the Black revolution. Pam Grier, Angela Davis and Katherine Cleaver, all three brown-skinned types, became the poster females of the Black revolution. It was a throwback to the days of the Cotton Club in Harlem, New York, where the beautiful browns and lighter women ruled the day.

Even in the Black revolution, where blackness was supposed to be highly celebrated and prized, the black or very dark-skinned female with broad features and thick body was shunted to last place. All color shades of Black women are subjected to the pain and suffering of *racial victimization*. The perception is that lighter-skinned Black females often get a little more relief because they do not have to carry the label of being ugly, at least in most parts of the Black community. They are closer in color and physical appearance to the White female and therefore under the rules of White supremacy are less of a *color threat*. This type is even more acceptable and passable if in addition to being light, she has long wavy hair, thinner lips, smaller hips and a flatter derri'ere. If, on the other hand, she has big lips, nappy hair, a huge behind and a broad nose, she is subject to some of the same degradation as her darker-skinned sister.

Black females, especially the darker ones, have suffered the greatest physical and color rejection. The very dark or near black, broader-nosed, bigger-hipped, thicker-lipped and kinkier-haired Black females have been relegated to the bottom heap on the beauty scale. It is very rare if ever that a very black-looking female with broad features is chosen as the most beautiful woman in the world or even in the Black community. Far too many Black people, males especially, have accepted the notion that whiter features are the first and most important criteria for beauty.

Lighter-skinned Black females with thin lips, straighter noses and thinner hips are given greater status and have more value among Black males in the Black community. Black men will still jump over five dark-skinned sisters to get at a light-skinned sister. In a crowd of Black women they will look for and spot the light-skinned woman first. To test the validity of this statement, ask the following question: how many Black men in this area of the world consider the very black-skinned females of Haiti or Congo as the most beautiful women in the world? The answer is very few. Yet many of these same Black men will include the Latina actress Jennifer Lopez, or J Lo, as among the most sexy and desirable. Until Black people begin to see the very black-skinned women of Haiti and Congo or even Mississippi as physically beautiful, the deep color rejection will remain and grow deeper.

Sexual discrimination against Black women, as we have seen, is tinged with the additional element of color tone or complexion prejudice against the darker female. During the era of chattel slavery, very descriptive derogatory labels were used to dehumanize and degrade Black females. During slavery, the majority of Black females had dark to very dark skin. The language used to describe them was laced with expletives like monkey and gorilla.

The dark skin, the broad nose and the kinky hair were used as signs of deep degradation. Such traits, then and now, trap these Black women deeply in the *colorized syndrome of racism*. They are victims of a color caste system. This is not to imply that light, tan and brown-skinned Black women do not face the same racial horrors. They do and are equal victims of racism under White supremacy. However, the *color dynamic* has a powerful impact in terms of how Black females see themselves and how they see each other.

RACE CODE WAR

On top of tons of social oppression and racial rejection, the dark-skinned Black female is the butt of many sexual and racist jokes, comedy routines and cartoon stereotypes. This is the Aunt Jemima face on the pancake box although it is interesting to note that the Black female on the Aunt Jemima box has been lightened-up to make her more appealing.

A noted example of this color code war debasement was the highly popular 1970's NBC hit television series "Sanford and Son." The role of the dark-skinned character, Aunt Esther, was played by the comedian Lawanda Page. She was routinely called degrading names by a very light-skinned Black male actor/comedian named Red Foxx. He even bellowed in one line from the show "that he could stick her face in dough and make some gorilla cookies." In essence the closer to the color white, the more acceptance and the less degradation. When the Black female begins to look whiter, the reference to gorillas and monkeys eases up a bit. The traditional dark-skinned Black female is the last to be considered physically beautiful. The greatest number of women on welfare and with low incomes are dark-skinned, broad-featured and large-sized women. The largest numbers of women that live in the so-called inner cities and are incarcerated are darker-skinned Black females. More than likely the greatest numbers of women that do not have men or get invited to social functions are dark and thick Black women. Sadly, thick and dark-skinned Black females are emerging and gaining acceptance is in the sordid world of pornography. They are being regularly featured as big booty harlots that love to have sex with any man or woman. This is a blatant continuation of color and racial degradation.

The attachment of the word black to any phrase communicates a stronger derogatory meaning. There is a difference, no matter how slight, between being a nigger bitch and a black nigger bitch. The difference is the skin color. A nigger bitch, as degrading as it is and as it sounds, can be a Black female of any hue.

However, a black bitch is a clear designation of a dark-skinned Black female. If she has much less melanin in her skin, she is called a yellow bitch, which is equally degrading. A White supremacist will use the expressions black bitch and black nigger bitch interchangeably; however, Black people will generally note the difference in color by using the corresponding expression. Black indicates that the female is dark skinned. It is rare if ever that a light-skinned Black female is called a black nigger.

The light-skinned Black will be called a nigger or nigger bitch or high yellow bitch. The color degradation sets up the sexual and racial degradation thus, it is imperative to remember that Black females, regardless of color, are beautiful. The lighter skin is not more beautiful or more ugly than the darker skin. The beautiful rainbow that Black women create cannot be equaled anywhere on the planet.

The tall dark woman with the short, nappy hair and big buttocks is beautiful. The small light woman with the long, wavy hair and flat behind is beautiful. The big-eyed brown woman with medium hair and buttocks is beautiful. The Black woman is the beginning of all life on the planet and no female anywhere on this earth can match her beauty. The differences in skin color are used to drive wedges, maintain interracial tensions and establish false beauty standards that pit one Black individual against another. Most dark and Black females probably do not feel that they are physically the most beautiful women in the world. The refusal to believe this is very sad because they truly are the most beautiful women in the world. I encourage them to secure pictures of Whoopi and Halle and look at them until you convince yourself that Whoopi looks as good as Halle.

Deep color rejection of blackness is part of racial conditioning under White domination. The charts below indicate how color has impacted the perception of beauty in modern society. The Racial Conditioning Chart shows how racially different females are perceived. The Color-Conditioning Chart illustrates how Black females of different shades are viewed. The Sexual Conditioning Chart exemplifies how Black females are chosen and desired based on color.

RACIAL CONDITIONING CHART for FEMALES

Female Categories	Image
White female	Mother, wholesome, smart, thin, most beautiful and most desirable

RACE CODE WAR

Yellow female	Attractive, the more white looking the better, submissive
Brown female	Good looking, sexual, fiery and hot
Red female	Fat, unattractive and not desirable except to rape
Black female	Fat, ugly, loud, boisterous, lustful and suitable only at night

COLOR CONDITIONING CHART for BLACK FEMALES

Black Female Categories	Color	Physical Features
Extremely undesirable	Very dark or black	Thick lips, broad nose, nappy/short hair
Undesirable	Dark brown	Thick lips, broad nose, nappy/short hair
Desirable	Brown	Medium lips, smaller nose, short/curly hair
Very desirable	High brown and tan	Thinner lips, smaller nose, curly/long hair
Most desirable	Yellow to near white	Thin lips, narrow nose, wavy/ straight/long hair

SEXUAL CONDITIONING CHART for BLACK FEMALES

Black Female Categories	Color	Physical Features
Extremely nasty	Very dark to black	Thick lips, broad nose, nappy hair
Very nasty	Dark brown	Thick lips, broad nose, nappy hair
Sexual	Brown	Thick lips, broad nose, nappy hair
Sexual and sensuous	Tan	Thinner lips, smaller nose, curly hair
Very sexually desirable	Yellow to pale	Thin lips, narrow nose, wavy/straight hair

Color Code War

IMPACT of the COLOR CODE WAR

Most Black people will not admit the impact that the color code war has on their lives in terms of their choices of mates, friends, employment opportunities and living environments. They would rather shoot you than admit that color is a strong determining factor in their selection of professional, social and romantic associates, employment options and places where they choose to live. They shout statements such as, "I don't think about color," or they will say, "It never crossed my mind what color she/he is." Yea, right!

Even in the year 2003 there are many Black social clubs, fraternities and sororities that will not even admit large numbers of very dark-skinned Black people to be part of their organization. To become a member of the club, the very dark individual must have some special status. He or she must have money, a good education, be famous or show some other criterion that establishes value and worth. This kind of color-based thinking starts with the establishment of values that are transmitted from a White-dominated culture. The general value theme that guides opinions and selections is the belief that the lighter the individual, the better and the darker, the less respected unless there is some special achievement. This is a manifestation of the color code war. It is the way the color code war impacts decisions of beauty and value and importance. Under this thinking and value system, certain colors have greater value both in the real world and in the perceived world.

In the color code war certain colors have perceived values. A perceived value is slightly different from a social value. The perceived value is an evaluation of an individual, group or population based purely on color. Social value is based on the collective image of a group or population. Perceived value does not take into account other variables such as education or income or social achievement.

For example, under the concept of White supremacy, a high brown-skinned individual will automatically have greater perceived value than a very dark brown-skinned person. Why? Whiteness or being closer to it is better and has greater perceived value. If he/she is light skinned, they will be perceived as good, worthy, industrious, prosperous and in good standing. If they are dark skinned, they will more likely be seen as a criminal or incompetent individual.

This contention was validated by a recent study conducted by Dr. Keith Maddox, Assistant Professor of Psychology and head of Tuft University's Social Cognition Lab. The findings of the study, "*Cognitive*

RACE CODE WAR

Representations of Black Americans: Reexploring the Role of Skin Tone," were released in April, 2002. The results were based on two studies that examined the role of skin tone or color in the perception and representations of Blacks.

This study was conducted using Black and White people. Dr. Maddox discovered that among both Black and White people the darker the skin color, the more the individuals are perceived as criminals, thugs and incompetents. Dr. Maddox said, "Our research shows that both blacks and whites associate intelligence, motivation and attraction to light-skinned blacks, and being poor or unattractive to dark-skinned blacks," According to the study, the most highly thought of Black people are those with lighter skin. They are generally thought of as having the highest and best qualities and are the most attractive/desirable. The following Human Complexion Chart is an indicator of how color is valued and perceived in the social order under White supremacy.

HUMAN COMPLEXION CHART

Decoding Key for Color Code Ratings and Meaning Under the Concept of White Supremacy

Supreme Value - The Best and Most Powerful

White is the highest standard of human development in the universe.

Extremely High Value - Very Important and Very Powerful

Pale white, while not the most beautiful color associated with Whiteness, still represents the highest image of human development.

High Value - Powerful and Very Important

While being classified as White is powerful, there are some issues between Whites about who is validly White. Regardless, any classification of White is still greatly superior and very valuable.

Color Code War

Favorable Value

The individual or group is on the borderline of being White. They are or could be maneuvering for entry into a full whiteness classification.

High Rating

While the person, group or population is not exactly White they are close to being White.

They are still considered higher than nonwhites because they are closer to White.

Preferred and Desired Stock

This means that while the individual or population is not White, it is striving to be White, which is more comforting and positive under the color rules of modern racism.

Advantageous

It is better to be any color of yellow because it is a sign of being closer to the ultimate goal of being White and powerful.

Very Noticeable

This means that the person is sensuous, sexy and highly sought after. This is the only other allowable standard of beauty under White supremacy.

Acceptable

This is next to the last level of reasonable acceptance. The high brown skin color gets too much notice and begins to subtly imitate Whiteness. However, the individual can still get inside the proverbial door of acceptance.

Measured Acceptance

You can enter into the realm of social acceptability but your behavior and attitude will be watched closely.

RACE CODE WAR

At the Door/Banging at the Door/Away from the Door/Outside

What does "the door" mean? The door symbolizes the barrier to acceptance in the color-based social system. The door is the barrier that must be passed through to get into the room.

Unacceptable/Totally Unacceptable

This means the individual, group or population has very little or no value in the social order.

Supreme Level of Abhorrence

This means that the individual, group or population is viewed as a threat to the existence of the social order.

COLOR	COLOR VALUE RATING	MEANING
White	Supreme Value	White is always the best
Pale White	Extremely High Value	Pale is superior but not the most attractive White color
Brownish White	High Value	Jewish or Gypsy White/ good White
Dark White	High value	Darker Whites such as Spanish/Italians still have great worth
Near White	Favorable Value	To be closer to White is much better
Very Yellow	High Rating	Lighter is better and more beautiful
Yellow Yellow	Preferred Stock	Yellow is acceptable and comfortable
Medium Yellow	Desired Stock	Yellow is mellow
Darker Yellow (almost brown)	Advantageous	Any part of yellow is mellow
Tan	Very Noticeable/Gets in the Door	Tan is sexy and very desirable

Color Code War

Dark Tan	Very Noticeable as Suntan	Dark tan is very sexy/rich looking
Light Brown	Acceptable	High Brown is sexy and Desirable
Reddish Brown	Measured Acceptance	Let them in but watch carefully
Medium Brown	At the Door	Medium brown is still not there
Dark Brown	Banging at the Door	Value begins to drop right here
Darker Brown	Away from the Door	Value rapidly decreases
Medium Dark Brown	Away from the Door	Value is almost nonexistent
Very Dark Brown	Outside	No value
Black	Unacceptable	Feared/menace/monster
Very Black	Totally Unacceptable	Predator/monster
Purple Black	Totally Unacceptable and Abhorrent	Super predator and animal
Black Black	Supreme Level of Abhorrent	Monster

BRAZILIZATION PROCESS: COLOR and RACE

There are major predictions that in the year 2050 racism will be eliminated because there will be only one color and that will be the color brown. This prediction is based on such things as the projected low birth rate of White people and the higher birth rates of Latino and Asian nonwhites and Black/White racial interbreeding. *However, the dynamics of eugenics, cloning and hidden biological advances are not calculated in these formulas.* Do not be fooled: White supremacists will not commit racial suicide. They will, however, create enough racial confusion through such things as promoting the development of racially hybrid populations to throw Black people further off balance. Brazilization is the newest method of racial integration that encourages race mixing to produce a new color strand.

The Brazilization process is named after the model of color assimilation practiced in the South American nation of Brazil. This

307

color and racial model encourages and promotes racial mixing at a certain level to produce racially or color hybrid populations. It has created so many color strands that new racial classifications have emerged. Along the way, all of this race mixing has further entrenched the idea that lighter or closer to white is socially acceptable, more beautiful, socially desirable and economically enhancing.

GOALS and OUTCOMES

Under the concept of Brazilization, the goal is to bring forth new colors as a strategy to replace racism. However, what is developing is greater color confusion, the gradual elimination of the darker-colored populations and an increase of individuals classified as White within the social order. It is a different racial management pattern than the color segregation model used in Europe, Australia and North America. Under the practice of Brazilization, the general population is encouraged to racially mix in order to produce greater ranges of skin color. While the goal of reducing racism is admirable, the problem is that the new colorism comes at the expense of dark-skinned Black people. In developing this new race/color amalgam, the darker individual and population has been marginalized and reduced while the lighter to brown-skinned population has dramatically increased.

No other population-Yellow, Brown, Red or White—is being asked to give up their genetic or cultural identity to gain greater social acceptance. This strategy implies that dark black people are socially unacceptable and must whiten-up to be passable. This is the worst kind of White supremacy, the deliberate breeding out of dark-skinned people.

The Brazilization process does several things: it reduces the actual number of people classified as Black; secondly, it creates additional color wars among Black people, because a color-based economic hierarchy will be established to engender and escalate resentment and anger; thirdly, a new buffer population will replace White people as the frontline defense against Black people.

The new racial populations will be separated and reclassified by skin tone or color. They will be placed under White people but above the darker-skinned populations to serve as racial/color buffers. This will create greater confusion and conflict. They will become the managers and directors in day-to-day interactions with Black people. To some degree this approach is already being tested in the so-called inner city. As White people move farther out into the suburbs, the colored replacement populations serve as the new racial managers.

Finally, the color division strategy will disorganize and deplete the Black numerical base by creating color confusion, color competition, racial division and intra-group race hostilities. Light-skinned Black people who will be reclassified as White, and they will compete on the basis of color against brown-skinned Black people who will be reclassified as tan. One of the major fallouts of the new color integration will be the loss of racial identity and any sense of where to belong. In the year 2003 and beyond, it is becoming harder and harder for Black people to identify as physically Black. The color strands are so numerous that many feel uncomfortable being classified as Black.

The new color strands and physical features have radically stretched the idea of what has been considered Black. The new questions are what is Black, who is Black and who is not Black? White supremacists have defined who is Black by cleverly defining who is White. Black people have never defined who is Black and who is White. The effort to change racial classifications from Black to multiracial or biracial could be an effort to increase the number of White people, decrease the number of Black people and stir mountains of confusion and racial estrangement.

Under the Brazilization process a range of colors and hues are produced and each color is classified differently. The result is an increase in the number of people classified as White, near White or non-Black. The closer to white skin, the better the economic advancements and social opportunities. Social and economic benefits will be accorded to each color group on a sliding scale. Of course, under the system of White supremacy, the top dog is White. The next highest are the near Whites, or mixed breed, populations.

On the bottom of the ladder are the deep chocolate-Black people. This pattern plays out all over the world wherever Black people have been colorized or scattered whether in India, Mexico, Australia or the United States. This condition is no fluke of history. It could not have escaped the eyes of color strategists all over the world. This model is more effective and deceptive because it gives the impression that racism does not exist since people can freely have sex without being lynched or pillaged. It is a form of quiet racial genocide for Black people and particularly darker-skinned Black people. This process is now occurring at a quickened pace in North America.

RACE CODE WAR

THE CALIFORNIA COLOR CODE

The most dynamic model of color hybrids building in North America is in the state of California, which has become a cross-racial breeding ground. The California racial breeding model was developed along the same lines as in Brazil. It is producing a whole new variety of colored humans with varying physical features and color mixtures. The rapid growth of the brown-colored Latino or Hispanic population in California has allowed the colorization scheme to speed up rapidly. In the process it is producing greater racial confusion for Black people. The final result will be the "whitening up" of Black people to make their offspring more acceptable under the new color order.

This form of racism will lead to the development of new color group classifications. It will be modeled on the Brazilization concept, where the closer to white, the greater the social and economic benefit. This means that Black people could be split into as many as ten color groupings or racial categories. Imagine the Black population divided by ten and reduced tenfold in terms of population, political power and cultural identity.

The concept of racial groups as known today will be completely obliterated. All except the most organized people, namely, the White supremacists, will be confused and disorganized. Many of the people who are presently classified as Black under the current White supremacy system will be reclassified and called something else. The racial propaganda machine is gearing up to manufacture a new concept of race based on the reclassification of Black people, thus creating divisions that can tear families apart as in slavery.

The selected cities below are areas where the colorization strategy is being tested or fully implemented.

CITY	RACIAL EXPERIMENT STRATEGY
Paris, France	Race mixing
Los Angeles, California	Race mixing to test new color strains
Rio de Janeiro, Brazil	Multi-race mixing—intra-race classifications
Sao Paulo, Brazil	Multi-race mixing—intra-race classifications
San Juan, Puerto Rico	Race mixing to produce new color strains
Panama City, Panama	Race mixing to produce new color strains

Color Code War

WHAT MUST BE DONE

The following are recommended actions to counter the growing development of the color code war in such areas as value, beauty and social importance.

Establish Equal Physical and Visual Images of Beauty

The peculiar color, economic, spiritual and psychological issues facing all Black people must be brought out of the social closet. No longer can we use the excuse that it might hurt the fragile unity of the race to discuss the topic or that skin tone is really not an issue with Black people.

If this issue is not effectively addressed, it will destroy Black people. There is already a very tense anger over this issue, which surfaces in many private relationships. Those who say that it is really not an issue with Black people are totally incorrect. It has been an issue for hundreds of years, but it has always been swept under the table. There are millions of dark-skinned and very light-skinned Black people, especially Black females, who have suffered the pains of racial confusion and identification, social rejection and deep self-hate based around physical appearance.

There is a quiet movement beneath the radar screen that is designed to physically separate Black people based on skin tone/color. Many of the light to high brown-skinned and Arab-looking Black people are moving out of the central cities. They are financially, physically and mentally separating from their darker-skinned brethren. This is a very quiet transition that very few Black people have openly talked about.

However, when coded language says that Black people moving into the suburbs, it is generally a reference to those Black people with income and education. A larger percentage of very dark Black people have not attained economic parity with lighter Black people. The evidence for this is based on an observational study of the higher percentages of dark-skinned Black people in low-income and substandard housing, low-wage jobs, urban school districts and prisons. And there is a higher percentage of lighter-skinned Black people living

311

in the suburbs and holding key leadership, professional and business positions.

The new theme should be that all shades of Black beauty are equal. However, in the short term the dark-skinned people will need greater affirmative action in order to catch up to their lighter brethren in terms of being perceived as beautiful. Dark-skinned Black females with broad noses, thick lips, big eyes and nappy hair must be extolled as the original beauties of Black culture. The equalization of all images must be posted in churches, schools, employment locations, beauty contests, etc. Light, dark, brown and red Black people need not fear high-profiling this issue; it will help bring all sisters and brothers into a unified whole.

Study and Correct Color Coded Images in All Formats of The Media

All too often the darkest individual Black-oriented movies or music videos serves as the bitch, loudmouth whore, buffoon, clown, hit man or sexual deviant. The opposite is often true of lighter-skinned Black people. They are often portrayed as the "best and the brightest." Both of these scenarios are totally and equally unacceptable. Pay close attention to the skin tone or color of the individual playing a role. See if other very dark or very light individuals within the movie or media format have similar roles. Demand that beauty come in all colors and that the use of only one color as the standard of beauty will not stand. Anytime this color-coded pattern is noticed it must be dealt with immediately. E-mails, letters, media conferences and community-based forums/workshops as well as active protests to the Hollywood studios and advertisers have enormous power to make constructive change. These color-coded images are extremely detrimental to Black self-love and collective development. The following are examples of color-coded roles.

ROLE	COLOR	FEATURES
Maid	Black or dark brown	Broad nose, thick lips
Loudmouth bitch	Black or dark brown	Heavy, with broad nose, thick lips

Color Code War

Hot mama	Black or dark brown	Big butt with broad nose, thick lips
Desired love interest	Light or near white	Thin to medium sized, long hair, straight facial features
Hero	Light or near white	Thin facial features
Comedian	Brown or dark brown	Big nose, thicker lips, nappy hair
Criminal	Black to dark brown	Broad features
Good mother	Light to yellow-brown	Thin features
Big Moma	Dark	Fat and loud
Leader	Light to light brown	Medium features

Establish a study group to track variables such as rates of employment, welfare, substandard housing and incarceration based on skin tone or color.

Determine if there is a statistical correlation between skin color, social acceptance/development and economic attainment. For example, how many dark-skinned Black people live in the ghetto and how does this compare with the percentage of light- skinned Blacks moving into the suburbs. This could indicate that a new racial division strategy based on color is emerging, which could further destroy the fragile unity among Black people.

Study the patterns, promotions and purposes of race mixing.
What is behind the great push for racial integration? For the last 100 years White supremacists have been pushing Black people as far away from them as possible. They segregated the schools, redlined living environments, denied housing loans and engaged in a host of others actions designed to place Blacks at the bottom of the social order. What is the purpose and basis of the radical switch that took place in the 1990s? Study, debate and teach others about the meaning and purpose of racial integration.
What does it have to do with racism?

Is segregation the only criterion and manifestation of racism? Does an integrated social order mean the elimination of racism or have we been tricked? What will come of race mixing and how will it impact on the future of Black people here and abroad?

RACE and COLOR RITUALS

Each day millions of people engage in hidden race and color rituals from the bedroom to the breakfast table without fully understanding the color, racial and social implications. In a society that places great emphasis on the dynamics of race and color, all people, places, things and events have the potential to become viewed within the context of a racial interpretation. It is only because racists have used color to degrade or uplift various racial populations that these observations become so very important to understanding modern racism.

Color reflects images of a racial population. In the 1970s and 1980s there were a series of commercials that used a singing group of dark raisins. The group sounded like the legendary Motown singing group, The Four Tops. This was using the color of the raisins, which were dark or black in most cases, although there are light- colored raisins, to send a racial message. Regardless to how cute or funny the commercial may have appeared, it still transmitted a clear race and color message. In this context there are a number of routine rituals that are engaged in daily that have strong messages and implications that are racially and color based.

A ritual is a habit, pattern, custom, routine, method or practice. Most rituals are practiced without much thought except in areas such as religious, fraternal or political activities. Rituals are only consciously thought about when they are interfered with. For example, drinking coffee in the morning before going to work or after getting to work is a ritual. It is only when the coffee machine is empty that the routine is disturbed or recognized. So long as the coffee is available and the electricity works, the drinking of coffee is not given a second thought. A racial or color ritual functions in the same manner. It is a daily routine that has racial and color overtones, meanings, purposes and desires. In most cases this ritual also goes on without giving it a second thought on the conscious level. But on the subconscious level its affects are very noticeable and powerful.

The following are definitions of race and color rituals.

Race Rituals

Social practices and personal behaviors that are performed regularly and involve the use of race to satisfy a need or desire to glorify a situation, signify a meaning or wish to degrade people, things, places and events.

314

Color Code War

Color Rituals
Social practices and personal behaviors that are performed regularly and involve the utilization and consumption of a color(s) to satisfy a need, glorify a situation, demonstrate a desire or degrade people, things, places and events.

Under the auspices of White domination the color and race rituals are part of the normal pattern of everyday life. They have become normal and acceptable forms of colorism that are hidden in plain sight. It is hard for many people to distinguish or to understand the racial and color implications of these regular routines.

However, it is important to recognize how these practices embed certain racial/color beliefs, hide or activate the expression of real racial/color desires and are used to manipulate racial and color issues in society. The messages are often hidden in the color of an object. For example, why are so many trash cans dark or colored black? Hidden in this color is a clear racial message about the value of Blackness and how it should be perceived. The color black has the most contradictory messages. The white supremacist loves and admires the color black yet hates and degrades it in the same instant.

The majority of office computers are white or very light gray. They are so light gray that they appear to be white. What are the color implications of computers being white or very light? Could it be a message that white or light means intelligence, brainpower and competence? Of course, that is the message because under the concept of White supremacy, white and light mean smart and superior.

Why are so few computers except lap-tops colored black? It seems that black would wear as well or better than white or light gray. Why not black? The computer is a super-brain instrument that is designed as a superior thinking force. Does it mean black or dark and intelligence do not compute or are not compatible? Turning on and using the computer has become a ritual that has deep color and racial inferences. These and other examples will be covered in this section on race and color rituals.

The Following Is a List of Selected Daily Race and Color Rituals
Drinking Coffee
Smoking Cigarettes

Eating Chocolates
Selecting of Dark or Light Meat at the Table
Telephone Calling
Dumping Trash in the Can
Using a Cell Phone
Turning on and Using a Computer
Turning on a Television
Using a File Cabinet

DRINKING COFFEE

The drinking of coffee symbolizes the ritual of digesting black color into a white body in the white supremacist mindset. This is a color ritual. The imbibing of coffee is using a liquid-colored substance to fulfill or gratify a desire for greater skin color. The old adage that drinking coffee makes you black is believed at the subconscious and perceptual experience level of many Black and White people. While many Blacks and Whites were dealing with the social and political ramifications of color and race, they were unknowingly consuming the taste of Black and White color issues at the food table.

Coffee has been the subject of many color and racial references in American society. According to most knowledgeable sources, coffee was discovered in Ethiopia around A.D. 800. This was during one of the golden age periods of African history. The racial and color connections did not began until coffee came to Turkey, where the proverb was:

Coffee should be black as hell, strong as death and sweet as love

When the rest of Europe got into the coffee picture around 1615, the attachments of color and race continued. The French statesman Tallyrand said that the recipe for coffee was:

Black as the devil, hot as hell, pure as an angel, sweet as love

The early references to the color of coffee triggered immediate and often conflicting associations with blackness in early white supremacist culture. Black conjured-up words like devil, horror, wicked and death. Yet it contradicted itself in the early stages with some whites decorating themselves in black to appear intellectual, chic, rich, powerful and social. However, the two most significant color sayings in Tallyrand's statement are *black as the devil and hotter than hell*. The pure as an angel and sweet as love sayings also have indirect color connections.

His statements are reflections of a not fully developed opinion about how to view Blackness in the early period of the development of White supremacist culture. This kind of contradictory thinking was corrected and effectively minimized and neutralized with the coming of modern racism.

The connections between the devil as a Black and hell as hot are interesting. The meaning of hot when decoded means not just hotness to bring out the flavor, but a hot climate such as Africa. It also helps to explain why the enslavement of Black people was easy to justify. They basically viewed Black people as sub-human or demon-like creatures. Otherwise what did the color of coffee have to do with the color of the devil?

Such clumsy color associations are examples of racial perceptions early in the formulation of White supremacy thought. The first question is why is the devil black? The second question is why was coffee opposed by many seventeenth-century Christians who wanted Pope Clement VII to label it as the devil's beverage. The only reasonable connection between coffee and the devil is the color. The dark or black color immediately triggered a racial and color connection: a black liquid equates with the devil and Black people. Only a racially based thinking process would be able to draw a relationship between the color of coffee and the color of a physical image of evil called the devil.

The color black also has an opposite side that has been played down or dismissed in White supremacist culture. Many Whites believe that the color black signifies rich, powerful, sexual, intellectual and chic. However, this feeling is not transferable to Black people except through derogatory uses of the color black.

Wearing black has been the hallmark of the coffee-drinking intelligencia for nearly 400 years. Back during the early Renaissance, the rich were dressed in flamboyant clothes made with expensive dyes and gold and silver decoration . . . Dutch

> *merchants also introduced coffee and chocolate to Europe around this same time ergo, you suddenly had the wealthy and educated merchant crowd and the artists they supported sitting around in coffee houses all dressed in black, drinking coffee and eating chocolate for a buzz.*
> —*www.araneum.bc.ca/black2.htm*

The interesting point is the connection between coffee, chocolate and the color black. These intellectuals, upperclass statesmen and women were wearing, consuming and bathing themselves in the darkest of colors. And yet they considered these colors prestigious and top-notch. They were digesting a black-colored drink, eating black-colored food and wearing the blackest garments.

The all-black dress creates a physically black look and reveals a hidden desire to have a physically black color. Wearing black outer garments gives the entire body the look of a black physique, except for the head and hands. Wearing the black robe and cap is very similar to the black cap and gown that is worn in thousands of annual commencement ceremonies.

This color association and affiliation would be parallel to a group of individuals sitting around eating marshmallows and white-colored salad dressing while drinking white milk and wearing white clothes. It would be easy to see that there was an embedded color message. The ideas and beliefs behind wearing black are based on the concept that if enshrouded in black, one would be considered rich, mystical, powerful, intellectual and in vogue.

White men and women during that period of Dutch history could achieve the desired black look and still be respected among their peers. Most White supremacists will deny that this look has anything to do with a special significance of the color black. They will point out hundreds of false reasons as to why this is not so. However, even today they continue to wear black as a symbol of honor and respect for the highest and most distinguished roles in society. And yet they still will not give the color the credit it deserves. Following are examples of how black is identified with segments of society in the modern era.

A. Black robes- Law, Religion, Entertainment
B. Black suits- Business, Law, Religion, Entertainment

Color Code War

C. Black dresses - Business, Law, Religion
D. Black shoes - Business, Labor, Law, Religion
E. Black Head dresses - Religion, Entertainment
F. Black ties – Social Life, Business

In the modern era coffee and the race question are highly intertwined and symbolically connected to issues of racial integration. The following are selected examples of sayings that use coffee as a racial metaphor:

SELECTED COFFEE/RACIAL METAPHORS WITH DECODED RACIAL MEANINGS

1. Cream in My Coffee / Do You Want Cream in Your Coffee? /You're the Cream in My Coffee
   <u>**Heavy sexual overtones including sperm ejaculation on black skin**</u> *and sexual intercourse with a Black individual to further racial integration.*

2. I Want It (Coffee) Black
   Message about real color desire and preference.

3. Dark and Rich
   Statement about real feelings regarding the color black.

4. I Take It Black/I Like It Black
   This is a real message about strength, power and the durability of Blackness. It is also a hidden message about the desire for color or color interaction such as sleeping with a black or dark individual(s).

5. Drinking Coffee Makes You Black
   A racial myth designed to poke fun at the relationship between the color of coffee and Black people.

6. The Devil's Beverage or the Devil's Brew
   The devil is black so therefore black is evil.

RACE CODE WAR

The use of coffee as a racial metaphor during the nineteen sixties was part of the language of integration in America. The pouring of cream into coffee stood for mixing White and Black people into the same social condition. Cream is white like semen. This meant that White males would be able to ejaculate White sperm into Black females, and Black males would be able to ejaculate into White females.

This had a deep meaning on the sexual perception plane. The coffee metaphor was often used to explain the dangers of integration. It was also used by Black people, especially those who called themselves black nationalists and were opposed to the integrationist tendencies and tactics of the Civil Rights Movement, to explain the dangers of race mixing. A black cup of coffee was integrated with cream/milk and paired with a white cigarette in the morning. A white cigarette and a cup of black, or integrated, coffee became a tandem in the morning before work. Caffeine and nicotine became addiction partners in the workplace. Coffee is dark or black and the majority of cigarettes, at least in this country, are white sticks that are sucked on in a manner similar to that of a female performing oral sex on a male penis or dildo.

SMOKING CIGARETTES

Another example of color and racial ritual is the smoking of cigarettes. White females were often pictured with a cup of coffee and a cigarette in the morning either at home or at work especially if there are separate locations for smokers in the workplace. The smoking of the white cigarette for females symbolizes the sucking of a white phallus. Black females have copied the habit of morning cigarettes and coffee in an attempt to emulate Whites or be more like the fabled Miss Ann the coded symbol of a white woman.

For the white male the smoking of a white cigarette it is an indication of power as symbolized by an erect white phallus. The cigarette is held and smoked upward when consumed. The upward direction is a symbolic erection that shows manhood, virility and potency, however misguided the symbol might be.

This was part of the great uproar over the commercial cartoon characterizations of Joe Camel and the Kool cigarette advertisements. The word Joe rhymes with hoe, blow, know, show, dough, low, roll, row and sow. These are all modern words that symbolize sex, money, toughness, smartness, cars and women. These are the things that cool means in the male mind. The word camel has the word came in the spelling, which comes real close to the word come, which is a modern word for male ejaculation.

Camel also has the spelling of the word male within it. This is a direct association with young males who are mostly White. This is surmised by the symbols of Joe Camel's lifestyle and suburban environment. It is similar to the terminology of Salem cigarettes. When scrambled, it too comes out as males.

The face of the Joe Camel cartoon character looks like a brown or dark penis. However, it is supposed to be the depiction of a camel. But upon closer inspection, it is rather obvious that J.C. is a male sexual organ!

The connection is: camels = males = penis= virility = women = power.

The initials J.C. are also interesting. These initials have a very powerful mental and mystical connection to an untrained and highly impressionable young mind. The most famous J.C. connection is Jesus Christ. The message is that smoking these cigarettes is like having a heavenly experience similar to cocaine, and it is the Christ-like thing to do. The camel symbolizes humping endurance during the act of sexual intercourse. The smoking or sucking of this magic cigarette is designed to bestow otherworldly powers of virility and manhood, primarily to young White males.

The cartoon Joe Camel may be decoded as *White-boy cool* and clearly indicates that his image was being targeted toward White youth. The creation of Joe Camel as a brown-colored phallus was clearly playing on the age-old belief that the darker phallus is the most potent. The camel is an animal associated with the deserts of northern Africa; the brown to dark brown color of Joe Camel indicated that he was a nonwhite character. This combination added up to a nonwhite character from an African environment, which gives a strong Black connection to this commercial scenario. To be cool means to be Black. To have black or colored testicles is the symbol of a real man.

White male children and youth are heavily influenced by the antics of Black males. They often desire to be like them in sports, coolness, dance, music, talk, fighting, getting girls and all the things that male youth concentrate on at an early age. The Joe Camel cartoon character played on the desire of many young White males to secretly be like Black youth or, when they grow up, to be like Michael Jordan.

This intense desire is most reflected in the White youth's emulation of Black hip-hop clothes, music, language, behavior and lifestyle. The Joe Camel character was the latest in a long line of products designed to overtly or covertly satisfy the desire for greater color consumption. White females smoked a lot of tobacco products called More cigarettes in the late 1970s, 1980s and 1990s.

This product was introduced by the R.J. Reynolds Tobacco Company (now RJ Nabisco).

Black females smoked these cigarettes for a different yet similar reason. The original More Cigarettes were dark—some would call them black. A lighter or whiter version of More cigarettes was introduced and referred to as White Lights. This version, however, did not have the same racial impact as did the original dark-colored More pack. The original dark version of More cigarettes declined in public fascination and acceptance for two reasons. First, because of the long-overdue assault on cigarette smoking and, secondly, because the dark cigarettes are blatant symbols of black penises.

Black women smoked or suck these oral items as a misplaced sign of sexual affection, connection and desire for Black males. Unfortunately, both Black and White women became addicted to these cigarettes and in return for their patronage were afflicted with deadly diseases and health problems.

White women smoked black cigarettes for a different set of reasons. First of all, the dark brown color of More cigarettes represented a radical color departure from the normal color of cigarettes on the market during that period. More cigarettes resembled a slimmer version of a cigar. There were many cigars on the market with various brand names, including one brand called Black Peter. What's interesting is that cigars are considered a male smoke. In the first half of the 20th century the smoking of cigars was considered a sign of wealth, prosperity, richness and, most significantly, virility, as cigars were passed out to other men on the birth of a child.

This was a color ritual, where the association of a thing and its color was given a specific value and significance in terms of an event.

Color Code War

The cigar is a black phallus symbol. The name of the Black Peter brand attests to the correlation between the cigar and sexual reference. The association of childbirth with a symbol of the black phallus is to accord the highest value of life to Blackness. *This was and is done in a glad-handed fashion, and this ritual is racially reinterpreted in order to hide the sacred relationship between the beginning of life and the sperm of the first man—a Black male with a black phallus.* The connection between males giving out cigars upon the birth of a baby is only explained to a limited degree within the sexual context.

The racial and color context has been overlooked or purposely skipped over. This birth celebration is a symbolic color and racial ritual of recalling how life actually began on the planet. It has been well documented that all human life began in Africa. The dark cigar is a phallic symbol. The male phallus is the originator of the birthing process. The phallus sets in motion the pregnancy experience. The first human beings came out of Africa. This subliminal association between the birth of humankind, resulting from a black penis, is quite revealing.

More cigarettes were marketed as black phallic symbols. They were/ are advertised using racial and sexually coded language. Words such as long lasting, long dark and brown and black and sleek are used to advertise these black oral items targeted at female smokers. The long-lasting reference is to the mythological lasting sexual powers of Black men in the boudoir.

These misguided beliefs were developed during slavery and continue today. There are now books and videos on the market that teach women, primarily White women (Black women already know), how to have sex with a Black man without getting tired or worn out. Since it is now okay to have sex with a limited number of Black males, White women are complaining about how long it takes Black men to have a sexual orgasm.

The phrase long, dark and brown is a clear reference to the fabled sexual organ of the Black male. This has been the subject of endless sexual dialogue, racist humor and social degradation. During the era of chattel slavery, the issue of the size of the Black male penis became a big item in racial characterizations of Black males as beasts, rapists, sex crazed animals and sub-humans.

During the first wave of sexual integration, White women wanted to feel the legendary Black penis. The smoking of dark cigarettes helped to open the door. It was part of the Virginia Slim syndrome of White female liberation. She could come out from under the shackles of sexual tyranny (decoded: stay away from the nigger males) imposed by her man.

More cigarettes were part of the new freedom to openly have an affair with a Black male. These cigarettes are packaged as black shafts waiting to be gorged and sucked by White females. This fulfilled latent desires of many White females to have sex with Black males. She could smoke a More cigarette as it became a surrogate, much like Elvis Presley, for interaction with a nonwhite or Black male. ***This is a racial ritual.*** It is interesting to note that More cigarettes appeared on the scene at exactly the same period when sexual integration between Black and White people began to expand and become acceptable on a limited basis.

This act of smoking (decoded: sucking a Black penis) did not go unnoticed by some of the White supremacists. The power of More cigarettes was so great that another product was launched to counteract its unexpected racial significance. The company that produced More cigarettes came out with a White version in an effort to capture a greater share of that market and to deal with possible psychological side effects at the sight of a dark brown cigarette inserted in a White mouth or deeply planted on White lips.

The Max cigarette was seen as a neutralizing force to the powerful More cigarette. Many wondered aloud about why so many females were smoking (decoded, sucking) these long, black phallic symbols. This is interesting because Black women have smoked (or sucked) white cigarettes for years and there were no complaints or rushes to judgment! This new counter-product was called Max. The Max cigarette was advertised as thick and light. Max is a name associated with Germanic culture.

It is safe to say that Max was the whitest of white phallic symbols. However, Max died. It did not last in the tobacco marketplace, probably because there were enough white cigarette phallic symbols to go around. And its message did not take hold because in the rush to interact with the forbidden fruit, White women simply did not want to try anything that would get in their way of interacting openly with Black males. This was part of an era that stressed the development of a sense of new freedom and new fun for many White females.

White women had been held at bay by many surrogate Black things and representations such as *Frank Sinatra, Elvis Presley* and even the *Osmond Brothers*, who, while arguably exceptional entertainers in their own right, were however White mimics of Black culture. They functioned as White imitators and substitutes for the real Black thing. These substitutes were designed to quench the unending thirst for color and for sexual integration with the darkest of all colors, Black males. More cigarettes appeared in the mouths of many White women who were involved in or desired to be involved in sexual integration activities with Black males.

Smoking the long, black cigarettes signaled an acceptance of and willingness to have sex with Black males. It was also an act of smoking, or sucking, a Black phallus. These cigarettes also triggered the implanted desire in many Black males to have sex with White females. This meant that the symbols of White purity, such as Cinderella and Snow White, were available for the choosing.

The smoking of the dark cigarettes was a signal that many Black males accurately picked up on. It was during this period that sexual interactions between Blacks and Whites greatly and openly increased. This same kind of thinking was imposed on Black women during slavery. During the brutal rape of Black women during chattel slavery, White supremacists had attempted to impose the acceptance of the White masters in the mindset of Black females.

This is also why there are thousands if not millions of White males who seek out and have sex with nonwhite females in the backroom at the workplace in the streets of the so-called inner city, and in hotels and casinos. Smoking white cigarettes is a method of replanting the idea of sex and sucking a White phallus into the minds of Black females. This is also a color and racial ritual. Smoking a white cigarette is a symbol of sucking a White male phallus. The marketers know how to tap into a mindset in order to satisfy, side track or delay a wanton desire through the creation of a product.

A subliminal racial embed often goes undetected in the conscious mindset. Yet, this sense of freedom enabled White people to declare a sexual revolution, which really meant open sex with niggers without getting in trouble or the nigger being lynched. They could fulfill hidden desires without being heavily ostracized.

The word More/Moor is also a reference to the ancient Moors who were mostly Black men and some dark-skinned Arabs. The Moors ruled Spain and northern Africa for almost 800 years! They were called Blackamoors and were very powerful, helping to bring Europe out of the Dark Ages into modern times. Therefore, in the history books and the collective mind of Black and White people is the knowledge of this past relationship. The White supremacists have attempted to cover up these historical facts by pretending that the Moors were white Arabs. However, there are many historians who effectively refuted and killed that grand lie. The Moors were Black men and dark Arabs who were half Black. The history of the Moors is replete with thousands of references to Whites as sub par and backward people. Spain was enriched by the Moors and had emerged from "backwardness" centuries earlier.

SANTA CLAUS

The most famous character associated with Christmas for the last 100 years is Santa Claus, also known as Saint Nicholas, Cris Cringle, Sinter Klass, Father Frost and Father Christmas.

One of the most troubling aspects is his name Santa. If the spelling of Santa is shuffled, several nonsensical or not clearly definable words appear: *Nasta, Ansta, Tansa, Snata* and none of these spellings add up to much. However there is one word that adds up to a whole lot and that is the word Satan. When the letters in Santa are slightly shuffled, the word becomes Satan.

Many studies have shown how the subconscious mind makes associations with the spellings of words. Is the belief in Santa a form of hidden devil worship or paganism? Have generations of people been manipulated to worship a satanic figure wrapped up as a good old fellow? Why would the name of the jolly St. Nick character in a bright red suit coming down a chimney be so close to the spelling of the name of Satan, which is one of the most recognized evil religious forces in the world? And why would it be injected into one of the most sacred holidays of the year?

Color Code War

Santa has become so popular that his image has moved the word Christ out of Christmas. The new word, or to be more exact the new letter, is an X. This is very interesting. One of the most popular expressions for Christmas is now Xmas. The X in Christmas stands for Christ, and it is an initial for the word Christos. The X is also used as an abbreviation for Christianity. It has a Roman or pagan quality, at least by Christian standards. However, in modern racism thought, the letter X has quite a different meaning. The letter X in White supremacy is a code for a derogatory, inferior or evil thing, event or people. The X means banned and not wholesome and positive. The most banned things in society are X-rated, which is one of the most popular uses for the X.

Things that are X-rated are generally connected to sex or to profanity, which is usually a sexually degrading term. The use of the X with Christmas gives the holiday a sexual tone and flavor. It is part of the ancient sexual celebrations at the end of the year. However, the use of the X is not always derogatory. Words like X-ray are constructive and meaningful uses of the X. But in the majority of the popular uses for the X it is used in a derogatory context. The X has moved Christ out of Christmas. This allows the commercialism aspect to take control during the Christmas season.

Other Selected Uses of the Letter X
X-rated
XXX-rated
X-brand / Brand X
X-Files
X-wife
X-husband
My X

How did Santa Claus, with a possible alternate spelling of Satan for his first name, become connected to the birthday of the Christ child? What does Santa Claus have to do with the birth of Christ? The birth of Christ is a good sign but it is offset by the rise of Satan through the creation of Santa Claus. It is spiritualism represented by Christ, as in Christmas versus the opposite, that is, the materialism that Santa represents and that Christ preached against.

RACE CODE WAR

The evil tried to keep the good from being born. This is the temptation of Christ. Santa is a code for materialism under a guise of charity and good deeds. Materialism is associated with greed, war, money, possessions, murder and many of the things that have caused some of the greatest wars. The act of Santa coming down the chimney into the house to deliver toys and gifts late at night is presented as a symbol of trust, charity, hard work and entrepreneurial spirit.

It is designed to associate the symbol of White older males with the concept of goodness, kindness charity and wonderfulness. But Santa coming down the chimney lays down another concept that is different from the notion of kindness and charity.

The chimney symbolizes the management of fire and heat. Santa is dressed in a red and white suit. The devil is often depicted as dressed in red as well as in black. The color red represents fire and brimstone, and the chimney is the way to hell. Santa comes *down* the chimney, which is in the same direction as going to hell. It is the struggle between good and evil, using the symbols of evil and good. The sack on his back symbolizes Satan's desire to plunder, pillage, loot, despoil and destroy. It helps to establish the symbol of respect for the old, wise, and wonderful White male with words of advice that say:

> *Oh, you better watch out, you better not cry, I'm telling you why, Santa Claus is coming to town. He knows when you've been sleeping, he knows when you're awake, he knows when you've been bad or good, so be good for goodness sake.*

The words of this song are interesting and dynamic. In some areas of the world a naughty child receives a lump of coal. A lump of coal is black. This means that a child is taught from early in life that black is evil and bad. The idea of bad is associated with blackness even during the Christmas season. This song is designed to incorporate into the mind at an early age that the White man is a good man with godlike powers. He is everywhere, with all-powerful eyes that see everything. The Santa Claus character is designed in the same manner as the White Jesus Christ with other symbols of White manhood.

The idea that he knows when you are sleeping suggests that he is everywhere watching. This is very interesting. The same concept is on the U.S. dollar bill, with the all-seeing eye. This is an early method of implanting the infallibility, reach and power of the White god and of the great images of Uncle Sam. Both Santa and Uncle Sam have long tentacles with godlike powers.

Santa is White, his short elves are White, Mrs. Claus is White and they live at the North Pole, a cold and white climate. Santa has a white head of hair, a white beard and reddish-white cheeks. He wears a red suit with a black buckle, black boots and a Masonic looking red cap. Santa (Satan) or the devil symbolizes the struggle between good and evil. Satan is the image of a devil hidden in Whiteness. In the White supremacist culture subliminal messages are the backbone of many racial transmissions. The image of the round, jolly White man clothed in the symbols of hell, with a name that, when unscrambled, spells the word Satan, is a message about race, evil and deception.

EATING CHOCOLATE

The power of dark-colored morsels entering the mouths of millions of youth is a powerful impact on the conscious mind. The color of chocolate has a very powerful racial meaning in the collective White mindset. The act of eating chocolate is ingesting the darkest color into a white or lighter-skinned being. There is an overwhelming desire for chocolate in White-dominated nations. The following is a listing of the names of selected chocolate flavorings:

ASSORTED CHOCOLATE
Coconut
Coconut Cluster
Vanilla Cream
Fruit and Nut Caramel
Butter Cream Caramel
Almond Cluster
Vermont Nut Cream
Chocolate Butter Cream
Roman Nougat
Raspberry Caramel
Strawberry Cream
Chocolate Butter Cream

RACE CODE WAR

Maple Nut Cream
Orange Cream
Peanut Butter Crunch
Apricot Cream
Molasses Chew
Chocolate Truffle

The two most competing colors and flavors in the White supremacist culture are vanilla, which is decoded as light, bright and white, and chocolate, which decoded means dark and black. These colors represent the two most dynamic forces in White supremacy. The massive consumption in 1999 of over 23 billion dollars worth of chocolate is representative of one of the most perplexing and dramatic color issues. White people as a whole consume more chocolate than any other group and in more ways than any other sweet product. This includes coffee, cocoa, soda pop, cookies, cakes, ice cream, candy bars, fudges and so forth. The priority selection and consumption of vanilla by Black people has a different kind of mental impact. Black people choose vanilla as a rejection of the color of chocolate.

They have been taught to believe that chocolate, while tasting good, is ugly and unattractive. To Black people, it is not considered as pretty as vanilla or white. The best illustration of this is in the selection of Neapolitan ice cream. It is sold as a three-flavor ice cream: strawberry, vanilla and chocolate sold together or contained in separate layers within the ice cream box. Each color is significant and represents a racial group in America.

This is part of the connection between color and race and everything in a race-and-color culture. The term neo means contemporary and the term politan sounds like the word politician. The ice cream colors/flavors are packed in separate sections within the same box to keep them apart. This reflects the racial and social conditions of segregation that exist during an era of racial management under White supremacist culture.

The radical color mixing of food and consumer items such as fruit drinks, ice creams, soda pops and clothes did not come until the social explosion of the Civil Rights Movement in the late 1960s. Food and consumer items were formerly part of a segregated culture and they reflected the desire of the White majority to create psychological racial distance. The mixing of the colors in fruit drinks or in toothpaste and ice cream progressed as racial interaction increased. The movement toward greater social diversity has also produced an intense mixture of color combinations in consumer items and consumer choices.

From telephones to washing machines, the swing toward mixing colors has created the new modern condition of White supremacy domination. Old color control barriers were broken and modified to make way for the new racial management approach. The old, stiff, White apartheid model had to give way to more refined manipulation. The three racial groups, White, Black and Red, were the most dominant in the news and at the center of racial and social debate during that era in American history. Whites preferred the chocolate, and Blacks wanted the vanilla. Black folks left the chocolate ice cream to melt and preferred to eat the strawberry and vanilla.

One of the most frequently used sources for chocolate is the Cacao fruit. The original outer color of the Cacao Fruit is not black or dark. Its color varies from yellowish brown to red. The seeds or beans inside the fruit are dark brown. The real question is would as much chocolate be consumed if the color of the substance were not dark? Is it the taste of chocolate or is it the color of chocolate that makes it so appealing and desirable? Coconut is a good tasting white colored substance and yet it is not as in demand as chocolate.

One of the most popular and desirable chocolate products is the candy bar. The chocolate- coated candy bar is one of the most popular sweet treats in the world. Millions of people of all ages, races and colors consume hundreds of thousands of tons of chocolate candy bars each year. Following Is a Selected List of Popular Candy Bars.

SELECTED POPULAR CANDY BARS and CANDIES

Snickers
See the following section.

Mars Bar
The darkness of space, the everlasting black holes in the vast universe with their unknown secrets and wondrous ways.

RACE CODE WAR

Three Musketeers
Blackness is linked to the greatest warriors and bravest men in European folklore. Today, the warrior is the boxer and the football player.

Payday
This is the lighter or whiter looking candy bar. It associates color with money and business. Payday is a workingman's candy bar. The word payday usually means a reward for something done.

Hershey Bar
Deep, dark chocolate power,

Baby Ruth
The color and racial significance of the baseball player Babe Ruth to a chocolate candy bar is very interesting. Babe Ruth had been called a nigger in certain areas of town because of his dark complexion, big nose and the look of a Negro.

Zagnut
The light/white taste will drive you crazy.

Butterfinger
Hidden in the word are the words butt, finger, butter, Niger, tut, beer, nut and other words with deep sexual and racial implications.

Milky Way
This is a sexual cosmic experience. The dark chocolate and white creamy center mean that eating this bar is an out-of-this-world sexual and cosmic experience.

Kit Kat
This candy bar is quietly modeled after a Black female in the cat-like style of an Eartha Kitt.

O'Henry Bar
This dark chocolate bar activates thoughts of O' John Henry, who was famous for driving steel drills into solid rock to build the railroad.

Color Code War

Fifth Avenue Bar
This name is associated with glitz, glamour, high fashion and wealth. Rich and dark or deep, rich chocolate make mental connections among chocolate, richness and glamour. This is the same as 15th and 16th-century Europeans who dressed in black to express richness and power.

Tootsie Roll
The name Tootsie Roll has certain sexual and by its dark brown color racial inferences. The word roll implies sex, fun, music and power. The word tootsie is a sexual reference for female. Is Tootsie Roll a subliminal reference to a black female?

NutRageous
The name stimulates thoughts that go well beyond a candy bar. The word nut in the modern social context has many uses from food to sex. The combination of sweet dark chocolate with nuts triggers in many mindsets an intense sexual, color and racial stimulation.

Reese Cup
Does the subtle association of sweet dark chocolate with a version of the nut (peanut) word quietly insert into the mindset the subliminal notion of black sexuality?

Mounds
The Mounds bar is dark brown with white coconut filling. Why is the outside of the candy bar dark brown and the inside white? The word mound also has deep spiritual significance. The ancient Indian burial mounds and the mystery of the mounds are linked to religious occurrences and supernatural events.

Almond Joy
Black, dark brown and pleasurable sex with the taste of the candy bar.

Nestlé's Crunch
Deep, dark chocolate power.

RACE CODE WAR

The brand names that are chosen for such things as dark chocolate candy bars reveal a lot about how color is desired and is ritualized in this society. The consumption of dark chocolate or dark-colored things is part of a daily color and race ritual for millions of people. People that crave chocolate are called chocoholics. It is also part of the very strange love/ hate relationship that determines how people and things that are very dark in color are perceived and treated. In this social order there are two central messages about blackness and darkness. The first and most powerful is that it is inferior and undesirable. The second and most hidden is that it is better and greatly desired.

These conflicting messages create great confusion about the role of dark color in this social order. A closer examination of one of the best-selling chocolate candy bars in the world illustrates this level of confusion and reveals the way the cloaked desire for dark color is satisfied.

The selection of any brand name is designed to send a very important message about the product and how it is to be perceived. No product or brand name is chosen by accident. There are extensive marketing tests to determine how the consumer will react to the product brand name. Most products are marketed using subliminal or unspoken social attachments that trigger certain emotions or consumer responses.

The mental association between dark chocolate and dark people is almost inescapable in a highly race-and-color-based society. The use of the words white or black or their related terms in any context in this society will activate a certain emotional and mental reaction. That is why the selection of Snickers as the brand name for a deep-chocolate candy bar is worthy of note

At first glance it sounds like the name is intended to signal that this chock-full-of-nuts candy is so good that it will cause you to giggle with great delight. (The word nut in a chocolate candy bar has deep sexual and racial implications. It has the same meaning as having sex with a dark or Black individual. Getting a nut inside the chocolate is the same as satisfying the deep need to experience sex with a Black or dark-skinned female or male. The subtle message is that this need can be satisfied when eating a nut-filled candy bar). Sometimes you feel like a nut and sometimes you don't!

If the objective is to cause the individual to giggle, then why not name the candy bar Delightful or Giggles? Either would be a wonderful brand name for a candy bar that tastes as good as the Snickers bar. The word snicker raises an immediate flag because it triggers associations with things other than candy. When the word snickers is repeated fast and often, some of the spellings or sounds that it morphs into are words such as nickers, snickas, sniggas and so on.

The sounds of the words nickers or snigger are too close for comfort to the spellings and resonance of the word nigger. When the letter s is removed from the word snigger, it has the unmistakable spelling of the word nigger. Whether this was the marketing strategy or the reason for naming the candy bar Snickers is little more than idle speculation. The attachment of a word like Snickers, with its word associations to a hardcore racial term like nigger, should have raised many questions.

Does this brand name reflect some unconscious desire to associate a degrading word for Black people with the consumption of dark color? If so, what is the hidden meaning? This social order has often called Black people cannibals, yet at the same time it subliminally links Black people to the oral consumption of dark chocolate. Is this part of the reason why everything Black people do or have is controlled and devoured?

Is the practice of this color and racial ritual the same as destroying and consuming Black culture? Is this part of the strange love/hate relationship with darkness/Blackness that the racial and color rituals expose? While Black is allegedly despised and called inferior, there is a great and unending desire to consume it or to be around it in some manner. This is part of the reason why so many Black people are confused about how White people think about color and race.

On the one hand, people are conditioned to fear darkness in this society, yet at the same time they continue to show an incredible need for the consumption of very dark things. Does this mad desire to consume color lead to other forms of mental derangement and emotional instability? Could this have been the reason why convicted serial killer Jeffery Dahmer murdered and ate the flesh of dark-skinned victims?

RACE CODE WAR

Was it just a coincidence that while Dahmer was engaged in these murderous acts he was also employed at a chocolate factory? What other rationale is there for calling a deep dark chocolate nutty candy bar a name that sounds so close to the word nigger?

The same flag should be raised about why the NBA team called the New York Knickerbockers, often shortened to Knicks. When the team was composed of mostly White basketball players, it was called the Knickerbockers. When the roster began to be composed of mostly Black basketball players, the name of the team was officially shortened to Knicks. This was a subliminal yet a very powerful change that slipped under the radar screen.

The word Knicks is close to the words hick, sick, pick, Rick, Dick and Mick. It is also interestingly close, when repeated in rapid succession, to the sounds of terms like niggs, nigs and niggers. The closeness of the sound of the word Knicks to nigs is just too close for comfort. Even the word Knickerbockers was unsettling because in some circles it was used as short-handed way to make fun of Black people. The switch to the shortened name just when the racial composition changed to Black basketball players should have drawn much greater attention.

RACE and COLOR at the TABLE

Color selection at the food table pinpoints very dynamic racial and color interactions. For example, the request for a piece of white meat or dark meat at the Kentucky Fried Chicken counter is no accident. It is a racially based decision. When Black people choose to have a slice of white meat instead of dark meat at Thanksgiving dinner, it is a racial and color message. When White people choose to eat dark meat rather than white meat during the annual Thanksgiving feast, it also makes a racial and color statement. What is the message? The choice of meat color indicates a subtle preference for which race or color is favored.

There is a strong correlation between the choice of meat color and the standards of beauty and sexual desire. The consistent choice of white meat indicates a preferential desire to have or be with people who have white or light skin. In many Black households it is not unusual to see adults and children ask for white pieces of chicken.

336

Color Code War

It is also not unusual for most or many Black patrons of fried chicken establishments to order the white meat of the chicken. The selection of white and dark colors in the choice of meat is a subtle racial and color issue. When the word meat is decoded, it means skin. The color of the meat means a specific racial population. The White-dominated meat industry understands the race and color implications behind these harmless appearing choices. The commercials play on the color and race theme.

Who can forget the pork commercial that mentioned the other white meat? This was a clear and direct reference to white skin, or White people. There was a racial message hidden in the commercial. The message was that white people were being ignored. The term "other" means less than or insignificant. The equating of pork with Whiteness is to show that, like pork, White people are fading into the background and not being given top billing. They must become more aggressive about being White. Was this a racial call to arms to step up and be White and proud?

In a racially charged social environment all references to color must be understood in the context of race, color and racial symbolism. The selection between dark meat and light meat is the same as the choice between black skin and Black people and white skin and White people. In the Black community lighter skin color is programmed as superior, more beautiful and desirable.
Of the top beauty selections among Black women most have been the lighter, keen-featured and straight-haired females.

White meat is also promoted as a healthier and better choice. In the White community the darker the suntan, the greater the social accolades. White people spend billions of dollars tanning, trying to get dark or darker skin color. When White people select the darker meat, it is a psychological desire to have darker skin. They subconsciously compensate for whiteness with such behaviors as consuming darker meat, chocolate and cola.

The same kind of racial and color reaction is involved in the choice of such things as milk and ice cream. In the Black community, vanilla and strawberry flavors have historically been the choice over chocolate ice cream. What does this symbolize? It is a rejection of Blackness as being ugly and undesirable. Under White supremacy domination, the most unsuspecting things, such as food, are used to send racial and color messages.

The following list is of selected foods, accessories and related appliances that illustrate race and color meanings at the food table.

ITEM	RACIAL MEANING
White Meat	Superior/Better/Healthier
White Salt	Salt of the Earth—The Best
White Bread	Enriched/ Fortified Substance for Life
White Milk	White Milk on Black Faces: Symbol of Civilizing Blacks
White/Vanilla Ice Cream	Best Ice Cream/ Best Orgasm During Sex
White Sugar	The Sweetest and Most Refined People Are White
White/Irish Potatoes	Irish or White Is the Substance of Life
White Starch	Correctness, Stiffness, Professional
White Beans	The Substance of Life
White Napkins	Cleanliness
White Paper Plates	Clean Food
White Paper Napkins	Cleanliness
White Porcelain Plates	Clean Food
White Pears	White Penis Symbol
White Table Cloth	Sacred and Holy Food
White Candles	White Erect Phallic Symbol Burning with Passion
Silver/Light Utensils	Whiteness Injected
White Crackers	White People
White Corn	Survival Food from the Red People / Theft of Land from Native Americans
White Popcorn	White Fire/ Passion
White Chocolate Cookies	White Power Over Black People
Vanilla/ White Cookies	The Most Desired and Sweetest People
White Grits	White Power and Strength
White Eggs	The Unifying Force
Angel/White Food Cake	The Best and Most Desired Female
White Cake	The Best and Most Desired Female
White Refrigerator	The Cold Northern Climate
White Oven	White Fire and Sexual Passion
White Wine	The Best Wine and Smoothest Passion

Color Code War

Dark Meat	Inferior People
Dark Pepper	Black People
Dark Wine	Sexy Wine
Light Beer	The Best and Healthiest Sexual Fun
Black Beans	Little Black Negroes
Graham/ Dark Crackers	Black and Sweet
Devil's Food Cake	Evil/ Sexy Cake
Brown/Dark Eggs	Inferior Unifying Force
Chocolate/Dark Cookies	Addictive and Powerful
Chocolate Milk	The Least Fortified and Enriched

One of the most effective methods of social bonding is the least suspected and detected, yet it is one of the three most pleasurable and desirable. The way to a human's heart is through the stomach. This old adage is quite correct. One of the most effective connection points to the mind is the stomach and taste buds. The subtle power of food has often been discounted, misunderstood or dismissed. Food is one of the most powerful social persuaders and political weapons in the known universe. Indeed, food has been used as a political weapon.

In the last 50 years, the world has seen thousands of images of starving populations. Somali, Chad, Ethiopia, Nazi concentration camps, Bosnia, India and other nations have suffered the pain of massive starvation. Food is one of life's most common denominators. Wars have been waged over the control of millions of acres of land. If people have nothing or little to eat, the rulers of that nation will face unending conflict and social disarray. On the other hand, when used properly, food can individually satisfy, collectively pacify, culturally socialize, politically mobilize and geographically unify.

Eating is a profound psychological, biological, emotional and spiritual experience. The process of individual consumption of food is extremely pleasurable and highly rewarding. The wonderful aroma of food can lift the sagging spirits of the most downtrodden individual or group. Food has an effect on the human body like no other substance, with the exception of water. The process of collective, group or family eating has an even greater reward. It can, in addition to being rewarding and pleasurable, become a great mechanism for bonding people together.

The old slogan that the family that eats together stays together has a lot of merit. The collective eating process has evolved into a socialization process. It is called a power lunch, power dinner, dinner date or old-fashioned family night out.

All of these food interaction processes result in great bonding of all participants. This is why so many marriage celebrations are held in food establishments, career advancements are made over dinners, and business deals are proposed and finalized over great steaks and fine wine. Food, combined with its design and presentation, is very important in the game of seduction.

The naming of food establishes a connection to culture, which can have very potent racial and political implications. The first response to this statement might be, "Well, it is because this is where the food comes from." In non-racial social environments this would be a reasonable response. However, under the conditions of White supremacy all things, people, places and interactions are racial and food is no exception. The food naming process is a racial and color weapon. Foods from Europe and North America are classified as superior and more desirable than foods from nonwhite areas of the world.

Food is also a passive weapon that allows the eater to subtly identify with a culture. If the food is considered tasty and has good presentation, it opens the door to other cultural interactions. When an individual becomes addicted to a taste, he or she will mentally desire to know more about the culture and the people. Food, like music, connects one to the power of another cultural model. Food is the gateway to cultural interaction.

People will often begin to study and learn to emulate the ways of a culture that creates superior food. White people have always laughed and turned their noses up at the food selection habits of other people, especially in nonwhite nations. There are countless television shows and movies that have shown White people turning up their noses at the names and types of foods in nonwhite regions such as Asia, the Pacific, the Aboriginal Outback, Japan, China, Africa and Latin America.

Whites have constantly put down other groups' foods. They say that French fries are better than Somali yams, and part of this is to get nonwhites to buy White food products and become dependent on them for food. The goal is to convince through taste, food presentation and nomenclature that Western or White food is superior.

However, in order to do so, the other group of people must be convinced that the White food is superior and therefore better to consume. The naming of food, however, has an additional purpose other than identifying its origin. The food naming process has become one of the most effective methods used to bind the various factions of White people into a single White identity. Food has become racial. The titles of food, food menus and names of drinks have become very racial and very political. There are in most average White and Black food establishments the following items:

American Cheese
English Muffins and English Stew
French-fried Potatoes and French Dressing
Greek Salad
Swiss Cheese
Italian Dressing and Italian Pizza
Jewish Bread
Irish Stew
Irish Potatoes
Swedish Muffins

The use of ethnic names such as American, French, Greek, Italian, English, Swedish and so forth to identify foods is part of the quiet blending, bonding and amalgamation process of various White cultures into one White social and psychological entity. The White supremacy process is the integration of disparate White parts into a collective White whole. If White supremacy is to remain intact, it must constantly expand to bring in new factions of White and light people and assimilate their expressions and modes of interaction. The White supremacy system must find ways to mold and create unity and harmony among participating White individuals, groups and nations. Food is one of the most effective mental, spiritual, physical and emotional binders because it creates an acceptance of all things White at the most important mental, physical and emotional levels.

RACE CODE WAR

There is White food and Black food. White food is English stew, French dressing, Greek salad, Italian pizza and so forth. In reality there is no White or Black food unless it is made with white or black coloring. However, under the conditions of White supremacy, all things, including food, are racialized and colorized. Therefore, the purpose of giving food racial identity is to make so-called White food appear superior and far more desirable.

This is why so-called Black food is considered low-class eating. Such things as hog maws and chitterlings do help the case against low-class eating. This kind of eating is called soul food. Soul food has its origin in the chattel slave trade, when Black people were given scraps from the White master's table and were fed a different diet. However, the word soul has no national or bonding identity.

The word soul according to *Webster's New Collegiate Dictionary* has many meanings from a spiritual and moral force to intensive sensitivity and emotional fever. So soul food is intensive and emotional food. All food consumption is emotional and intensive. All food is soul food because it nourishes and replenishes both the human body and the soul. There is nothing identifying or bonding about the word soul. The term soul food is, however, unintimidating and allowed by a White-dominated and supremacist culture. However, the word soul says nothing about its identification with a certain race or group. As a matter of observation, White Italians seem to eat with as much intensity and fervor as any group of people. Yet their food is called Italian. And Italians in America still call their food Italian. One of the most famous food sayings, or at least it's supposed to be a food saying, is the statement *that's Italian! What about saying that's African!* The response would be off the hook.

Other word attachments have too much racial firepower, direct racial identity and intimidating qualities. The words African, Black, Negritude and others would cause Whites to accept Blacks at an emotional, pleasurable, cultural, social, mental and spiritual level. This would mean that every time some White person orders or eats an African cookie or Nigerian salad he or she would experience a pleasurable and positive feeling about Black people. This is parallel to how Black people take in positive vibes about White people when they eat Swiss cheese.

Color Code War

Food and food names are constant reminders of emotional, pleasurable attachments between White people and Black people. However, a White supremacist understood the power of food nomenclature in the nineteen sixties and for a limited time glorified unhealthy soul food.

Again the word soul has no direct racial identification or recognition. Many Whites would have—because of their training in Whiteness—emotional and social problems saying, without forethought or afterthought, "Give me some African or Black dressing on my salad." For example, a radio show entitled "What Do You Know" was aired on WCBE, a public radio station in Columbus, Ohio, at 11:00 a.m., Saturday, July 15, 2000. The host was Michael Feldman. He used a very interesting reference during a live and dated broadcast from Chicago. He had just had a dynamic and powerful blues band perform with a powerful Black vocalist and lead singer. Immediately after giving the great lead singer and the dynamic blues band some well deserved accolades, he said, "Well, now we go from blues to smut." This was supposed to be a comical reference to a Chicago-based food chef who bills himself as the king of smut. In this case smut was the name of a Mexican dish he specialized in preparing.

However, in this association between a Black blues man and the king of smut it was not hard to see the color connection. The "What Do You Know" game contest, which followed and is a regular feature on the show, presented a contestant from the audience, a White female graduate student in the Kellogg Business School at Northwestern University. When offered a chance to taste the Mexican dish, she replied a couple of times in a disgusted manner, "Oh, it's so black." If the word French or Greek had prefixed the dish, her reaction might have been quite different. But to eat food with an African origin creates an immediate and often dramatic departure from the White norm. It instantly causes the eater and others standing or sitting near by to think about what is being consumed.

White people have been trained to think that they invented almost every major food. And Black people have become so conditioned to eating foods with White racial titles that they do not give a second thought to how it has conditioned their thinking on an emotional level. The consumption of pizza gives one a favorable opinion of Italy. The consumption of French fries gives a favorable opinion of France. But the racist mind immediately goes to work downgrading anything African.

CONCLUSION

Where Do We Go from Here? *What Can Be Done?*

The revelation of the existence of modern racism driven by racial code words, color codes, symbols and images requires that changes must be implemented if we are to achieve a world based on justice. If the goal is the discontinuance of White supremacy and racial domination, then all forms of racial and color code wording must be stopped. What can be done to address the issues that are identified in this work? Revelation without recommendation is pointless. The following are simple and very doable initiatives that, if implemented, could have a dramatic impact on the racial and color code issues identified in this book.

Initiatives

Check and assess the use of identified race/color code language in newspapers, television, radio, motion pictures, books, music, education, workplace environments and daily conversations.

Compile a listing or a workbook of the identified words, terms, phrases.

Send copies of the listing or of the workbook of identified code words to various heads of major corporations, motion picture and advertising executives, local/ national media outlets, the heads of education groups/ systems, government officials, political leaders and community groups. Ask that they discontinue the use of these words, and inform them that this language is used in a coded format to describe Black people in a derogatory manner. Offer correct words to use, which relate an accurate story.

Monitor the use of the words on a daily basis in all social and media interactions to see if their usage has been curtailed or eliminated.

Openly challenge or convene community forums to address the continued linking of words in dictionaries and thesauruses like dark and black with derogatory meanings, and bright and light with positive associations.

Push for the discontinuation of the linking/ association of words like white, bright, black or dark as descriptions of human behavior e.g., dark side, dark personality, black thoughts or bright student. Inform the public that these are color and racial code terms that are deeply embedded in the language to maintain modern racism and therefore must be rooted out. Inform them that the continued use of this language maintains racism and colorism.

Ask people or leaders to define what they mean when using such terms as inner city. Does this term mean a geographical location or are they using it to describe in a degrading manner the people that live in a certain area of the city?

Challenge and counter how we define ourselves in the Black community. Words like bitch, dog and so forth cannot be allowed to stand as fun-loving or tell-it-like-it-is expressions.
This kind of verbal or written slang is extremely detrimental to the psychological and perceptual development of Black people.

Establish local Black Anti-Defamation Chapters that address the issues of racial code wording, racial imaging, the use of racial symbols and race rituals in the practice of modern racism. There must be an organized effort to bring these issues to public attention. The chapters would monitor and hold perpetrators accountable for images that are considered degrading, defaming, demeaning and misleading about Black people.

BLACK ANTI-DEFAMATION COUNCIL
A group(s) of individuals that monitors and deters the practice of using racial code wording, racial symbolizing, racial colorizations and racial imaging to defame Black people

The council studies, monitors and recommends a course of activity to effectively respond to the use of racially based words, images, symbols and messages in all areas of life. The council assesses the level of racially degrading material within a defined geographical area. An assessment

Conclusion

method can be constructed to enable the group to determine the degree of racially degrading material, i.e., racial imaging, racial sexual colorizations, racial code wording and racial symbolism, that may exist within a neighborhood or area, including alcohol and tobacco billboard advertisements.

These assessment instruments would be called racial code assessment instruments. They would be used to gauge the level of racially offensive material that is promoted, allowed to exist and proliferated in a targeted area or community. Local councils can be created right in your neighborhood and can be linked all over the world through the existence of modern Internet technology.

Information can be exchanged about the use of racially coded language and its affects in different regions of the city, country and world. In this day and age the word travels fast and long. It has immediate power to halt the spread of certain kinds of practices and behaviors. If these monitoring activities are maintained over a period of time, degrading images, messages, practices and behaviors can be neutralized and eventually discontinued. Then it will be possible to set the stage for the reestablishment of dignity and respect for Black people. We can no longer sit or stand idly by and miscalculate the power of words in terms of their ability to shape or misshape our world. This is the lesson that we failed to learn form other groups. Black people are always talking about learning from the Jewish experience during the Nazi Holocaust. But where are the Black or African American Anti-Defamation organizations? The Catholics, the Arabs and other groups have these kinds of agencies. Defame means to harm the reputation by libel or slander and it is time to end it. A synonym of the word defame is malign. There are clearly no people in the history of this nation or of the world that have been more maligned, besmirched and slandered than Black people. We can never be sure what defamation could lead to. It is not so far-fetched a notion that these images and code words left unchecked could lead to dire social consequences for an entire group of people. There should be a network of local Black anti-defamation councils. The purpose of an organized anti-defamation effort would be to monitor, manage and correct such things as misleading racial images and the use and practice of racial code words.

347

There Are Other Things That We Can do to Counter the Affects of Racial Codes Under the System of Modern Racism
Study and teach others about racial domination/ White supremacy

Speak, write and act against racism and White supremacy

Challenge religious or moralistic beliefs that perpetuate teachings and images that are racist

Read and decode White- and Black-oriented newspapers daily or on a weekly basis. Do not use slogans, sayings or words without first understanding their meaning

Do not use catch phrases without understanding their meaning and definition

Do not repeat words without understanding their meaning

Always ask for the meaning of new words and phrases that you have not heard before or do not know

Always maintain a pleasant and respectful speaking tone and manner

Never let anyone or any situation push your verbal or physical response button. Always keep your cool

Always strive to mentally, emotionally and verbally manage the situation and not allow the situation to manage you

Never engage in telling others about your personal affairs unless seeking counseling from a certified individual who by law has to maintain confidentiality

Do not carry unnecessary messages—it produces unnecessary conflict

Always request clarity or seek the definition of what is meant by the use of certain words before responding in public or in private interactions

Conclusion

Minimize time spent clowning and joking and maximize work and productivity

If you are male, do not spend inordinate amounts of time chasing and entertaining females; spend that time working on constructive projects

If you are female, do not spend inordinate amounts of time desiring to be entertained or chased by Black males; spend that time engaged in constructive thoughts and activities

Never use color-coded words like negative, fair, bright, or light to describe things or deeds

Do not joke about race or color issues—it is never a laughing matter

Do not laugh at racial or color jokes—the joke is on you

Never verbally overreact to a hostile racist or color statement; remain calm and ask questions about what is meant by the use of the words and what is the user's objective for using them

Never verbally overreact to a subtle racist statement; remain calm and ask questions about what is meant by the use of the words and what is the user's objective

Give measured and correct responses to all racial statements, questions and issues and tell the truth to the extent possible

Study your worded response in given racial situations; revisit what you said and evaluate the consequences of the language that you used

Refrain from using the racial code words identified in this work when talking to Black or White people

When words are used to describe the behavior of Black people or

White people, always ask what is meant or why that language was used

RACE CODE WAR

Do not lie about issues related to race, color and racism

Never assume that you know what an individual means based on the words that are used; always ask questions until it is clarified

Do not joke about sexual issues – it just might get you into big trouble

Minimize the use of sex language except during intimate sexual situations between consenting adults; even then understand the words that are being used

Do not use degrading sex or race language ever, no matter how tempting

Do not ever join in attacks on other Black people no matter how inviting or angry you might be at the individual; when asked about a situation, only respond with fact-based statements

Always listen carefully before speaking or responding

Always ask questions before giving answers; even if you think you know the answer, listen and understand the question first

Do not become the entertainment of the party—your life is no joke

Teach Black children to prioritize solving the problems of Black people Teach Black children about modern racism and how to effectively decode their social environment

Following Are Ways to Counter Racial Code Language in Music. The areas of music and politics are chosen as illustrations of what to do in various areas of life to effectively counter the effect of racial and color codes. The two columns consist of Do Nots and Do's. Do Nots are behaviors that must be discontinued if we intend to have an effective impact on racially degrading lyrics and music. Great recording artists and entertainers such as the King of Pop, Michael Jackson, have revealed the extent of racism in the music industry and how racially degrading music is pushed into the Black community.

Conclusion

The Do Nots

Do not buy, promote or attend concerts that feature artists and songs that call Black females whores and bitches and contain other degrading lyrics and terms.

Do not buy, promote or attend concerts that feature artists and songs that call Black males dogs, no-good and contain other degrading lyrics and terms.

Do not write or listen to lyrics that glorify guns or shooting other Black people.

Do not write or listen to lyrics that glorify the selling of drugs or engaging in degrading acts of sex.

Do not play or allow to be played songs in the presence of young children that degrade Black people sexually, glorify violence, use curse words, urge substance abuse or use racial codes, words, symbols or images.

Do not support or purchase any music that glorifies Black males' cursing, shooting each other, selling illegal drugs and engaging in sexual abuse of Black womanhood.

Do not support or promote music videos that use excessive curse words or feature nude or near nude Black females, illegal drugs, gangsterism, pimping, jewelry and fast cash.

Do not attend or promote concerts that promote violent messages and devalue Black life.

Do not promote, buy albums or attend comedy concerts with artists that poke fun/ degrade Black people.

Do not pose for musical promotional pictures or posters that are sexually, culturally or racially degrading.

Do not support artists that continue to put out degrading lyrics and music.

RACE CODE WAR

Do not buy musical magazines or publications or visit Internet web sites that degrade Black people.

Do not buy products of commercial sponsors that underwrite publications that degrade Black people sexually, glorify the sale of illegal drugs, violence and gangsterism.

The Do's
Organize efforts to ensure that all music played over the airwaves that degrades Black people is greatly minimized or taken off. Five or six people with determination can have great impact on what is played over public airwaves.

Promote music that creates greater awareness of the plight of Black people both here and abroad.

Promote music that helps Black people solve their individual and collective problems.

Write lyrics and music that solve the problems between Black females and males in a constructive manner.

Promote and heavily support with dollars recording artists that use positive, uplifting and constructive messages to improve the mindset of Black youth and expose the use of racially coded language.

Develop and organize individual or community music review teams that evaluate and monitor the quality of Black music videos and recordings that are played on the radio, in clubs, at concerts and sold in record stores. Set up a rating review system that checks for racial code words and other racially degrading material.

Issue and publicize a community ratings system for the music, recording artists and recording companies that are positive or baneful to the interest of Black people.

Convene, attend or support local, state or national conventions that deal with issues related to degrading musical images, songs and videos.

Conclusion

Monitor the television channels and Internet sites that play demeaning Black music or Black music videos.

Hold contests for the best and most effective slogans, sayings and stickers that denounce degrading music and put forth constructive lyrics.

Develop plays, write scripts, make videos that reveal how degrading music is made, promoted and encouraged in the Black community.

Develop information about who or what groups make money off the derogatory images and where they invest their money.

Issue annual music reports about racially degrading material at events such as the Dr. Martin Luther King Day activities.

Develop specific measurements to gauge the social imaging impact of degrading music on Black youth and adults.

Meet regularly with radio stations and recording executives to let them know that their music must be held to high standards for the betterment of Black people.

Buy publications that promote constructive artists and music that unites Black people.

Develop intense public media campaigns against racially degrading music.

Challenge and hold accountable artists, publicists and recording companies that use the rationale that *music is a reflection of life in the streets* in order to continue to promote degrading songs. Hold them accountable by monitoring their music in clubs, radio programs and advertisements. Write letters, send e-mails, make phone, beeper and cell phone calls, write articles for the Black and White press, hit on web sites, etc. Do not fall prey to the outdated rationale that you are censoring art. The derogatory imaging of Black people must be challenged whatever it is called. In the final analysis, don't be fooled by a handful of people who want to make money. It is in their interest to keep Black people following the illusions and not challenging or confronting the use of demeaning images to misdirect our development as Black people. Reduction in the support of derogatory/degrading Black music will lead to the restoration of positive dialogue and constructive action in the music industry.

Following Are Ways to Counter Racial Code Language in Politics
Ask questions about, study very closely and break down the language used by elected officials: they are taught to use words in such a manner that captures your mind. It is language designed to reflect how you feel about an issue or to redirect your thinking about that issue. The best-trained politicians use code language that is sprinkled with certain words designed to persuade the audience without them knowing that it is happening.

Read extensively and question political positions on critical issues that have tremendous impact on Black life in the present and in the future.

Conduct community forums that regularly teach, inform and assist residents to understand how politicians and political systems work and impact their lives on a daily basis.

Support attempts to develop and prepare Black people to speak and deal with issues of racism on every level.

Support efforts to mobilize Black people to counter the use of degrading racial images in political television commercials during campaigns.

Support work that raises referendums to address the issues of racial imaging, racial profiling and racial symbolism.

Establish support efforts in Black neighborhoods to welcome, hold dialogues, work on Black-on-Black relationship problems and dissect Black experiences in Africa, India, Australia, Canada, South America, the Caribbean, New Zealand, Pacific islands and Europe-

Do not assign a godlike status to Black, White or any other elected officials. Elected officials are not rulers. They are the representatives

Conclusion

of the people. In the case of Black elected officials, their role is to speak and act in the best interest of Black people.

Do not support politicians who do not work hard or do not have a measurable plan and timetable to eliminate the existence of the ghetto and other institutions of racism in plain sight that have the effect of racial warfare against Black people.

Do not support any representatives that do not give a regular and verifiable report of their efforts and progress in addressing Black concerns at the local, state or national level.

Do not vote for or give money to politicians that do not prioritize economic assistance and foreign aid for Black people in Africa, South America, India and other Black nations.

Do not financially support or vote for Black elected officials who do not push a Black agenda with specific programs and measurable outcomes.

Withhold financial support and do not vote for political candidates who do not have specific and measurable physical, commercial and investment development action plans for predominantly Black living environments.

Do not allow any candidate or existing office holder to use identified racial code language or symbols in their political campaign literature or commercials or as part of their legislative agenda.

I thank you for reading this book, and I hope you will use what you have gleaned to make a difference.

CLOSING WORDS OF THANKS

Thank you for buying, reading, thinking about or talking about this book. I hope it has help to broaden your understanding and energized your efforts to deal with the existence and affects of modern racism and colorism. The intent of this work is to expose a communications format design to mislead, degrade and demean people based on racial identity and skin color. It my greatest desire and fondest wish that one day in the near future all forms of racial domination and color supremacy will be eliminated from the face of the earth. In order to achieve this all people must work and understand the power of words, symbols and image to abuse and destroy.

Racism and colorism are the greatest barriers to the achievement of a new world of justice and peace. These age-old scourges must be attacked with great vigor and relentlessness.
We must mount effective campaigns all over the world to stop the spread of modern racism.

I believe in justice for all people. I will continue to monitor very closely racial code words, images, symbols and messages and its affect especially on black people. Ladies and gentlemen, brothers and sisters our struggle continues until we have collectively wiped out racism, colorism and all of its subliminal social and culture remnants from the face of this planet. With the help of almighty God and with your deep and unbending commitment we can achieve the greatest victory in the history of this world.

GLOSSARY
OF RACE CODE WAR TERMS

The following is a selected list of words and definitions that are used in this book to describe the issues of race and color. This racial glossary is intended to increase the understanding of how modern racism works.

Black **A color identification label for people of African descent.**

Black Mindset **Effective method of thinking used to offset the domination of White supremacy.**

Black Slave Language **Submissive racial communications.**

Black Thought **Effective mental responses to White domination.**

Brazilization **The neutralization and confusion of targeted racial populations with miscegenation.**

Chattel Slave State **Districts, provinces and states established and preserved for the physical** enslavement of Black people.

Chemical Conspiracy **Organized effort to direct the placement of illegal and controlled substances to targeted racial populations and their living environment.**

Code **A system of signals used for secret or deceptive communication. Symbols, letters, numbers or words that are used to represent assigned and often secret meanings.**

Code Book **A book containing a list of symbols, letters, numbers, words or expressions for use in secret or deceptive communications.**

Code Name **A word or term used as a code designation for secret or deceptive communication purposes.**

Code Word **A code name or code group name used for secret or deceptive communications.**

Code Word Identification Process **The systematic attachment of words, images, symbols and colors to a population in order to convey racial messages.**

Codify **To reduce to a code, classify and systematize.**

Color **The visual shade, tint and complexion of people, things and places**

Color Based **Words used to identify the skin color of an individual, group or population for purposes of discrimination and degradation**

Color Branding **Stigmatizing and attaching derogatory labels to certain color and racial populations.**

Color Code **The standardization of meanings and values of different tones, shades and tints.**

Color Code War **The classification of skin tones and shades in order to practice racial domination.**

Color Communications **Visual, written, sign, audible and verbal languages used to transmit messages about skin pigmentation, shade, tone and tint.**

Color Communications Perspective **The observation, examination and interpretation of how pigmentation, shade, tone and tint are used to transmit messages, ideas, speech and behaviors about race.**

Color Conditioning **Attaching derogatory emotions and thinking to certain shades/ tones/races.**

Color Confusion **Organized and purposeful social confusion regarding race and ethnicity.**

Color Culture **A social order based on maintaining of the superiority of certain skin pigmentations and shades/tones.**

Glossary

Color Degradation **The linking of certain colors with people, things, places and events to debase and demoralize.**

Color Demonization **The classification of certain tones and shades as evil and wicked.**

Color Dynamic **The social interaction between different skin shades and tones among individuals, groups and populations.**

Color Exploitation **The use of skin tones/ shades to degrade targeted racial populations.**

Color Frame of Reference **A philosophical worldview based on skin pigmentation.**

Color Genocide **The elimination of individuals, groups and populations based on skin pigmentation.**

Color Identification **The appointment and classification of individuals, groups and populations by skin pigmentation.**

Color Identity Words **Words that are used to identify with, indicate and describe the pigmentation of people, things or places.**

Color Implication(s) **The use of tones/shades to imply derogatory racial meaning.**

Color Interpretation **Judgments and opinions about individuals, groups and populations based on pigmentation.**

Colorism **The concept and practice of using skin pigmentation, tones, shades and tints to assign values and standards for people, things, places and events.**

Colorization **The attachment of values that define people and their living environments based on skin pigmentation.**

Colorization Process **The system of assigning values to people, things, places and events based on color.**

RACE CODE WAR

Color Language **Verbiage that uses skin tones and shades to degrade certain populations.**

Color Matters **Social, religious, political, educational and economic issues that are directed toward certain individuals and populations based on their color.**

Color Myth **The spread of lies and half-truths that are designed to besmirch individuals and populations based on skin color.**

Color Order **The attachment and assignment of superior and inferior rankings based on tone and shade.**

Color Perspective **A racial view on all interactions between White and Black people.**

Color Point of View **A philosophy that attempts to understand social interactions and culture on the basis of color.**

Color Reference **Thought and action that seek to degrade individuals, groups and populations based on skin color.**

Color Rituals **Social practices and personal behaviors that involve utilization and consumption to satisfy a need, glorify a situation, demonstrate a desire or degrade a colored population and their living environment.**

Color Supremacy **The belief in and practice of the superiority and domination of certain skin shades, tones and pigmentations.**

Color Threat **The belief that certain populations are evil, menacing or dangerous because of skin pigmentation.**

Color Trigger Symbols **Embeds, emblems, insignias, designs and labels that convey racial messages.**

Color War(s) **A campaign of warfare against targeted colored individuals, groups and populations.**

Glossary

Color Words **Verbal and written language that values and devalues people, things, places and events by attaching and linking them to certain tones/ shades.**

Communication Interpretation **Opinion, judgment, conclusion or analysis of communication interaction among individuals, groups and populations.**

Communication Perspective **Observation, examination, classification and interpretation through verbal, written, visual and auditory forms of language to create, express and transmit social ideas, thoughts, behaviors, philosophies and messages.**

Control Words **Communication that expresses domination and in-charge thoughts, behaviors, actions and mannerisms.**

Destruction of Racial Esteem **The persistent annihilation of the mindset of a targeted racial population.**

Direct Racial Word **Verbal and written derogatory communication against a targeted racial individual or population and their living environment to provoke a violent or emotional reaction.**

Effective Action **Constructive, meaningful and positive activities designed to counter the impact and use of racial code words, symbols, images, colors and other subliminal messages in all areas of life.**

Effective Behavior **Constructive and positive conduct that counters and defeats the purpose and impact of racial code words, racial images, racial symbols, racial colors and racial messages.**

Equal Communications **Language interaction that establishes, promotes, sustains and maintains racial justice and eliminates White domination and supremacy.**

Equal Power **Communication dialogue among individuals, groups and populations of comparable might and force.**

RACE CODE WAR

Equitable Principle **The percentage of the ownership and control of material wealth should be equal to the percentage of a targeted racial population within a geographical area.**

Hardcore Racial Language **Oral, written and sign language that transmits harder-tone racial communications designed to provoke and create violent and emotional reactions.**

Hardcore White Supremacist **A more direct racist who does not condone or support the model of modern racism.**

Illusion of Inclusion **The practice of setting up massive racial con games.**

In-Charge Language **Dialogue that uses control words.**

Ineffective Action **Destructive and derogatory activities and conduct which support the purpose and impact of racial code words, racial images, racial symbols, racial colors and racial messages.**

Ineffective Response to Injustice **Impotent reactions to White domination.**

Level of Crime Allowed to Exist **The degree of injustice permitted among a targeted racial population within their living environment.**

Low-Level Chemical Peddlers **Street-level hucksters of illegal and controlled substances in targeted racial neighborhoods.**

Miseducation Justification **Language used to justify racial injustice in education.**

Modern Racism **A mutated and sophisticated method of racial domination also known as White supremacy.**

Nigger **A racist slang term used to degrade, demoralize, destroy and belittle Black people.**

Glossary

Nigger Talk   Conversation that is degrading, demoralizing and destructive to the self-esteem of Black people.

Order of Things   The establishment and maintenance of White domination and superiority and Black dependency and inferiority here and abroad.

Planned Racial Annihilation   The deliberate and measured disintegration of targeted racial populations and their environments.

Planned Racial Confusion   The deliberate and measured discombobulating of targeted racial populations.

Purposeful Backwardness   Deliberate and persistent maintaining of regressive socioeconomic conditions for targeted racial populations.

Purposeful Disadvantagement   The planned and persistent maintaining of the socioeconomic inferiority of targeted racial populations.

Purposeful Neglect   Planned and persistent social disregard of targeted racial populations.

Purposeful Racial Disintegration   Directed and persistent effort toward the dissolution of targeted racial populations.

Purposeful Racial Stereotyping   Directed and consistent derogatory labeling of targeted racial populations.

Purposeful Suppression   Persistent and directed curtailment of targeted racial populations.

Race   The classification of individuals and populations by genetic and physical color similarities.

Race Based   A philosophy, purpose and agenda for maintaining existing racial domination.

RACE CODE WAR

Race Code **The use of non-racial words to substitute for words, symbols, colors, images and behaviors that deceive and degrade Black populations.**

Race Code War **An uninterrupted campaign of racial domination using deceptive / coded communications. This includes the use of Racial Communications, Racial Code Words, Word Bombs, Racial Symbols, Racial Images, Racial Sex Images, Words and Symbols, Sexual, Color and Racial Triggers, Color Codes, Color Symbols, Color Images and Hidden Racial, Sexual and Color messages.**

Race Relation(s) **Refined methodology and deceptive behavior for controlling interaction with Black people.**

Race Rituals **Social practices and personal behaviors that involve the use of symbols to satisfy a want or need, glorify a situation or degrade a racial population and their living environment.**

Race War **An uninterrupted campaign of warfare against targeted racial individuals, groups and populations.**

Racial **Things related to the issue of race.**

Racial Annihilation **The purposeful genocide or destruction of an individual, group or population based on race.**

Racial Behaviors **Social demeanor and comportment that are assigned to certain races of individuals, groups or populations.**

Racial Brand **The purposeful attachment of disparaging labels to certain targeted populations based on race.**

Racial Characters and Characterizations **Degraded and demeaning depictions of targeted populations based on race.**

Racial Chemicals **The linking of illegal and controlled substances to targeted populations based on race.**

Glossary

Racial Chemical Conspiracy **The organized and purposeful distribution of illegal and controlled substances to exploit and destabilize targeted populations and their environments based on race.**

Racial Chemical Victimization **The targeting of certain race populations and their living environments as scapegoats for the use of illegal and controlled substances.**

Racial Code Words **Non-racially identifiable words, terms and phrases that are used as surrogate language in order to send yet conceal false, misleading or degrading messages about targeted populations based on race.**

Racial Code Wording **The process of using non-racially identifiable words, terms and phrases as surrogate language in order to send false, misleading or degrading messages about targeted populations based on race.**

Racial Colors **The assignment of derogatory color labels and identities to targeted Black populations.**

Racial Communications Perspective **The point of view that uses all forms of language to create, express, transmit and engage in racist ideas, philosophies, thoughts and behaviors.**

Racial Communications **Written, oral and visual interaction between White and Black people based on the language of White superiority and Black inferiority.**

Racial Communications Weapons **Words, symbols, images, colors and messages that establish derogatory or misleading mental and visual depictions of targeted racial populations.**

Racial Concepts **Thoughts, ideas, beliefs, creations and impressions that explain, justify, promote and maintain racial supremacy.**

Racial Conditioning **The process that attaches racist stigmas, labels, brands and stereotypes in order to exploit populations and their living environments based on race.**

RACE CODE WAR

Racial Confusion **The practice of purposely deceiving, misleading and confounding individuals, groups and populations for racist purposes.**

Racial Conquer Mentality **Belief in the manifest destiny and domination of racial supremacy.**

Racial Conquest **The purposeful and planned domination of one race by another.**

Racial Containment Facility **Facilities that are primarily designed to incarcerate large numbers of individuals identified as part of a targeted population based on race.**

Racial Control **The domination of individuals, groups and populations based on race.**

Racial Control Words **Linguistic communication that expresses thoughts, behaviors and actions designed to control populations and their living environments based on race.**

Racial Culture **Racist lifestyles that are practice to maintain power and control.**

Racial Deception **The utilization of falsehoods and misinformation to deceive and abuse targeted populations based on race.**

Racial Decoding **The unscrambling and exposing of coded words, symbols, images, colors, messages and behaviors that are used against targeted populations and their living environments based on race.**

Racial Demonization **The utilization and connection of offensive images to degrade targeted individuals, groups and populations and their living environments based on race.**

Racial Destabilization **The purposeful/ organized destruction, disintegration, and annihilation of targeted individuals, populations and environments based on race.**

Glossary

Racial Dynamic Highly dysfunctional interactions between White and Black populations.

Racial Economics A system of unequal material wealth based on race differences.

Racial Exploitation The purposeful victimization of targeted individuals, groups and populations based on differences of race.

Racial Frame of Reference An anatomy of thinking, believing and acting designed to improve, develop or maintain the dominance of a certain racial population.

Racial Genocide The elimination of an individual, group or population based on race identification.

Racial Group The grouping of people by physical, genetic and skin color similarities.

Racial Identification The categorization of individuals, groups and populations based on physical, genetic and skin color similarities.

Racial Images
A. Explosive visual, written and verbal images designed to debase, degrade and destroy targeted populations and their living environment based on race identity.

B. Visual, linguistic and sensory depictions, characterizations and illustrations designed to convey a covert or overt racist message.

Racial Imaging The purposeful and targeted visual, verbal, linguistic and sensory depictions, characterizations and illustrations designed to convey a covert or overt derogatory racist message(s).

Racial Implications A derogatory judgment determination/action that has great significance to the development or survival of a targeted racial population.

Racial Inference **Words, statements, symbols and images designed to send information about race and color issues.**

Racial Injustice **Discrimination, abuse, degradation and exploitation based on race.**

Racial Injustice in the Classroom **The practice of race abuse, deception and exploitation in formal educational settings.**

Racial Interaction **Social intercourse between Black and White people.**

Racial Interpretations **Judgments, opinions and inclinations that are designed to victimize a targeted population based on race.**

Racialization **The perceptual connection of racist images, ideas and behaviors to characters, events and locations.**

Racialized **The acceptance and perceptual connection of racial images, ideas and behaviors to characters, events and locations.**

Racial Justice **The elimination of White supremacy and other forms of racial domination.**

Racial Language **Oral, written and sign language that transmits racially based information about Black people.**

Racial Management **Modern White supremacist domination through the use of control language, deceptive behavior and social manipulation.**

Racial Manipulation **The misuse and exploitation of a targeted racial population.**

Racial Meaning **Actions, behaviors, thoughts and language that have racially based goals and purposes.**

Racial Message **Information designed to degrade and defame a targeted population and their living environment based on racial identity.**

Glossary

Racial Metaphors **Symbols, images and comparisons that are designed to transmit racist messages.**

Racially Motivated Behavior **Engagement in activities designed to inflict harm or degrade an individual, group or population because of their racial identification.**

Racial Myths **Derogatory distortions designed to besmirch the character and image of a targeted racial population.**

Racial Order **Social arrangement and hierarchy based on racial designation.**

Racial Point of View **Thought and philosophy that describes social interactions and culturefrom the perspective and interest of one race over another.**

Racial Politics **A system of political interaction and vote getting based on the manipulation of targeted racial populations.**

Racial Population **A mass, group or community of people classified and categorized by racial designations.**

Racial References **Thought, action and behavior from a racial point of view.**

Race Rituals **Social practices and personal behaviors that are performed regularly and involve the exploitation of a racial population to satisfy a need, glorify a situation, demonstrate a desire or degrade people, things, places and events.**

Racially Based **Ideas, behaviors, speech and actions that are developed from a racist premise.**

Racially Based Dialogue **Language that ordains the psychological acceptance of racial domination.**

Racial Scenario(s) **Daily game-playing between Black and White people living under the conditions of White domination.**

RACE CODE WAR

Racial Statement **Words linked together to convey a hidden racist meaning or intention about a targeted population.**

Racial Stereotype **The derogatory branding and labeling of a targeted population based on race.**

Racial Subjection **Conquest, captivity and enslavement based on race.**

Racial Supremacy **The implementation of beliefs, practices and systems that postulate the superiority and domination of a certain racial group or population.**

Racial Symbols **Things that stand for or express indirectly hidden or overt racist meaning and purpose.**

Racial Thought **Opinions, sentiments and ideas based on the supposed superiority or inferiority of a certain racial population.**

Racial Trigger Symbols **Communication embeds and devices designed to unleash and activate derogatory emotional and behavioral racial reactions.**

Racial Trigger Words **Communications designed to unleash and activate derogatory emotional and behavioral racist reactions.**

Racial Warfare **The uninterrupted campaign of racism that has the effect of degrading, destabilizing and confusing Black people here and abroad.**

Racism **The belief in and practice of racial domination, discrimination, degradation and oppression.**

Racists **Individuals, groups and populations who believe in and practice White supremacy /racial domination.**

Sexual Conditioning **Stigmatizing and attaching derogatory sex labels and perceptions to targeted racial populations.**

Glossary

Sexual Degradation The purposeful creation and use of sexual stereotypes to debase individuals, groups and populations based on racial differences.

Sports Talk Dialogue about sports issues that is used as a cover to attack and degrade Black athletes.

Sports Trigger Symbols Symbols designed to unleash and activate emotional and behavioral reactions regarding Black participation in sports.

Sports Trigger Words Linguistic communications designed to unleash and activate emotional and behavioral reactions regarding Black participation in sports.

Stabilization The establishment of a well-balanced society without racism, racist involvement, racist intervention and racist hindrance.

Submissive Communications Acquiescent and compliant verbal and written responses to White supremacy domination.

Targeted Racial Populations A mass, group or community of people, classified and categorized by race, that is marked for exploitation, manipulation, destabilization or extermination.

Unequal Communication Communication interaction that establishes, promotes, sustains and maintains racial injustice and White supremacy.

Unequal Power Communication between individuals, groups and populations of incommensurate might and force.

White A race and color designation designed to identify a certain population.

White Authority Domination, command and control based on classification as a White individual, group or population.

371

RACE CODE WAR

White Christmas **The whitenization of a spiritual and religious holiday.**

White Domination **The worldwide control of Blacks and other nonwhites under the system of White supremacy.**

White Female Insertion **The injection of false White female sexual images into the perceptual minds of Black males.**

White Male Insertion **The injection of White male sexual images into the perceptual minds of Black females.**

White Mindset **A method of racial thinking used by White supremacists to organize other Whites to support and implement White supremacy domination.**

Whiteness **The belief and postulation that all things classified as white are better or superior than things of any other colors**

Whitenization **An indoctrination of thought that postulates that White is superior.**

Whitenization Process **The implementation methodology and system for the promotion of whitenization amongst all people, in all things, institutions and systems.**

Whitening **Thought, speech, and behavior that transforms in the figurative and literal sense people, things, places and events from their original state to a state of whiteness.**

White Supremacist **Those persons classified as White who believe in, practice and implement White domination over all people, things, places and events worldwide.**

White Supremacist Mindset **A psychological, behavioral, cognitive and psychic frame of reference designed to establish and maintain White domination over all people, places and things worldwide.**

Glossary

White Supremacy **The organized and purposeful belief in and practice of White racial domination over all people, things, places and events.**

White Supremacy Domination **The purposeful control and practice of racial domination of Black and other nonwhite people.**

White Supremacy Language **Organized and purposeful linguistic communication that postulates the covert and overt domination of persons classified as White over all people, things, places and events worldwide.**

Word Bombs **Explosive language devices used to degrade and defame targeted racial populations.**

Word Raid Attack **Derogatory language designed to attack a targeted racial population.**

RACE CODE WAR

READING LIST

Al-Mansour, Khalid. *Betrayal By Any Other Name*. First African Arabian Press, San Francisco, 1993.

Afrika, Llaila. *Nutricide*. A&B Publishers Group, New York, 2000.

AMX Videos. *The Fantasy Fest; Vote for Bush,* Vol. 7. Colorado Springs, CO, 2000.

Ani, Marimba. *Yurugu*. African World Press, Trenton, NJ, 1994.

Arnheim, Rudolf. *Art and Visual Perception: Psychology of the Creative Eye*. University of California Press, Berkeley, CA, 1971.

Barnhart, Robert. *Dictionary of Etymology*. Harper Collins Publishers, New York, 1995.

Bauer, F.L. *Decrypted Secrets: Methods and Maxims of Cryptology*. Springer-Verlag, Berlin, Heidelberg, Germany, 1997.

Bayley, Harold. *The Lost Language of Symbolism*. Carol Publishing Group, New York, 1993.

Bennet, Lerone. *The Challenge of Blackness*. Johnson Publishing Company, Chicago, 1972.

Biedermann, Hans. *Dictionary of Symbols*. Penguin Books USA, New York, 1994.

Birren, Faber. *Color Psychology and Color Therapy*. University Books, New Hyde Park, NY, 1955.

_____. *Selling Color to People*. University Books, New Hyde Park, NY, 1956.

Bowden, Mark. *Doctor Dealer*. Warner Books, New York, 1989.

Reading List

Brietman, George. *Malcolm X Speaks*. Grove Press, New York, 1965.

Browder, Anthony. *Nile Valley Contributions to Civilizations*. Washington, DC, 1992.

Brown, H.E. *Pimps in the Pulpit*. In-Step Publishing, Washington, DC 2002.

Butler, William, and Keeney, Douglas. *Secret Messages*. Simon and Schuster, New York, 2001.

Carruthers, Jacob H. *Intellectual Warfare*. Third World Press, Chicago, 1999.

Chomsky, Noam. *Propaganda and the Control of the Public Mind*. Recorded at Harvard Trade Union Program, Cambridge, MA.

Clarke, John Henrik. *Marcus Garvey and the Vision of Africa*. Random House, New York, 1973.

Coon, Carleton. *The Origin of Races*. Alfred A. Knopf, New York, 1962.

Coppola, Francis Ford. *The Godfather*. Paramount Pictures, 1972.

Council on Black Internal Affairs. *The American Directory of Certified Uncle Toms*. CBIA and DFS Publishing, 2002.

Diop, Cheika Anta. *The Cultural Unity of Black Africa*. Third World Press, Chicago, 1978.

Dixon, N.F. *Subliminal Perception: The Nature of a Controversy*. McGraw-Hill, London.

Evanzz, Karl. *The Judas Factor*. Thunder's Mouth Press, New York, 1992.

Fardan, Dorothy. *Message to the White Man and Woman in America.* United Brothers and Sisters Communications Systems, Hampton, VA, 1991.

Ferber, Abby. *White Man Falling.* Rowman and Littlefield Publishers, New York, 1999.

Frazer, J.G. *The Golden Bough: A Study in Magic and Religion.* Macmillian, London, 1967.

Fuller, Neely. *The United Independent Compensatory Code/System Concept.* Washington, DC, 1974.

Hacker, Andrew. *Two Nations: Black and White, Separate, Hostile, Unequal.* Ballantine Books, New York, 1993.

Hall, R., Wilson, M. and Russell, K. *Color Complex.* Harcourt Brace Jovanvich, New York, 1992.

Harris, Elliot. *The Un-American Weapon: Psychological Warfare.* M.W. Lads Publishing, New York, 1967.

Hirschfeld, Magnus. *Racism.* Kennikat Press, Port Washington, NY, 1973.

Hutchinson, Ofari Earl. *The Assassination of the Black Male Image.* Simon and Schuster, New York, 1994.

Jochannan, Yosef Ben. *Africa: The Mother of Western Religion.* Alkebulan Books Associates, New York, 1970.

Jones, Del. *The Black Holocaust: Global Genocide.* Hikeka Press, Philadelphia, 1992.

Key, Wilson Bryan. *The Age of Manipulation.* Madison Books, Lanham, MD, 1989.

_____. *Media Sexploitation.* Prentice Hall, 1972.

_____. *Subliminal Seduction: Ad Media's Manipulation of a Not So Innocent America.* Signet, New York, 1973.

Reading List

Kovel, Joel. *White Racism, A Psychohistory*. Vintage, New York, 1971.

Langer, Walter. *The Mind of Adolf Hitler: Secret Wartime Report*. Basic Books, New York, 1972.

Lutz, William. *Double Speak*. New York Times, New York, 1981.

Maddox, Dr. Keith, and Gray, Stephanie. *Cognitive Representations of Black Americans: Reexploring the Role of Skin Tone*. Personality and Social Psychology Bulletin, 2002.

Massey, Gerald. *Ancient Egypt: Light of the World*. Kessinger Publishers, Montana, 1992.

McLuhan, Marshall. *Understanding Media*. McGraw-Hill, New York, 1967.

Montagu, Ashley. *The Concept of Race*. Collier Books, London, 1970.

Norman, Bruce. *Secret Wartime*. Dorset Press, New York, 1987.

Pasteur, Alfred, and Toldson, Ivory. *Roots of Soul*. Anchor Press Doubleday, Garden City, NY, 1973.

Pinker, Steven. *The Language Instinct*. Morrow, New York, 1994.

Plump, Sterling. *Black Rituals*. Third World Press, Chicago, 1973.

Rodney, Walter. *How Europe Underdeveloped Africa*. Tanzania Publishing House, Dar Es Salaam, 1972.

Rogers, J.A. *Sex and Race,* Vols 1-3. Helga Rogers, 1952.

_____. *Nature Knows No Color Line*. Helga Rogers, 1952.
Rowan, Carl. *The Coming Race War in America*. Little Brown, New York, 1996.

Ruhlen, Merit. *Origins of Language*. John Wiley and Sons, New York, 1994.

Singh, Simon. *The Code Book.* Doubleday, New York, 1999.

Smitherman, Geneva. *Black Talk.* Houghton Mifflin, New York, 1994-2000.

Snowden, Frank. *Blacks in Antiquity.* Bellnap Press, Cambridge, MA, 1970.

Soukhanov, Anne. *Word Watch.* Henry Holt, New York, 1995.

Stoddard, Lothdrop. *The Rising Tide of Color.* Blue Ribbon Books, New York, 1920.

Sultan, A. Latif, and Naimah, Latif. *Slavery: The African American Psychic Trauma.* Latif Communications, Chicago, 1994.

Webb, Gary. *Dark Alliance.* Seven Stories Press, New York, 1998.

Welsing, Francis Cress. *The Isis Papers: The Keys to the Colors.* Third World Press, Chicago, 1991.

Williams, Chancellor. *Rebirth of African Civilization.* Third World Press, Chicago, 1993.

_____. *Destruction of Black Civilization.* Third World Press, Chicago, 1976.

Willie, John Bizarre. *Benedikt Taschen.* Verlag Gmbh. Germany, 1996.

Woodson, Carter G. *The Mis-Education of the Negro.* African American Images, Chicago, 2000.

Wright, Bobby. *The Psychopathic Racial Personality.* Third World Press, Chicago, 1984.

Wrixon, Fred. *Codes & Ciphers.* Prentice Hall, New York, 1992.

Yette, Samuel F. *The Choice.* Berkeley Publishing, New York, 1971.

Notes

Notes

Notes

Notes